The Changing Function of Compliance

As risks arising within the business environment grow in size and complexity, so too do the regulatory requirements put in place to manage them. The pace of regulatory change is itself a significant business risk, and compliance departments are under increasing pressure to keep up with the change and adapt their organisations accordingly. This new edition of what has become an indispensable guide to regulation compliance brings readers up to date with changing areas of focus and provides guidance for regulated firms and regulators alike.

The Changing Function of Compliance considers the relationship between regulation and compliance as well as key influences on both, offering insight into the effectiveness of current approaches and addressing practical compliance challenges. It explains the purpose and development of regulatory risk management and the existing regulatory environment, and provides a detailed exploration of the compliance function, explaining how the role might be strengthened and how best to approach the role to enable it to be effective. This practical and accessible handbook includes a mix of hands-on advice, examples and research based on the experiences of practitioners, educators and regulators drawn from across a wide range of jurisdictions and sectors.

This book is an essential read, whether you are concerned about the growing and changing implications of regulatory risk, the benefit of leveraging additional value from your compliance function or your own compliance role or ways of transforming and sustaining the function to ensure its continued relevance to the business.

Sharon Ward is an experienced regulatory compliance specialist. A compliance professional since the mid-1990s, Sharon is a former senior practitioner active in the development of professional education in this field throughout the past two decades, initially in her operational roles with the International Compliance Association and thereafter as its Chief Examiner (GRC). She has developed, taught on and written for a range of governance, risk and compliance-related programmes to Master's level, both in the UK and internationally, contributing to key industry initiatives. Formerly Module Director for the Financial Services Compliance elective of the Chartered Banker MBA (CBMBA) and Editor of the *Journal of Business Compliance*, Sharon is a fellow of the ICA and of the Chartered Institute of Educational Assessors. Her work in this area continues through research, development projects, teaching and assessment.

"Sharon Ward has produced a defining book for the function and role of the Compliance function in the twenty-first century. Since its development from an internal control department to a more influential advisory role, there has been a tumultuous process of scandal, business misconduct and regulatory response that is still ongoing. The debate as to the nature of its activities, influence and strategic value within organisations bears the hallmarks of the birth of a profession. Her book is as timely as it is instructive; it is an invaluable read to accompany any effort to understand the value and role of the Compliance function, and a must-read for practitioners and legislators alike."

Anthony Smith-Meyer, *Editor-in-Chief,* Journal of Business Compliance, *Adjunct Professor of International Management and Organisational Behaviour at Miami University, MUDEC Campus, Luxembourg, and Founder of TheGovernanceProject.org*

The Changing Function of Compliance

A Handbook to Managing Regulatory Risk

Second Edition

Sharon Ward

Routledge
Taylor & Francis Group

LONDON AND NEW YORK

Designed cover image: © Getty Images / everythingpossible

Second edition published 2024
by Routledge
4 Park Square, Milton Park, Abingdon, Oxon, OX14 4RN

and by Routledge
605 Third Avenue, New York, NY 10158

Routledge is an imprint of the Taylor & Francis Group, an informa business

First edition published by Gower 2015 and by Routledge 2016

British Library Cataloguing-in-Publication Data
A catalogue record for this book is available from the British Library

ISBN: 978-1-032-55648-2 (hbk)
ISBN: 978-1-032-55577-5 (pbk)
ISBN: 978-1-003-43130-5 (ebk)

DOI: 10.4324/9781003431305

Typeset in Minion
by codeMantra

Contents

Figures

Foreword

A distinctive and increasingly recognisable role for the Compliance professional has emerged over recent decades. Those working in these roles have a fundamental part to play in how business is conducted, shaping the approach to regulatory compliance within regulated firms and, in doing so, influencing the attitude towards it and the business culture that develops as a result. A robust culture of ethics and integrity within business is being increasingly demanded by all; in fact, by more and more stakeholders, it is not only demanded, it is expected. Yet challenges to achieving this are ever present in an increasingly complex global regulatory and business landscape. Better harnessing the benefits of compliance activities, together with the abilities of the professional compliance personnel who perform them, is an obvious next step.

The professionalisation of the compliance industry lies at the heart of ICA's activities, with supporting and developing those who work within these roles being at the core of what we do. As such, it remains our ongoing commitment to advancing both standards in compliance and the standing of Compliance practitioners. In doing so, we actively support measures taken to promote the role of Compliance and to educate business about the benefits to be gained from better utilising the pool of knowledge and experience Compliance professionals offer. In this timely text, the crucial role the Compliance function plays within individual businesses, the wider regulatory and business environment, and between regulators and regulated businesses, is demonstrated and championed. In encouraging the further enabling of the function and highlighting the benefits to be achieved in doing so, it reinforces many of the points that lie at the heart of our own approach. In making clear the link between regulatory risk and compliance risk; in identifying the impact of the Compliance role beyond that of individuals and individual firms through to the wider regulatory environment; in charting the development of the function and the many influences upon it; in detailing current best practice in Compliance activities and approach; in providing comment on and analysis of the practical impact that changes in the regulatory arena have had; in showing how both the role and Compliance professionals themselves have developed as a consequence; and in concluding with an array of recommendations for future development of the role itself and the role of key stakeholders in doing so, this text recognises that the Compliance field and the demands placed on those who work within it will continue to develop to reflect the world in which we live and work and that, through our many different activities, we can all help shape this to the mutual benefit of all stakeholders, regardless of their individual objectives.

As the way in which both Compliance and how those working in this field are viewed continues to mature, we support the author in her view that there is a clear need for key stakeholders to take hold of the reins of the profession's development and, in doing so, channel their commitment to embedding the ethos and approach we are all agreed is necessary to develop the business culture of fairness and the regulatory outcomes we are all aiming for and desire.

Bill Howarth
Former Chief Executive and Life President
International Compliance Association

Much has happened in the business environment since Bill Howarth kindly provided the Foreword to the first edition of this text. In this most recent edition, we retain the content and focus of previous editions, whilst revisiting certain key elements to provide updates on developments and insight into current challenges and practice.

Dedication and Thanks

My thanks to all who assisted in this project in so many different ways. Too many to count, you know who you are and how greatly I have appreciated your input. With particular thanks, however, to MJH and HS for their insightful contributions and for giving so freely of their time during the production of the first edition of this text, without which it would never have gone beyond an idea nor been finalised. I couldn't have done it without you. Thank you again MJH for your help with this most recent addition, and to those who undertook proof reading, most notably CW and DJH. Any inadvertent mistakes or oversights do, of course, remain my own. Lastly, my thanks to my former colleagues at ICA for their support and encouragement in the early stages of this endeavour and to current and future students who continue to act as a spur to its production and update. You remain an inspiration and a continued source of encouragement in all of our professional endeavours.

Acknowledgements

In producing this text, a significant debt is owed to the many individuals, groups and bodies who have written, or contributed to, a vast array of papers, studies, research, investigations, commentaries and so forth on the numerous topics that impact compliance and the Compliance role, not least those such as regulation, supervision, governance, risk and ethics. I have drawn extensively on such output, much of which has been cited in the body of this text or referred to in the accompanying bibliography; where specific reference has been made to these works for the purposes of illustration and education, every effort has been made to ensure these are appropriately attributed and referenced. Further detail and information on any such work may be located via the information and links provided, all forms of copyright of such material remaining with the relevant authors. I am indebted too to the many Compliance professionals, spanning numerous industry sectors and jurisdictions around the world and comprising senior and junior practitioners, educators, regulators and commentators, who have shared their views on this developing profession with me in so many different capacities over many years; in doing so they have helped shape my own views and continue to do so.

Introduction

OVERVIEW

As the business environment has grown in size and complexity over recent decades, so too have the risks arising within it. Reflecting this, regulatory requirements put in place to help manage these have increased, bringing with them their own challenges. As a consequence, the role of regulatory Compliance functions in regulated firms, tasked as they are with assisting in the management of risks arising from adherence to (or more specifically *non*-adherence to) such regulations, has grown in prominence.

The role of regulatory Compliance functions in regulated firms has grown in prominence.

The holders of Compliance roles and the activities they undertake provide a vital operational link between regulators and the board of regulated firms; i.e., the two principal stakeholders who have a key interest in ensuring regulatory risks are effectively managed. Compliance activities provide valuable oversight and assurance to these key stakeholders that the requirements they have set in support of their respective objectives have been adhered to. However, although the view that 'good compliance is also good business' is now generally recognised within regulated firms – and as a consequence the Compliance function is seen as an essential component in a successful assurance framework – the function itself and those who work within it nevertheless remain an often underutilised resource. There is a tendency to focus on the impact of their actions solely within individual regulated firms, yet the activities of an effective Compliance function – with its close links to governance, operational/business risk management and its underlying support of ethical cultural development – have far more to offer. Greater understanding of the practical

An effective Compliance function – with its close links to governance, operational/business risk management and its underlying support of ethical cultural development – has far more to offer.

DOI: 10.4324/9781003431305-1

Compliance role and of the skills common to those working within this area will increase recognition of how this function can be further enabled to:

- assist all stakeholders within the regulatory environment in which business takes place and in which regulated firms operate in achieving their risk management aims,
- make clear the significance of this for the financial services industry as a whole.

BACKGROUND

One of the most widely acknowledged consequences of the global financial crisis of 2008 was the severe damage done to the reputation of the financial services industry. As the industry embarked on a global struggle to recover its reputation, it has subsequently and regrettably been hindered by the unfortunate regularity with which additional reputation-damaging scandals have punctuated the international and national news. While much has been written on the specific causes of these, their emergence has given weight to the belief that the ethos and values at the heart of the industry have become distorted, providing a fertile breeding ground for many problematic practices that have become embedded, seemingly intractably. In many ways, the global crisis encouraged a spotlight to be firmly focused on this age-old area of business, bringing to light practices and attitudes that were, by any objective measure, unacceptable, but which had been allowed to proliferate seemingly unchallenged during the preceding years. Business relies on confidence and trust,[1] yet the events around the crisis and the emergence of subsequent scandals and failings in related business areas in the years since have shaken the faith of both direct and indirect stakeholders in this industry. There has been a growing realisation that the regulation and business practices intended to manage the many risks inherent within this vital industry were simply not up to the task.

This has made us all look again at what we expect and want from our financial services industry. Across all stakeholders, from the public to regulators to business leaders, there appears to have been, for some time now, a genuine determination to bring about change, recognising that the future success and reputation of the financial services industry depends upon it. Whatever the underlying drivers, we know there needs to be positive transformation. We have had many questions to ask ourselves as to how we could and should bring about this transformation. Should our focus be on enhanced rules and regulations? On improving systems and controls? These existed at the time of the last crisis (and the crisis before that...), but when tested, were found wanting. What then of enforcement and the action to be taken against those who fail to comply with requirements in respect of the rules, regulations, systems and controls that underpin business activities? Again, though widely thought to be robustly in place, when challenged, these too have often been found to be flawed.

Inevitably, calls for a reappraisal of the industry itself, its activities, its motives and indeed our expectations of individuals who work within it grew in the years following the 2008 crisis; with the strength of these calls and spurs to action punctuated by the emergence of further problematic events. In response to this, governments and regulators around the world reviewed, and are continuing to review, regulatory regimes and practices at both a national and international level to address perceived shortcomings. These aim to allow future risks to be identified more effectively and proactively and to clearly demonstrate that

Increasing acceptance of the specific and significant role of individuals, not only in potentially being the source of future problems but also in supplying the solution to the difficulties that have been experienced across the industry.

The most carefully crafted systems and controls in the world are only as strong as the individuals involved in supporting them.

lessons from the past have been learned. New and enhanced requirements have been put in place, including obligations for transparency in business activity, increased focus on governance and greater levels of censure for non-compliance. Most significantly for the issues addressed in this text, however, is increasing acceptance of the specific and significant role of individuals, not only in potentially being the source of future problems but also in supplying the solution to the difficulties that have been experienced across the industry. Conduct risk is currently high on the regulatory agenda, and there is an increasing shift towards focusing on the role of the individual in terms of requirements and responsibilities, as well as those of the collective, such as firms and industry sectors, for example. With this has come an understanding that efforts at remediation should not be confined to enhanced structures and frameworks alone, but also focused on the very heart of business itself, that is, the people and the roles they perform. This recognises that the most carefully crafted systems and controls in the world are only as strong as the individuals involved in supporting them. Essentially, rules and enforcement are all well and good, but they are only effective if they are underpinned by ethics, with ethically motivated individuals, working with integrity, operating genuinely effective mechanisms intent on developing and supporting the rules and enforcing consequences where weaknesses or wrongdoing are identified. Focus should be on embedding integrity and ethics in all working practices, with consideration of the environment that is created and supported. Increasingly, this view is being reflected in the stated aims of industry reforms. This is also where the Compliance function and the activities and approach of the Compliance professionals who work within this arena have a greater role to play, particularly in respect of helping to manage the risks that inevitably emerge.

REGULATION, RISK AND THE ROLE OF COMPLIANCE

The level of regulatory demands on businesses has grown exponentially in the years since the global crisis. This shows little sign of dissipating. From a workload perspective, there has been a resulting impact on those within the various sectors that make up the industry. Surveys of Compliance practitioners have regularly cited matters relating to the level of regulatory change as being of concern, highlighting this as one of the major risks for regulated business. The growing impact of regulatory change and the level of regulatory risk arising from this is increasingly high on the board agenda of most regulated firms.[2] As with any risk within business, however, it is the *management* of this risk, rather than the *avoidance* of it, and the mechanisms through which this is achieved, that are of particular importance. All parties involved have a role to play in ensuring their efficacy; much has been said on what can be done to improve risk management within the business environment, encompassing what to look at, what to change and how prevention of past problems can be assured. Regulators and regulated businesses are faced with many challenges in their efforts to manage not only the risks arising from regulatory changes but also the practical consequences of them.

In this text we develop this theme, looking specifically at:

- *who* is involved in the management of regulatory risk
- *why* it is necessary
- *how* it can be achieved and improved upon
- as well as setting this *who*, *why* and *how* within the context of environments that directly influence this activity.

In particular, we focus on these topics as they relate to the role of the regulatory Compliance function and those who work within it. As we see the role of the function developing, so too do we see the face the function presents to business changing through the actions and approach of regulatory Compliance professionals.

In today's regulatory climate, with its focus on conduct and demonstrable oversight, regulatory risk is a significant business risk for regulated firms and regulators alike. For the two main parties (or stakeholders) with an interest in preventing regulatory risk from manifesting, the consequences of not doing so are considerable:

- For regulated firms, intent on achieving certain business objectives, both the threat of, or actual, regulatory action would impact on achievement of these objectives, increasing the likelihood of reputational damage. Reputational issues are prominent amongst general business risks and, of course, the ultimate consequence of a regulator taking action against them would be the loss of their licence to conduct business, logically resulting in cessation of that business.
- For the regulators, with key strategic and operational objectives to work towards, there are also issues of reputation to consider as there is an expectation within these that regulators will adhere to national and international requirements, together with any recommendations and guidance in respect thereof.
- Furthermore, in an even broader context, the need for the regulator to take action, although in many ways a sign of strength (exemplifying the regulatory regime in action) could, paradoxically, if there were too many such incidents, have detrimental consequences for the reputation of the jurisdiction. This would ultimately impact on the ability of both the regulator and the regulated businesses to achieve their objectives, providing a strong impetus for both to ensure regulatory risks are proactively managed on an ongoing basis.

As we explore the management of regulatory risk within this text we therefore do so from two perspectives: what can be done within regulated firms to limit the possibility of this risk manifesting, and what can be done more generally within the regulatory environment to support this. In doing so, we raise awareness of the Compliance function's role. Compliance risk is closely related to regulatory risk; in essence, the realisation of a compliance risk increases the likelihood of realising a regulatory risk. Accordingly, the management of these risks is linked; the activities of the Compliance function are the means by which regulators and firms can be assured that both are *equally* and *effectively* managed.

THE CHANGING FACE OF COMPLIANCE

The regulatory Compliance function is one that deals with risk management every day. Though just one amongst a number of assurance, oversight and internal control functions performed within regulated firms, as a distinct operational area it is one that has gained in prominence over recent decades and is increasingly recognised as a fundamental part of good business practice. Individuals working in compliance-related roles can increasingly be found in regulated markets across the complete spectrum of industries beyond financial services, including medicine, professional services, pharmaceuticals and food, to name just a few.

Ostensibly, the responsibilities central to the Compliance role lie within a distinct and fairly narrow remit; in practice, however, the activities they undertake in order to meet these responsibilities encompass a far broader arena. This has much wider relevance for, and benefit to, the firms that employ them. These benefits also extend to the various agencies with whom the firm interacts and, indeed, to the wider business environment. The Compliance role has adjusted and developed its remit over many years, reflecting its changing operational environment and the demands placed upon it. Linked to this, the activities and approaches prioritised by the function have shaped the skill set required of the individuals who work in these roles. As we anticipate and respond to further impending change in the regulatory environment, we need to consider what could and should the future role of Compliance be.

Compliance is a role, now embedded within business, which can be further leveraged to provide additional practical advantages for the benefit of all industry stakeholders.

The thesis that underpins this text is that Compliance is a role, now embedded within business, which can be further leveraged to provide additional practical advantages for the benefit of all industry stakeholders. As such, this is a role that requires increased attention and awareness so that these benefits are more readily recognised, and as a result, are more likely to be realised.

In order to appreciate the benefits that can be gained from further enabling and developing the Compliance function, it is helpful to provide context to the purpose and activities of the role as well as understanding around what constitutes the activities and approach of the function more specifically. The three parts of this text have been structured with this in mind, broadly spanning matters that relate to the historic, current and future aspects of the Compliance role:

1. To place the role of Compliance within context, in Part I we begin with an examination of the purpose of regulation and assess how effectively these aims have been achieved within the existing regulatory environment. Next, because the regulation that applies in a particular sector or jurisdiction does not, of course, develop in isolation, we examine the influences and key influencers on the development of regulation and provide a brief history of the development of the Compliance role arising from this. Risk and, more specifically, regulatory risk management within the regulatory environment is then explained and the specificity of the Compliance role is contrasted with those of other more general risk management activities in business.

2. In Part II we commence a deeper exploration of the Compliance role, looking at current approaches and identifying the factors that have particular influence on it. We explore the practicalities that relate to the role, illustrating what is required for initial formation of a Compliance function and then its subsequent development. We conclude with exploration of different compliance activities and the required approach to the role overall to enable it to be effective.

3. Part III then moves beyond the current position, considering the implications of our present focus and future plans. We make clear why Compliance matters and to whom, then consider practical compliance challenges and how these might be addressed. Finally, we discuss how the Compliance role can be strengthened and explain why this is necessary. We conclude with some bold recommendations for the enhancement of the role, highlighting actions that can be taken by key stakeholders, showing why enabling the professionals working within this area will make a valuable contribution to achieving the business environment's stated aim of restoring confidence, and thereby support the fundamental aims of regulation.

USING THIS TEXT

The division of this text into three distinct parts enables it to be used in a variety of ways, depending upon the needs of the reader. For the benefit of those who are either completely new to the topic or simply wish to appreciate all the different elements of the content collectively, the grouping of the topics means that it can be read in Part and Chapter order. Other users, however, may wish to read the text out of sequence. For example, those who predominantly wish to understand the historical and contextual background to the Compliance role and how it developed can focus on Part I; new or aspiring compliance practitioners or others who are specifically interested in the practical aspects of the Compliance role can turn directly to Part II; those whose interests lie in understanding how the role might be further developed can focus on Part III. Read collectively, or individually, it is intended that each of the Parts and Chapters will provide practical insight into the Compliance role and its purpose within business today.

NOTES

1 Dictum Meum Pactum – My word is my bond…
2 Albeit it could be argued this needs to be higher on the agenda of others, with recent and ongoing examples referred to later in this text suggesting closer attention might usefully have been paid to such.

Part I

Compliance Context

To appreciate what the role of Compliance is and how it might be developed to our collective benefit, we need to consider it in context. In Part I of this text we explore the *regulatory environment* which acts as the backdrop to all the material in this text, considering different elements as they contribute to compliance context overall:

- In Chapter 1 we begin by exploring the aims of regulation and the objectives of those who are affected by it. We examine the impact of regulatory failure and the effect of changes arising from this. We reflect on what is meant by 'risk' in this context – specifically regulatory risk – and why management of it is necessary for, and beneficial to, both the regulatory environment within which business activities take place and the different parties involved.
- Chapter 2 focuses on the financial services regulatory environment, building on the topics covered in Chapter 1. We look at the constituent elements of this environment, consider what and who the main influences and influencers are and their impact on the different stakeholders involved. We consider how the regulatory environment is shaped by this, exploring a practical example. We also examine the specific role of the Compliance function – a key influence in its own right – understanding its origins and highlighting key periods in its development. In doing so, we chart its expansion and show how increasing complexity and regulatory requirements introduced and expanded in response to this have given rise to a new profession.
- In Chapter 3, we examine the science and art of regulatory risk management, exploring risk in the regulatory environment and addressing how this can most effectively be managed. We look at the activities necessary to achieve this and the roles of the main stakeholders involved, examining risk in regulatory approaches alongside corporate governance considerations, while reflecting on compliance risk in the context of regulatory risk.

These chapters provide a broader context to our consideration of practicalities in the Compliance role which will be explored in Part II Compliance Focus.

DOI: 10.4324/9781003431305-2

Regulation and Risk

UNDERSTANDING TERMS

Let us begin by exploring some of the main terms that form the basis of discussions in this text: what do we mean by 'risk' in the context of business? Why do we need to 'manage' it? And how is this linked to 'regulation'? A primary consideration here is around the purpose of business: put simply, it is to achieve particular goals, of which making a profit and continued viability of the business operations are usual. The overriding risk considerations in this context relate to threats to the achievement of financial goals and, ultimately, to the business failing and ceasing to trade. The effective management of risk is an inevitable part of business and is therefore vital if business operations are to be successful. This applies at all levels and for all sizes of business, from the smallest to the largest of transactions: failure to effectively manage risk can result in failure to achieve business aims and ultimately lead to failure of the business itself. Of course, in thinking about this, we have to remain aware that the risk landscape is ever changing and is currently much more dynamic than it perhaps has ever been. We must therefore be conscious of the need to evaluate a wider range of business risks and continuously reflect on the most appropriate means of managing these.

One means of managing risk is to put in place measures to ensure that business is transacted in a particular way and thereby reduce the likelihood of potential risks being realised. These measures – a means to *regulate* the way in which business is transacted – might take a variety of forms. They could be derived directly from within the business itself through internal regulations.[1] But as risks arising from the conduct of business are not confined solely to the business itself but may impact a wider set of stakeholders, such measures might be set not only directly by the business but also imposed by external parties, such as in the form of laws or regulations. Requirements intended to manage risks arising from the business may therefore be set by a number of parties, including external entities who have wider responsibilities than just the particular element of which the business is a part,[2] or by regulatory bodies with responsibility for a particular industry sector in which the business operates. The regulations set internally by the business would then themselves reflect the aims of the applicable laws and regulations set by the external parties.

DOI: 10.4324/9781003431305-3

Regulations, of whichever type, place distinct requirements on the way in which business can be carried out. This can have both positive and negative consequences. Consider this example:

Internal or external requirements that activities be carried out within certain parameters might result in the business being viewed more positively by its customers, but these requirements might be at an additional cost to the business. This could be viewed as a negative, particularly if the business considers the costs to exceed the benefits gained from positive customer perception, which would especially be the case if those benefits were effectively unmeasurable. In response to this, those businesses subject to external regulation might challenge the regulations as being unfair, which might then impact on the aims of the internal or external regulators who implemented them in the first place.

In this context, the risk to ongoing business operations can be considered as *regulatory risk*: the risk that there will be an impact from laws or regulations (for example, in respect of removal of authorisation to operate, or changes to laws or regulatory requirements or allowances which might lead to losses, increased costs of doing business or restrictions in business activities, and so on) that will have an effect on business operations, and if negative ultimately to the degree that achievement of financial goals will be hampered and potentially cause the business to fail.

This then leads us to a focus on the related *compliance risk* arising from this which – in this context – is the potential for a regulated business to fail to comply with all the various regulatory requirements, which are essentially the demands placed upon it as a condition of it being allowed to operate.

Balancing the impact of regulation is an important consideration for both regulators and regulated alike.

Balancing the impact of regulation is an important consideration for both regulators and regulated alike, with consequences for the practical management of both regulatory and compliance risk.

REGULATION, RISK AND THE FINANCIAL SERVICES INDUSTRY

The financial services industry is a significant worldwide business, providing jobs for millions and generating billions in monetary terms for the world economy.[3] At both a global and national level, the industry plays a significant role in practical day-to-day operations, offering an environment in which business can be transacted. It is not unreasonable to take the view that without the opportunities afforded by financial services to the many parties involved, business in the form we recognise today – personal, public, national, international and global – would not be possible. Financial services are a core component of modern business activity.

Underpinning all this activity is a complex web of regulation, intended to support the goals of the industry and ensure operations within it are transacted effectively and in an acceptable manner. As to what is acceptable and who the arbiters of this should be, this is not solely the preserve of the financial services industry itself. Due to the nature of this industry and its role, both within business and the world economy, its operations have a broad range of influence. Its activities impact on us all and therefore have systemic implications. The potential for such extensive, system-wide impact across a range of markets, the economy or society as a whole heightens the need to manage the risks inherent within this industry. Therefore, the role of regulation in this market has widespread significance for many, not only those directly involved.

REGULATION

To appreciate the relevance of regulatory and compliance risk management in this broader context and, in turn, appreciate the role of the Compliance function itself in relation to this, it is necessary to consider the purpose of regulation and the needs of participants within the regulatory environment from which regulation emerges.

Although it is a term somewhat open to interpretation, regulation for the purposes of this text is taken to mean 'a rule or directive made and maintained by an authority and/ or the action or process of regulating or being regulated'.[4] Specific definitions vary, but ask the average individual, who will undoubtedly have been subject to regulation in one form or another (such as, for example, 'Do not park here: Subject to a Fine!' or 'Your tax return must be returned on time or you will be subject to penalty' and so on), and they will certainly be able to hazard a guess as to what regulation signifies: namely, statements or instructions either to do or not to do something, at pain of falling foul of certain requirements and being penalised as a result. Consequently, regulation can have quite negative connotations, with its overtones of control and restriction.

> **Regulation for the purposes of this text is taken to mean 'a rule or directive made and maintained by an authority and/or the action or process of regulating or being regulated'.**

But take a step back and think: where would we be without it? In a world with no rules in which each and every one of us could do exactly as we wished, when we wished, what would the consequence be both for ourselves and for everyone else? Would the result be roundly positive for us all? Is it likely that we could all do as we pleased without our choices affecting others? Or would the result be something more akin to chaos? As with many things in life, the true outcome would likely be some combination of both. Historically, however, given the needs of the many, rather than the few, sets of 'rules' to govern behaviour have been introduced. These rules have either developed organically as equitable agreement has been reached between the parties involved about particular behaviours or requirements, or alternatively have been implemented through the use of force (violent or otherwise). Society has then further developed these rules, either formally through laws, or informally through accepted social norms. Although deeper consideration of this interesting subject is beyond the scope of this text, the emergence of rules, guidelines and accepted practice is of relevance to our discussion and should be borne in mind. All of these factors support the fundamental purpose of regulation, which is intended to impose some form of order on interactions, reflecting the mutual goals, whatever these might be, of the participants (or, as they are increasingly known, the *stakeholders*).

Agreements as to the way in which matters will be transacted have continued to develop for different aspects of life over many thousands of years. Business operations have of course been subject to the same process. Broadly, such agreements are concerned with managing the interests of those involved, helping to ensure that all, ideally, have an equal opportunity to achieve their aims. In simple terms the ideal transaction goals could be described as follows:

- *Seller* – wishes to sell a particular product or service and, in doing so, receive fair and adequate recompense (profit) for the resources utilised to produce it;
- *Buyer* – wishes to purchase a particular product or service and, in doing so, make fair and adequate payment for it.

Inevitably, aspects of this 'simple' exchange will be open to interpretation. The goals of each party will likely not necessarily be as idealised in the commercial environment as might be wished or as are presented in this scenario.[5] In addition, there are of course other influences on each transaction (and indeed other stakeholders involved). These issues will be explored shortly. But if we extrapolate the key aims and desires of the parties to this simplified transaction, it provides us with a straightforward summary of what regulation is intended to achieve, essentially:

- Creating an agreed set of rules and requirements, known to each party;
- Providing clarity and openness, thus encouraging fairness and equality.

If a transaction was undertaken on this basis, what would the outcome be? If it allows each party to transact with more confidence, it will encourage participation. This will in turn encourage more participation, more buying and selling, and so the cycle continues, and with increased commerce potential for increased profit. This promotion of confidence in the market, whichever market that happens to be, encourages wider participation than might otherwise be the position if such agreements (that is, regulation) as to the way in which the transaction should be undertaken were not in place.

STAKEHOLDERS IN REGULATION

When we speak of stakeholders in the regulatory environment, who exactly are we referring to? Think about those who have an interest in it, who are affected by the actions that take place within it and the decisions that support those actions. The diagram on the following page provides a simplified overview of the main groups that we might consider as stakeholders in regulation.

The aims and objectives of these stakeholders and the consequent impact of their activities on the regulatory environment will be explored in Chapter 2. For now, think about how the creation and support of confidence in, and trust of, the market for all stakeholders underpins the purpose of regulation (Figure 1.1).

Considering the purpose of regulation in the context of the aims and objectives of these stakeholders, the key characteristics of an effective regulatory environment could be described as follows (Figure 1.2).

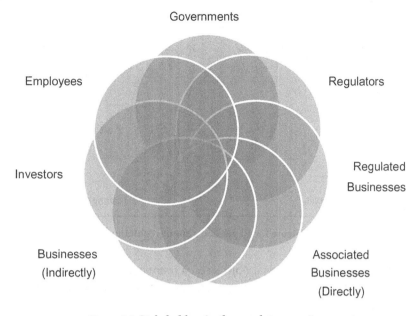

Figure 1.1 **Stakeholders in the regulatory environment**

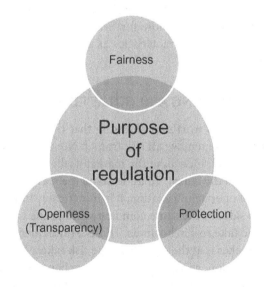

Figure 1.2 **Purpose of regulation**

Of course, depending upon the market and its significance for its stakeholders (itself an important point, which we will return to) other key aims might be:

- the containment of problems arising within the market, so they do not impact on other parties, both within and (and perhaps more importantly?) outside of it;
- ensuring the health (business, financial and so on) of all involved (particularly those with significant influence or power), so that other participants in the market (particularly those less knowledgeable or powerful) are not harmed.

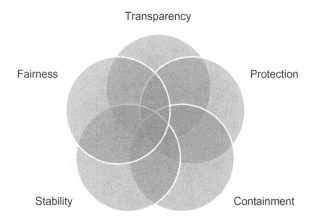

Figure 1.3 **Expanded aims of regulation**

Upon incorporating these additional objectives, a more accurate depiction of the characteristics of an effective regulatory environment might be as per the expanded aims of regulation (Figure 1.3).

These objectives, with varying emphasis depending upon the particular market or sector referred to, lie at the heart of the regulatory objectives of regulators in jurisdictions across the world; objectives we will explore further in Chapter 2. In the meantime, let's look at the implications of these characteristics as we consider their relevance for the development of regulation.

STRUCTURING A REGULATED MARKET

Before proceeding further, it is worth emphasising that the introduction of regulation into a market will not of course remove all risk from it. Nor is it intended to do so. Given the inherent nature of risk and, indeed, of the market itself, this would be an impossible goal, doomed to failure from the outset. To understand the reason for this, we need to appreciate that risk does not operate in isolation; it is inextricably linked with reward. Risk and reward exist as two sides of the same coin and without the opportunity to gain reward there is no reason to take risk in business. This is a fundamental principle of market economics; the reward-seeker is at the same time the risk-taker. This applies to both parties involved in the transaction, as they both seek to exchange something they have for something they do not. However, in participating in the transaction, both parties want to maximise their reward and minimise their risk. This would be fine if both parties participated from a position of equality. In reality, there is invariably inequality between them, which enables one to enjoy disproportionate rewards at the expense of the other suffering disproportionate risk. But what regulation can do, through emphasising transparency, fairness and protection, is 'level the playing field' between the different participants by setting out the 'rules of the game'. At the very least, those intent on participating will then appreciate what they are becoming involved in. In doing so, regulation, regardless of form, encourages market stability and contributes to the means by which negative issues can be effectively contained, thus limiting their impact on the wider environment.

Nevertheless, the existence of regulation to provide structure to a market does not directly equate to an equal understanding of the market for all participants, for how could it? Within many markets, except perhaps the most basic, some participants will be deemed experts and others amateur; there will thus always exist a strong element of unevenness in such environments. The development of legislation needs to take this into account, while accepting that with or without regulation there will always be asymmetries of knowledge. Regulation seeks to manage such inequalities to a greater degree than would otherwise exist by focusing on creating a fair environment through the transparency of requirements and means of redress and in doing so, protects consumers and the markets themselves.

There are many who would argue that formal regulation is unnecessary.[6] Such arguments maintain that the market, in whichever area it exists, will find its own way and, out of this, will form a set of practices acceptable to its participants. Arguably, this is reasonable where the particular market being considered is of minimal importance to anyone else, other than those directly involved. There may thus be a case for leaving well alone and either letting that market decide for itself or allowing it to be governed by non-specific regulation. For example, in the UK the need to regulate the sale of luxury 'brand name' goods might not be seen as a necessity by all, regardless of our view as to whether they are worth the sums charged, but their sale is nevertheless subject to the Consumer Rights Act, which covers the buying and selling of goods and services. However, where activities within a market have wider implications – such as, for example, as is the case with financial services, where the activities of the market have an impact not only on those directly involved but also on non-participants – this requires a different approach if the intrinsic risks are to be managed to the benefit of all stakeholders, including those not directly participating.

FINANCIAL SERVICES REGULATION

The unique role and widespread nature of financial services in business operations today convey upon it a significant level of responsibility. Furthermore, the long-term nature of many financial services products introduces another level of risk: that in addition to their impact in the present time, they can have either an ongoing impact in the future or, somewhat like an unexploded bomb, have a sudden impact many years hence when the product reaches its maturity.

Thus it is not so straightforward to recognise the inherent risks in financial services products as it would be for, say, immediate consumables, such as food products for example, where it would quickly be apparent whether or not these were fit for purpose. Or even perhaps with a more costly purchase, such as a car, where again it would be likely to become more quickly evident that there were problems than with, for example, the provision of a pension or long-term savings product. There exists within financial services, therefore, an even greater need for transparency and for rigorous standards to be adhered to.

The existence of financial services regulation is intended to help provide parity between the different parties in terms of each understanding of what is and what is not acceptable and where a perceived victim of wrong-doing can seek redress. This does not mean, however, that there is always consistency in approach or application. Nevertheless, given the significance of this industry, there is a necessary and not unreasonable expectation that appropriate measures are put in place to manage its risks effectively. Responsibility for doing so lies with the governments of the world, both collectively and within their respective national boundaries, and with the bodies they have set up and charged with this. As a result, regulators exist at an international and national level, and at local and sectoral levels to reflect the myriad complexities of the industry. Regulated entities are subject to supervision and to a range of disciplinary measures should they not adhere to specified requirements. An industry has developed around regulation itself and it is an established part of business life.

WHEN REGULATION FAILS

Given its overriding purpose and a general agreement on behalf of stakeholders that regulation in some form or another is necessary, what happens when regulation fails or is perceived to have failed? The distinction between *actual* and *perceived* failure is in fact an important one and we will return to this topic, but first, we will consider the impact on the regulatory environment and the stakeholders within it when it is known or believed that the aims of regulation – that is, to support the existence of a fair and open market in which all can securely participate – have been compromised in some way. Consider the almost immediate consequence of stakeholders realising or believing that the market is not as they understood it to be. This can be summed up in a single phrase: loss of confidence. Think about the following example, with which you will no doubt be familiar.

A Crisis of Confidence

The events of the global financial crisis at the end of the 2000s sparked worldwide crises of confidence in the financial and financial services markets. The ramifications of this were felt by us all, as the shock waves of the financial fallout spread and continued to filter through during the years that followed. At an **individual level**, for example, many were impacted through job loss or inability to access credit. At a **national level**, many jurisdictions saw the failure of long-standing institutions and billions of pounds wiped off share values. At a **global level**, both the immediate impact of the crisis and the contagion effect which contributed to many subsequent crises that arose in different jurisdictions or sectors had ramifications for other jurisdictions and sectors and for the global economy as a whole. All of this effectively highlighted the increasingly interconnected nature of the worldwide markets and the consequences thereof.

Once confidence in a market is lost, the implications are significant and can be disastrous. Confidence is the lifeblood of commerce and once undermined, irrespective of the market, cannot easily be restored. There have been numerous examples over recent

decades that have contributed to a growing loss of confidence in certain individuals, organisations, sectors, industries and even nations. For example[7]:

Mis-selling of pensions and mortgages (UK), BP oil spill incident, US Savings &
Loan crisis, Greece Bailout, 1987 stock market crash 'Black Monday', Barings and
Nick Leeson, MMR vaccine, Long-Term Capital Management (LTCM) collapse,
1987 Asian Financial Crisis, MPs' expenses scandal, Dot.com Crisis, Enron fraud
scandal, Iceland bankruptcy, Worldcom scandal, Siemens Bribery Case, Bank
of Credit and Commerce International (BCCI) scandal, Parmalat bankruptcy,
JP Morgan Chase Bank – Cease & Desist orders by the Federal Reserve, Shell
Transport, Martha Stewart Insider Dealing Case, UBS and Kweku Adoboli,
Lehman Brothers collapse, Northern Rock run on the bank, Citibank enforce-
ment over AML weaknesses, Citigroup and Robert Casoni insider trading, LIBOR
rigging, Eurozone crisis, Madoff Scandal, Societe Generale and Jerome Kerviele,
Co-operative Bank and Paul Flowers, Standard Chartered fine in respect of Iran
Transaction Regulations, HSBC Money Laundering case, Panama Papers, Wells
Fargo, Cambridge Analytica, Wirecard, Theranos.[8]

Consider the impact on general market confidence of these few cases alone. Note both the
wide range of topics and different business sectors involved – scandals are not restricted
to one type of business. These examples illustrate how issues arising within particular
industries can have a detrimental impact on confidence, not only amongst those directly
affected by the particular issue but more widely still. Such events raise concerns amongst
stakeholders, leading to fear and mistrust, which may spill over into other areas too and
thus contribute to greater business detriment overall.

One notable consequence of a loss of confidence or trust in a particular market is
withdrawal from participation in the market itself. An example of this at a commercial
level was the reluctance of the banks to lend to each other during the 2008 credit crisis as
concerns grew as to both their own financial health (or rather their potential ill health!)
and that of their contemporaries. The impact of this was marked and, from a purely
commercial perspective, resulted in a slowing down of the wheels of commerce and thus
the generation of profit. In many cases, there was realisation of losses, which in some
instances proved catastrophic. Loss of trust in key markets, such as financial services,
invariably has severe implications for us all. A post-crises example was the situation in
Europe in the 2010s, with confidence in the Eurozone and the continuance or otherwise
of the Euro very much a topic for concern, particularly so in certain countries.[9] This inevitably impacted upon investment into the countries affected and therefore the support of
business and job creation within those countries, with consequences for both states and
individuals. Countries experiencing challenges respond in different ways, for example
in the post-crisis years of the early 2010s, during a so-called period of austerity in the
UK, there was an increased level of focus on the relationship with the EU. In the 2016
'Brexit' vote, the population voted to depart this relationship, with significant implications for all stakeholders involved, not least in respect of activities pertinent to this text,

including provision of financial services and activities therein, with work in this area ongoing. More recently still, the widespread uncertainty around how the challenges arising from the Covid-19 global pandemic, particularly in the early days of 2020, brought its own challenges, as governments and agencies around the world reacted at different speeds and with differing areas of focus; the consequences of this were felt by all of us, businesses and individuals alike.

The fact that issues arising in a particular sector can affect not only the sector directly involved, but also others less obviously linked, is a significant one. The ramifications of this can be severe and widespread, affecting business in many ways. In the financial services sector, for example, the almost non-stop emergence of problem after problem, scandal after scandal, in the period immediately following the global financial crisis, in the previous decades and indeed since then, has eroded public confidence to such a degree that the likelihood of a return to the once strong level of belief and faith in financial institutions seems almost impossible to imagine. As a result of the tumult of scandals, issues, problems and difficulties, this industry (and indeed those working within it) is increasingly viewed in a negative manner by the wider public. When put together with scandals emanating from other industry sectors, there has been a growing increase in public dissatisfaction with the efficacy of regulation generally. Regulatory scandals, mismanagement of business and the perceived weakness of the regulatory approach have contributed to an increasingly pessimistic view. What can be done to tackle this?

> **There has been an increase in public dissatisfaction with the efficacy of regulation.**

REALITY VERSUS PERCEPTION

Necessity certainly focuses the mind. When the perception of the effectiveness of regulation is weakened, demonstrating the benefits and strength of it is more important than ever, and never more so than in the financial services sector. To many, particularly the uninitiated in the sector – that is, the wider public with whom regulated firms do business – *perception is all*. Irrespective of what the *actual* position is, *how* it is perceived is deemed to be the truth.[10] As a consequence, consider the following statement:

> **When the perception of the effectiveness of regulation is weakened, demonstrating the benefits and strength of it is more important than ever.**

There might be a regulation in place to prevent a certain action or activity, but as this is not seen to be used or, if used, is not perceived as effective, then the perception overall is adverse and, when distilled down, supports the view that all regulation is ineffective.

The types of failings and scandals previously referred to, of which there have been and continue to be far too many over the years, have greatly contributed to this perception. The perceived weakness of the regulatory regime in preventing these is likewise a key factor.

Although much ire for the events of the global financial crisis was laid at the excesses of 'greedy bankers',[11] failure of the regulatory system to rein in these excesses was also perceived as significant in determining the nature and scale of how events developed. In the extreme, in view of the tax and other revenues generated by the financial services sector, there are some who might argue that *over*regulation, or rather too close an examination of the business models in operation, is not desirable[12] and thus we come back to those related issues of trust and perception. Responding to these calls for action through the development of additional legislation is an inevitable response and there have been many moves in this direction. However, this harks back to our earlier comments on the need for balance, and care must be taken by policymakers to consider the wider impact of such developments fully before implementation.

ADDRESSING THE CHALLENGES

Many efforts have been made to address the perceived and accepted failings within business over the years. Sadly though, this is something that goes through cycles of failings, leading to regulatory action followed by other (or indeed the same) failings followed by regulatory action and so on,[13] almost on a loop, but with a little perceived level of consistent success, being reactive rather than proactive. One of the chief conclusions to be drawn from the continuing emergence of such problems is that problems continue to occur despite the introduction of ostensibly tougher regulation and the ongoing requirements arising from it, together with the continued efforts of regulators and other stakeholders at jurisdictional and sectoral levels, plus the activities of assurance, control and oversight functions within individual regulated businesses. The inevitable inference, therefore, is that elimination of such problems is unlikely. But if in addressing this we do what we have always done, we will inevitably keep getting the same result. Consequently, we need to change what we are doing in some way in order to achieve a different outcome. With that in mind, what can be done to remove, or at least limit, the effect (the risks) of these problems for all those who have a stake in the business marketplace? Will what is currently being proposed, developed and acted upon be sufficient?

As we ponder this question, it is perhaps useful to keep in mind that a key role of government in a capitalist economy is the provision of a framework to curb capitalism's excesses. To quote partially from Sir Winston Churchill, 'The inherent vice of capitalism is the unequal sharing of blessings ....'.[14] We might also add a variation to his observation on democracy and say that '*Capitalism* is the worst form of *economics*, except all those other forms that have been tried from time to time'.[15] Churchill's acerbic wit aside, both these observations neatly help to highlight the weaknesses inherent in a market economy. Good regulation should prevent the excesses inherent in a market system borne of capitalism and human nature. By taming these excesses, regulation aims to provide a framework within which all participants can equitably participate.

PRESENT VERSUS FUTURE FOCUS

Regulation reflects the aims of the stakeholders involved. Of course, in the drafting of laws and regulations, the focus inevitably tends to be on the issues that are prominent at the time[16] and, more often than not, these require subsequent enhancements when they do not fully meet their stated objectives. However, this is only to be expected given the complex nature of the issues involved: there is no single perfect solution. It is also worth remembering that the focus of any change at any given time will necessarily be on these prominent issues at the possible expense of others that, while seemingly minor at that moment, may be impacted by other factors and turn into prominent issues in the future.

The events of recent years have given us much to think about in terms of our approach to regulation and there has been much change as a consequence. Change is ongoing, with influential bodies and regulators around the world re-examining these issues, putting in place new approaches and planning further modifications as illustrated by the volume of activities and initiatives. The range and depth of the output over time of just one of these bodies, the Basel Committee on Banking Supervision (BCBS),[17] illustrates this effectively:

- Basel III.
- Methodology for assessing and identifying global systemically important banks (G-SIBs) regulatory consistency.
- Framework for dealing with domestic systemically important banks (D-SIBS).
- Regulatory Consistency Assessment Programme (RCAP).
- Liquidity Stress Testing.
- Supervisory expectations regarding audit quality of banks.
- Revised core principles for banking supervision.
- Supervisory framework for measuring and controlling large exposures.

In the years following the global crisis, at both global and national levels, efforts have been made to demonstrate that lessons have indeed been learned.

In the UK, for example, there was a complete overhaul of the regulatory regime in the early 2010s and a demonstrable shift away from so-called 'light touch' regulation towards more active intervention, with the new regulators issuing pronouncements in support of this. In *The Prudential Regulation Authority (PRA) approach to banking supervision*[18] paper published by the Bank of England, Prudential Regulation Authority in October 2012, it was made clear that there was a shift in emphasis: 'the PRAs approach will rely significantly on judgement ... will be forward looking ... will focus on those issues and those firms that pose the greatest risk to the stability of the UK FS system'. In terms of Threshold conditions,[19] which set out the regulators' expectations of regulated firms, it was made clear that 'The PRA will expect firms not merely to meet and continue to meet the letter of these requirements but also to consider the overriding principle of safe and soundness'. This 'safe and soundness' element provides insight into this regulator's views on priorities around the operations of regulated firms. In support of this, in his *The new approach to financial regulation* speech in May 2013, Andrew Bailey, the then Deputy Governor of the PRA,[20] made the point that:

the financial crisis has through adversity reminded us of the importance of banks to the functioning and health of the economy and their role as providers of critical financial services ... The crisis has been a searing experience for banks and regulators, precisely because at times they have both failed to fulfil this central objective of maintaining safety and soundness and hence the continuous supply of critical services to the public …

Since then, we have seen regulators maintain focus on such matters, while adjusting to reflect current priorities such as, for example, responding to challenges as varied as the Covid-19 pandemic, the rise in fraud and increasing levels of technological developments. More recently still, events such as the war in Ukraine, the rise in energy prices and the ongoing global economic challenges will need to have been considered. All such have continued to shape the regulatory landscape, with different elements given priority at different times while contributing to the development of the regulatory environment overall.

Continuing our UK example, there have been significant and ongoing developments in this jurisdiction over recent years. This has been not least in response to the decision on the part of the British public to leave the EU following the 'Brexit' vote, with consequences for the financial services regulatory environment and stakeholders therein. Following a tumultuous period in the years following the vote in 2016, the unwinding of the close framework that existed between the UK and the EU was required, spanning numerous industry sectors including financial services, with inevitable impact on business operations in a practical sense: uncertainty, lack of clarity, the need to continue 'business as usual' against a shifting backdrop. All of this will have impacted the nature of risk arising within the business environment, with relevance for its management and the roles of those tasked with this. During this time *The Future Regulatory Framework (FRF)* was 'established to determine how the financial services regulatory framework should adapt to the UK's new position outside of the European Union (EU), and how to ensure the framework is fit for the future'[21] with two consultations, the first in October 2020, and a second which closed in February 2022. Alongside this, the Financial Services Act 2021 was implemented in April 2021, representing a 'major milestone in shaping a regulatory framework for UK financial services outside of the EU'.[22] The Financial Services and Markets Bill, intending to implement the FRF proposals, was unveiled in July 2022 and is due to come into law some time in 2023. Those working in the roles discussed within this text will need to maintain ongoing awareness of the developments as regards specifics of this Bill and the objectives of the FRF, with consideration to their relevance for their organisation and sectors, as these continue to significantly impact how the future regulatory and Compliance environments develop within this jurisdiction.

We will explore some of the actual initiatives and activities at both global and national level as we move through this text. However, a key element of more recent thinking is increasing focus on an aspect of the regulatory structure that actually lies at the very heart of business and is worth our focus at this point. Namely, the people, their ethics and behaviours. Elevating the attention paid to individuals' activities and behaviours, to matters of ethics and integrity and to the role they play within financial services, and other such shifts in thinking, provides scope for a change in regulatory approach that will have wide-reaching ramifications for us all. Viewed objectively, this shift in focus has emerged not only from those directly involved (such as regulators), but from the wider stakeholders – the consumers, investors and ordinary people – demanding change to establish a market that more accurately reflects the risks inherent within it and the intended aims of regulation that we have discussed in this chapter.

This shift in focus is a good illustration of how the regulatory environment is influenced and how it continuously adapts to meet the needs of its stakeholders. What – and indeed who – these *Influences* and *Influencers* are, and their consequences for stakeholders, is explored in Chapter 2 as we continue our consideration of context in the development of the Compliance role.

NOTES

1 For example, in the form of policy, systems and controls that reflect the aims of the business.
2 Such as the laws of the jurisdiction in which the business is based, for example.
3 The International Monetary Fund website provides some interesting data on this topic.
4 Adapted from Oxford Lexico definition www.lexico.com.
5 There is also the likelihood of shifting stakeholder roles to consider, for example their role as buyer/seller – or indeed more widely their role as influencers on the market – will likely change at different times or in different circumstance, with them being one type of stakeholder at a particular point, a different one at another, and thus influencing the market in different ways.
6 There are numerous commentaries and texts on just this topic for those interested in exploring it further, a number of which are included in the Bibliography.
7 A small sample is provided here for illustrative purposes only. Those not familiar with some of these cases can access ample information on each by simply typing the name into an internet search engine.
8 At the time of writing the collapse of a cryptocurrency firm FTX has been announced, with it being reported in court documents that the newly appointed FTX CEO John J Ray III, with his many years of experience working with companies through bankruptcy, including Enron, had said: 'Never in my career have I seen such a complete failure of corporate controls and complete absence of trustworthy financial information as occurred here'. Note this article www.cbsnews.com/news/ftx-bankruptcy-john-ray-ceo-failure/. It will be interesting to watch the progress of this case.
9 Such as Greece.
10 It could be argued that the growth in social media engagement and activism over the past decade, its expanded reach and usage, may increasingly be contributing to shaping understanding of what truth, objectively, is believed to be or perceived to be. We will explore this point and related topics further in Chapter 2 when we discuss *Influences*.
11 Comments and headlines along these lines have been frequent in the years since the global financial crisis, referenced at all levels. For example, note: www.parliament.uk/search/results/?q=Greedy+Bankers; and keep in mind when considering *Influences* and *Influencers* in Chapter 2.
12 Advocating instead something more akin to a lighter touch form of regulation, which, as its name suggests, advocates a lighter rather than a hard approach to regulation in terms of setting out requirements, putting in place restrictions on activity, and so on, considered to have been adopted in the early part of the decade prior to the global financial crisis of the late 2000s, for example in the UK banking industry. In hindsight, this approach was roundly criticised and we explore aspects of this criticism later in this text.
13 We will discuss some key regulatory actions in subsequent chapters of this text.
14 The quote then concludes 'The inherent virtue of socialism is the equal sharing of miseries', which is a matter for personal politics and a whole other discussion.
15 For the correct quote substitute 'Democracy & Government. From a House of Commons' speech on 11 November 1947.
16 For example, the Uniting and Strengthening America by Providing Appropriate Tools Required to Intercept and Obstruct Terrorism Act of 2001 (USA PATRIOT Act) signed into law on 26 October 2001, shortly after the terrible events of 11 September that year. This significantly increased focus on terrorism, money laundering and financial crime prevention.
17 Note the BCBS website available via www.bis.org at www.bis.org/bcbs/index.htm?ql=1/.

18 See www.bankofengland.co.uk/publications/Documents/other/pra/bankingappr1210.pdf/.

19 The minimum standards for becoming and remaining authorised.

20 Now Governor of the Bank of England.

21 Financial Services Future Regulatory Framework Review: Proposals for Reform – Response to the Consultation – July 2022, HM Treasury assets.publishing.service.gov.uk/government/uploads/system/uploads/attachment_data/file/1092499/FRF_Review_-_Proposals_for_Reform__Government_Response_-_July_2022_.pdf.

22 www.gov.uk/government/news/milestone-for-uk-financial-services-as-bill-receives-royal-assent.

2

Influences and Influencers

THE FINANCIAL SERVICES REGULATORY ENVIRONMENT

The regulatory environment we have in place today did not emerge in isolation from other factors. It developed over many years, a consequence of the shifting influences which have shaped it over time. In their different ways, each of the factors that combine to create the existing regulatory environment has an effect on the approach to the management of risk and on the roles and activities of those involved. Ultimately, therefore, this regulatory environment impacts the overall business environment which operates across the globe. Whether we think of practical failings, scandals or the development of regulatory responses arising from these, the factors that contribute to the current regulatory environment impact how the risks intrinsic within the business environment are perceived and influence our responses to them. An understanding of such factors, whether direct and indirect in their level of influence, can help us appreciate the environment in which the management of regulatory and compliance risk takes place.

Accepted norms and requirements naturally play a key role in business and have done so since man first bartered a fish for a rabbit, or whatever the first trade may have been. During that time, these have adapted to reflect the prevailing business environment. The business environment itself will have been cultivated by many seemingly unrelated factors which have nevertheless conspired to shape its development. In this regard, the financial services environment is no different from any other and a variety of factors that influence it come together to form the regulatory environment within which regulated business takes place.

In order to understand this environment – and consequently appreciate the need to manage regulatory and compliance risk and the role of Compliance in relation to it – it is useful to examine the wider *influences* that have helped shape it over the years and recognise that these continue to do so:

- considering the roles they play;
- identifying any specific responsibilities that might arise from those roles;
- contemplating what their bearing on the regulatory environment is and why;
- examining their relevance for regulatory and compliance risk management.

Emerging from this, we can observe the rise of the Compliance function, note its areas of focus and consider its development within the risk management framework of the

DOI: 10.4324/9781003431305-4

regulatory environment. For the purposes of focused consideration of a particular regulatory environment, many of the practical examples referred to within this chapter are drawn from a specific jurisdiction, the UK, with those from other jurisdictions supplied in support where necessary and/or to make or expand on a particular point.

INFLUENCES AND INFLUENCERS

It is fair to say myriad influences combine to create the regulatory environment; the combination of these and their effect is considerable. The following diagram provides a simplified overview of the main elements that make up this environment while illustrating how wide-ranging they are (Figure 2.1).

Constitution, Sector, Culture, Crisis, Economics, Experience, Jurisdiction, Laws, Codes, Guidance, Type of product or service, Legal system, Regulatory Models, Industry, Objectives, Politics, Precedent, Regulation, Regulatory Framework, Rules, Scandals, Technology, Type of market, World Events, Investigations, Attitude.

Figure 2.1 Influences on the regulatory environment

Each of the elements that contribute to the regulatory environment more generally – as well as developments in regulation specifically – can be strongly affected by a range of influences.

An awareness and appreciation of the *actual* or *potential* impact of such influences allows us to understand more readily the setting within which regulatory and compliance risk must be managed.

All of these create the backdrop for further developments and must be taken into account if the regulatory environment is to be properly understood. Each of the elements that contribute to the regulatory environment generally – as well as developments in regulation specifically – can be strongly affected by a range of influences. Influences in this context are those matters, real or imagined, that have an effect on the regulatory environment. Without being too specific at this stage (we will consider the detail of this topic when exploring the Compliance environment in Part II) our focus here is on high-level influences that may or may not be directly related to financial services, but which nevertheless have in common an impact on the thinking and/or approach of stakeholders within the regulatory environment and/or the activities thereof. Consequently, they act as a stimulus for change, providing pressure or inspiration, that, in turn, has some bearing upon developments within the environment and thereby influence upon its resulting form. An awareness and appreciation of the *actual* or *potential* impact of such influences allow us to understand more readily the setting within which regulatory and compliance risk must be managed.

In addition to these more general influencing factors, the regulatory environment is shaped not least by the stakeholders who contribute to it through their activities, but also by how they respond to the issues that inevitably arise as a result. These stakeholders are the *Influencers* of this chapter's title, and it is their actions and approach that impact the development of the regulatory environment. The extent to which they can *impact* the regulatory environment is largely reliant upon their level of *influence* over it. However, as will be explored in this chapter, such influence may not always be as clear-cut as it first appears.

As the range of influencers in the following diagram illustrates (Figure 2.2), not all of this influence need be direct in the sense that the stakeholder is closely involved in setting or supporting the actual *structure* of the financial services environment (such as would be the case for regulators or international standards bodies, for example).

International bodies, Employees, Advisors, Regulated Institutions, Government, Institutions, Industries, Media, Criminals, Credit Rating Agencies, Investors, Lobby Groups, Management, Campaigners, Regulators, Politicians, Courts.

Figure 2.2 **Influencers on the regulatory environment**

Influences and influencers may be influential in a broader, possibly less tangible sense (such as in the case of media coverage or technological developments, for example). This is an important distinction, as practical experience has shown again and again that it can be the intangible issues which have the greatest impact. The issue of perception and its impact on confidence discussed in Chapter 1 is a particularly useful example of this.

Some of these influences and influencers will now be considered, demonstrating the importance of these in the development of the regulatory environment overall.[1]

Influences

- *Constitution and legal system*: the constitution of a jurisdiction, reflecting its history, will undoubtedly have had an impact upon the development of law within that jurisdiction. The type of legal system in place: common law, civil or administrative – will shape on the way in which law is practised and laws implemented.[2] This will in turn have influenced the form of regulation adopted (for example, civil law and common law jurisdictions take a different approach).
- *Crises*: periods of crisis, either national or international, contribute to the development of the regulatory environment in multiple ways, encouraging the prioritisation of certain issues over others, or promoting certain agendas or actions. For example, at an international level, the European sovereign debt crises of the early 2010s raised the possibility of Eurozone countries defaulting on their debts, causing widespread concern in markets around the whole world, i.e., not just in the Eurozone itself. This prompted different jurisdictions to review and adjust their monetary relationships with each other. Various banking crises that have occurred in different countries around the world, e.g., Argentina in 2001 or Japan in the late 1990s, are other useful examples. More recently still, the worldwide crisis resulting from the spread of the Covid-19 virus provides a clear practical illustration of the need for the regulatory environment to rapidly adjust, for example in relation to the regulation in place around the development, trials and delivery of vaccines.

- *Culture*: the cultural practices that exist within a particular environment (that is, the way in which things are done, what is considered acceptable and what is not) perform a pivotal role in business and have undoubted relevance for the regulatory environment. Business practices in many parts of the world differ as a result of these cultural influences and knowledge of these is important if the background against which business is transacted is to be understood. As an example, think of HSBC's 'The world's local bank' advertising strategy, introduced in 2002 and prevalent for many years thereafter, which sought to gain commercial advantage through its portrayal of a worldwide bank which, although multinational, still had the flexibility to understand the local nuances of each market it operated in. Of course, regulatory development is not always in line with wider societal development – as in other respects it is so often playing catch up and, as a consequence, its focus on matters such as culture, may lag somewhat behind what is currently being prioritised elsewhere.
- *Economic*: economic factors, such as increases in competition or trade reforms for example, will impact upon decision-making within a jurisdiction or sector and affect which matters are given focus and priority. Again, responses to the Covid-19 pandemic provide pertinent examples in this regard.
- *Experience*: this plays a vital role, particularly in how the regulatory environment is perceived by participants. Major lessons from history (such as the 1929 stock market crash or dot-com bubble of the early 2000s, for example), or experiences within a particular jurisdiction or sector (such as rising house prices or times of economic hardship, for instance), will have a definite impact on future regulatory developments and, in turn, on the regulatory environment, whether positive or negative. For example, if there has been a problem with a particular financial product or service, such as a scandal or reporting of regulatory failure in respect of it, this will remain in the minds of potential consumers and other stakeholders, or indeed regulators who had to deal with the fallout, for some time and will in turn influence future reform – a practical example might include if people have experienced a run on a bank (such as that on Northern Rock in the UK in 2007), or a currency devaluation (note the case of Zimbabwe during the last decade, for example), this might naturally incline them to be cautious. Conversely, experiences perceived as positive, of which unfortunately there appear to be far fewer (at least in comparison to negative experiences) have the opposite effect, encouraging participation (see World Events, below). A useful example of this is that found in countries during periods of growth and boom, such as in America in the 1950s or in the Western world in the few years preceding 2007. Recent and ongoing activities around investment/speculation (dependent on your viewpoint) in cyber currency, such as Bitcoin, for instance, is an interesting ongoing example when set against the backdrop of worldwide geopolitical and similarly significant events of recent years, combining as it does elements of both.
- *Guidance*: linked to, but separate from, formal laws or regulations, guidance is often a feature of the regulatory environment. Emanating from a number of different sources (see international bodies, regulators, industry groups, and so on below, for example), guidance focusing on various topics (such as a particular product or service, or a particular sector, for example) supports formal requirements and assists stakeholders in their implementation.

- *Investigations or reviews*: decisions to focus on particular issues (for example the Walker review into corporate governance in banks and other financial institutions in the UK in 2009,[3] the international investigation into LIBOR[4] rigging from 2013, and so on) although often arising from existing concerns, can broaden awareness and so spread the level of concern, prompting further calls for action.
- *Jurisdiction or sectors*: different jurisdictions and different industry sectors within them may have specific requirements or issues that will impact the regulatory environment that exists to support them. For instance, business undertaken in so-called 'off shore' jurisdictions often focuses on specific activities,[5] and therefore particular issues are sometimes prioritised over others (such as certain jurisdictions being used as tax havens, for example, or having been targeted by financial criminals in the past, so requiring tighter security or focus).
- *Laws and codes*: implementation of new laws, though perhaps intended to address current or past real or perceived issues, nevertheless has an impact on the existing and subsequent environment. They shape the environment in which the regulator operates, having direct consequences for their own objectives and the tools available to them to achieve those objectives. Whether already in place or those planned, these provide shape to the structure of the regulatory environment. For example, the *UK Corporate Governance Code*, the latest version of which was published in 2018, which sets out standards of good practice in relation to board leadership and effectiveness, remuneration, accountability and relations with shareholders.[6]
- *Objectives*: the aims of a particular jurisdiction and, by extension, the objectives with which regulators in that jurisdiction are tasked, strongly influence the regulatory environment. For example, if one key aim of a jurisdiction is the prevention of financial crime in that jurisdiction, this is likely to be enshrined within law and be apparent within the approach taken by the regulator.[7]
- *Politics*: influences of a political nature can be significant. Following the election of new governments, in most instances there is a change in regulatory approach. For example, in the UK, the appointment of the Conservative/Liberal coalition government in 2010 was followed by a fundamental change to the existing regulatory model. Prior to that, when the Labour Party won the 1997 election, this was swiftly followed by an announcement of a complete change in the regulatory system and the formation of a new regulator. On an ongoing basis thereafter, parties in office or indeed opposition parties, will raise issues on the political agenda that can often have a significant impact on the regulatory environment.
- *Precedent*: although, as is often said, 'past performance is no guarantee of future performance', what has gone before undoubtedly influences future plans. Once a precedent has been set for an action or approach, it is likely that this will be adhered to in subsequent developments unless there is a particularly strong reason for not doing so.
- *Regulation and rules*: the formal regulation that exists in a particular jurisdiction provides a central pillar of the regulatory environment. The types of rules put in place, be these conduct-of-business-related (such as rights, suitability of recommendations and discretionary dealings, the standard of advice and disclosure regarding charges, for example) or prudential (capital reserves, liquidity standards, and so

forth), focus attention on specific issues and in so doing shape the regulatory environment to reflect these. Together with other key aspects (see regulatory framework, below, for example) these provide the formal context within which regulated business is carried out.

- *Regulatory framework*: this is the framework within which regulators operate, comprising their legal powers as enshrined in law, their objectives arising from these, the regulatory model adopted in support of this and the approach to regulation taken by them in the implementation of their powers. Each of these elements will be addressed in greater detail in the Influencers section of this chapter.

- *Regulatory models*: the type of regulatory model that exists in a particular jurisdiction will have a marked effect on how regulation is carried out and experienced within that jurisdiction. There are broadly four commonly accepted models, which will be discussed in Part II of this text as they apply to the Compliance environment specifically. However, at this juncture, it is sufficient to say that those experiencing regulation under one model will have a different experience to those experiencing regulation under another. The model in place will therefore have an impact on approaches within it. As a consequence of the global downturn of recent years, governments around the world looked again at their regulatory models and regulatory approach, both of which directly impact the regulatory environment. It is also important to keep in mind that the level of regulatory maturity will differ from jurisdiction to jurisdiction, sector to sector, and this too will impact the model and approach to implementation.

- *Attitude to risk*: attitude towards risk within the jurisdiction, in many ways a reflection of the jurisdiction's prevailing culture, will impact the regulatory environment, providing a range of influence, some overt and some more subtle. This will have consequences for the implementation of safeguards and support mechanisms, for example, or encourage participation in lesser or more risky business activities.

- *Scandals*: as discussed in Chapter 1, financial services-related scandals, fraud and corruption, bank or key institution collapses and the issues arising from these (such as unclear allocation of senior management responsibilities, weaknesses in systems and controls, fraud and false accounting, and so on) impact public and general confidence. Not only that, but they heavily influence the areas of focus within the regulatory environment during the subsequent period after the scandal has emerged.

- *Technology*: some developments have a worldwide impact, a good example of which is technology. As technological abilities have increased, so too has the way in which this has been utilised as a channel for financial services (sales, distribution, communication, and so forth). Impacts can be as simple as the speed with which business can be undertaken, the spread of news and knowledge and so on, with resulting positive and negative consequences (benefits of promptly hearing important news, for example, contrasting with the regularly reported concerns about decreasing and more limited attention spans. Another useful example is opportunities for easier access to information and services contrasting with the increasing occurrence of fraud). The need to keep up with developments has had a marked impact on the regulatory environment overall, widening the remit of regulators and increasing the need for awareness and understanding of the implications of these. Popular throughout Europe and also in both Asia and Africa, mobile technology is a good practical example of this, providing the opportunity for delivery and receipt of payments via mobile phones. While this gives access to millions of individuals who would not otherwise have access it also provides further regulatory challenges to ensure fairness, limit the potential for criminal use and so on. Technology gives rise to new types of threats, which in turn shape regulations. An example of this is the proliferation of issues relating to information security,[8] which in themselves give rise to a whole host of additional requirements and considerations within the regulatory environment. There is of course also the increased risk arising from relying on technology and what happens if it fails, for example in the outage of cloud services of which we have seen a number of examples more recently.

> **Technology gives rise to new types of threats, which in turn shape regulations.**

- *Type of market, product or service*: the characteristics of these will shape regulatory requirements. It may be necessary, for example, for some products or services to be subject to more detailed and prescriptive legislation due to their complex or problematic nature, while others might be deemed more straightforward and so have a less complicated legal framework.
- *World events*: world events (challenging ones such as wars and various crises for example, including for example the supply chain blocks in the Suez Canal, the Covid-19 crisis, the war in Ukraine, or ones perceived as positive such as the moon landing in 1969 or the Berlin Wall coming down some two decades later, or – to continue the Covid-19 example – roll out of a vaccine and widespread lifting of Covid restrictions as a consequence) affect the level of comfort and optimism the public feels generally. This impacts on actions in seemingly unrelated areas, such as their attitude to risk, which can have knock-on effects on the popularity of certain markets, whether they are directly involved in the particular issues or not.

This summary, while not exhaustive, sets out a number of the main influences on the regulatory environment. Particularly significant influences to note are:

- the objectives of the jurisdiction or sector
- current legislation and regulation
- powers granted to regulators and how these are supported via law
- the regulatory framework (spanning models, responsibilities and approach) that is in place as a result.

To help appreciate the impact of all these influences in broad terms, it can be useful to reflect on different levels of influence. The following diagram (Figure 2.3) indicates these,[9] grouped on the basis of the following:

1 *Most significant influence*: from impacts to the environment in general through to impacts on regulated organisations specifically, each influence categorised as most significant has a marked role to play in shaping the regulatory environment.

2 *Significant influence*: next in order of significance are those factors that provide additional structure to the regulatory environment, together with those that, while not directly involving financial services matters, nevertheless have a marked influence upon the regulatory environment that supports this industry.

3 *Some influence*: finally, influences that, though far less direct than those previously discussed, nevertheless have a definite role in influencing. Influences of this nature tend to impact the way in which approaches are agreed, whether consciously or unconsciously.

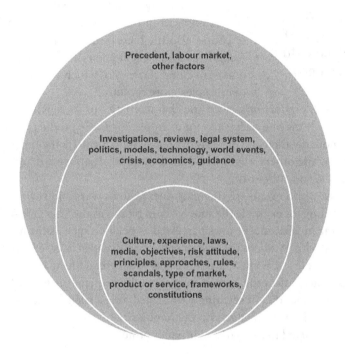

Figure 2.3 Different levels of influence (influences)

Influencers

Against this backdrop of influences that shape the regulatory environment, we will now consider the *influencers* that are responsible for their creation and maintenance. As with the influences themselves, the level of influence afforded to influencers is largely dependent upon their role within the regulatory environment. Accordingly, the level of impact they have will differ depending upon circumstances. Some of the main influencers are as follows.[10]

• *Campaigners and lobby groups*: those campaigning on particular issues play an important role in influencing the attitude of various stakeholders and thus shaping the regulatory environment. For example, those campaigning on behalf of the elderly, if sufficiently vocal, can draw focus towards activities within the market that relate to this particular audience, such as pensions, equity release schemes and so forth, thereby inevitably shifting attention away from some other group. There have been some notable successes on the part of campaigners in relation to financial services 'scandals' over recent years which have seen positive outcomes in targeting attention to their chosen issues.[11]

- *Courts*: rulings by the courts and the consequences of these for future legal developments can be instrumental in shaping a key area of the regulatory environment.
- *Credit rating agencies*: the judgements made by such agencies on the strength or otherwise of a particular business, jurisdiction or individual can have a profound impact and consequently contribute to activities within the regulatory environment.[12]
- *Criminals*: though not perhaps the most obvious group of influencers to consider when thinking about regulation, the actions of criminals (both known and those yet to be discovered) significantly impact the regulatory environment, as many of the activities undertaken within it are specifically designed to counteract their criminality. A huge amount of resources are poured into preventative measures and therefore the role of criminals (both actual and potential) in shaping the regulatory environment is significant.
- *Employees*: as discussed at the outset of this text, the structures and procedures in place to support the business environment are only as strong as the individuals who operate within them. The contribution of employees to the development of the regulatory environment is, therefore, substantial.
- *Government*: governments, having given the power to the regulators to regulate in a particular sector, have an interest in ensuring the effectiveness of those regulators. They are also able to undertake or encourage specific initiatives aimed at supporting their own goals.[13]
- *International bodies*: as well as giving thought to all of these influences and influencers within their own regulatory environment, regulatory policymakers must also give consideration to the activities of policymakers elsewhere. Awareness and understanding of international initiatives being developed around the world and the influential bodies responsible for them are therefore necessary for regulatory professionals because, in the ever-connected business environment of today, these inevitably impact activities in other jurisdictions. There also needs to be awareness of the numerous bodies[14] at an international level that have produced initiatives intended to help standardise the actions of stakeholders involved in the worldwide economy, as these inevitably influence the actions and approach of individual regulators. Such bodies, or the initiatives arising from them, can be either sector-focused (for example, banks, insurance and so on) or subject focused (for example, Anti-Money Laundering, Corporate Governance and so on). Example international initiatives include a focus on topics such as coordination, financial stability and money laundering prevention. Such initiatives impact upon the development of financial services regulation in individual jurisdictions, although the extent of this will necessarily be determined not only by the topic itself but also by each individual jurisdiction's approach to it.
- *Industries/sectors*: certain industries/sectors are more active in promoting their approach to regulation. This can be for many reasons, such as concerns regarding

reputation (following previous scandals, perhaps) or because their activities have particular resonance with the wider public (food or environmental agencies, for example). With that in mind, their activities and areas of focus can have a level of influence that spreads to other areas.

- *Institutions*: the activities and business focus of partially or non-regulated institutions can have notable consequences for regulated institutions and the wider regulatory environment. Awareness of them, particularly where their activities might overlap in the view of consumers, is therefore important.[15]

- *Investors*: investor focus on, or preferment for, a particular type of business, product or service will inevitably have consequences for each directly and for the regulatory environment more generally. This may result from increased attention and subsequent activity (in terms of promotions, for example, from the business perspective or increased supervision, perhaps, from the regulator) on the preferred types of business, products or services at the expense of alternatives. As a consequence, the preferred types are raised in prominence which may bring with it certain positives or, conversely, negatives depending upon the particular circumstances overall. Either way, investor focus or preferment can be influential in shaping the approach that develops. This might also be considered linked to the activities of shareholders, whose increased level of activity over recent years (challenging director remuneration for example) can influence decisions made and actions taken.

- *Media*: this is an influence that might not readily have sprung to mind a decade or so ago, but is one that is now widely recognised as being deeply influential in a number of spheres. Benefiting from technological developments, the media has expanded its presence through its many different outlets. Its activities in publicising issues, problems and crimes wherever these arise, with a great deal of immediacy, have ensured that the general level of awareness of such matters is far higher now than previously. This, alongside the increasing tendency for media activities to be a feature in the armoury of those seeking to promote particular causes (see Campaigners and lobby groups), results in the media playing an increasingly powerful role in shaping both actual current and future developments of the regulatory environment and the general perception of it. It is important to recognise, however, that the media is not neutral in its approach, and its agenda, whatever that may be at any given time, invariably influences this. Consider that individuals can now have a media 'voice' and essentially be their own journalist, and that relatively small groups can have their views and priorities amplified through the nature of social media; what might be the consequences of less robust fact-checking alongside this? What might this mean for the changing nature of risk and, consequently, risk management? Increasingly we are seeing polarisation of opinion[16] and it is useful to reflect on what might be the effects of this on the regulatory environment and its stakeholders.

- *Politicians*: the actions of politicians in drawing attention to certain topics and shaping responses to particular issues can be considerable, which in turn will have a marked impact on the regulatory environment. However, focusing on issues deemed particularly newsworthy or in line with the general public opinion can also be a popular tactic. In doing so, the aim will not solely be addressing that particular issue, but also raising their own profile or enhancing their reputation. As such, the often partisan nature of their activities should be considered with caution.

- *Regulated institutions*: such institutions are required to adhere to certain regulatory requirements in order to retain their licence to trade. Their adherence or otherwise to these requirements can heavily influence the subsequent development of the regulatory environment that surrounds that sector. For example, non-compliance with requirements can ultimately lead to regulatory action or to outcomes that have even wider consequences, such as is the case in relation to scandals or world events (see Influences, above).

- *Regulators*: the powers granted to regulators reflect the overarching objectives of regulation. The powers are intended to create an environment where the attainment of those objectives is possible. Regulators are granted authority for their activities via the relevant entity or entities with law-making powers in the relevant jurisdiction(s) or sector. For instance, the statutory objectives, remit and scope of the FCA in the UK were set up under the Financial Services and Markets Act 2000[17] as amended by the Financial Services Act 2012[18] and more recently the Financial Services Act 2021.[19] The aims of the regulators are set out in their objectives and, in order to meet these aims, each regulator is awarded a number of powers. Although the manner in which these are exercised differs from jurisdiction to jurisdiction and sector to sector, the main functions of the regulator are broadly similar: standard setting, authorisation, supervision, enforcement and cooperation with other regulators. The way in which regulators approach their role in the execution of these powers heavily influences the regulatory environment within which regulated activities take place.

As with Influences earlier in this chapter, to help appreciate the impact of specific Influencers, the following diagram (Figure 2.4) provides an indication of their level of influence,[20] grouped on the basis of the following:

1 *Most significant influence*: the most significant influencers are those with the power to directly shape the regulatory structure and approach.
2 *Significant influence*: next, those whose activities inform the actions of those who directly shape the regulatory structure. These can be broadly divided into two subsections: professional and public, though of course there can be an element of crossover.
3 *Some influence*: last, but by no means least, the third level of influencers. While these have been categorised as having some influence, but have not been placed in the most or significant categories, this needs to be approached with a caveat: this categorisation is very much linked to the wider environment and the broader background against which their actions take place. For example, over the past decade following the global financial crisis, industry groups focusing on certain issues (such as the aforementioned Payment Protection Insurance in the UK example) achieved a temporary promotion in importance, enabling them to be even more effective than they would have been previously. Given the heightened awareness of regulatory and financial services' shortcomings that provided fuel for public opinion on the one hand and, on the other, a desire to be seen to be doing the right thing on the part of regulated firms, this combined to result in an even greater level of influence on the regulatory environment overall.

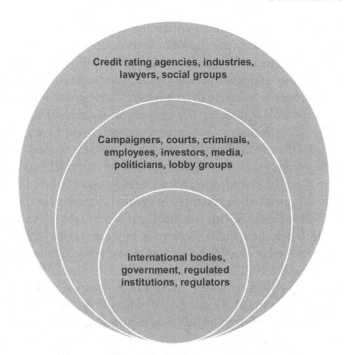

Figure 2.4 **Different levels of influence (influencers)**

INTERCONNECTIVITY OF INFLUENCE

In exploring influences and influencers, one of the most significant lessons to be drawn from recent years and one that warrants emphasis in the context of this text, is the interconnectivity of these and relevance from a risk perspective. For example, while many of the *potential* impacts of systemic risks were recognised prior to the global financial crisis, the consequences of the *actual* impact of such a widespread event were not so fully understood and this has significant relevance from a regulatory perspective. Similarly, and more recently, many nations had given consideration to the potential impact of events such as pandemics, but it was in the unfolding of an *actual* pandemic, and a global one at that, that acted as a spur to immediate activity including regulatory development. The importance of achieving such understanding from both a macroeconomic and macroprudential perspective cannot, however, be underestimated. To do so, it is necessary to appreciate the interconnected nature of all of the various influences and influencers discussed.

The work of an influential global body can provide a useful illustration to support our understanding of this. Back in July 2007, the Group of 30 (G30)[21] began a

17 jurisdiction review of financial regulatory approaches … prior to the current market turmoil that has impacted many countries around the globe. We began the project at a time when the efficiency and efficacy of financial regulation and supervision were being actively discussed and debated.

In the executive summary of the report of their findings, *Structure of Financial Supervision: Approaches and Challenges in a Global Marketplace*[22] published in 2008, they made the point that:

> Today, those issues are even more salient and important for national and international financial supervisors and policymakers as they seek to restore financial stability. This report is being published during a period of extensive global focus on the benefits and challenges of various supervisory approaches ... The marketplace has seen a marked shift from domestic firms engaged in distinct banking, securities, and insurance businesses to more integrated financial services conglomerates offering a broad range of financial products across the globe. These fundamental changes in the nature of the financial service markets around the world have exposed the shortcomings of financial regulatory models, some of which have not been adapted to the changes in business structures. These developments require central banks, supervisors and financial ministries to assess the efficacy of the particular supervisory structures in place in their home countries or jurisdictions ...

This goes on to set out their belief that the study demonstrated:

> the commonality of the challenges faced by supervisors around the globe and illuminates the many different structural solutions adopted by supervisors addressing these common challenges within their own particular economic, political and cultural contexts.

In the years since the findings of the above review were issued, the ramifications of the global financial crisis continued to unfold, magnifying the impact of many of the issues referred to within this extract. The effect on all stakeholders within the regulatory environment has been significant, with international bodies and interested groups continuing to seek solutions to the challenges that have arisen, not only internationally but also at a grassroots level. This has impacted on individual jurisdictions and regulated firms within them. Existing ways of doing things have been scrutinised and have resulted in structural changes in a number of jurisdictions. Priorities have also been reconsidered, both in terms of specific actions and areas of ongoing focus linked to mitigating against the recurrence of issues identified. Another report issued by the G30, in 2018, provided insight not least in its title to where thinking regarding priorities and areas of focus lay at that time: *Banking Conduct and Culture: A Permanent Mindset Change*. This focus was reflected at a national level, for example in the UK with its increasing focus on matters relating to culture and conduct from the mid-2010s onwards.

Development of regulation has continued in response to events. This is consistent with the approach of the past, with a tendency to be rather *reactive* in nature (as opposed to *proactive*), as it addresses the issues and concerns arising from those events. As we move forward in the regulatory environment – taking decisions, agreeing on actions and shaping future experiences – we need to consider the likely consequences of such activity and whether this will achieve what we wish it to achieve, or whether the increasing focus on activities of a more proactive nature will yield more effective results.

Moreover, it is fair to say that focus has often lent towards distinct aspects of regulation, homing in on a specific issue rather than taking a more holistic view encompassing wider contributory factors. There has seemingly been a failure for us to fully appreciate the bigger picture and the impact of one aspect of regulation on another. While such

Focus has often lent towards distinct aspects of regulation, homing in on a specific issue rather than taking a more holistic view.

There is the danger of failing to consider the developments arising in other areas and their potential for future systemic or specific impact.

interconnectivity issues have become increasingly recognised in recent years, we need to be cautious about repeating our mistakes. This includes those regulatory *reactions*, such as focusing only on addressing already identified problems. In this there is the danger of failing to consider the developments arising in other areas and their potential for future systemic or specific impact. In this case, were past performance to be indicative of future performance, such an approach could prove problematic; as well as guarding against further failures in those problem areas now known about, we also need to guard against potential failures in other, not yet problematic, areas. We could consider these to be 'unknown unknowns'[23] and consideration around these is needed if we are to form a sufficiently robust set of responses.

The contrast between today's business environment and that of many years ago, during which initial development of regulation as we understand it commenced, is another area of import. This difference has arisen as a result of the many influences that have impacted upon it over time, as highlighted earlier in this chapter. The regulatory environment is a reflection of those influences; for good or ill, the regulatory environment we have now is one which has evolved from past events and the decisions, actions and experiences of that past. Inevitably, therefore, it is an environment that is vulnerable to focusing predominantly on the needs of

For good or ill, the regulatory environment we have now is one which has evolved from past events and the decisions, actions and experiences of that past.

It is an environment that is vulnerable to focusing predominantly on the needs of the moment at the potential expense of wider, longer-term requirements.

the moment at the potential expense of wider, longer-term requirements. For example, the immediate regulatory needs arising from an event or scandal naturally impact upon the resultant form of and approach to regulation. This then impacts subsequently on the approach to its implementation, directly impacting the regulatory environment, both initially and then on an ongoing basis. The obvious downside to this is that this process invariably takes time, such that by the time the original regulatory 'problem' has been addressed, another has arisen and leads to regulation constantly being in a state of 'playing catch up'. There is also the fact that in the period since regulations were put in place, a multitude of events and developments will have occurred. These will have impacted upon and changed that regulatory environment, consequently changing regulatory needs to a greater or lesser degree. Such change continues and the future regulatory environment will be similarly shaped by events and decisions happening now, with a resulting necessity for further regulatory developments and changes to the regulatory approach overall. And so, again, the cycle continues.

Remember, this is nothing new. A useful means of understanding how and why different factors can impact the development of a regulatory environment – and thus appreciate whether changes currently being contemplated will achieve their intended objectives – is to consider a practical example. With that in mind, the following gives a brief overview of regulatory developments in the UK financial services industry over a 30-year period from the early 1980s to the early 2010s, highlighting events and actions of different stakeholders. It focuses in particular on events over three decades, highlighting key episodes and flagging points of note, showing how these have shaped the regulatory environment we find today. Drawing on work completed in the early 2000s, it is intended to provide insight into the development of regulation in jurisdictions generally and to provide an illustration of the impact of the influences and influencer-inspired issues discussed earlier in this chapter.[24]

The Development of a Regulatory Regime

Recent decades have borne witness to a tumultuous period within the UK financial services industry. Before we look at the detail of this period, it will be helpful to highlight the position preceding this, so as to provide a little context. After the revisions to the regulatory structure and the implementation of the 1986 Financial Services Act (FSA 86) in the 1980s, subsequently followed by the comprehensive overhaul of the late 1990s and the implementation of the Financial Services and Markets Act 2000 (FSMA) in 2001, it might reasonably have been expected that many of the difficulties and irregularities of the previous periods had been corrected. Yet this proved not to be the case, as the events of the late 2000s financial crisis and the period since have clearly shown.

Prior to each of these periods of revision (and this has been notable again since the 2008 crisis), there were calls for reform and for the inadequacies of the existing regimes to be rectified. These two overhauls of the regulatory system, which included detailed reviews to assess requirements, the introduction of new laws and the creation of new regulatory bodies, were intended to answer these calls for action and address the inadequacies of the existing systems. Given the degree to which these achieved their aims, to what degree can we be confident that the most recent regulatory overhaul and ongoing activities in this regard will be any more successful in achieving their intended aims? In considering this, it is useful to revisit key periods in the development of this regulatory environment so as to more readily understand the changes made and why, and thereby appreciate the likelihood of success of current and planned changes.

Background to the FSA 86 Regulatory Environment

During the preceding centuries, regulation in the UK was largely via self-regulation. However, over time and increasingly during the late 1970s and 1980s, it became apparent that consumers of financial products had not received the desired quality of service. For example, concerns grew about that provided to less sophisticated investors in respect of advice by Financial Advisors, whose income was largely dependent upon sales to these financially naïve investors. Following a number of high-profile scandals,[25] there was considerable debate regarding the effectiveness of regulation.

Additional regulation was considered necessary, indeed overdue. Neverthe-less, over-regulation in many ways was deemed to be as potentially problematic as under-regulation and obtaining a balance was considered important. This desire for a balanced approach was asserted by the government on many occasions, which made clear that regulation should be no more than the minimum necessary to pro-tect the investor. In 1981 Professor Laurence Gower was commissioned to under-take a review and in 1982 published a report that was critical of the existing system, providing recommendations for action, which were subsequently supported by his 1984 *Review of Investor Protection* report. Following the production of the initial findings, there was resistance against any attempt to introduce an SEC-style (Secu-rities and Exchange Commission) US regulator to the UK financial industry and therefore many of Gower's planned recommendations failed to progress further. In January 1984 he made his final recommendations and in 1985 those relating to investor protection were further defined in a Government White Paper[26] as (1) ef-ficiency, (2) competitiveness, (3) confidence and (4) flexibility, the first three clearly mirroring the objectives of regulation overall, the fourth reflecting what those working within the industry were looking for.

The Government paper recommended replacing the *Prevention of Fraud (Invest-ments) Act 1958* with an investor protection Act. This ultimately became the FSA 86, implemented some two years later. Clearly, the positive aspects of self-regulation were recognised when considering the regulatory system during the period lead-ing up to FSA 86, as an attempt was made to retain these benefits while widening the monitoring and regulatory sanctions available. This was intended to provide a system of self-regulation within a statutory framework. The Treasury was given responsibility for oversight of financial services regulation and in turn delegated many of these powers to a designated agency called the Securities and Investments Board (SIB), which later became the Financial Services Authority (FSA). This body recognised a number of 'front-line' bodies and organisations that conducted regu-lation of investment business on a day-to-day basis. These included self-regulatory organisations (SROs), covering different market areas, alongside, but separately from a number of recognised professional bodies (RPBs), recognised investment exchanges (RIEs) and recognised clearing houses (RCHs).

Given the overall focus of the FSA 86, regulation of investment business had a wide remit. However, remaining central to it was protection of the investor, recog-nising that there existed different types of investors, ranging from those who could be expected to understand financial dealings through to those who might have little knowledge or understanding. Good and effective regulation was considered even more important where the investor concerned was financially unsophisticated, that is, for retail rather than wholesale clients, and the differences between these types of investors was a key consideration in the regulatory approach at that time.

Although following many of the forms of self-regulation which had existed pre-viously, the FSA 86 in practice leant more towards an autocratic, rule-imposing style, rather than that most usually found with self-regulation. The development of core rules and ten principles further defined the regulatory environment in which the industry operated and signalled a significant change in approach. However, in a concerted effort not to bring about the dreaded SEC-style of regulator that had clearly been favoured by Professor Gower, but decried by the City, the aims of the Act had, in fact, been watered down considerably. Despite the very definite benefits it brought, it was widely held that it did not go far enough in meeting its core objective of properly regulating investment business and calls for further change grew in intensity in the years following enactment.

Background to FSMA Regulatory Environment

As a consequence of this, a thorough overhaul of the regulatory system in a number of areas was demanded. This demand was fed by a sequence of events and regulatory failures significant enough in the eyes of the world to earn the label 'scandals'. For example:

- **Maxwell**: in 1991 extensive fraud was discovered in the administration of the Maxwell Group's pension funds. The fund management company were regulated by one of the then regulators, the Investment Management Regulatory Organisation (IMRO), who were heavily criticised in a report compiled by the House of Commons following an investigation into the affair. Although IMRO had conducted a review of the company only some five weeks before problems were identified, they had found nothing wrong.
- **Pensions mis-selling**: while the problems of Maxwell were fresh in the minds of all concerned, the industry began to focus on pension mis-selling issues. This was to become one of the most significant scandals of recent decades, if not simply in monetary terms, then undoubtedly because of the impact on consumers and their confidence in the industry. The subsequent review was costly, time-consuming and people-intensive.

Such scandals fuelled the view that the industry as a whole was rife with poor – if not downright illegal – practices, involving questionable activities on the part of participants and failure to act on the part of regulators. Numerous papers were produced and investigations undertaken that raised concerns not only about the scandals but also about the complexity of the system. For example, Lord Atkins commented in July 1993 on how the excessive volume of dispute resolution schemes bewildered investors.[27]

Following the investigation into Maxwell, Andrew Large, the Chairman of the Securities and Investments Board (SIB), produced a report of his findings in summer 1993.[28] This highlighted concerns that the regulatory system was not achieving what it had set out to do. It also flagged the responsibilities of the regulator regarding the financial market. Overall, the main view of the report was that, although the regime introduced by the FSA 86 could achieve investor protection, changes were needed both in attitude and regulatory approach.

One of the main intentions in forming the FSA was to fashion a regulatory presence providing more effective regulation allied to better protection and education for consumers, under an umbrella of greater transparency and responsibility. Underpinning this was a need for legislation that updated FSA 86 and addressed issues arising from it. The emergence of this new form of regulatory agency (or 'super regulator') with a widened range of powers, enshrined in law, was intended to move the overall method of regulation away from its self-regulatory roots and, in so doing, address the perceived weakness of the self-regulatory model.

A draft of the Financial Services and Markets Bill (FSMB) was published for consultation in the summer of 1998. Its long and arduous journey through the legislative process was cause for speculation throughout the industry: most notable was the unusual step of it being scrutinised by a joint committee during its review by the House of Commons. As a result, in its final state, it was a large and unwieldy piece of legislation, running to hundreds of pages. However, once fully enshrined, the Act gave a legal basis to the reforms of the financial services regime and, under the FSA, the merging of regulation for the different areas of banking, investment, insurance and so on heralded significant upheaval for the industry.

The formation of the single regulator was not without its detractors, but recognition of the need for action was strong. The Financial Services and Markets Act (FSMA) came into being in 2001. Its intended aims were supported by the four key objectives of the FSA and were designed to incorporate and address the main area of regulatory focus for the financial services industry. One of the primary intentions of the new regime was to move towards a more integrated and transparent approach, though in their early progress report[29] three specific risks to the four regulatory objectives were flagged:

- External environment
- Consumer and industry developments, and
- Regulated institutions.

While FSMA and the statutory authority of the FSA were definite indicators of the legalistic approach to financial services regulation in the UK, the way in which this was done is of note. The FSA, through its development of the system under FSMA, reintroduced the idea of the regulated business making judgements and achieving compliance through recognition of need and right, harking back to the basis of self-regulation. It was therefore apparent that, in fact, a less prescriptive form of regulation was in favour, allowing those working within the industry a more flexible approach to the manner in which they complied with regulations.

Rather than clearly specifying how rules should be adhered to, guidelines were provided and industry practitioners complied through interpretation of them, considering what was appropriate for their particular type of business. For example, the FSMA did not formally incorporate the wholesale versus retail distinction, although it did allow for this. The advantage of internal involvement in decision-making, rather than the requirement simply to follow rules laid down by an outside agency, had been recognised.

Conclusion

There were many reasons behind the changes in approaches, not simply those arising from a need to rectify omissions under the previous regimes. The industry today is familiar with direct regulation and supervision, which is very different to the situation only a few decades ago. It follows, therefore, that; due to the lack of familiarity with the process and requirements, there was a need to be prescriptive, as demanded by the FSA 86. It then came to be considered that those operating within the industry knew what was needed in terms of approach and requirements in order to meet the objectives of regulation, and therefore regulation could afford to be less prescriptive and more flexible[30] while ensuring there remained in place a definite regulatory framework within which to operate.

Subsequent events and investigations post-global financial crisis have shown the effect of this revised approach and acted as a trigger for calls for further change in the regulatory structure in the years that followed.

We will return to subsequent changes in a moment but ahead of that, continuing the themes explored during the example, it should be recognised that the opportunity for proactive consideration of what is required in terms of regulatory enhancements – and thus what the best approach to this should be – is a luxury not afforded to many. Regrettably, given the fast-changing nature of the regulatory environment, it is rare that a jurisdiction is allowed the opportunity to take a leisured approach to the development of its regulatory system (the need for speed in the regulatory response to Covid-19 measures is a pertinent case in point).

One exception that can be usefully reflected upon, however, was found in the Australian experience in this regard. A paper published in 2006 that discussed the integration of financial regulatory authorities in Australia[31] provides insight into the matters to be considered during the development of a regulatory framework. It includes commentary on the origins of modern financial regulation in that jurisdiction following the Financial System Inquiry which took place in 1996 – an inquiry 'not prompted by any particular failure or financial crisis – indeed it came at a time of steady growth and relative calm in the Australian markets'. This is an atypical experience and is considered worthy of particular note. The inquiry (known as the 'Wallis Inquiry' after the respected Australian businessman, Stan Wallis, who chaired it) considered 'what should be the shape of Australia's financial system regulation, without any pressure to redress a systemic or other regulatory or financial failure'. The paper highlighted the consideration and subsequent adoption of the 'twin peaks' model of regulation attributable to Michael Taylor (a 'former officer of the Bank of England and a director of a course in financial services regulation at London Guildhall University in the mid-1990s') – the very regulatory model subsequently adopted in the UK and in a number of other jurisdictions worldwide.

As a means of further understanding the significant impact of influences and influencers on the regulatory environment, it can be useful to consider in detail a jurisdictions response to a particular set of events. We will do that now in continuing our reflection on the development of the regulatory environment in the UK, exploring a key initiative from the early-mid 2010s, the formation of the *Parliamentary Commission on Banking Standards (PCBS)*.

The reasons for its formation were unfortunate as it was established in the wake of the emergence of the LIBOR scandal in July 2012,[32] the fallout from which raised fundamental questions about standards that existed within banking practice. The purpose of the Commission was to conduct an inquiry focusing on professional standards and culture in the UK banking sector. It was then required to make recommendations for action. It published its report *Changing Banking for Good*[33] on the findings of this inquiry in June 2013. The following extract from the summary of this report sets out the Commission's approach and its main areas of focus:

> The UK banking sector's ability both to perform its crucial role in support of the real economy and to maintain international pre-eminence has been eroded by a profound loss of trust borne of profound lapses in banking standards. The Commission makes proposals to enable trust to be restored in banking. These proposals have five themes, as set out in the report[34]:
>
> - making individual responsibility in banking a reality, especially at the most senior levels;
> - reforming governance within banks to reinforce each bank's responsibility for its own safety and soundness and for the maintenance of standards;
> - creating better functioning and more diverse banking markets in order to empower consumers and provide greater discipline for banks to raise standards;
> - reinforcing the responsibilities of regulators in the exercise of judgement in deploying their current and proposed new powers;
> - specifying the responsibilities of the government and of future governments and parliaments.
>
> No single change, however dramatic, will address the problems of banking standards. Reform across several fronts is badly needed, and in ways that will endure when memories of recent crises and scandals fade.

The inquiry's findings, though in many ways not unexpected, did not make pleasant reading. The summary of the report noted that 'The UK banking sector's ability both to perform its crucial role in support of the real economy and to maintain international pre-eminence has been eroded by a profound loss of trust born of profound lapses in banking standards'. The Commission made a number of proposals to enable trust to be restored around banking, three of which are particularly pertinent to the themes discussed in this text:

- 'making individual responsibility in banking a reality, especially at most senior levels;
- reforming governance within banks to reinforce each banks responsibility for its own safety and soundness and for the maintenance of standards;

- reinforcing the responsibilities of regulatory in the exercise of judgement in deploying their current and proposed new powers'.

Arising from these themes were, amongst many others, recommendations for an enhanced version of an 'Approved Persons' regime (the statutory regime first introduced under the FSMA 2000 around the regulation/approval of individuals), a 'senior persons regime, which would ensure that the key responsibilities within banks are assigned to specific individuals; a licensing regime alongside the senior Persons regime', 'a more effective sanctions regime against individuals'; individual and direct lines of access and accountability to the board for the heads of risk and compliance functions, and much greater levels of protection for their independence. And for the regulators too:

> emphasis on individual responsibility … needs to be matched by the replacement of mechanical data collection and box ticking by a much greater emphasis on the exercise of judgement by the regulators, supported by more effective oversight and empowerment tools.

Not forgetting governments: 'resisting the arguments from opponents of reform who will claim that any further change to banking will represent an upheaval too far or that risks have been eliminated and "this time is different"'.

Within the body of its report, of its 11 chapters it had topics worth highlighting in the context of our discussions in this text:

- one chapter focused on bank governance, standards and culture,
- another on regulatory and supervisory approach, and
- another on sanctions and enforcement.

The significance of these in the context of the enquiry's purposes was duly noted.

The ramifications of the Commission's findings continue to reverberate and a number of initiatives arose in its wake. We will touch on others throughout this text but at this point, it is useful to note that since then, the Senior Managers and Certification Regime has been introduced, with a focus on two key elements: responsibility and accountability. There has also been an increased focus on Culture, both within organisations and within the banking sector more widely.

Essentially, though focused on the banking sector, the findings of the review, its recommendations and the responses to it from various stakeholders were significant for all sectors in financial services within the UK and indeed beyond. All such activities, all of different types but aimed at addressing the weaknesses and perceived gaps that had become apparent in the regulatory approach at a national level, did much to further embed the efforts being made internationally and vice versa. In doing so it is believed the review impacted positively on the wider business environment.

Consideration of the factors within the examples previously presented should help consolidate understanding of the issues covered thus far in this chapter while providing background to the next topic to be addressed within it: the emergence of the Compliance role.

THE RISE OF THE COMPLIANCE FUNCTION

On a practical level, at one end of the regulatory spectrum, the implementation of regulation and the subsequent need to verify adherence to it placed additional pressure on regulators; at the other, regulated businesses were required to devote additional resources to evidencing compliance with an increasing volume of requirements.

All of the influences and influencers discussed so far, together with myriad others, combine to create the regulatory environment in which business is transacted. The rise of the Compliance function reflects the shifting priorities resulting from the changes and challenges that have emerged in response to these. As financial services developed during the latter part of the twentieth century, they exploited the opportunities afforded by technological developments along the way. Its products and services became increasingly complex and consequently placed additional obligations on all of the stakeholders involved. The volume of regulation considered necessary to support this increased complexity and minimise the number of potential risks grew appreciably. This impacted on the industry in a number of ways and to a degree that dwarfed previous experiences.[35] On a practical level, at one end of the regulatory spectrum, the implementation of regulation and the subsequent need to verify adherence to it placed additional pressure on regulators; at the other, regulated businesses were required to devote additional resources to evidencing compliance with an increasing volume of requirements.

And so the plethora of new regulations that arose in the late 1970s and into the 1980s, together with the need to comply with it, placed increasing emphasis on an existing area of risk within financial services, namely regulatory risk. It also helped further define another risk within this context, compliance risk:

- From the regulator's perspective, the management of regulatory risk became a more prominent consideration because of the potential implications for the regulator of having to take action.
- From regulated firms' perspective, the management of compliance risk, particularly as this related to the regulatory requirements emanating from regulators, became more defined as a distinct area of operational risk[36] and required focused resources.

Both these risks were to play a significant role in the development of operations within financial services businesses over the ensuing decades. This spawned the creation of a new role: that of the individual within a regulated business tasked with ensuring adherence to regulatory requirements, namely the Compliance Officer.[37]

Not all jurisdictions or sectors moved at the same pace towards formalisation of the compliance role. For example, in the UK prior, to the FSA 86,[38] staff dedicated to ensuring adherence to regulations were generally only to be found in larger firms. Even then, this was usually undertaken in conjunction with other business activities.[39] Therefore, people working in such roles would fit their Compliance activities in and around their other responsibilities.[40] More often than not, they prioritised the latter, particularly where they were part of the businesses' direct operational endeavours. Over time, however, as products and services became ever more complex and the surrounding regulation ever more burdensome, the presence within a regulated firm of an individual whose role it was to focus predominantly on this area of activity became increasingly familiar. This development was mirrored in jurisdictions and sectors around the world over the subsequent decades, with many watching closely as compliance-related activities developed in the US and Western Europe.[41]

Eventually, the emergence of this role was supported by the issue of more specific regulatory guidance. Continuing with our UK example, the FSA 86 brought the role of the Compliance Officer increasingly to prominence. Following the formation of the FSA, there was an increased focus on senior management responsibilities within regulated organisations. Individuals appointed to key positions, that is, functions with significant influence within the organisation, were more clearly designated as such and this included the Compliance Officer position. It was made clear that there was a 'fundamental requirement that compliance officers have a sound knowledge of the rules of the relevant regulatory body/bodies and their impact upon the business'.[42]

Over time, and in conjunction with activities in individual jurisdictions and sectors, general guidance dealing with the specific activities of the function began to emerge.[43] An important example of this was a paper issued in 2005 by the aforementioned Basel Committee on Banking Supervision (BCBS), one of the growing number of international best practice bodies. The BCBS's paper *Compliance and the compliance function in banks*[44] addressed the management of compliance risk. It also identified areas of responsibility and set out a series of principles[45] for the effective achievement of these. Just as relevant for other regulated sectors, this document examined how and why this risk can and should be effectively managed. It also made clear where responsibilities lay for doing so within the regulated firm (in this case, a bank). It recommended the formation of a Compliance Function, stating that 'a bank will be able to manage its compliance risk more effectively if it has a Compliance Function in place …'.

The *Principles* in that paper incorporated best practice guidance to help banks during the initial design and implementation of a Compliance Function and during its subsequent operation. This spanned areas such as responsibilities of the Board of Directors and Senior Management for compliance, and compliance function principles, as well as other key matters. These *Basel Principles*, though without legal force, were widely recognised as effective indicators of good practice and this continues to be the case. Consequently, they are used as a set of guidelines, not only by members of the BCBS but also more widely by those in other sectors seeking a framework for the operation of their compliance function.[46]

As compliance requirements became more prominent, more firms began to further define the role within their own organisations. Still, however, the main emphasis was predominantly on the monitoring and 'policing' aspects of the role, with a focus on checking. Compliance functions became unenviably tagged with the nickname 'the Business Prevention Unit', which subsequently proved difficult to shake off.

FROM 'BUSINESS PREVENTION UNIT' TO BUSINESS ENABLER?

As the type of activities undertaken by the Compliance function grew, so increasingly did the size of the actual functions themselves. In larger firms, there were some compliance functions spanning hundreds of staff, involved in a range of compliance-related activities. However, just as other business practices change and develop, so too did this approach to staffing the function. Realisation dawned that compliance checking on this scale was not always an effective means of managing compliance risks, and indeed that there was no general correlation between size and effectiveness[47]: As is always the case, the approach required to be effective depended on the needs of the particular business. It is fair to say though that larger, more systemically impactful organisations, with an increased level of regulatory focus, may have been more likely to go down the route of proportionately bigger functions.

Care therefore needs to be taken in this regard. It could be that the very existence of Compliance as a distinct function within an organisation can, in being seen to act as a 'safeguard', perversely generate the view within firms that compliance 'is not my responsibility, its theirs' and thus compliance considerations are not then an area of day-to-day focus for most managers, or built into their standard business practices. Such approaches erroneously support the view of the Compliance function being responsible for compliance within a firm, rather than the firm itself and the staff working within it being responsible for this in their own areas of operation.

This realisation encouraged a move towards more effectively embedding responsibility for ensuring compliance within business operations more directly, essentially within the heart of business activity and 'the way things are done'. In this, Compliance acted as a monitor and expert advisor, assessing performance and taking action where needed. Alongside this was an increase in Compliance involvement in supporting an effective culture within the business function. Additional best practice guidance and recommendations were issued at an international level and incorporated into requirements at the national level.[48] These emphasised the need for an enhanced Compliance role with appropriate autonomy and resource, as a means of enhancing the effectiveness of risk management within regulated firms. This resulted in a discernible shift in what was now required of the function and how it was viewed.

The 'three lines of defence' model, a well-known risk management approach,[49] reflects this. This model has become a recognised and generally accepted risk management tool within financial services, albeit one that has been subject to some criticism and further development in recent years. We will discuss these criticisms and developments in some detail in Chapter 3. At this point, however, note that in simple terms, under this model the business is recognised as the first line of defence in risk management, and Compliance the second. The model can be broadly summarised as follows:

- *First line of defence*: operations within business units, including internal controls.
- *Second line of defence*: oversight and assurance functions such as Compliance and risk management units.
- *Third line of defence*: dedicated independent assurance functions, for example internal audit.

All activities reinforce the overriding purpose of the Compliance function: to assist the firm in the management of its compliance risk and, consequently, avoid the realisation of regulatory risk.

Consider the role of the Compliance function within such a model. Having developed substantially over recent decades, the role of a modern Compliance function differs substantially from its initial form. Though it still incorporates checking within its remit, it does so alongside a range of additional activities. The focus of these is to proactively support risk management within the firm. All activities reinforce the overriding purpose of the Compliance function: to assist the firm in the management of its compliance risk and, consequently, avoid the realisation of regulatory risk.

It is important to note here that the activities of the Compliance function were never – and never could be if they were to achieve their intended aims – solely about checking or policing; it is just that it took a while for everyone to recognise this. In order to be effective, compliance activities necessarily considered not only systems and procedures, but also people and their behaviour. As such, establishing and developing relationships, both internally and externally, was always part of the Compliance role. It is a part which became increasingly important over time.

Key points to note in respect of the development of the Compliance function at this stage are:

- The role of the Compliance function has changed over time and continues to develop in response to the regulatory environment in which it operates.
- The Compliance approach has become proactive, anticipating issues and addressing them before they become significant, rather than only being reactive to them.
- The activities of the function are linked to the strategy of the regulated business. All the different factors that influence the compliance environment still require monitoring, which remains a core aspect of the Compliance role. This is, or ought to be, defined from a strictly risk-based perspective, utilising the Compliance resource available to the best effect to achieve the intended outcomes.
- As the approach to regulatory requirements and business needs has seen a shift more towards the desired (or required) outcome,[50] the compliance approach too has moved on from its initial mechanical tick-box methodology. It is more interested in the objective (or outcome) intended or achieved.
- The Compliance function is integrated into the business via both strategy and operations, rather than working as a distinct separate entity remote from day-to-day business. The old image of compliance is long gone, or certainly should be! As a result, Compliance is no longer viewed simply as an administrative monitoring function, but as a strategic business function that can genuinely enhance business operations.

The detail of the Compliance role, including its activities and approach, is explored in Part II, considering additional best practice guidance in the context of the Compliance function itself. How the Compliance role can be further enhanced to the benefit of all regulatory stakeholders is then the subject of Part III.

With our focus remaining firmly on Compliance context at this stage, we now need to consider more fully the topic of regulatory risk management and the roles of those involved in this; this is the focus of our next chapter.

NOTES

1   This list is not exhaustive, and the topic areas explored in alphabetical order for ease of reference – no indication of priority is given at this stage.

2   You may find it useful to research the contrasting regulatory regimes in jurisdictions with different legal systems (for example Austria, Ireland and the Netherlands) for an example of these.

3   We will discuss this further later in this text but for now note D. Walker's (2009) Treasury Report.

4   London Interbank Offered Rate, the global benchmark interest rate – further details of this scandal will be explored later in this text.

5   For example, refer to the discussion in this IMF working paper (Zoromé 2007).

6   See Financial Reporting Council (2012).

7   Note that, conversely, if a jurisdiction or sector makes the decision to prioritise certain issues it may decide to adjust its regulator's objectives to reflect this, such as in the UK in 2010 when the objective of maintaining financial stability replaced an existing objective that focused on promoting public awareness of the financial system.

8   Information security can be defined as the practice of defending information/data (in whatever form – physical, electronic, and so on) – from unauthorised access, use, disclosure, disruption, modification, perusal, inspection, recording, destruction and so forth.

9   Note that this range of influences, while reasonably comprehensive in terms of coverage, is not exhaustive as there will inevitably be additional influences not included – this diagram and subsequent coverage should therefore be considered indicative only. In addition, although an attempt has been made to provide an indication of the level of influence, invariably there is a degree of overlap in practical application.

10 Again, these are explored in alphabetical order for ease of reference – no indication of priority is given at this stage.

11 The Payment Protection Insurance (PPI) campaign in the UK being a notable example.

12 For example, consider the coverage of an inquiry focusing on the accountability, transparency, methodology and impacts of these (UK Parliament 2010).

13 For example, in 2011 in the UK, *Project Merlin* was agreed between the government and four of the major UK banks, aimed at curbing bankers' bonuses, promoting transparency in respect of executive pay and promoting lending to businesses.

14 The main international bodies, with the broadest and most influential remit, are summarised in Appendix 1.

15 The growth of Payday Lenders in the UK illustrates this point: over a number of years there were efforts to provide clarification on this type of activity, with tightening of regulatory requirements under the Financial Conduct Authority (FCA) in the mid-2010s.

16 Levy, G. and Razin, R., 2020. Social Media and Political Polarisation. *LSE Public Policy Review*, 1(1), p. 5. http://doi.org/10.31389/lseppr.5.

17 Information can be found at: www.legislation.gov.uk/ukpga/2000/8/contents.

18 For information see UK Government (2013).

19 www.legislation.gov.uk/ukpga/2021/22/contents/enacted.

20 Note that this range of influencers, while comprehensive in terms of coverage, just as with influences discussed earlier, is not exhaustive as there will inevitably be additional influencers not included – this diagram and subsequent coverage should therefore be considered indicative only. In addition, although an attempt has been made to provide an indication of the level of influence, again invariably there is a degree of overlap in practical application.

21 An 'independent global body comprised of economic and financial leaders from the public and private sectors and academia'. 'The Group of Thirty, established in 1978, is a private, non-profit, international body composed of very senior representatives of the private and public sectors and academia. It aims to deepen understanding of international economic and financial issues, to explore the international repercussions of decisions taken in the public and private sectors, and to examine the choices available to market practitioners and policymakers'. Information extracted from the G30 website, more about this group can be found online; see www.group30.org for more information.

22 See Group of Thirty (2008).

23 Now in fairly common usage, this phrase, contrasting with 'known unknowns' is attributed to the then United States Secretary of Defence Donald Rumsfeld in his response to post-9/11 questioning by the US Department of Defence.

24 The information included is presented for educational and illustrative purposes only and makes no claims to be fully complete in its description of the various events referred to. For those interested in exploring these further, a number of useful resources are detailed in the Bibliography accompanying this text.

25 Such as those referred to in Chapter 1.

26 UK Government (1985).

27 Morris (1995, p. 5).

28 Ibid., p. 12.

29 FSA, *Building the New Regulator*, pp. 3 and 9.

30 The so-called 'lighter touch' approach referred to earlier in this text.

31 Cooper (2006).

32 The BBC website provides a useful timeline of this here: www.bbc.co.uk/news/business-18671255 and some detailed specifics relevant to our text focus are explored in Chapter 7.

33 See UK Parliament (2013).

34 Parliamentary Commission on Banking Standards – House of Lords Library.

35 Including the need for new pieces of legislation, increased focus on specific areas, additional concerns as a result of issues and scandals emerging, to name but a few. It also spawned the production of lengthy rule books which required updating manually on a regular basis whenever a rule was amended, adjusted or removed.

36 A risk incurred by an organisation's internal activities.

37 As Keith Darcy (2013) explained in his article 'Ethics and compliance: Birth of a profession', in 1991 the United States issued Chapter 8 of the Federal Sentencing Guidelines in respect of crimes it the workplace, which raised two new risks 'a personal threat and a corporate threat. The Personal risk meant that executives could become subject to civil and/or criminal charges' while 'the corporate threat resulted from the fact that companies could be subject to mandatory fines of up to $290 million'. As a result of this, and the implications of new developments not being lost on those with an interest in this area, the Ethics and Compliance Officer Association was formed in the US that same year.

38 Which, remember, came into force in 1988.

39 In Taylor (2005) the origination of the role of the Compliance function and Compliance officer in the UK is described, using the phrase 'alphabet soup' to describe the plethora of regulators (and consequently requirements) that were in place at that time. The 'comparatively little knowledge or expertise' of those in Compliance posts at that time was also noted, with everyone finding their way as best they could.

40 As a result, Compliance activity at that time was sometimes referred to as a 'Friday afternoon role'.

41 Appendix 2 provides a summary of current worldwide Compliance-related associations, organisations and professional bodies. It is interesting to note that a number of such, either formally or informally, were formed and contributed to on an ongoing basis by those working directly in Compliance practitioner roles as they sought opportunity to share thoughts on developments in this field, find practical solutions to shared challenges and of course opportunity to come together with others in this emerging profession.

42 Taylor (2005).

43 A summary of good practice guidance and recommendations is set out in Appendix 3 and this will be explored more fully in Part II.

44 Accessible at: www.bis.org/publ/bcbs113.pdf.

45 Referred to throughout this text as the *Basel Principles*.

46 We will explore these further in Part II.

47 Note commentary within www.mckinsey.com/capabilities/risk-and-resilience/our-insights/the-compliance-function-at-an-inflection-point for example.

48 These will be discussed further in Part II.

49 Refer to www.iia.org.uk for further detail.

50 As will be explored further in Part II.

3

Regulatory Risk Management

RISK IN THE REGULATORY ENVIRONMENT

Risks within business must be managed, both those risks that are already well known and accepted as part and parcel of business practice and those that are newly arising, or indeed newly recognised. As a further consequence of our collective experience of recent years, the management of risk within business, both from a regulatory and a business standpoint, and at both an international and local level, has become increasingly accepted as being invaluable to the effective operation of the wider business environment. Risk management is now firmly established as a vital component of good business practice. For both regulators and those subject to regulation, greater recognition of the interconnected nature of the markets has brought with it improved respect for the role regulation plays, or ought to play, within those markets. However, an inevitable outcome of this is an awareness of the need for enhanced focus on the effective management of risks relating to regulation and thus greater focus on regulatory risk in its entirety.

The regulators of the financial services industry play an important role in managing the risks inherent within this industry, whether it be risks with which the industry is familiar or those that are emerging. The stated aims of these regulators, the requirements they put in place and the approach they take to their role make a substantial contribution to how effective risk management is within their field of responsibility. Be this at the national or international level, this has consequences for all stakeholders in the industry. Equally, those who are subject to such regulation also have an important role in ensuring that regulatory requirements are adhered to and that business is conducted appropriately. Again, how effective they are in doing so has consequences for us all.

This scenario illuminates the two risks that are central to the theme of this text; related, yet also distinct: regulatory risk and compliance risk. Effective management of both, and the mechanisms through which this is achieved, will pay dividends to those directly involved and to the financial services industry as a whole.

Risk Definitions

Before we focus on how we might manage regulatory risk, let us revisit what we mean by this. We need to consider the many different issues involved and then, having understood those, we can then think about what can be done to manage this risk and who

DOI: 10.4324/9781003431305-5

should be involved in doing so. In examining this topic we will consider regulatory risk management from a broad perspective (that of the regulator) and from a more focused perspective (within a regulated firm). This will allow us to contemplate the issues implicit within and from different viewpoints and lead on to an exploration of the effective management of compliance risk within a regulated firm. But defining 'risk' is in itself a complex concept, so before focusing on specific aspects of risk, it would be useful to examine this.

The basic economic principle of any business, regardless of size, is the investment of resources with the intention of generating a profit. However, profit is not guaranteed. If the business is unsuccessful, the worst-case scenario will be that when it is recognised there is no realistic prospect of success, resources can be withdrawn intact and the only loss is the time spent on the venture. However, the loss of some or all the resources invested is a real possibility. In this sense, there is only one real risk: that of financial loss. But this is an oversimplification and does little to help us understand what factors we need to consider in managing the risk of that financial loss manifesting. Rather, we need to be able to say something like 'financial loss arising from …' and then we will have identified something that can be managed and controlled. Consider the following:

Drilling down through the business's operations, repeatedly making this statement as we go, will create a whole list of statements, which will in turn generate linked sub-statements, which will in turn … and so on. Collectively, these statements will describe the multitude of factors that, if not recognised and effectively managed, will result in financial loss for the business in question. Furthermore, examining all these statements, will if it has not already become self-evident from the process itself, identified links between them. By understanding the structure of these statements, we can then reassign the term 'risk' to aspects of the business's operation which then turns 'risk' from the abstract (albeit measurable) concept of 'financial loss' to something less abstract, and so more manageable and controllable.

Using the above concept, if we then imagine risk as a pyramid, with financial loss at its apex, then the body of the pyramid is the sum of the 'financial loss arising from …' statements, as we have linked them and drilled down through the business to its most basic operational components.

Having said all of that, the concept of 'financial loss arising from …' is perhaps a little unwieldy. As such, we see in use terms such as 'risk triggers', 'risk events' or 'risk realisation events' and such like, which describe the same sort of thing. Whichever terminology is used, the key purpose is to enable informed decision-making around how to separate out different operational areas of the business, identify specific risks arising and create management and control structures around them. Since the purpose of identifying risk is to then create controls to mitigate or manage the risk, that is, the *management* part of 'risk management', this leads us to both the skill and the danger of risk management: being able to differentiate between *risk* and *control*. Here, the danger is the trap of confusing the reversal of controls as being the risks themselves. For example:

We might identify 'unauthorised transactions' as being a risk, but this is in fact the reversal of a control, that is, the control being the 'authorising of transactions'. The underlying risk in this example is the potential for financial loss arising from transactions being outside a set of prescribed criteria for the activity concerned. The purpose of 'authorising the transaction' is therefore to ensure that only those that meet the prescribed criteria proceed and those that don't are prevented from doing so. In this regard, we can see that an 'unauthorised transaction' could still meet all the prescribed criteria and thus be entirely legitimate, hence why it would be inappropriate to say that 'unauthorised transactions' is the risk. We can also see that authorising the transaction is in itself unnecessary, it only becomes necessary as a means to manage the risk of transactions falling outside the prescribed criteria being processed, where such processing exposes the business to financial loss or the risk of financial loss.

Obviously, this is a simple example. In the real world, the effective application of risk management involves an understanding of each business area and the nature of its trans-actions in order to identify the inherent 'risk triggers'. Thus, in our example, it is likely that the control of 'authorising' the transaction has been put in place as a means to prevent a range of possible 'risk triggers' being realised.

This leads us neatly to our next point. We said that authorising the transaction in the example above is in itself unnecessary, a choice has been made to do so and doing this has resource implications. Thus it is clear that the implementation of any control comes at a cost to the business. Skilful risk management, therefore, includes an assessment of the cost of having the control versus the potential cost, i.e. the ultimate financial loss, of not having it. This equation helps to determine what is often described as a business's 'risk appetite'. This is the point at which the perceived cost of control exceeds the perceived potential for financial loss; the business accepts that by not imposing certain controls, it may experience some losses from those transactions that circumvent or slip through its system of controls.

We opened Chapter 1 by exploring the terms 'regulatory risk' and 'compliance risk' in the context of business. The realisation of such risks, if not effectively managed, could lead to financial loss for the regulated business in which these occur. As such, they are areas that sit within the body of the risk pyramid referred to earlier and it is the 'financial loss arising from …' questions or 'risk triggers' that exist within these two inter-related areas that we need to examine and understand more specifically. Although we will look later at some specifics of risk management as they are relevant to this text, for those wanting to explore risk management in greater detail, there are many sources of material available, such as, for example, that contained within the Institute of Risk Management website.[1]

Risk in the Regulatory Environment

Risk impacts all stakeholders in a business. Clearly, therefore, those involved in the regulatory environment that supports that business have an interest in ensuring such risk is effectively managed and that appropriate controls are in place to do this. How positive actions or, conversely, failings in one sphere of business can impact business in another – and indeed how the behaviours of those involved can have a bearing on other, seemingly unconnected, areas of business – has been made clear to us all by the events of recent years.

From our general examination of risk, it should be evident that regulatory risk is only one of many risks faced by regulators and regulated businesses. Before focusing on regulatory risk specifically, it would therefore be useful to briefly consider some of the other significant risks within the regulatory environment. Risks that may be of relevance for our area of focus centre on operational issues and include those such as:

- *Reputational*: the risk that the reputation of a jurisdiction, sector or regulated firm will be harmed and thus ultimately result in financial loss.
- *Business continuity*: also known as *business interruption* or *disaster recovery* risk. This is the risk that business activities may be prevented or cease altogether due to calamitous or unforeseen events as wide-ranging as fire, criminal activity, technology failure and so on.
- *Criminal*: the risk of prosecution for either a regulated business or individual due to criminal activity.
- *Legal*: civil action due to negligence, breach of contract and so on.
- *Operational*: this relates to the failure of a regulated business's operations, spanning both system and control failings and those of individuals within the organisation.

Primary amongst these is *reputational* risk, as should any of the other risks manifest, they would in themselves likely result in reputational risk. Although inherent in any business model, this risk materialised in spectacular fashion following the global financial crisis, with what some would say has been a near-catastrophic effect on the worldwide economy. When institutions with lending central to their business model decline to lend to each other, due to issues of trust and concern about reputation, causing the engine of commerce to splutter and requiring a good deal of lubrication in a variety of forms to get started again,[2] it is not difficult to arrive at the view that reputational risk and the widespread difficulties that arise when it manifests have a significant impact on the regulatory environment and all the stakeholders within it. Manifestation of reputational risk almost inevitably follows the manifestation of the majority of the other risks apparent in the regulatory environment.

Given our area of focus, we need to also consider risks in a broader sense, beyond the confines of an individual business, and this brings *Systemic* risk into our sphere of consideration. This is, for example, the risk that failings, or the fear of failings, in one regulated business might spread to other such firms in the same sector, and then potentially to other sectors within the jurisdiction and then to other jurisdictions, causing a contagion effect (exactly as happened in the 2008 global financial crisis).

Such risks, as well as resulting in immediate practical business concerns, also have an impact on public confidence, causing problems well into the future. Considering how risks, particularly those of a systemic nature, might impact on the generally accepted objectives of financial services regulation gives some idea of the magnitude of the impact on the industry should these manifest, with undoubted consequences for:

- Maintaining confidence.
- Ensuring the fairness, efficiency and transparency of markets.
- Protecting consumers and investors.
- Reducing systemic risk.
- Ensuring the soundness of financial institutions.

Regulatory Risk and Compliance Risk

Having gained a broad appreciation of risk generally, let us now turn our attention to the two risks central to our discussion within this text, considering these in the narrower regulatory context as defined in Chapter 1:

- *Regulatory risk*: Firms are required to comply with specific laws and regulations. They need to maintain up-to-date awareness of them as they apply to their own particular business operations. Ongoing adherence to regulatory requirements emanating from these is necessary to ensure continued authorisation to conduct business and regulatory risk is the risk of having this authorisation (or licence) withdrawn or curtailed by the regulator. Changes in laws and regulations might impact on the possibility or desirability of continuing certain forms of business (for example, increasing costs or necessitating alteration of business models) and this is also a regulatory risk. Essentially, the risk to the regulated firm is that action will be taken by the regulator for non-adherence to regulatory requirements, with the ultimate sanction being the removal of authorisation to operate. There are also risks from the regulator's perspective relating to this particular risk which, because of the wider consequences for the regulatory environment, are relevant to our theme and will be explored further shortly.
- *Compliance risk*: Regulated firms are required to put in place measures to ensure regulatory requirements are met. The Compliance function's role is to be part of the management, control and assurance structure set up to do this and, as such, the principal role of the Compliance function is to assist the regulated business in the management of its Compliance risk. Compliance risk can be viewed as the risk of failing to comply, resulting from operational factors such as inadequate controls, training, conduct and so on.

While both risks are broadly recognised by the regulated business as subsets of its overall operational risks, once businesses recognise regulatory risk as promulgated in this text, the implications of both these specific risks for the regulatory environment become much clearer and appreciation of their relevance even greater. The two principal stakeholders in the management of regulatory risk in this context are:

1. regulators themselves, and
2. the board of directors of regulated firms.

Therefore, the management of regulatory risk needs to be considered from two perspectives, with each of these parties adopting practical strategies to limit the possibility of this risk materialising:

- From the *regulated firm*'s perspective, considering that the regulatory risk is the risk that action may be taken against it by the regulator for failure to comply with specified requirements set by them, with the likely impact of such action resulting in the firm not being able to achieve its objectives.
- From the *regulator*'s perspective, considering that regulatory risk is the same as for the firm, but the consequences are different. The manifestation of regulatory risk in this context would result in the failure of the regulator to meet its own objectives, with the reputational impact of that, potentially, leading to a loss of mandate. However, the risk that the regulations agreed, implemented, supervised and enforced by the regulator in pursuit of the achievement of their own objectives are inadequate, and thus pose a risk to the regulator's ability to achieve its aims, is also of wider significance. There are implications for the regulators that link to strategic risk with consequences not only for the regulator in not achieving its objectives, but also for the economy. Since the regulators' aims are, in part, concerned with the national and international economy, losses that could arise from such inadequacies could be significant.

With our appreciation of risk in general, and regulatory and compliance risks in particular, we can now discuss their management in a more meaningful context.

Stakeholders in Managing Regulatory Risk

By virtue of their fundamental purpose and their consequent objectives, that is, their *raison d'être*, regulators have a specific interest in the impact of risks on the regulatory environment and, consequently, on their management. The activities they undertake support this. Likewise, the executive board, in their role of leading and directing the business under the terms of their firm's authorisation by the regulator, has overall responsibility for the management of risk within their business. They delegate this to the CEO of the firm, who in turn delegates it to *all* management within the firm.[3] This reflects the 'three lines of defence' model previously discussed, with the first line of defence including the managers who are responsible for the management of risk in their area of business. Responsibility for the day-to-day oversight of the management of risk is delegated to operational or assurance functions within the business, as will be discussed further shortly.

For the purposes of this text, we shall consider the role of the regulator in regulatory risk management to reflect both the regulator's general role plus its specific objectives and purpose, as exemplified in its approach and practices. Broadly, these reflect the aims and objectives of all stakeholders within the regulatory environment as a whole, as exemplified in the aims and objectives of regulation. Let us contrast this with the role of the regulated firm in respect of regulatory risk management. This reflects both the firm's own objectives and purpose, as exemplified in its approach and practices together with those of the various stakeholders within it. In comparing and considering them in this way, a significant degree of overlap is apparent, resulting in very similar practical day-to-day objectives.

We will shortly consider the role that each of these two stakeholders plays in regulatory risk management within the regulatory environment. Before doing so, however, let us ensure we are clear on the risk management process and its constituent elements.

The Risk Management Process

The risk management process is the means by which risks may be identified, managed and, should they arise, mitigated. Note here that there is no suggestion that risk will be completely eliminated. But as we recognise from our discussions earlier in this text, managing risk is fundamental to the effectiveness of the regulatory environment and the regulatory purpose overall. Essentially, risk management in this context is a continuous cycle with the intention of aiding the understanding and management of risk both within the firm and also, from the regulator's perspective, in the regulatory environment in which that firm operates. Considering the aims of risk management and risk management techniques in particular, what should we keep in mind when considering the management of regulatory risk from both these perspectives?

Those who are less familiar with the process of risk management generally will find the output of the Institute of Risk Management[4] useful. *A Risk Management Standard*[5] provides a clear definition of risk and risk management, together with a thorough exploration of the different stages. It supplies a very useful set of guidance on this topic and can be freely downloaded in a number of languages. This may prove useful to readers interested in aspects of this topic that are beyond the scope of this text. Another useful set of guidelines is published by the International Standards Organisation.[6] *ISO 31000: 2018 Risk Management* sets out guidelines on managing risk faced by organisations, and is not industry or sector specific.

In broad terms, and to summarise what can be a detailed and multi-layered process dependent upon the nature of the risk approach and the aims of the stakeholders who are party to it, there is an accepted cycle of action to manage risk which broadly spans five stages, as shown in Figure 3.1.

Increasingly detailed and layered models will be in use in different sectors and within individual organisations, with aspects of the cycle drilled down further and developed to allow for particular priorities and areas of focus. An example of the drill down can be seen in the aforementioned IRM Risk Management standard which includes Risk Analysis and Risk Evaluation as part of Risk Assessment, with Risk Identification, Risk Description and Risk Estimation as part of Risk Analysis. This is then followed by Risk Evaluation, Risk Reporting and Communication, before Risk Treatment and then on to Risk Monitoring and Review. This breakdown of the process at certain stages allows for a more granular consideration of Risk and activity in relation to each stage and will, ideally, reflect the particular operational environment in which it is used – in the context of our discussions in this text, for example, aligned to the organisation's strategic objectives.

One of the main points to note from the simplified diagram included here in Figure 3.1 is the continuous nature of the process, with the consideration stage providing input

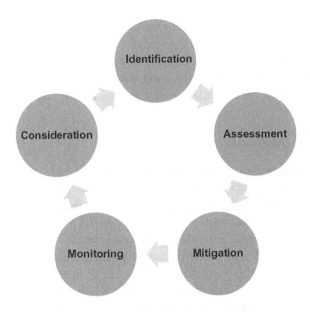

Figure 3.1 Cycle of risk management

through to the identification stage and so the cycle begins over again. In essence, these stages 'cycle' through the process of identifying and mitigating the risks identified. It is also important to note that the output of each stage effectively feeds into all of the other stages, thus informing the next steps and contributing significantly to the efficacy of the process overall.

If we consider the first two of these stages, identification and assessment, in the context of the regulatory environment, the key requirements are *knowledge* and *understanding*: *knowledge* of all the different factors that could impact on the environment and *understanding* of the impact they might have. This is where an appreciation of the many different influences and influencers discussed in Chapter 2 is beneficial. Recognising the role each influence and influencer has to play and building an understanding of their activities and impact into the risk assessment process for the business increases the likelihood of the process being robust. This in turn increases the likelihood that it will be of practical benefit.

A thorough risk assessment to allow for granular identification of risks is important. A risk not identified is, in essence, a risk unknowingly accepted, with ramifications for the organisation that could be felt immediately or lay dormant for an extended period, potentially not causing any problems at all but, if the unidentified risk then manifests, the consequences of this have to be dealt with and the impact may be extensive and problematic.

As with any business, risks within the financial services industry are not static. At different times, some are more of a threat, priority or opportunity than others and require additional focus. Expansion of the assessment stage to further drill down into specifics, for example considering matters such as VUCA (an acronym for Volatility, Uncertainty, Complexity and Ambiguity; considerations that increasingly form part of risk assessment[7]) can be crucial in ensuring that the risk management approach overall is appropriate in the context of the organisation *at that specific time*. This emphasis is necessary, underlining the point that risk management is not a static exercise. Is it acceptable to put in place a 'reasonable' risk management process that reflects a 'reasonable' degree the needs of the organisation and then follow *ad infinitum*? No, it is not. To be effective, it is important the risk management process is regularly revisited and developed to reflect what is needed. Prioritisation of the risks arising, once they have been identified, is important if they are to be managed appropriately. This has to be borne in mind throughout, on an ongoing basis, from the initial risk management planning stage, right through each of the subsequent stages, with the threat/opportunity/priority implications regularly re-assessed. In this, the intended objectives of risk management in the particular context should remain a constant feature, so that there is a clear appreciation of what the process is seeking to achieve.

Identification of risks, actual or anticipated, should be based on robust intelligence, with decisions around management being undertaken on an informed basis. So, for example, consideration of risks for a business should be based on intelligence *from* the business, as well as intelligence gathered more widely. This intelligence can arise from any number of sources. In attempting to produce as thorough a risk assessment as possible, efforts should be made to ensure all relevant sources are included. This is a vital stage of the process to identify the implications, as failure to do so can skew results. Consider this simple example.

One part of the firm identifies a problem with a particular product. They are aware that it will likely cause issues at some point down the line and intend to address these issues shortly. They do not, however, flag identification of this problem outside their immediate area of the business. Alongside this, the review procedures in place, which should have identified potential or actual problems in that business area, were either not sufficiently robust or were not adhered to. The rest of the business, and those tasked with undertaking the risk assessment for it, were not, therefore, aware of that problem in that business area. Consequently, the risk assessment produced for the organisation overall was inaccurate. As a result, an area of the business that might have been assessed as requiring action was instead assessed as satisfactory, providing a false level of assurance. This has consequences for the business decisions made and potentially for the organisation overall, depending of course on the nature of the problem that had not been factored into the assessment.

From a practical standpoint, effective risk management and the production of reliable management information (MI) as an output of it is helpful not only in mitigating risks but also in the provision of intelligence as part of the overall business decision-making process, including that relating to priorities and opportunities. Consideration of the various factors that go into the risk assessment and management process supports an approach crucial to the effectiveness of regulatory and indeed business operations. Termed 'horizon scanning', this essentially means 'keeping an eye on' current or emerging developments that may have a future bearing or influence, and this includes current or emerging developments from both within and without the organisation. An awareness of actual or potential issues that may impact on the regulatory environment or the regulated firm is necessary if those responsible for them are to be able to appropriately plan for and support the issues that arise.

Of course, it is not possible to be aware of all potential risk factors at all times in order to build these into the risk management approach. In the previous chapter, in discussing influences, we spoke of 'known unknowns' and linked to these there are 'unknown unknowns'. In our risk assessments, there will undoubtedly arise factors of which we are unaware, and these might even include so-called 'Black Swan' events, from the concept of *Black Swan Theory.*[8] Nevertheless, it is realistic to plan an approach to risk management which considers the types of issues and influences that:

- more routinely and commonly occur in a business or environment of that type, and
- that have previously occurred within an individual business,

and for it to be reasonably robust as a consequence, albeit requiring ongoing development. For example, from a regulator's perspective, firms providing particularly complex products or services, that are based in a problematic sector or that have a track record of problems, would be expected to be assessed as higher risk than more straightforward businesses and therefore to have an internal risk management system that reflected this. In regulated firms, parts of the business dealing with more challenging activities or staffed by less experienced individuals might be deemed higher risk. Essentially, prioritisation of the risks within the risk management system should reflect the risk environment in which it operates.

As the risk management cycle is under way, execution of the actions to manage each risk produces results that can be used to continue to inform the risk management process. This will help to ensure it remains current and relevant. Some form of workflow tracking can assist in identifying actual or potential issues within the embedded approach and how these might be addressed. Once relevant data is circulating, something must of course be done with the output. Recent and ongoing developments in risk management and subsequent enhancements have been driven by technology, as with so many other aspects of business. The current ability to analyse vast streams of data, identify patterns[9] and so on, and the immediacy with which this can be done, is very different from what was possible at the time many of the traditional approaches to risk management were put in place, hence significant development in this area over the past decade or so. An awareness of current and emerging trends is imperative if legitimate stakeholders are to keep pace with them and be able to capitalise on the output these systems are now able to provide. However, while the ability to generate ever more detailed and finessed data is admirable, the generation of such information for the sake of it is not sufficient or beneficial: it is what is done with the information that is more important. Too often there are examples of mounds of information being generated, but little being done with it,[10] which benefits no one. Furthermore, once material is generated – thus providing an audit trail and documentation that demonstrates there are issues – something actually needs to be done with that material otherwise those responsible are being neglectful in their duties to manage identified risk. And from a regulatory perspective,

From a regulatory perspective, identification of a risk but electing to take no action in relation to it could be viewed as a risk decision in itself.

Most risk management regimes include some form of historical analysis, but in its most useful form, this is structured in a manner which supports current and anticipated needs, producing meaningful data that can be actively utilised.

A crucial element of an effective risk management process is that it must allow for flexibility.

identification of a risk but electing to take no action in relation to it could be viewed as a risk decision in itself.

An effective risk management approach should consider combinations of the many methodologies available. It should assess what is most appropriate given the field within which risks are to be managed and build this into the overall approach. For example, most risk management regimes include some form of historical analysis, but in its most useful form, this is structured in a manner which supports current and anticipated needs, thus producing meaningful data that can be actively utilised. At the other end of the scale, predictive modelling[11] can be of very definite benefit in certain fields yet rather less so in others.[12] Clearly, a combination of approaches, tailored to the specific area under scrutiny, should be considered most effective. Capitalising on the mechanisms currently in place also provides opportunities for refinement of the risk management approach over time.

Finally, a crucial element of an effective risk management process is that it must allow for flexibility. It should be able to change and adapt its approach depending upon the identification of issues and the needs arising as a result. Too rigid an approach can result in too narrow a focus that, while possibly meeting a distinct set of requirements initially, will not be able to meet the broader objectives of risk management within the regulatory context, that is, mitigating the related regulatory and thus compliance risk, and respond effectively to change as required.

PART 2

The Role of Risk in Regulatory Approaches

Regulators require regulated businesses to adhere to the regulatory requirements that have been set for the jurisdiction or sector in which that business operates and they expect to (and are expected to) take action if it is found that those they regulate do not adhere to these requirements.

The regulator (or regulators) within a jurisdiction will have a number of aims intended to support the creation and subsequent maintenance of a particular business environment. These aims are defined within the regulator's objectives and supported through the establishment of a regulatory framework that comprises formal structures, regulations and a series of activities.

To be effective, the following should be prerequisites of the regulator's position:

• *Objectives*: the objectives of the regulator and their responsibilities as a consequence of these objectives must be clear.

- *Powers*: legal powers that provide the regulator with the authority to be effective in their regulatory role. The powers granted to regulators reflect the overarching objectives of regulation and are intended to create an environment where attainment of these is possible.
- *Resources*: the allocation of sufficient resources to allow the regulator to successfully exercise their powers.[13]

Given their remit, regulators, as with all businesses, are mindful of this latter prerequisite, i.e. the use of resource, considering how this can best be utilised to meet their aims. This is usually undertaken through some form of risk assessment of the various organisations and individuals it regulates. Although not the only method of regulation,[14] increasingly, the approach to the regulation adopted by regulators has been on this basis.[15] This was a logical step for the financial services industry, given its growing complexity and the inevitable issues arising from resource limitations.

In her 2004 paper, *The Development of Risk Based Regulation in Financial Services: Canada, the UK and Australia*,[16] Professor Julia Black considered such developments. Black looked at the approaches of regulators in three jurisdictions, whom she considered to be the 'main proponents of risk-based regulation':

- The UK Financial Services Authority (FSA).
- The Canadian Office of the Superintendent of Financial Institutions (OSFI).
- The Australian Prudential Regulation Authority (APRA).

Black's paper summarised the motivations of each for developing risk-based approaches to regulation and observed that these motivations were notably similar. These included:

> Political pressure following financial collapses; the need to create a new organisational culture within a recently formed regulatory body; the need to bring supervisory practices in line with developments in financial institutions' operations and risk management practices; the need to deliver 'integrated' financial regulation; a need to improve internal managerial control, to prioritise resources and shift regulation onto a more proactive footing; and a concern to manage the expectations politicians and the wider public had of what regulation could and should achieve.[17]

From the perspective of nearly two decades since publication of that paper, it is interesting to reflect that such drivers remain topical and relevant.

> Following analysis of the methodologies and approaches, the paper highlighted a number of outcomes. One of these focused on culture and people, and raises a point that has particular resonance for us in the context of our focus: 'Implementation remains patchy within the organizations: re-skilling and changing organisational cultures is taking time'. We shall return to considerations in this area in due course.

Finally, the report offered a number of reflections on the operation and (potential) implications of the risk-based approach. These included:

> The danger of focusing more on diagnosis than cure; the importance of organisational culture in implementing risk-based regulation; risk-based frameworks can create risks; the danger of

inappropriate reliance on firms' internal controls is reduced but not removed in risk-based approaches; and, in making it clear what issues are not regulatory priorities, risk-based regulation can have a potentially contentious political message.[18]

Here again, we see recognition of key considerations around the adoption of a risk-based approach, with potential downsides needing to be carefully weighed against anticipated upsides.

Black's work in this area has continued.[19] In her presentation to the OECD in 2008,[20] Black elaborated further and highlighted a number of challenges to implementation and also lessons for regulators; challenges which are interesting to note in the context of our overall focus on the management of regulatory risk. These included:

- *Challenges to implementation* (flagging those such as the challenge of combining simplicity and complexity; data issues; balancing structural internal risk processes; culture; managing blame).
- *Main lessons from current experiences* (including topics that spanned starting out issues – such as focusing on risks not rules, ensuring sufficient powers, knowing what the goals are; through dealing with transition – including the amount of time required, organisational challenges, considering how the organisation will respond to risk assessment; together with challenges of maintenance and need for communication, both internally and externally).

Under challenges, a point particularly pertinent to our focus was flagged: 'going beyond the individual firm in assessing risk' and under main lessons noted, that there was a 'need to recognise that risk-based processes require regulators, and politicians, to take risks'. Useful points to ponder as we continue our consideration of regulation and risk in the regulatory environment and how these impact the Compliance role.

Echoing these aims, a number of international standards have developed which focus on supervisory approaches and methods, essentially tools by which regulators manage risk within their sphere of responsibility. This includes the BCBS's *Core Principles for Effective Banking Supervision*[21] (originally produced in 2006, reviewed and revised in 2012,[22] with the standard then incorporated into the Basel Framework) and the International Association of Insurance Supervisors' *Insurance Core, Principles, Standards, Guidance and Assessment Methodology* (adopted in 2011, most recent update 2019) which specify international expectations of supervision in certain sectors. Interestingly, although sector-focused, many such recommendations continue to be considered and adopted more widely as they are recognised as benchmark approaches with equal relevance in other business or industry sectors. In recent years, there has been an even greater focus on creating a more unified and targeted approach to regulatory oversight and supervision in general, with a number of recommendations and best practice requirements resulting from the initiatives of key bodies,[23] arising from experience and current areas of priority. An example of this is the formation of the European System of Financial Supervision (ESFS) in 2010, which included the European Systemic Risk Board (ESRB), and the publication of a revised version of the 2003 International Organisation of Securities Organisations (IOSCO) *Objectives and Principles for Securities Regulation* the

In recent years, there has been an even greater focus on creating a more unified and targeted approach to regulatory oversight and supervision in general, with a number of recommendations and best practice requirements resulting from the initiatives of key bodies, arising from experience and current areas of priority.

same year.[24] More recently, we should note the Financial Stability Board consultative report on Regulation, Supervision and Oversight of Crypto-Asset Activities and Markets issued in 2022.[25]

Risk assessment forms an important part of the supervisory framework overall, beginning with the initial authorisation of firms or individuals to conduct business within the area of that regulator's responsibility and then supervision of their activity on an ongoing basis to ensure continued compliance with requirements. Regulatory risk differentiation and actions with respect to this is, essentially, risk management by the regulator. Examples include:

- The Probability Risk and Impact SysteM (PRISM),[26] the risk-based framework for the supervision of regulated firms used by Ireland's Central Bank. Under PRISM^{TM}, the most significant firms, i.e., those with the ability to have the greatest impact on financial stability and the consumer, receive a high level of supervision under structured engagement plans, leading to early interventions to mitigate potential risks.
- The Canadian Office of the Superintendent of Financial Institutions (OFSI),[27] where the concentration of supervision will depend on nature, size, complexity and risk profile and the potential consequences should the supervised entity fail.
- The Australian Prudential Regulatory Authority (APRA)[28] risk approaches. The Supervision Risk and Intensity Model (SRI) has recently replaced the long-standing Probability and Impact Rating System (PAIRS) and Supervisory Oversight and Response System (SOARS) models.

Mindful of their obligations, both statutory, and in a broader sense, regulators will want to build a thorough understanding of each regulated firm.

Note the commonalities of these approaches in relation to risk-based supervision, with a focus on what are perceived to be key risk areas; these reflect the risk assessment methods of many other regulators around the world. Essentially, mindful of their obligations, both statutory, and in a broader sense, regulators will want to build a thorough understanding of each regulated firm. They are concerned with the achievement of their own objectives and approach risk management with a key point in mind: what risk does this firm/individual/activity pose to the regulator achieving their own objectives?

Remember, in this context, regulatory risk is a risk not only to the business (that is, of sanction from the regulator) but to the regulator too, in that if they have to censure a firm, there are implications for both the regulator itself and for the jurisdiction or sector for which it is responsible. For example, consider the impact on the regulator of its success in identifying, and sanctioning, a significant number of firms in its jurisdiction. This success can be double-edged: if it is regularly identifying problems and censuring firms, does that mean it is doing a wonderful job and that its jurisdiction can be seen as a safe and sound place to do business because all the 'bad' businesses have been found out and disciplined? Or does it mean that the underlying culture of the jurisdiction is poor and that the regulator is merely successful at the tip of the proverbial iceberg in a jurisdiction that should thus be avoided? The other possibility is that the regulator is in fact unsuccessful in ensuring firms comply in the first place, questioning its credibility amongst those whom it regulates. Balancing regulatory action and consideration of the risk approach by the regulator requires consideration of the consequences for *all* the regulator's objectives.

Risk Governance in a Regulated Firm

As leaders of the firm, board members and senior management have overriding responsibility for how it operates, with their decisions and approaches driving the day-to-day activities of the business. From a regulatory standpoint, they take responsibility, firstly, for ensuring the firm is operating in a manner which meets the authorisation requirements set by the relevant regulator and, secondly, that it continues on this basis once authorised. An important means of ensuring that all of these requirements are adhered to is via the governance approach within the organisation. At a national or sectoral level, it is expected that global requirements in respect of corporate governance[29] will have been translated into standards and legislation locally. It is expected that relevant requirements emanating from the regulator or regulators will have been adopted within firms in terms of approach within individual businesses, and that their approach will be apparent within policy, procedures, systems and controls. The method of doing so will necessarily vary depending upon applicability of requirements for the sector or business type.[30]

Essentially, governance provides the mechanism through which a business can operate. The decisions taken by the business in respect of objectives and approach should be made within an appropriate corporate governance framework. The effectiveness of such a framework is central to the success or otherwise of the business in meeting all of its many objectives, including those relating to regulatory requirements: any gaps and weaknesses will be reflected in its operations.

Within this framework, the regulator will expect to find systems of control that are appropriate for the management of the different types of risk inherent within the business. This would include regulatory and compliance risks. Remember, the executive board retains overall responsibility for ensuring risk is effectively managed within the business. Alongside their own role in this process, the board and senior management must consider the contribution to be made to the management and oversight of risks by other functions and individuals within their organisation (such as assurance functions, front line business and other significant units), embedding this within the approach they expect from the business overall.

The executive board retains overall responsibility for ensuring risk is effectively managed within the business.

Responsibility for day-to-day risk management is delegated by the board of directors to management, but given the significance of the issues involved here, why would they delegate in this manner? From a simply practical perspective, it is not possible – or indeed appropriate, given

Activities of functions such as Compliance, Risk, Internal Audit and so on, play their part in providing assurance to the board that activities within the business are as they should be.

their overall role – for the board to have detailed involvement with each and every aspect of the business on a daily basis. Typically, therefore, they delegate oversight of risk and controls to a sub-committee of the board, and delegate responsibility to the business's second and third lines of operations to monitor and report on levels of assurance to that committee, with individual business operations acting as the first line. This is where the activities of functions such as Compliance, Risk, Internal Audit and so on, play their part in providing assurance to the board that activities within the business are as they should be.

The means by which the various types of risk are managed in an organisation will differ depending upon the nature of the risk and the size, structure and complexity of that organisation. Some will have dedicated risk management functions, others will have separate functions focusing on specific risks, while others will incorporate aspects of risk management into the remit of other oversight, control or assurance functions. For example, the majority of (large) firms will have a separate Internal Audit function but may combine other assurance areas, such as fraud or Compliance. Essentially, however, it is increasingly recognised that it is not the structure *per se* that is key, but how effective it is in ensuring the achievement of its intended objectives. Whether activities are centred around a single function or split across several, the remit and activities of the various risk assurance operations need to share a common purpose and agreement of intent, covering:

- *Clarity*: of objectives and of accountability.
- *Commitment*: of all involved, both functions and individuals, with this commitment central to the organisation's strategy and code of conduct.
- *Information exchange*: between the various functions, communication of commitment throughout the organisation, ongoing reporting on achievement of objectives and feedback at all relevant levels of business.
- *Action*: change in approach or corrective action if objectives are not achieved.

Whatever the chosen structure, the oversight and assurance functions should aim to closely align with the strategic objectives of the business. Think back to the discussion on the general risk management process in Part 1 of this chapter and the Institute of Risk Management overview previously referred to. Essentially, the activities of such functions are the control mechanism within the business designed to provide checks of, and support for, the systems and controls that have been implemented with the aim of achieving the board's business objectives, but day-to-day responsibility for managing risk within the organisation remains with the business itself.

This approach is an important part of the aforementioned 'three lines of defence' model. Widely adopted, its practical application within business continues to develop. Background to this is useful to note, particularly so in light of more recent developments.

In January 2013, the Institute of Internal Auditors (IIA) produced a Position Paper that focused on this model,[31] stating that it:

> provides a simple and effective way to enhance communications on risk management and control by clarifying essential roles and duties. It provides a fresh look at operations, helping to assure the ongoing success of risk management initiatives, and it is appropriate for any organisation – regardless of size or complexity. Even in organisations where a formal risk management framework or system does not exist, the Three Lines of Defence model can enhance clarity regarding risks and controls and help improve the effectiveness of risk management systems.

The paper usefully summarised the model and how it might be utilised. However, while the practical benefit of having three lines of defence to manage risk within a regulated organisation is evident, it is not without its pitfalls.[32] As with the application of other forms of risk management, one danger of having a second and indeed third line of defence is the risk that the first line fails to place sufficient focus on their own responsibilities, because it believes it can rely on the two other lines behind it. This is a risk that the business should be particularly mindful of and consider as they develop their risk management approach.

Recommendations for the development of the three lines of defence model and its practical application were not new. Deloitte Australia published an interesting paper in April 2012,[33] which raised some pertinent questions about it and expanded upon an approach it termed 'Three Lines of Assurance'. In this, they discussed the traditional three lines of defence model that 'focused on providing assurance "upwards", with business units providing assurance to senior management and boards that controls and processes are operating as intended. This type of assurance was typically high level, infrequent and fairly static in nature'. They made the point that:

Recommendations for development of the three lines of defence model and its practical application are not new.

> Organisations with this traditional three lines of defence model found themselves ill equipped to adapt to the new norm of volatility and uncertainty, particularly as pressure for greater levels of agility, assurance and risk reporting increased. Our study found that there has been a change in the organisations' demands for assurance.
>
> Accordingly, organisations now demand more timely assurance that flows not only 'upwards' but also across divisions and functions and provides management with the information required to make better business decisions and to do so in real time. As cost pressures emphasise the need for leaner and more effective teams, this has also meant that organisations have had to become smarter in how they provide assurance and what they provide assurance on. In general, this has meant the desire for assurance to be built into the first line or operational processes so that the second and third lines can focus on providing 're-assurance' rather than being the only level of assurance.

This study also observed that 'Few organisations have a robust and integrated understanding of how the various sources of assurance come together across the three lines to enable the business to make more informed business decisions' and, particularly pertinent for our discussion, made the point that 'Compliance risks are a good example of this assurance ambiguity, where despite its prominence and rising importance, ambiguity still surrounds its impact, how it is monitored, managed and embedded into the business'.

A paper produced in December 2013 by Ernst & Young (EY), *Maximising Value from Your Lines of Defense: A Pragmatic Approach to-establishing and Optimising Your LOD Model*,[34] also considered this topic and addressed a number of questions in respect of the practical application of the model, such as the potential for gaps in coverage, redundant controls, confusion given the amount of information generated and, most importantly, 'siloed' risk functions, which reduces value and increases cost. Such points will be examined in Part II when we consider practicalities of the Compliance role. Approaches spanning a number of the second and third lines of assurance have become increasingly commonplace, such as GRC (Governance, Risk and Compliance) initiatives for example, arising largely from the practical necessity of avoiding potentially problematic omissions or overlaps by aligning activity to improve efficiency across three interrelated areas of business.

In 2020, the IIA updated the Three Lines of Defence model.[35] Now termed the 'Three Lines Model', within this the word 'defence' has been replaced with 'assurance'. Though this may be deemed a fairly minor adjustment it represents a sizeable shift in emphasis, better-reflecting intentions and enhancing clarity and purpose in terms of practical usage. In the context of our discussions within this text, it is a notable modification that more robustly supports, in terms of language, the role and activities of the Compliance function.

From a Compliance perspective, in applying the three lines of assurance model or a variation of it, it is important to recognise that the Compliance function is not solely focused on compliance risk alone, rather it plays an important part in the management of *all* risk within the regulated organisation. Compliance responsibilities and activities will inevitably overlap significantly with other aspects of the business's aims and objectives.

Compliance responsibilities and activities will inevitably overlap significantly with other aspects of the business's aims and objectives.

Its 'second line' role highlights the practical importance of the Compliance function as part of a regulated firm's risk management strategy: one that is of interest not only to the regulated firm itself but, as we have seen, also to their respective regulator (or regulators). With this in mind, there is a broad agreement that, within both the regulatory environment more broadly and within regulated firms individually, just being compliant, i.e., simply adhering to requirements alone, will not be sufficient if intended aims are to be achieved.

It is encouraging to note that attitudes towards these issues appear to be maturing. In the aforementioned article from Deloitte, it was observed by the authors:

> We found that as risk management practices matured, organisations were asking more acute questions such as 'Do we have the right risk information at the right time and is it provided to the right people? Do we have the right levels of assurance across the business?' This process of evolution, where risk management becomes more attuned to the environment and needs of the business, has resulted in organisations recognising the opportunities and limitations of their current practices. They are beginning to reflect on the differences between effective risk management and mere monitoring; in many areas, risk management teams are now beginning to revisit their original notions on what were traditionally perceived to be effective risk management practice.

Such an approach certainly appears to be a promising development. For those interested in thinking further about the types of questions to put to boards in support of compliance-related risk management activities, both the IRM document referred to previously in this chapter and another focusing on *Risk Appetite & Risk Tolerance*[36] has some excellent points to make and questions to ask of the board in relation to their attitude to risk management.

All that said, it is important to remember that compliance risk is not necessarily always high on the list in terms of focus within the business – risks such as reputational, financial and so on tend to take precedence. Be that as it may, in a practical sense, compliance risk is central to effective business operations and this needs to be recognised by the business: if compliance risk escalates to regulatory risk then the very right to operate as a business could be at risk. During the past decade, there has been a 'growing regulatory scrutiny of the manner in which firms identify and manage regulatory risks …'[37] and given the frenetic pace of regulatory change over recent years,[38] interest in firms' activities in relation to management of the risks arising from this is unlikely to lessen. Boards need to recognise the 'compliance' and thus 'regulatory' risks implicit within other risks and approach their management of these appropriately in order to meet their overall business objectives. With that in mind, their close involvement with the actions of the Compliance function in this respect is vital and the 'board should review, challenge and ultimately sign-off on regulatory risk assessments'.[39]

> **If compliance risk escalates to regulatory risk then the very right to operate as a business could be at risk.**
>
> **Boards need to recognise the 'compliance' and thus 'regulatory' risks implicit within other risks and approach their management of these appropriately.**

Therefore, setting the tolerance level for this set of risks will have been aided by the objectives set for the Compliance role. Compliance activities can give the board greater control over potential exposure to risk within the business and also a greater appreciation of vulnerabilities in this regard, allowing them to make informed decisions for the business overall.

Compliance Benefit

To recap, in preventing or limiting the likelihood of compliance risk relating to regulatory requirements being realised within a regulated business, the Compliance function is assisting not only the regulated business itself but also the wider regulatory environment in the sector and jurisdiction within which that business operates. In particular, Compliance activities support the main objectives of the regulator or regulators in that sector and jurisdiction and, in so doing, impact positively upon the regulatory environment, thereby assisting in the management of regulatory risk by reducing the likelihood of it being realised in that jurisdiction. This in turn helps the regulator to achieve their objectives, which creates a more positive environment overall, and so something of a virtuous circle is created. In this way, the benefits of an effective Compliance function can be seen to support the overall objectives of regulation and, in so doing, provide benefit to the financial services environment as a whole.

Compliance Focus

In order for the aforementioned benefits to be realised, however, it is important that the Compliance role is carried out appropriately. Compliance must always aim to balance its approach, as achievement of the management of compliance risk is only really successful if it is achieved alongside realisation of the firm's objectives. Compliance is not an end in itself, it is a means to an end, and if the business does not meet its objectives and make profit, then it will fail, which is not in the interests of Compliance or indeed of the regulator of that business. Finding this balance adds another interesting dimension to the role of the Compliance function. The function's remit, structure, approach, activities, personnel and the way in which all of these work together within the regulated business, while taking into consideration wider regulatory needs, will contribute to the level of the Compliance function's effectiveness. An appropriate understanding and appreciation of the Compliance environment and the appropriate positioning of the role to reflect this is therefore needed.

Compliance must always aim to balance its approach.

Compliance is not an end in itself.

This will be addressed in Part II of this text as we consider what comprises 'Compliance Focus'.

NOTES

1   www.theirm.org.
2   Such as central bank intervention in the form of quantitative easing, for example.
3   ISO 31000:2018 Risk management – Guidelines www.iso.org/standard/65694.html emphasises a pertinent point in this regard 'Top management is accountable for managing risk while oversight bodes are accountable for overseeing risk management'.
4   Available at: www.theirm.org.
5   Available at: www.theirm.org/what-we-do/what-is-enterprise-risk-management/irms-risk-management-standard/.
6   Available at www.iso.org/about-us.html. ISO 'is an independent, non-governmental international organisation with a membership of 167 national standards bodies'. Note the content of the ISO 31000:2018 Risk Management Standard, available from www.iso.org/standard/65694.html, which provides guidelines on managing risk faced by organisations.
7   Note the report referred to at www2.deloitte.com/kh/en/pages/risk/articles/risk-management-in-vuca-environment.html for further information.
8   After the very interesting book *The Black Swan: The Impact of the Highly Improbable* by Nassim Nicholas Taleb, published in 2007, that essentially makes the points that there exist certain kinds of rare and unpredictable events, known as outliers, that have an extreme impact and of the human inclination to retrospectively find simplistic explanations for these events. Highly recommended for those who have a particular interest in this subject area.
9   The growing field of 'Analytics' for example.
10 As an interesting article (Krell 2011) succinctly puts it: too much information, not enough analysis of that information!
11 This is the process by which a model is created or selected with the aim of trying to most accurately predict the probability of an outcome.
12 One of which is particularly relevant to our discussion in this text, as predictive modelling as a methodology has in the past been fairly widely used in the financial services industry. Unfortunately, some of the failures and scandals discussed earlier in this text provide examples of the downside of essentially being reliant on models that are 'backwards' looking. For example, the activities of the Credit Rating Agencies S&P, Moody's

and Fitch re the Collateralized Debt Obligation (CDO) market in 2008 and some years before that, the Long Term Capital Management (LTCM) debacle.

13 There is also of course the consideration around the costs and benefits of regulation which need to be kept in mind, note for example Figure 3 on the topic of regulatory impacts ec.europa.eu/smart-regulation/impact/commission_guidelines/docs/131210_cba_study_sg_final.pdf alongside the supporting text on the topic more broadly.

14 Other methods might include laws which impose burdens, laws which directly confer rights and/or provide protection, self-regulation and so on.

15 An approach now common to many sectors, including Food Safety and Environmental protection, for example.

16 Black (2004).

17 Extracted from said article. Ibid.

18 Again, extracted from said article. Ibid.

19 Note www.lse.ac.uk/law/people/academic-staff/julia-black for a comprehensive list of publications.

20 Note that the references included here have been provided for illustration purposes but for further consideration of these points it would be useful to access the full detail of the points in this presentation.

21 See Bank for International Settlements (BIS 2012b) and as discussed in Chapter 2.

22 See International Association of Insurance Supervisors.

23 Such as those in Appendix 1.

24 See IOSCO (2010).

25 www.fsb.org/2022/10/regulation-supervision-and-oversight-of-crypto-asset-activities-and-markets-consultative-report/.

26 Further information on this topic can be found here: www.centralbank.i.e./regulation/processes/prism/Pages/default.aspx.

27 Further information on this topic can be found here: www.osfi-bsif.gc.ca/Eng/Docs/sframew.pdf.

28 Further information on this topic can be found here: www.apra.gov.au/Pages/default.aspx.

29 The European Corporate Governance Network (ECGI) is an excellent source of information on matters Corporate-Governance-related, including requirements in individual countries around the world. See: www.ecgi.org/index.htm.

30 For example, the UK Governance Code does not apply to all firms, only for listed companies, and therefore there is a whole tranche of regulated firms in the UK that do not have to comply with these.

31 Institute of Internal Auditors (2013).

32 In fact this methodology was criticised in 2013 in the previously highlighted UK Commission on Banking Standards review.

33 See www.deloitte.com/view/en_AU/au/insights/browse-by-job-title/coos/2165412188ed6310VgnVCM100-0001956f00aRCRD.htm.

34 See www.ey.com/GL/en/Services/Advisory/Maximizing-value-from-your-lines-of-defense.

35 www.iia.org.uk/resources/corporate-governance-basic-overview/application-of-the-three-lines-model.

36 See http://theirm.org/publications/documents/IRMRiskAppetiteExecSummaryweb.pdf.

37 KPMG (2012, p. 14).

38 Note the most recent Thomson Reuters *Cost of Compliance* report issued in 2022 (S. Hammond and M. Cowan) which flags Keeping up with Regulatory Change as the number one Compliance challenge that boards face currently. The UK FCA's Business Plan 2022/2023 also cites Setting and testing higher standards as one of its three priority commitment areas, supporting the view that this is an ongoing consideration.

39 KPMG (2012, p. 15).

Part II

Compliance Focus

Just as regulatory developments take place within the context of an environment that has been shaped by numerous factors, so too do Compliance operations. In Part II we narrow our context considerations, moving on from those elements and requirements relating to the regulatory environment more broadly, to explore those that create and comprise the operational environment within which the Compliance function works – the *compliance environment* which underpins the focus of the function:

- In Chapter 4 we examine factors that contribute to this, looking at influences upon it (both external and internal) and considering what the function's current operational environment looks like.
- In Chapter 5 we dig deeper into the operational aspects. We look at the components of a Compliance framework to examine their inter-relationship and consider how each contributes to the effectiveness of the whole.
- In Chapter 6 we concentrate on Compliance activities and approach specifically, exploring their role within the framework. Having previously looked at how the various components which comprise the Compliance framework work together, in this chapter we will undertake a detailed examination of how the framework could be utilised to promote its overall effectiveness.

Collectively, these chapters provide detailed insight into what constitutes compliance focus, ahead of our consideration of Compliance Development in Part III.

DOI: 10.4324/9781003431305-6

4

The Compliance Environment

BACKGROUND

So as to learn from practical experience, Part II contains multiple examples and is supported by information provided in a series of reports, reviews, studies and pieces of analysis based on the experiences and views expressed by Compliance practitioners, together with information gathered from formal and informal interviews with them. Drawing on material and comment from Compliance professionals in jurisdictions around the world, who operate in different industry sectors and work at different levels ranging from senior through to junior roles, these resources span multiple topics encompassing compliance, risk, governance, ethics and culture – collectively they combine to provide a comprehensive appreciation of the role of the Compliance professional today.

BALANCING ROLE

The practical role of the Compliance function within a regulated business is to perform a balancing act between two entities.

In many ways, the practical role of the Compliance function within a regulated business is to perform a balancing act between two entities, each with their own objectives, purpose and needs:

- the board of directors of the regulated business (as expressed in their business objectives, code of conduct, agreed risk appetite and general attitude);
- the regulator (as expressed in their standard setting, authorisation approach, supervisory and enforcement practices).

Consequently, the Compliance function's chief role is operating as a bridge between these two distinct stakeholders, providing assurance to both that sufficient care is being taken to help ensure that their respective objectives, purposes and needs are being met and alerting them to situations where they are not.

As many of these objectives, purposes and needs overlap (ensuring the business activities of the firm meet certain standards and that those within it act with integrity, for example), theoretically this should not prove too much of a challenge. However, from a practical perspective, there can be many of these. Some of these challenges and practical

DOI: 10.4324/9781003431305-7

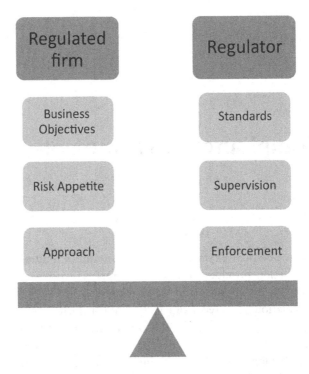

Figure 4.1 The balancing role of compliance

solutions for their resolution are addressed in the final Part of this text, with its focus on Compliance development. At this stage, however, let us explore the various factors that make up the Compliance environment.

The Compliance environment is, essentially, the Compliance function's operating sphere environment, reflecting the general objectives, purpose and needs of both the regulator and the board of directors of the regulated firm. Understanding of this will allow us to map the specific Compliance environment that applies to the particular firm in which the Compliance function is located and appreciate the context for the setting of its objectives.

THE COMPLIANCE ENVIRONMENT

To be able to achieve its own objectives – which we will expand on shortly – the structure of the Compliance function and its operations should reflect its operating environment, that is, the setting within which the Compliance function works. Once this is understood, the Compliance function can then build a successful framework that supports its objectives and allows it to perform its role effectively. For our purposes, this framework can be termed the *Compliance framework* and we will explore this in detail in the next chapter. However, before we begin to contemplate what this should consist of and how it should be constructed, we need to first consider the different factors that contribute to the aforesaid Compliance environment in which the framework operates.

Because the Compliance environment reflects the wider environment within which the regulated business is based, its constituent factors will in many ways mirror those that influence the regulatory environment more generally. Within the Compliance environment, these factors can be broadly categorised into two distinct sets of influences: namely, those that are *external* to the business and those that are *internal* to it, with the latter able to be further separated into influences arising generally from the business and those emanating from the Compliance function itself. Examples of these factors are set out in Table 4.1.[1]

The specifics of these, which will be different for each Compliance function, directly impact on the function's role. They need to be taken into account both initially and on an ongoing basis to ensure the function is fit for purpose. In the following sections, we examine each of these different factors and highlight their relevance for the Compliance framework.[2]

EXTERNAL FACTORS

From an external perspective, there are fixed factors (such as current regulatory requirements, structural models, approach and so on) and other more general, and potentially more fluid, but nevertheless relevant factors (such as world events and competition issues, for example), that shape the Compliance environment. Of these, the former provide the cornerstones for the Compliance framework with factors such as applicable legislation and the regulation arising therefrom being particularly important. An understanding of these, together with an appreciation of other aspects of the regulatory framework, including regulatory powers, models and so forth, are necessary to appreciate the regulatory approach that applies in a particular jurisdiction. Chapter 2 of Part I explored their level of influence and significance to the regulatory environment. We shall now look at them in the context of the Compliance environment.

Jurisdiction and Sector

The jurisdiction in which the regulated organisation is based and in which it does business will have a significant impact on the Compliance environment, as will the industry sector in which it operates.[3] For example, the constitution and legal system that is in

TABLE 4.1
External and internal factors

External factors	Internal factors	
	Business issues	Compliance issues
• Jurisdiction	• Nature, size and location of business	• Strategy
• Industry sector	• Business objectives	• Structure
• Legislation	• Corporate governance issues	• Resource
• Regulatory model and structure, approach, requirements and powers	• Activities of other oversight and assurance functions	• Remit
		• Attitude
• Specific Compliance function requirements	• Attitude of board and senior management	• Approach
	• Views of staff	• Experience
• International and national developments	• Previous experiences of compliance	• Culture
• World events	• General culture within the organisation	
• Technological developments		
• Competition		

place, and the laws that apply because of this, are relevant considerations in mapping the Compliance environment. In addition, the type of business that is undertaken and any particular restrictions around this would also need to be factored in. Essentially, there are a whole host of considerations relating to the jurisdiction or sector that have relevance for the Compliance environment and these need to be taken on board.[4]

Regulatory Structures

> **The regulatory structure that exists within a particular jurisdiction influences the span of responsibilities for the relevant regulator or regulators.**

The regulatory structure that exists within a particular jurisdiction influences the span of responsibilities for the relevant regulator or regulators. They receive their mandate and the powers to achieve this through law. There are broadly four recognised models of financial supervision in use around the world that define the structural approach that exists in a particular jurisdiction or sector:

- Under the *Institutional* model of regulation, a firm's legal status (as a bank, for example) determines which regulator supervises it. Individual regulatory authorities or regulatory divisions exist for distinct categories of financial services business. This is the traditional approach to the regulatory structure. Examples of jurisdictions that have adopted this model, either currently or previously, include Hong Kong and Mexico.
- The focus of the *Functional* model is on the function of the business, with the supervisory oversight determined by the nature of the business transacted by the firm, rather than by the firm's legal status. Under the functional model, a business operating in different sectors within the financial services industry would expect to find itself scrutinised by more than one regulator, with each regulator being concerned with its particular business sector. Examples of jurisdictions that have adopted this model, either currently or previously, include Brazil and Italy.
- Under the *Integrated* model (also known as the single regulator or unitary model), a universal regulator for all types of business and all sectors of financial services exists. Examples of jurisdictions that have adopted this model, either currently or previously, include Germany, Japan, Qatar and Switzerland.
- The *By Objectives* model is focused on what are believed to be the main objectives of the jurisdiction. Under this model, the key aims that the regulators are seeking to achieve define the structure. There is a separation of regulatory functions to reflect these aims, with individual regulatory bodies focused on a particular purpose. For example, one might focus on monetary policy, a second on prudential regulation, another on the conduct of business and so forth. The model known as 'Twin Peaks' is an example of regulation by objective, with one regulatory body focusing on conduct of business and another on prudential matters. Examples of jurisdictions that have adopted this model, either currently or previously, include the Netherlands, Australia and the United Kingdom.

Inevitably, there will be upsides and downsides to whichever structure is adopted by a jurisdiction, [5] some of which are depicted in Table 4.2.[6]

TABLE 4.2
Potential positives and negatives of different regulatory structures

Model	Pros	Cons
Institutional	• Traditional • Well established • Unambiguous	• Doesn't reflect prevailing business models – i.e. few firms have such simplified models • Doesn't work as effectively where products cross sectors • Potential inconsistencies in application of rules
Functional	• Consistency of rules applied by regulator • Regulatory arbitrage is therefore avoided	• Difficulties arise where activities cross jurisdictions • Can be difficult to see which activities fall under which regulator
Integrated	• Streamlined focus of supervision • Avoidance of conflict between parties involved • Comprehensive oversight of the jurisdiction	• Can be too large for span of responsibilities • Too many issues to cover • Might result in key matters being overlooked • Tendency to be bureaucratic
Objectives	• Focused • Allows equal priority to key issues	• Practical impact on firms of having multiple supervisors • Possible overlap between supervisors or conversely, matters falling between supervisors

What is key for the jurisdiction is the selection of a model that provides the best 'fit' for the pursuit of *its* (i.e. the jurisdiction's) objectives. The type of structure in place has a distinct impact on the regulatory environment and directly influences how, on the one hand, regulation is *conducted* by the regulator and on the other, how regulation is *experienced* by the regulated firm. Both of these subsequently influence the Compliance environment and consequently the approach to the Compliance function.

Information on which model is in place in which jurisdiction or sector can usually be found on the relevant regulator's website.

Approaches

The way in which regulation is conducted, regardless of the regulatory model adopted in a particular jurisdiction, can be termed the 'regulatory approach'. Broadly speaking, the regulatory approach will follow one of two models and will thus be either *rules-based* or *principles-based*, the main elements of which can be summarised as follows:

Rules-based	Principles-based
Under a rules-based approach, the regulator lays down set rules with which regulated businesses must comply in order to continue to operate within the jurisdiction or sector. The regulator then assesses the firm's compliance with those rules.	Under a principles-based approach, rather than requiring compliance with a set of detailed rules, regulators agree a broad range of 'principles' (i.e. beliefs governing behaviour) under which regulated businesses must operate. Firms must interpret what compliance with the principles will require and regulators will assess the degree to which the firm adheres to these.

While ostensibly jurisdictions operate under one or other of these approaches, in reality, most jurisdictions are, from a practical perspective, operating under a mixture of both. This is evident from the approaches to regulation that exist in different jurisdictions.

There are many reasons for this, which are largely to do with the practical application of regulatory requirements as they arise from the upsides and downsides (arguments for and against) of each approach. Let's consider these further:

- *Rules-based*: this has tended to be the preferred approach in either newer jurisdictions or when dealing with new and/or more complex services or products. The benefits of this are evident to both the regulator and the regulated: the latter can identify more clearly what is and what is not acceptable, while the former has clarity over whether or not a firm has met the specified regulatory requirements.

- However, the downside from the regulated firm's viewpoint can be the lack of leeway in the approach they may take. This, from a business perspective, can be considered problematic and potentially detrimental for some types of business (for example, those competing against firms from less prescriptively regulated sectors or jurisdictions). Within the firm itself, the need to comply with specific rules can lead to a 'box ticking' mentality with the focus on ticking off rule compliance rather than keeping in mind the intention behind the rules (the so-called 'spirit' of the rules). This can actually reduce the effectiveness and the objectives they were intended to achieve. From the regulator's perspective, the issue of coverage and keeping rules up to date with developments can be challenging, as, realistically, there cannot be a rule for every possible set of circumstances or, indeed, change of circumstances, and therefore keeping such a rulebook up to date becomes an onerous and challenging task in itself.

- *Principles-based*: the benefits and downsides of this approach are, essentially, the opposite of those of rules-based. As such, this tends to be preferred by jurisdictions who perceive themselves as being more mature or long established. The most significant practical benefit for the regulated firm is that in working under a broad set of principles rather than detailed rules, they have more room for flexibility in how they will interpret adherence to a principle and thus how they can approach a practical business issue. Necessarily, more thought is involved in this approach (rather than straightforward adherence to a rule), since those within the business may be more creative. This will also require clear documentation of how a particular decision was arrived at, particularly given that a principles-based approach is often accompanied by a requirement to demonstrate why a particular action or decision is considered to meet the requirements of the principle.

- From the regulator's perspective, while there is less absolute certainty over whether a firm has specifically complied with a particular requirement under a principles-based regime, this does provide a better opportunity to assess whether the action or decision of the firm in a particular instance has resulted in the relevant principle achieving its stated objective. If not, there might be a need for the provision of guidance to clarify matters for the sector or jurisdiction. Another advantage of the principles-based approach is that a set of principles will always be far less voluminous than an equivalent set of rules, so it does away with the burden of maintaining and updating a comprehensive rulebook. Similarly, the greater flexibility afforded by the principles-based approach means that it will be far more able to accommodate changing circumstances, thus a given set of principles is likely to be far more durable and long-lived. This in itself helps to give some certainty to business decision-makers, rather than them having to second guess this week's new or amended rules.

The regulatory approach strongly influences how regulation is conducted by the regulator and how regulation is experienced by the regulated firm.

In more recent years, there has been a move towards an enhanced version of the principles-based approach, focusing on the outcomes achieved. This *outcomes-based approach* essentially shifts the emphasis from general compliance with a principle to specifically demonstrating how complying with it has led to the intended outcome. For example, under an outcomes-based approach, a principle focusing on acting with integrity would require the regulated firm or individual to demonstrate that by acting in a certain way they would achieve this – that is, that they would be demonstrably acting with integrity. From a practical perspective, such an approach requires regulated entities to more clearly demonstrate the impact of their approach and how this aligns with the intent behind the principle.

As with the regulatory structure, the regulatory approach strongly influences how regulation is *conducted* by the regulator and how regulation is *experienced* by the regulated firm. It is therefore important that the individuals with responsibility for ensuring compliance within the business are fully aware of the regulatory approach in place and appreciate the requirements arising from it.

An indication of which approach is in place in a particular jurisdiction or sector can usually be found on the relevant regulator's website.

Regulatory Requirements

Knowledge of the regulatory requirements pertaining to the jurisdiction and sector (that is, knowing the rules and the powers in place to ensure adherence to these) is necessary to appreciate what is expected of the regulated business by the regulator, allowing the Compliance function to structure its own approach accordingly. Once again, information on each of these topics can usually be found on the relevant regulator's website.

Legislation
In order to understand the Compliance environment, it is important to have an appreciation of the legislative structure that it sits within. In simple terms, the key components of this are as follows (Figure 4.2).

Figure 4.2 Legislative structure

Legislative Structure

Primary legislation is the chief source of law in a particular jurisdiction. Under a jurisdiction's constitution, parliament (or legislature) is allowed to pass the statute.

In the majority of jurisdictions, the legislature holds the necessary power to delegate law-making powers to others and this delegated law is often referred to as secondary legislation. This secondary legislation builds upon the broad requirements of the primary legislation, by providing more detail and making it more straightforward to implement. It is also of benefit on an ongoing basis, as making any necessary amendments to secondary legislation is generally far more straightforward than would be the case for amending primary legislation, which can often be extremely time-consuming and convoluted.

In addition to principles, rules and codes, the regulatory authority often provides guidance to regulated businesses. This can be issued for many reasons, for example, because the regulator wishes to clarify specific points for the avoidance of doubt, such as providing clarification on the application and purpose of a specific requirement, because findings indicate there may be confusion over the interpretation of requirements or because concerns have arisen regarding activity in a particular area.

Following on from primary and secondary legislation, are principles, rules, codes and guidance, which are the instructions set by regulators for the businesses and individuals they regulate:

- Principles reflect the broad objectives that should be met and are often supported by more detailed rules
- Rules provide detailed and specific requirements that should be met
- Codes and guidance, or similar, focus on either specific aspects of regulation, providing additional clarity or definition, or exist to promote particular actions or behaviours.

Taken together, these support the requirements of the regulator.

The principles, rules, codes and guidance that are set or issued by regulators will necessarily relate to particular requirements within the context of the overall regulatory approach. Such requirements typically focus on two areas:

- *Prudential* requirements focus on the soundness of the regulated firms and the 'prudent' operation of the business. Typical areas of focus include protecting customer assets, ensuring capital holdings meet at least a minimum level, regulatory reporting, solvency requirements, financial returns, and so on.
- In contrast, *Conduct of Business* requirements relate to the daily operations of regulated business and the way in which these are conducted. Typical areas of focus include treating customers fairly, conflicts of interest, financial promotions, advertising, handling of customer assets, customer agreements, and so on.

Within the above, the specific focus will vary depending upon the issue at hand, but invariably matters involving the following two areas will be relevant to the Compliance environment:

- Regulations that relate to *Corporate Governance* will reflect issues such as managing risks and the efficient conduct of business, together with the imposition of minimum standards to do so.
- Requirements in respect of *Internal control* will focus on systems and control-related issues and necessarily vary depending upon the size and nature of a particular business.

In summary, then, primary legislation sets out the fundamental powers that underpin the regulatory environment (such as regulator focus, the span of responsibilities, liabilities and so on), thus the authority of regulators is enshrined in that legislation. It is then further delineated in the subsequent legislation, regulation, guidance and so on arising from it. Integral within this is the function of the regulator, what its objectives are and what it is intending to achieve for that jurisdiction or sector; topics we will now explore.

The Regulator's Function
The main function (or role) of regulators is summarised in Figure 4.3.[7] Think of them as a framework intended to support the overall aims of regulation.

The Regulator's Powers
Regulators in a given jurisdiction or industry sector act (or should act) as gatekeepers to that jurisdiction and/or sector, denying initial entry or ongoing participation to those who pose a threat to the achievement of the regulatory objectives that have been set. Although the specifics of the powers granted to regulators to enable them to achieve their intended objectives vary from jurisdiction to jurisdiction and sector to sector, the span of their role will be similar, irrespective of where they are located, and will broadly cover the areas shown in Figure 4.4.

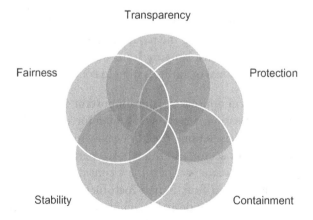

Figure 4.3 **Aims of regulation**

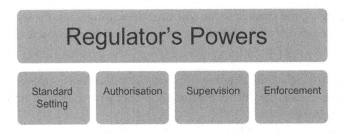

Figure 4.4 Regulator's role

Let's explore each of these:

- *Standard Setting* powers support the main aims of regulation. Regulators are required to agree upon and make clear what the expectations are within their jurisdiction/ sector to ensure the fair conduct of business and clarify what is required in practice.
- The *Authorisation* process acts as a barrier to entry into the market. In authorising firms and individuals to conduct financial services business, regulators ensure those entering the market meet the expected standards at that point. Given their role and their own specific objectives in support of this, it should be evident that regulators will wish to only have regulated firms that meet the required standards operating within the jurisdiction or sector for which they are responsible. Those who do not would pose a threat to the regulator achieving their own objectives. With that in mind, regulators set specific requirements that need to be met before authorisation is granted.
- Having ensured that firms and individuals who wish to conduct financial services business meet the expected standards at the outset, regulators need to make sure that these standards continue to be met. This assessment is carried out through the *supervision* process, which involves monitoring and reviewing the activities of those firms and individuals the regulator has authorised.
- Finally, in order to encourage continued adherence to the expected standards for the jurisdiction/sector, an effective regulatory regime must contain robust and visible sanctions for those that do not. The *enforcement* aspect of the regulator's powers addresses this requirement, providing the regulator with the opportunity to sanction those identified as not meeting the required standards once authorised. It does this through a variety of means, ranging from warnings for minor infringements through to, ultimately, removal of authorisation to conduct business.

The regulator's risk assessment approach[8] is an important mechanism supporting the regulator's powers of authorisation, supervision and enforcement. The approach taken by regulators in a particular jurisdiction or sector heavily influences the regulatory environment in that jurisdiction or sector and thus those operating within the Compliance environment. The practical consequences of this are considered in the next two chapters.

In addition to these four main functions (which focus predominantly on activities within a jurisdiction), it is also at least desirable, if not essential, that regulators cooperate with other regulators outside their own jurisdiction. Cross-border communication and regular cooperation with other regulators across jurisdictions are increasingly necessary, due to the ever more international and inter-related nature of business activity. Such an approach, as well as benefiting the regulator within a particular jurisdiction in the performance of their own role, supports the general purpose of regulation. It does this by recognising that regulatory activities in one jurisdiction cannot be considered in an isolated fashion, as they impact on activities in others.[9]

Another important point to consider is accountability. As regulators have the power to agree or remove authorisation, they effectively determine whether regulated business can take place or not within their jurisdiction or sector. As such, they have a significant amount of power. Alongside this power, however, sits a weight of responsibility – all stakeholders in the market need to be satisfied that the regulator is exercising its powers both effectively and equitably. Accordingly, accountability – and transparency in respect of this – in relation to the regulator's activities is essential.

These latter points in particular reflect the significance of the regulatory role in each jurisdiction, the first of these being of interest at an international level, given the interconnectivity of the marketplace, and the second being of particular relevance to those regulated organisations within the jurisdiction. Overall, however, the detail of the particular jurisdictional requirements tends to be tailored according to how a regulator exercises their powers in that jurisdiction and the mechanisms they put in place to support them. Each of the regulatory powers impacts on the effectiveness of the others and all of these need to be considered against how the regulator approaches their role. It is this which will have the most significant impact upon the effectiveness of the regulatory regime.

As with structure, approach and regulatory requirements, information on the regulator's powers that apply to a particular jurisdiction or sector can usually be found on the relevant regulator's website. It is also useful to note recent speeches, details on thematic reviews, current initiatives, publications, annual reports/plans, enforcement action or press notices from the regulator as these often provide an insight into the actual approach being adopted, together with an indication of the regulator's current and intended areas of focus. This can prove useful in understanding the prevailing priorities and themes that will influence the Compliance environment at any given time.

Statutory Compliance Function Requirements

Most jurisdictions have certain statutory requirements in respect of the Compliance function and those who work within it. These are incorporated into the rules, principles, guidance and other requirements of the regulator, both initially at authorisation stage and then subsequently during the supervisory process. Understanding – and, of course, complying with – such requirements are essential to the makeup of the Compliance environment and are therefore a fundamental consideration in mapping it. For example, in some jurisdictions the formation of a Compliance function is a specific *requirement*, while in others it is a *recommendation* only; in some there is a *requirement* to have a specific individual charged with heading this function, in others it is *recommended*. The general approach is the recommendation, with guidelines provided on what is needed, but an indication that firms should put in place what is appropriate for that particular firm depending upon its nature and scale.

> **In some jurisdictions, the formation of a Compliance function is a specific requirement, while in others it is a recommendation.**

Nor are the actual activities of the role or the requirements of the individual 'set in stone', i.e. specifically mandated or restricted. Again, there is usually an indication of expectation which firms are then required to interpret and apply depending upon what is appropriate for their individual circumstances while being mindful of the overall objective to manage compliance risk (in line with a firm's stated risk appetite).[10]

Finally, it is useful to note that, in general, statutory responsibilities cover both the *proactive* and the *reactive* aspects of the Compliance role. We will explore the implications of these requirements across the next two chapters.

Other 'Regulatory' Bodies

It is useful to keep in mind that it is not just the output of the main regulators *per se* that impact on the Compliance environment – there is more the Compliance function needs to be aware of. As was discussed in Part I in relation to the regulatory environment and referred to earlier in this Chapter, there are a number of bodies, both national and international, that have responsibilities in these areas. Such bodies issue rules, principles, codes and guidance on a host of topics, often sector or topic focused, that need to be taken into account in the mapping of the Compliance environment. Some examples that could be considered in the context of impact on this might be those such as:

- Bank for International Settlements (BIS)
- Basel Committee on Banking Supervision (BCBS)
- European Central Bank (ECB)
- European Systemic Risk Board (ESRB) and European Supervisory Authorities (ESAs): European Securities and Markets Authority based in Paris (ESMA), European Banking Authority (EBA) and European Insurance and Occupational Pensions Authority (EIOPA)
- Financial Action Task Force (FATF)
- Group of International Finance Centre Supervisors (GIFCS)
- International Monetary Fund (IMF)
- International Organisation of Securities Commissions (IOSCO)

However, it is important that those assessing the factors that contribute to this environment identify and consider those that are specific to each individual jurisdiction or sector.

International and National Developments

General Issues

Emerging issues and agreed approaches at both an international and national level will influence the Compliance environment, impacting either directly (the timetable for implementation of international legislation, for example) or indirectly (new legislation in an entirely different sector or jurisdiction, perhaps, which may impact at some point on the 'filter through' principle, whereby though it may not have immediate relevance, will impact further down the line and therefore needs to be considered). An awareness of developing trends and intended priorities is necessary to ensure the relevance of the function's activities – 'horizon scanning' to maintain awareness of matters of interest or potential impact in the short, medium or longer term.

A useful way to do this is to keep up to date on the various activities in which regulators and other influential bodies are involved. This can be done by looking at their websites and the various publications that are produced by them. Different regulators produce a host of material indicative of its areas of focus. This can be topic/sector/jurisdictional related and might include reports, research, information on planned and current consultations, feedback on consultations that have taken place, newsletters (topic or sector related), guidance (topic or sector related), press releases, information relating to enforcement action, speeches and so on. For example:

- At an *international* level, awareness of the output of influential international bodies such as those referred to above, those relating to the progress of key directives (MiFID, Basel III or Solvency II, for example) or key initiatives (such as actions to strengthen international regulatory supervision, sanctions, and so on) are often produced in report form, summarising recent activities while setting out next steps and intended timeframes. Speeches and press releases accompanying these are also useful in assessing which aspects of the various activities are receiving particular attention.

- At a *national* level, the regular output of national regulators is similarly useful in ensuring awareness of current and future focus. The Central Bank of Ireland, for example, has issued a wide range of publications that reflect its work, including the economic letters series, modelled on similar publications released by some institutions in the Federal Reserve System in the United States. These economic letters comprise short notes on particular domestic economic considerations, standard economic approaches and relevant policy issues pertinent to the Irish economy and are addressed in a concise and accessible manner.[11] The Autorité des Marchés Financiers (AMF), which regulates participants and products in France's financial markets, produce reports, research and analysis, the output of working group activities, guides, newsletters and many other such publications.[12]

Awareness of publications such as these and the areas on which they focus can help stakeholders appreciate current and potential issues that may impact on the Compliance environment. The content of speeches and the topics covered in annual reports, business plans and so on are useful means of keeping up to date with current thinking and priorities on the national and international stage.

Compliance-Specific Issues

As well as keeping abreast of current and ongoing developments generally, the Compliance function should of course take note of guidance and best practices relating to Compliance activities specifically. The influential international bodies referred to the above issue guidance on a range of topics which, although not legally binding, represent good and accepted practice. Some very useful international guidance on the role of the Compliance function and those who work in this area has been produced, summarised below.[13]

Based on the output of a variety of studies and consultations, several papers focusing on the Compliance function and compliance activities have been issued by some of the influential international bodies highlighted in Chapter 2. Widely recognised examples include:

Body	Paper
International Organisation of Securities Commissions (IOSCO)	*The Function of Compliance Officer* – July 2003[14]
Basel Committee on Banking Supervision (BCBS)	*Compliance and the Compliance Function in Banks* – 2005[15] *Implementation of the compliance principles: A survey* – August 2008[16]
IOSCO	*Compliance Function at Market Intermediaries* – March 2006[17]
European Securities and Markets Authority (ESMA)	*Guidelines on Certain Aspects of the MiFID Compliance Function Requirements* – July 2012 and most recent 2020[18]
International Organisation for Standardisation (ISO)	*ISO 19600:2014 Compliance management systems and most recent ISO 37301:2021 Compliance management systems*[19]

Although produced by bodies spanning multiple financial services sectors and jurisdictions internationally and with specific relevance to individual sectors and groups of regulated businesses, these papers have relevance to all regulated financial services firms, wherever located. Recommendations contained within them are indicative of good practice and will be reflected in the requirements of regulators in individual jurisdictions/sectors because the implementation of such guidelines into national requirements is usually overseen by regulators as part of their ongoing assessment of compliance in respect of the regulations that apply in their jurisdiction/sector. Accordingly, it is anticipated that all firms – both those directly required to adhere to the guidance and those who are not directly affected by it – would reference this guidance as a means of checking their own approach, allowing them to adjust it if necessary, depending on what is appropriate for their own organisation.

In addition to these international initiatives, at the national level, there is best practice guidance that is of relevance regarding the Compliance role in addition to statutory requirements set by national regulators. The following are examples of such guidance:

Body	Paper
National Occupational Standards (NOS)	*National Occupational Standards in Compliance* – 2006, updated 2011 and 2018[20]
British Standards Institute (BSI)	*Compliance Framework for Regulated Financial Services Firms – Specification*, British Standards BS8453:2011[21]

As with the international best practice guidance, the recommendations in these papers are not binding regulatory requirements. They are intended to provide interested parties with guidance on the most effective approaches to be taken in relation to the Compliance Function and the Compliance Officer's role.

Much of this content has been incorporated into specific requirements for Compliance function activities at national and sectoral level. Consequently, an awareness of such best practice guidance and any updates to it can provide the function with an indication of where the general expectations of the role are internationally and where developments are occurring.

We will consider this guidance more fully when we focus on the compliance role, activities and approach.

Other External Factors

As with the regulatory environment, there are many external issues of a less obvious nature that contribute to, and impact upon, the Compliance environment. What these are depends upon the nature of the business, its sector, its jurisdiction and so forth. Accordingly, an ongoing awareness of such events, activities and issues that might impact or influence the activities of the function should be maintained.

In considering the factors that might impact, the Compliance function should cast its net widely, rather than confining its focus only to those matters that are obviously connected to the Compliance or risk management role. For example, how might technological advances be used to positive effect on the firm? How might an increasing desire on the part of the public for transparency and openness be demonstrated by the firm, thus promoting it in the eyes of potential customers? How might output such as that of regulators, of prevailing news stories, and so on, provide insight into current hot topics? Or how, perhaps, might noting the activities and approach of competitors in a firm's particular field and the roles, products and services they offer and then observing the market's response, whether positive or negative, give an idea as to whether or not similar strategies should be adopted or care taken to avoid them? We can be sure that many of the scandals that have emerged within certain organisations in financial services over recent years will have prompted individuals with compliance responsibilities in other organisations to look again at their own organisation's approach to such issues (or others linked to them), satisfying themselves as regards this or deciding to take any necessary remedial action.

INTERNAL FACTORS

Just as with external factors, from an internal perspective there are both specific features and also more subtle elements that determine the compliance environment:

- Specific features that tend to be of a more 'fixed' nature include those such as the nature, size, location and complexity of the business; what its business objectives are; the activities of other oversight and assurance functions, and so on.
- Less 'fixed' rather more subtle elements that are perhaps more fluid in nature include those such as the attitude of the board (both executive and non-executive) and senior management, both more widely and towards the Compliance function specifically; views of staff; the firm's previous experiences of compliance issues (and any prior regulatory attention or sanctions it has been subject to); the general culture within the firm.

Again, just as with external factors, the level of influence and significance of each is reflective of that discussed in respect of the regulatory environment more generally. As intimated earlier, these can be further broken down into issues arising from the business in general and those from the Compliance function specifically, each of which we will consider as part of our focus on this topic. At this stage, we will consider the environment as it might exist prior to a Compliance function being set up and thus focus on how issues arise from the business in general. Firstly, specific, more fixed features:

Nature, Size, Location and Complexity of Business

The type of business carried out, in which business sector, where located, whether small, medium or large, conducting business in single or multiple jurisdictions – essentially what the business is doing and how complex the business it is doing. All of these hard facts have a *direct* impact on the Compliance environment. The nature, size, location and complexity of the business, where it is transacted and so on, will all influence the types of issues that need to be considered: for example, does legislation emanating from multiple jurisdictions have relevance? Do extra-territoriality requirements (i.e. laws valid beyond a jurisdictions territory) apply? Just as regulatory requirements, models, approaches and so on act as the cornerstones of the Compliance framework from an *external* perspective, the nature, size, location and complexity of a business are the *internal* equivalents. These will be a considerable driver as to requirements and will be a key determinant in the risk decision-making process.

Business Objectives

What are the aims of the business? What is it seeking to achieve in respect of meeting regulatory requirements? What is its risk appetite? What are its objectives in terms of the management of risk generally, and the management of regulatory and compliance risk specifically? A clear appreciation of these factors and of the business objectives overall provide tangible, concrete indications of what is expected of the Compliance function and are therefore a fundamental consideration in the establishment of the framework.

Corporate Governance

Given their purpose in support of how a firm is run, the internal governance structures that are in place within the business organisation, how these operate day-to-day and the various mechanisms that support them are crucial elements within the Compliance environment, specifically with regards to strategy, structure, resource, remit and reporting lines.

Activities of Other Assurance Functions

The remit of other assurance functions, such as internal audit for example, will necessarily impact on the role of the Compliance function and therefore the Compliance environment more generally. From a purely practical point of view, the existence of multiple assurance functions, all with their own remit and areas of responsibilities, provides scope for overlap of activity or, perhaps more worryingly, gaps in coverage – essentially, issues that the implementation of governance, risk & compliance[22] initiatives collectively, a grouping that has increasingly developed over time in response to the practical challenges of work in this area, are intended to address. Indeed, widespread adoption of approaches such as the Integrated Assurance model,[23] building on the 'three lines of defence' model (which has itself been further developed and, as discussed in Chapter 3, is now known as the 'Three Lines Model'[24]), encourages coordination of various work streams, streamlining reporting and simplifying oversight. Essentially 'combined' or 'coordinated' assurance, the intentions behind this include the provision of improved risk coverage and maximising control efficiencies, combined with better use of resources. It does this through aligning/integrating assurance processes across different functions (while retaining separate reporting lines), thus providing improved assurance to the audit and risk committees. In formulating the Compliance framework, therefore, consideration must be given to the roles and remit of other assurance functions, so as to make the best use of the resource available to the business, while at the same time meeting regulatory requirements in respect of each of the functions.

Next, the more subtle and fluid elements.

Attitude of the Board and Senior Management

The attitude of the board and senior management is vital to the success of the Compliance function. Although not immediately tangible, it is nevertheless an important component of the Compliance framework. A Compliance function that has these senior staff clearly on their side, supporting their actions and approach, will have a far greater chance of success. The *Basel Principles* could not have put it more succinctly when they said

> Compliance starts at the top. It will be most effective in a corporate culture that emphases standards of honesty and integrity and in which the board of directors and senior management lead by example. It concerns everyone within the bank and should be viewed as an integral part of a bank's business activities.[25]

Views of Staff

To a significant degree, how staff within the business view the role of the Compliance function will be influenced by the attitude of the board and senior management, and of other influential staff within an organisation. Simply put, if senior members of the organisation demonstrate their support for the function, both in word and actions, staff members within the business are more likely to do so. There are also other pertinent drivers that impact the views of staff and are themselves representative of the priorities of decision-makers within an organisation, such as reward mechanisms, perhaps, or the level of priority given to training and development in respect of compliance-related activities. For example, if reward mechanisms include compliance quality measures then they will likely have a significant impact on attitude, whereas if they do not it could be said that a message is being delivered as to how seriously such matters are viewed. Consideration to such therefore needs to be part of the thinking around how the Compliance framework is developed and delivered in its entirety.

Previous experience of compliance activities and approaches, garnered either from the current firm or from other roles elsewhere, also greatly influences the way in which Compliance is viewed. Whether a junior or senior staff member, negative past experiences will undoubtedly influence the perception of Compliance, its role, personnel working within it and the benefits of the function; conversely, positive past experiences are more likely to have a positive impact.

General Approach and Culture within the Organisation

The general approach and culture within an organisation will have a marked impact on the Compliance environment and needs to be considered when shaping the approach to constructing an effective operational framework. For example, communication styles, considering language usage, tone and delivery mechanisms, what feels 'usual' within that particular organisation should be reflected in the approach adopted by Compliance, so taking into account aspects such as, for example: what is the approach to training within the firm? Are staff members regularly involved in it? Do they contribute to it? If so, it might be useful to adopt a similar approach to Compliance training. What about the issue of blame? What is the general culture within the firm towards errors: is it an open sort of organisation where staff are comfortable to flag these in order to ensure they are addressed? Or does a blame culture exist, encouraging a tendency to cover up issues? Awareness of the prevailing approach and culture within the organisation and consideration of Compliance requirements in this context can help ensure the Compliance framework is better positioned and also able to cater for issues arising from these, so in turn be more effective.

These specific features and more subtle elements combine to create the practical backdrop to the Compliance function's role. They have a clear impact on the Compliance operating environment and therefore need to be borne in mind when developing the Compliance framework that is intended to support the function in achieving its objectives. Alongside these, there are a number of factors specifically concerning the Compliance function itself that also need to be taken into account.

INTERNAL FACTORS IN RESPECT OF THE COMPLIANCE FUNCTION

As with general business factors, some of the factors that specifically pertain to the Compliance function are again specific and tangible (for example, as a result of decisions arising from within the business itself) and others are far less so (such as the way in which compliance-related operations are carried out by the function, for example). Essentially, these drill down into the *purpose* of the function and what it is seeking to achieve through its various activities. First, there are a number of specific features specifically relating to the Compliance function, such as:

Strategy

Essentially, the intended risk management strategy within the firm – and the role the Compliance function is expected to play in this – form the basis of the Compliance strategy, underpinned by regulatory requirements. This is a central component in the function's operating environment and thus a key consideration in the development of its framework.

Such a strategy should not, of course, be developed separately from the rest of the business: a clear appreciation of the strategy and activities of other relevant functions – from business operations through to the roles of the board – will be necessary to ensure areas of overlap or gaps in responsibility are minimised and that the resulting Compliance strategy appropriately reflects the intended overall objectives. Parties to its development might usually include those such as board members, senior staff working within or leading the Compliance or Risk functions and other key operational and assurance functions. However, as with so many other aspects, all such will need to be considered relative to the specifics of the business and its organisation.

Structure

The structure of the function will have an impact on the performance of the Compliance role. How it will be structured, where it will be located and how this fits within the business structure all need to be considered.

Resource

The funding of the Compliance function and the allocation of resources across its activities and approach needs to be carefully considered. Of course, resource for one function or particular objective of the business is not something that should be looked at entirely separately from that of other functions or objectives. Decisions made in this regard will inevitably have consequences for the Compliance function which will in turn shape its activities and will thus need to be thought about as part of the framework planning. The extent and usage of resources should be a reflection of the risk appetite of the firm – a low appetite for compliance risk might necessitate a more highly resourced function and vice versa, while the less resourced function is the greater consideration to the risk-based approach that will need to be given to ensure it is appropriate. This of course mirrors the approach of the regulator in this regard, as discussed in Chapter 3 in its exploration of regulatory risk management.

Remit

The remit of the function, what it is expected to achieve and be responsible for, plays a significant role in the Compliance environment. The Compliance framework will therefore be heavily influenced by it. On a linked note, however, from a prioritisation perspective should remit come before resource or resource before remit? Here we have chosen to be realistic in our ordering approach: no organisation has a limitless budget and therefore the remit of the Compliance function will of course be impacted by the resource available, both in terms of funding and, as a consequence, staffing. Conversely, resource allocation can be driven by a combination of the risk appetite of those at the head of the firm and the remit of the Compliance function derived from this. Resource should never be the primary driver of focus, of course; accepting there is a reality to the amount of resource that is available this would then require the board to reset its appetite formally, based on what could practically be delivered within this and what exposures remained as a consequence. A risk-based approach to the remit set could be applied which can thereby reduce the amount of resources required, provided it meets with the risk appetite set by the board. On this basis the function might choose to approach the board to request additional resources, recognising that without it the function cannot deliver compliance in line with the risk appetite they have set for the organisation; one or the other would need to be adjusted.

In addition to this, *required* activities (as determined by the regulator) will be different in one jurisdiction or sector compared to another, therefore needing a different approach from the Compliance function. These different requirements and the activities that relate to them all form part of the Compliance environment. What is most important, therefore, is that those tasked with leading the Compliance function and developing the Compliance framework must consider all these variables so that they are able to build a Compliance approach within the regulated firm that (1) genuinely reflects the needs and (2) meets the objectives of the Compliance environment specific to that organisation. This is most definitely a case of one size does not fit all. While there will of course be similarities in requirements and the activities undertaken as a consequence of these requirements, the areas of difference and nuance necessary within the approach are what will make the difference between a so-so Compliance function and one that is genuinely effective in meeting its objectives.

Clear-cut matters relating to strategy, structure, resource and remit will be explored further in the next chapter as we explore the practical Compliance framework. But we also need to consider the factors of a more subtle and fluid nature arising from within the Compliance function itself. Essentially, these reflect those same subtle elements highlighted previously as emanating from within the business:

- Attitude
- Views
- Experience
- Culture

The attitude and approach of those within the Compliance function will contribute greatly to how it is perceived by the business and consequently to its success. These are driven by the experience of those within the function and the culture that exists within it, which are therefore important topics to focus on in setting out the framework. Historically, such topics have tended not to receive the same level of priority and attention as the more specific and defined factors have. They are inevitably far less clear-cut in terms of what, how and when things need to be done. However, effort expended on these aspects of the function is certainly warranted if its objectives are to be achieved. We will discuss this issue in depth in Chapter 6.

MAPPING THE COMPLIANCE ENVIRONMENT

In summary then, those tasked with setting up or developing a Compliance function should:

- Research each of the *external* and *internal* factors relevant to their particular organisation.
- Having done so, they should then be able to map the outcome of this research to reflect the Compliance environment specific to that regulated organisation.
- This then provides a platform on which to build the Compliance framework that will support the function in the achievement of its goals.

Set out below is an example checklist for this purpose, with indicative content on the points to consider in its completion. These are provided simply for illustrative purposes, however, and it is important to further develop such a checklist to ensure it spans all relevant factors that impact on the Compliance environment for a particular firm.[26]

Factor	Points to consider
Compliance environment	
Stage 1 – External factors	.
Jurisdiction and industry sector	For example, what are the specific requirements for the jurisdiction and/or sector? Where is the regulated firm located: single jurisdiction or multiple jurisdictions?
Regulatory structure	For example, what structure is in place? For example, is the jurisdiction operating under a classic institutional model or one of the other three accepted models?
Regulatory approach	For example, what is the regulatory approach in this jurisdiction? Does it lean towards principles or rules based, for example?
Regulatory requirements	For example, what are the specific regulatory requirements in that jurisdiction or sector? Where can this information be found?
Regulatory powers	And so on …
International and national developments	
Other external factors	
Stage 2 – Internal factors (General Business)	
Nature, size and location of business	
Business objectives	
Corporate governance	
Activities of other assurance functions	
Attitude of Board and Senior Management	
Views of staff	
Previous experiences of compliance	
General approach and culture within the organisation	
Stage 3 – Internal factors (Compliance function specific)	
Strategy	
Structure	
Resource	
Remit	
Attitude	
Views	
Experience	
Culture	

COMPLIANCE FRAMEWORK

Once the various factors that impact upon the Compliance environment are understood and mapped, the practicalities of the Compliance framework can then be developed, safe in the knowledge that this will (or should) appropriately reflect the function's operating environment.

The specifics of a Compliance framework are explored in the next chapter.

NOTES

1   While this list is not exhaustive, it is intended to provide a reasonably comprehensive overview of the types of factors that specifically contribute to the Compliance environment, drawing from those that influence the regulatory environment.

2   One of the most effective means of appreciating the consequences for the Compliance environment of the different factors that influence it is through consideration of real-world examples, when the effect of influences such as those discussed in Part I are in practical evidence. Readers may therefore find it useful to spend a little time researching a sample of regulatory regimes and approaches in different jurisdictions around the world – for example note those in Austria, Ireland and the Netherlands for a good level of contrast. This helps to put the Compliance environment issues into context as they fit within the regulatory environment more broadly.

3   This is along similar lines to those discussed under general influences on the regulatory environment in the aforementioned Chapter 2 of Part I.

4   Note again the contrasting regimes of Austria, Ireland and the Netherlands as referred to previously for some examples of how these apply.

5   *The Structure of Financial Supervision: Approaches and Challenges in a Global Market Place*, a paper issued by the OECD Group of 30 in 2008, provides useful insight on this topic. Updated information on the countries referred to therein can be found at www.oecd.org.

6   Adapted from use in Unit 1 of the *Financial Services Compliance Elective Module* of the CBMBA programme, by S. Ward.

7   For more detail on this topic note the content of Part 1.

8   Addressed in detail in Chapter 3 of Part I.

9   The workings of the range of global and international influential bodies referred to in Part I and Appendix 1 attest to this.

10 An example of national legislation in respect of the Compliance function, covering the rules, requirements and approach of national regulators (using the UK as a case in point) can be found in the FCA Handbook within Senior Management Arrangements, Systems and Controls (SYSC) spanning matters relating to application, policy and procedures and the compliance function. Note that the detail is accessible via the regulator's website and the relevant rulebook (fortunately now usually offered online, allowing ease of access and review) as is most often the case nowadays, even in the smallest of jurisdictions.

11 Based on extract from Central Bank of Ireland website at: www.centralbank.i.e./publication.

12 Based on extract from AMF website at: www.amf-france.org/en_US/L-AMF/Missions-et-competences/Presentation.html/.

13 Also, for ease of reference, included as a separate Appendix – note Appendix 3.

14 Accessible at: www.amvcolombia.org.co/attachments/data/20100630220810.pdf.

15 Accessible at: www.bis.org/publ/bcbs113.pdf.

16 Accessible at: www.bis.org/publ/bcbs142.pdf.

17 Accessible at: www.fsa.go.jp/inter/ios/20060510/02.pdf.

18 Accessible at: www.esma.europa.eu/sites/default/files/library/guidelines_on_certain_aspects_of_mifid_ii_compliance_function_requirements.pdf.

19 An overview can be accessed and the full standards purchased at: www.iso.org/standard/75080.html.

20 Accessible at: www.ukstandards.org.uk.

21 An overview can be accessed and the full standards purchased at: https://knowledge.bsigroup.com/products/compliance-framework-for-regulated-financial-services-firms-specification/standard.

22 Commonly known collectively as GRC, as highlighted in Part I.

23 Note www2.deloitte.com/cn/en/pages/risk/articles/assurance-health-check-and-digitization.html for further information around this.

24 Note www.iia.org.uk/resources/corporate-governance-basic-overview/application-of-the-three-lines-model – aspects of this model will be discussed further in later chapters.

25 A key example of international best practice guidance *Compliance and the Compliance Function in Banks – 2005* (BIS 2005).

26 Note that for the purposes of this text, all the various factors have been explicitly listed. However, as anyone who has ever worked in business will know, there are certain topics – attitude of the board and senior management, for example – that might be somewhat more difficult to quantify.

5

The Compliance Framework

EXPLORING THE FRAMEWORK

As addressed in the previous chapter, the term 'Compliance framework' in this text refers to the core elements of the Compliance function that underpin activities in pursuit of its objectives. In considering this, it is important to remember that there is no single 'correct' framework: the framework implemented within a particular firm should ultimately reflect the individual business. Typically, however, it will consist of the elements found in Figure 5.1, drawing on the factors discussed in the previous chapter.

These represent the main practicalities of the Compliance role. We will begin by addressing the initial aspects of setting up a Compliance function and then discuss ongoing requirements, exploring the following topics, as listed in Table 5.1.

INITIAL FORMATION

As highlighted previously, there are several sets of best practice guidance relating to the Compliance role that has been produced over the years since this distinct role for compliance-related activity began to emerge. In addressing the practicalities, activities and approach, all of these sources are considered in both this and the following chapter and have informed the content throughout. However, for the purposes of continuity and clarity, the predominant source referred to is the well-established and widely recognised *Basel Principles*.[1] While these were developed with banks in mind, they are universally accepted as being a best practice basis for all financial service businesses, and so have been referred to throughout this chapter. Where there are specific points to be made regarding the wording of other guidance, these too are included.

Each of these sources provides direction and explanation on *why* certain approaches should be followed. To more fully appreciate *how* these are being implemented in a practical context, and which variations of different approaches work most effectively, it is useful to hear from practitioners in this field who have real-world experience of implementing these requirements. Accordingly, this chapter draws attention to practical information

DOI: 10.4324/9781003431305-8

Figure 5.1 **Compliance framework**

TABLE 5.1
The main practicalities of the compliance role

Initial formation	Ongoing development
Strategy	Developing the framework
Policy setting	Communication
Independence	Relationship management
Structure	Supporting and strengthening the framework
Remit	
Resource	
Reporting lines	
Conflicts of interest	
Compliance plan	
Systems and controls	
Reporting and information flow	
Promoting the framework	

and feedback gathered in doing so, drawing on a mix of reports, reviews, studies and pieces of analysis based on the experiences and views expressed by such practitioners, together with information garnered from formal and informal interviews from some with them. Frequently amongst these is a reference to the Thomson Reuters annual *Cost of Compliance* surveys.[2] Currently, in their 13th year, they provide a regular snapshot of the challenges experienced and anticipated by Compliance practitioners and the span of their production allows for reflection on how priorities and actions have shifted in response to emerging challenges.

Let us begin by considering the main practical aspects of setting up a Compliance function within an organisation.

Strategy

At the outset, a clear strategy needs to be agreed and set between relevant stakeholders. To be effective, Compliance strategy must align with the overall strategy and approach of the regulated business within which the Compliance function is situated, including in relation to the risk management strategy. This is a view recommended in the *Basel Principles* which made the point right at the outset of its guidance that (the firm) 'should organise its compliance function and set priorities for the management of its compliance risk in a way that is consistent with its own risk management'. While there will be commonalities across the approach of Compliance functions, irrespective of jurisdiction or sector, a single solution in terms of approach is not sufficient. Therefore, ahead of constructing a Compliance framework, in addition to practical considerations (such as the structure, reporting lines and the systems and controls that need to be put in place, for example), issues arising from the overall strategy and approach of the regulated business need to be borne in mind. Considering matters such as the firm's business aims, plans for development, areas of focus, strategies for expansion or contraction and so on, and incorporating these into aspects of the approach of the Compliance function where necessary will help the function provide a better and more consistent level of support to the business. Taking this approach will also help gain business backing for the Compliance function, which historically has been something of a challenge for Compliance, and enable activities of the function to be demonstrably linked back to the achievement of business objectives. As always, it should be remembered that Compliance and therefore the role of the Compliance function is not an end in itself; it is there to help the business succeed in a compliant way.

One of the practical publications referred to previously focused on this area of business[3] emphasised this point by stating

> A viable and effective Compliance strategy should be driven by the business's regulatory risk profile and the risk appetite set by the Board, ensuring an appropriate compliance role, adequately resourced and directed in enabling the business to manage and mitigate its own risks.

Note the emphasis here on 'viable and effective' – it is not sufficient simply that the Compliance Strategy reflects the business regulatory risk profile and risk appetite, but in order to be viable and effective it needs to ensure an appropriate role for compliance, with resource and focus (in the form of the directed point referred to) aiding the business in managing and mitigating its own risk. A report produced a few years later on, once some of the regulatory developments referred to in earlier chapters of this text had started to bed in,[4] raised the importance of an effective Compliance strategy from the regulator's perspective, noting that those who lead this area are 'now much more frequently involved in corporate strategy, advising on whether and how strategic and business model considerations are likely to satisfy the supervisors' judgments' and emphasising practical considerations to support this, for example 'exploit technology tools in order to improve the efficiency of compliance operations and expand the firm's ability to manage and monitor its compliance risk' or 'the recruitment and development of talent in the Compliance function to align to overall business strategy'.

The alignment of the Compliance strategy with the business strategy is required to ensure appropriate focus of the function from the outset and demonstration of relevance and efficacy on an ongoing basis, both internally and externally, with particular significance for our two key stakeholders. The most recent Thomson Reuters *Cost of Compliance* report[5] – with its expanded title of 'Competing Priorities' echoing in many ways the balancing act required of the Compliance function previously referred to – cites volume and implementation of regulatory change as being the greatest compliance challenges the respondents to its survey anticipate currently. Looking back through the survey output of the past ten years it is interesting – though possibly not unsurprising given the focus of the role – to note the durability of this as a particular challenge, with it appearing in one guise or another during that time, from tracking regulatory change,[6] volume and pace of regulatory change,[7] continuing regulatory change[8] and keeping up with regulatory change.[9] Clearly, it remains a priority for Compliance practitioners, feeding into the approach adopted by the Compliance function, and considerations in this regard will therefore need to inform the Compliance strategy adopted.

We will return to the points regarding resourcing, the use of technology and focusing shortly. Ahead of that our next area to think about is the setting of Policy in support of the Strategy agreed upon.

Policy Setting

With the Compliance strategy determined to reflect the overall business strategy articulated by the board, clear compliance policy can then be developed, giving due consideration to all the relevant factors that influence the Compliance environment, as discussed in the previous chapter. Essentially, this draws together the inter-related aims of the board, senior management, oversight and control functions, assurance functions, business units and key individuals therein, setting out the Compliance-related requirements necessary to support the achievement of them.

On a related note, matters of *accountability* versus *responsibility* should be kept in mind when setting policy and agreeing approach: the board is accountable for overseeing the management of compliance risk[10] and senior management is accountable for the effective management of compliance[11]; although delegating day-to-day responsibility for such matters to the Compliance function, the board and senior management still retain accountability. This should be clearly reflected within the compliance policy set.

Best practice guidance expands on requirements in pursuit of these aims, specifically in relation to the effective management of compliance risk and also for establishing and communicating a compliance policy, ensuring it is observed and reporting thereon. For example, the role of senior management in respect of compliance policy is set out in *Principle 3* of the *Basel Principles*, neatly summarising what the policy should contain and who is responsible for ensuring its appropriate production: 'establishing a written compliance policy' that should contain 'all the necessary principles to be followed and the main processes for identification and management of compliance risk throughout the organisation' and in ensuring this policy is adhered to, senior management must also make sure: 'that appropriate remedial or disciplinary action is taken if breaches are identified'. *Principle 3* then goes on to include recommendations on how this should be achieved, again emphasising senior management's responsibility for: 'establishing and communicating a compliance policy, for ensuring that it is observed and for reporting to the Board of directors on the management of the bank's compliance risk'. Accordingly, as well as setting out intended aims and the requirements resulting from these *Principles*, policy should make clear the consequences of non-compliance for all parties involved.

As to the responsibility of the Compliance function itself for setting the compliance policy, regulators in different jurisdictions or sectors might set more detailed requirements on not only the policy itself but also on its production. Broadly speaking, however, the key message is that the Compliance function's role is not to set it directly *per se*, but to be actively involved in its development and setting. They should provide guidance on requirements, input on necessary areas of focus and then subsequently, once set, advise on enhancements where needed. The aforementioned *Future of Compliance* analysis flags the increasing importance of the various different stakeholders in setting such a policy, noting that 'With increasing expectations from the regulator that senior executives will be involved in the oversight of regulatory compliance matters, a process for Senior Management approval for all risk policies is essential'.[12] The quote from the *Changing Role of Compliance*[13] report referred to in the previous section underlines this point on a practical level, citing the board's expectations regarding Compliance function input being expected. The *Cost of Compliance* Surveys provides useful insight into the board's ongoing concerns around dealing with regulatory demands and changes in this regard, with such topics regularly featuring in the challenges flagged as being most of board concern (with keeping up with regulatory change being the main challenge noted currently[14] as with the Compliance Officers, and variations on this an ongoing feature over the past decade). Considerations ought also be given to those who provide input to the policy to ensure views are sufficiently broad and diverse, as this will help avoid 'group think'. Overall, the formation of the Compliance policy should clearly be a collaborative process to ensure that the overall management of compliance risk within the firm reflects its overall objectives and is thus effective in supporting their achievement. In doing so, it will support the achievement of the respective objectives of the stakeholders who are party to this.

To recap then, just as with everything else relating to Compliance, in order to be effective, the Compliance strategy and policy setting must be reflective of the Compliance environment, with consideration to the specific features of it and the 'fixed' nature of these. It is important to keep in mind, however, that this does not mean *solely* in terms of these specifics but also needs to be considered in terms of the *use* of the language, systems, reporting mechanisms and so on that support it, including the development of the Compliance plan and the activities and communication thereof, if it is to be effective. We will explore this point later in this chapter. At this juncture, however, we need to emphasise that what the Compliance strategy and policy overall is aiming to do is:

- Link, via the risk assessment process, Compliance activities and the resources invested in them to the business goals of the organisation as per its strategy.
- Articulate these in the Compliance policy and the procedures that are put in place to support them.

The initial formation of the function should be based on an approach with independence and a status that reflects independence at its core, be properly resourced and have defined areas of responsibility.

With these in mind, the central tenets of the Compliance function as per the *Basel Principles* should be noted. Within these are three key features, considered vital to the effective performance of the Compliance role:

- Independence.
- Adequate resources.
- Clear areas of responsibility.

At a minimum, the initial formation of the function should be based on an approach with independence and a status that reflects independence at its core, be properly resourced and have defined areas of responsibility. Let's explore these three features in more detail.

Independence

Independence is the hallmark of an effective assurance function. When viewed in their more traditional role of 'monitor' within regulated organisations, assurance functions are regarded differently and independently from the main part of the business. Given this aspect of their role, this is a reasonable view and one which, to a large degree, is necessary for the effective performance of such a role. Note, however, that independence in this context does not mean isolation: we shall return to this observation shortly.

The necessity for the Compliance function to be independent is a view emphasised in both guidance on requirements and feedback from practical experience. In the BCBS *Implementation of the Compliance Principles*,[15] the six measures to promote independence of the function were listed again, building on what was included in the original. So key are these to the effectiveness of the Compliance function that it is worth repeating these here:

1. Requiring a head of compliance to be appointed (that is, an executive or senior staff member with overall responsibility for coordinating the identification and management of the bank's compliance risk and supervising other compliance function staff);

2. That compliance function staff perform only compliance responsibilities (or, where this is not practicable because of the small size of the entity, that appropriate measures be taken to avoid potential conflicts of interest);

3. Requiring that the compliance function be given the right, on its own initiative, to communicate with any staff member and obtain any records or files necessary to enable it to carry out its responsibilities;

4. Requiring the compliance function to be given a formal status within the bank (responsibilities, independence, access to information, direct access to the Board of Directors or a committee of the Board...);

5. Prohibit remuneration of compliance function staff that is related to the financial performance of the business lines for which they exercise compliance responsibilities; and

6. That the supervisor and the Board of Directors be informed of the departure of the head of compliance and the reasons for such departure.

More recently, the MiFID requirements and guidelines[16] make clear that 'firms should ensure that the compliance function holds a position in the organisational structure that ensures that the compliance officer and other compliance staff act independently when performing their tasks'[17] with a clear point to make regarding what should happen when this is not the case: 'where senior management deviates from important recommendations or assessment issues by the compliance function, the compliance officer should document this accordingly and present it in the compliance reports'. Both the MiFID legislation and the ESMA guidance that supports it are also explicit on the independence implications of combining the compliance function with other internal control functions, stating that a: 'firm should generally not combine the compliance function with the internal audit function' again providing guidance on what should happen if the approach adopted is not in line with this:

The combination of the compliance function with other control functions may be acceptable if this does not compromise the effectiveness and independence of the compliance function. Any such combination should be documented, including the reasons for the combination so that competent authorities are able to assess whether the combination of functions is appropriate in the circumstances.

The guidance goes on to make the point that:

Compliance staff should generally not be involved in the activities they monitor. However, a combination of the compliance function with other control units at the same level (such as money laundering prevention) may be acceptable if this does not generate conflicts of interests or compromise the effectiveness of the compliance function.

And emphasising again that: 'Combining the compliance function with the internal audit function should generally be avoided as this is likely to undermine the independence of the compliance function because the internal audit function is charged with the oversight of the compliance function'. This is useful to reflect on taking into account how the 'Three Lines of Defence' model has been utilised in a practical sense supporting risk management within regulated organisations, how this has developed to its current 'Three Lines Model' approach with a focus on assurance and, within some companies, has been further expanded to incorporate additional lines that better suit those particular organisations individually.

In practical terms, and one to consider when putting in place reporting lines, the previously cited *The Future of Compliance* analysis makes the point that

> Compliance should enjoy direct access to the board (or to a sub-committee tasked with overseeing regulatory risk) in the event that issues need escalating. Such direct access would be defined as the facility to approach the board (or board sub-committee) other than via a third-party such as senior management.[18]

A jurisdictionally focused example of the recognition of the importance of independence of this role from a regulator's perspective was evident in requirements that emerged with the focus on improving standards in the UK financial services environment in the mid-2010s. A key initiative 'Strengthening accountability in banking: a new regulatory framework for individuals'[19] highlighted the need for firms to allocate responsibility for 'ensuring and overseeing the integrity and independence of the compliance function...' Wording within the current FCA rulebook under SYSC 6.1 highlights the need for the Compliance function to be able to 'discharge is responsibilities properly and independently'[20] and sets out a number of conditions to support this – reference to this provides useful contextual insight into how legislation and recommendations from influential bodies translate into defined requirements on the part of a particular regulator, while also emphasising Compliance function independence as an important factor within the Compliance framework.

Structure

As with so many aspects of the Compliance function, best practice guidance recognises that the structure of the function will depend upon the size and nature of the business: 'There are significant differences between banks regarding the organisation of the Compliance Function'.[21] There is a recognition that this will influence how the function is organised:

> In larger banks, compliance staff may be located within operating business lines, and internationally active banks may also have group and local compliance officers. In smaller banks, Compliance Function staff may be located in one Unit. Separate Units have been established in some banks for specialist areas such as data protection and the prevention of money laundering and terrorist financing.[22]

The ESMA guidance echoes this in stating 'when ensuring that appropriate human and other resources are allocated to the compliance function, investment firms should take into account the scale and types of investment services, activities and ancillary services undertaken by the investment firm'.

Rather than stipulating how the function should be structured, the emphasis is on the approach being appropriate for the particular organisation. There are, however, recognised Compliance models that should be considered:

- A centralised Compliance function (where the main Compliance activities take place and operate from a central point, with the function retaining direct control) is a fairly common structure and is probably the most widely recognised.
- A decentralised model (where responsibilities for a number of Compliance activities are delegated from the central point) is becoming more common. This can take a variety of forms, including individual Compliance functions in other parts of the business linked into a central hub, which retains responsibility overall, or alternatively a number of different Compliance departments working independently of each other, perhaps focusing on particular aspects of the role, either reporting into a central point or taking on specific responsibility, delegated to them from the central point.

Consideration at this stage ought also be given to the formation of an appropriate set of committees to act as support to the compliance and risk-based approach that has been agreed. For example, required committees such as those for risk and audit, or others such as remuneration and so on, dependent upon the needs of the business.

Overall, decisions made in respect of structure and related matters need to reflect the situation within business. As organisations become more diverse, operating in different sectors and jurisdictions, to many it makes sense not to have a single central function, but to position the function or its activities where it is believed they will be most effective. As with so many aspects of business, however, there are inevitably pros and cons to each approach and some of these are set out in Table 5.2.

TABLE 5.2
Potential positives and negatives of different compliance function structures

Centralised structure	Decentralised structure
Pros	*Pros*
• Traditional approach, familiar to many and easy to understand.	• Within businesses, so closer to the ground, therefore is aware of and able to respond more quickly.
• Able to provide direct oversight to the compliance activities and so may be viewed as safer.	• Clear areas of responsibility.
• Helps create a consistent approach and attitude.	• Tailored solutions.
	• More accessible.
	• Better/stronger/easier relationships.
Cons	*Cons*
• Can be unwieldy in size.	• Possible duplication of effort and/or resource.
• Inflexible/unresponsive to change and/or new developments.	• Can be viewed as less safe as Compliance Officer not in direct control.
• Remote/unapproachable/difficult to access.	• Possible inconsistencies of approach between businesses.
• Can encourage view of 'compliance' being the responsibility of the 'compliance' function.	• Maybe more expensive if each business needs a high-level individual.
	• Possible loss of independence.

The structure of the Compliance function and its position within the organisation will be influenced by many factors, a number of them historical, and these will inevitably have shaped the development of the general structure within the organisation. For example, a company with a strong central structure is likely to position Compliance in a similar manner, while those that are more decentralised in their structure might adopt an approach akin to this for their Compliance function. However, it is not the structure of the function that is most important of course, it is its effectiveness.

With that in mind and depending upon the structure of the Compliance framework, the Compliance function itself may not always be directly involved in all Compliance-related activities. Where this is the situation, best practice guidance emphasises that the allocation of all responsibilities should be clear and unambiguous, with clear reporting lines providing mechanisms for information exchange:

> In some banks, for example, legal and compliance may be separate departments; the legal department may be responsible for advising management on the compliance laws, rules and standards and for preparing guidance to staff, while the compliance department may be responsible for monitoring compliance with the policies and procedures and reporting to management. In other banks, parts of the Compliance Function may be located within the operational risk group or within a more general risk management group. If there is a division of responsibilities between departments, the allocation of responsibilities to each department should be clear. There should also be appropriate mechanisms for co-operation among each department and with the head of compliance (e.g. with respect to the provision and exchange of relevant advice and information). These mechanisms should be sufficient to ensure that the head of compliance can perform his or her responsibilities effectively.[23]

Allocation of all responsibilities should be clear and unambiguous, with clear reporting lines

The BCBS survey referred to previously identified the organisation of the Compliance function as one of the two major issues faced by firms implementing a Compliance framework.[24] This was seen as a particular concern for small to medium-sized firms and the issues arose in a number of areas: 'the determination of what are appropriate resources for the compliance function in relation to the size, complexity and nature of the business; the relationship between internal audit and compliance; the independence of the compliance function', all of which we will discuss in further detail later in this chapter. This finding, however, demonstrates the many practical challenges faced by those seeking to structure a Compliance function effectively, a view endorsed subsequently by *The Future of Compliance* analysis which noted that 'The importance of designing and operating the right compliance model is growing'.[25] This analysis also observed that 'Due to the increased regulatory supervisory focus on firms, we are seeing a notable increase in the extent to which the regulator challenges firms' Compliance structures'.[26] The authors of that paper agree, however, that

> there is no single optimal Compliance model. Models tend to be tailored to firms' specific profiles. Global, diverse operations tend to be organised on a decentralised basis, as this provides the business with a greater degree of compliance insight into, and oversight over, local operations.[27]

They also proffered the view that 'The majority of organisations should have some degree of Compliance representation within divisions and/or business units. This can range from embedded Compliance resources within the businesses line to divisional Compliance teams advising and overseeing the business lines' activities',[28] a point worth noting in focusing on this area as it reinforces the view that the Compliance function, although independent, is not being isolated if it is to be effective.

Whichever structural model is adopted, practically speaking, thinking around this structure should clearly reflect the function's role in the risk management and assurance framework of the organisation, supporting its purpose accordingly. The 'Three Lines Model' provides a useful basis for this, one that is widely adopted. For example, a review conducted by a regulator[29] identified that 'Without exception, every firm in our sample operates a structure modelled on the three lines of defence (LoD) and the compliance function is defined consistently as a second LoD function'.

In summary, in agreeing and subsequently developing the structure of the Compliance function and the compliance model that supports it (both within the business generally and within the function itself), care must be taken to ensure this reflects the needs of the business, not only from a strategic perspective but also from a practical perspective.

Remit

The remit of the Compliance function and the type of activity carried out by it will depend upon the Compliance policy set, and the responsibilities and activities of other functions within the business, including those involved in operational, assurance and control matters. In order to be clear on the Compliance remit, therefore, there should be a clear demarcation between the various functions:

> The responsibilities of the bank's compliance function should be to assist *senior management* in managing effectively the compliance risks faced by the bank ... If some of these responsibilities are carried out by staff in different departments, the allocation of responsibilities to each department should be clear.[30]

As they cover related areas, the activities of other oversight and assurance functions will necessarily impact on the activities of the Compliance function and the remit of all such ought to have been set with these in mind. An awareness of the objectives and roles of other such functions is therefore required.

Within these, there will be certain statutory responsibilities, as well as responsibilities emanating solely from within the business, but generally the remit will span:

- Provision of advice.
- Guidance and education.
- Identification, measurement and assessment of compliance risk.
- Monitoring, testing and reporting.
- Statutory responsibilities and liaison
  - the compliance programme.[31]

We will explore these in detail in the next chapter, but it is of interest to note that this was the second major issue identified in the BCBS survey into the *Implementation of the Compliance Principles*, with firms highlighting 'the scope of compliance risks'[32] proving to be an issue when implementing a Compliance framework. The extracts from the *Cost of Compliance* surveys discussed earlier also emphasise the continuing challenges arising from regulations and changes thereto. This again demonstrates the many practical challenges faced by those seeking to be effective in this key area of business.

Resource

The resource allocated to the function must be adequate to meet the demands placed upon it, both by the business and other parties to the Compliance environment: 'The resources to be provided for the compliance function should be both sufficient and appropriate to ensure that compliance risk within the bank is managed effectively'.[33] The majority of this resource will relate to personnel, although there will also be investments in terms of technology, developments and so on. Enhancement in technological capabilities has had a significant impact on resourcing considerations for Compliance over recent years. As a resource that is central to business strategy, the function must be appropriately staffed, comprising sufficient numbers and levels of experience to have a reasonable expectation of meeting the function's objectives. We will explore staffing and related matters in the next chapter.

Reference to resource requirements has appeared regularly in various pieces of compliance literature, linked as it is to so many aspects of the Compliance role. The MiFID Guidance, for example, makes the point that 'Investment firms should ensure that the compliance function takes a risk-based approach in order to allocate the function's resources efficiently',[34] and that 'the compliance function should be allocated a budget that is consistent with the level of compliance risk the firm is exposed to'.[35] *The Future of Compliance* findings emphasise the point that 'quality and quantity of resources is a critical success factor for any Compliance function to fulfil its responsibilities …',[36] a point we will elaborate on shortly. Inevitably, however, there will not be an unlimited flow of resources available to the function. While the function has to balance all of its many activities in deciding how to apportion its resources effectively once made available to them, the firm itself will be 'attempting to strike a balance between reducing overheads and maintaining a robust and effective Compliance function'.[37]

The *Cost of Compliance* surveys make some useful observations on the subject of Compliance budget. In 2012, it found that 93% expected their budget to remain the same as the previous year or to increase, with 11% expecting a significant increase. A very similar finding was noted in 2018 with 94% expecting the budget to stay the same or grow, and 14% expecting a significant increase. More recently, the 2022 findings indicated 62% expected an increase, 12% significantly more, in contrast to 2021 which was 52% more, 10% significantly more. Note the overall direction of travel here. The latest survey highlights the expectation for some compliance functions to 'do more with less'. The reasons for this will vary, but it is useful to consider how resourcing matters are linked to other factors, for example growing concerns about the availability of staffing with an appropriate level of expertise to work in this key area of business, with a lack of skilled resources identified as one of the main challenges for Compliance professionals in 2021 and 2022. How firms will elect to deal with such challenges will also vary, with increasing consideration being given to how technological developments may be harnessed to do so. For example, a finding linked to this was noted in the *Compliance function in wholesale banks* survey[38] observing that

> The dominant change over the past few years has been a dramatic increase in monitoring and surveillance activity, whether manual or substantially automated. The corresponding resource changes are the investment in systems and an increase in headcount in these areas.

Clearly, agreeing appropriate Compliance resource is an issue, and is a factor to be considered at an early stage in developing the compliance framework and on an ongoing basis thereafter. A useful insight into practical mechanisms for securing Compliance budget is provided in *Measuring the Value of Compliance: Winning Arguments for Securing Compliance Budget*[39] which was undertaken as a benchmarking exercise, the results of which were published in the *Journal of Business Compliance*.[40] The research focused on an issue that continues high on the agenda of Compliance professionals irrespective of the industry: securing resources for the conduct of ethics and compliance programmes that provide the required level of assurance that internal policies and procedures intended to demonstrate regulatory requirements are adhered to. Increasingly tight budgetary constraints have increased resistance to the allocation of funding to verify what many consider ought to be implicit practice within regulated businesses. Consequently, consideration of 'cost to business' concerns versus 'value add' requirements are never far from the minds of those who have budgetary allocation responsibility. As a result of this, those tasked with securing such funding often encounter a level of resistance to their efforts. This research project sought to consider mechanisms by which the value of such programmes could more effectively be communicated, thus easing the process for all concerned and increasing the likelihood of securing appropriate resources to meet the requirements of all interested parties.

The research indicated a commonality amongst respondents in respect of the type of information provided in support of applications for funding. When explored further, this appeared to result from the ease with which such information could be obtained, rather than because of its efficacy in supporting the funding-seeking objectives. However, it was apparent that the greater the level of detail contained within this information the better this was in terms of how positively it was perceived in supporting the funding request. This led to the conclusion that focused evidence-based requests, rather than those resulting from generalisations, were more effective in securing a successful outcome. Conversely, the research found that not all forms of evidence were considered equal: contributions by expert *external* parties, such as consultants, were not as effective as might be expected, with contributions from *internal* experts such as other oversight and assurance functions (Internal Audit or Risk departments, for example) being notably more influential.

> **Focused, evidence-based requests, rather than those resulting from generalisations, were more effective in securing a successful outcome.**

While on the subject of resource, it would be useful to touch on the topic of *outsourcing*. Highlighted under *Basel*

Principle 10: 'Compliance should be regarded as a core risk management activity within the bank. Specific tasks of the compliance function may be outsourced, but they must remain subject to appropriate oversight by the head of compliance'. Outsourcing is an increasingly common practice in the compliance world, but one that can be a source of concern and requires careful consideration from a risk management perspective. The ESMA guidelines make clear that 'Investment firms should ensure that all applicable compliance function requirements are fulfilled where all or part of the compliance function is outsourced',[41] and in the guidance, the point is made that 'Outsourcing of the compliance function within a group does not lead to a lower level of responsibility for the *senior management* ....'[42] This neatly summarises the key requirement in respect of outsourcing: similar to the issues regarding responsibility and accountability discussed earlier in this chapter, vis-à-vis the board and the Compliance function. The main point here is that while activities can be outsourced, responsibility and accountability cannot. Returning to our *Cost of Compliance*[43] survey, respondents make clear that 'outsourcing needs continued compliance focus' while highlighting ongoing risk management concerns in relation to this. Regulators too recognise risk management challenges inherent in outsourcing activity, with a useful example of regulator output in respect of this being that from the UK's FCA in 2020, updated 2022.[44] This highlighted matters around operational resilience and expectations accordingly, making clear what firms were required to comply with in respect of key aspects such as material notifications, intra-group outsourcing, data security and risk management in relation to this, requiring appropriate systems and controls to be put in place accordingly.

Reporting Lines

The first point to consider is reporting lines in the sense of to whom, directly, the function – and in a practical sense, that means the head of the function – reports to. The *Basel Principles* have a clear view on this:

> The head of compliance may or may not be a member of Senior management. If the head of compliance is a member of Senior management, he or she should not have direct business line responsibilities. If the head of compliance is not a member of Senior management, he or she should have a direct reporting line to a member of Senior management who does not have direct business line responsibilities.[45]

It is important to recognise that, as with the optimal structure within the Compliance function itself, what would be appropriate in one organisation might differ greatly from that appropriate in another (depending as ever on the size, nature and complexity of the organisation) and, just as with the structure, it is what is appropriate that is the key requirement. The *Basel Principles* have a view on this topic also and how this might work practically, stating:

> In some banks, the head of compliance has the title 'compliance officer', while in others the title 'compliance officer' denotes a staff member carrying out specific compliance responsibilities. In cases where Compliance Function staff reside in independent support Units (e.g. legal, financial control, risk management), a separate reporting line from staff in these Units to the

head of compliance may not be necessary. However, these Units should co-operate closely with the head of compliance to ensure that the head of compliance can perform his or her responsibilities effectively.[46]

This evidently links with the emphasis placed on the independence of the function, as discussed earlier in this chapter.

Regulators consider the standing of the head of Compliance within the regulated firm to be of particular importance. For example, the UK's FCA SYSC requires the allocation of a director or senior manager to the function of responsibility for oversight of the firm's compliance and reporting to the governing body in respect of this.[47] The role of the Compliance Officer is designated as a Senior Management Function (SM16) and is an Approved Person[48] under the Senior Managers and Certification Regime (SM&CR).[49]

Consequently, the Compliance Officer's role, whether undertaken by an individual with that specific title or otherwise, is increasingly recognised as a senior position in its own right. As a consequence, a greater number of Compliance Officers report directly to the board or are members of the board themselves. For example, in *The Future of Compliance* report, the authors note that while: 'There is a range of possible Compliance reporting lines, some being stand-alone, others reporting through Risk and still others via Legal Counsel' though clearly making the point that 'paramount is that firms must be able to demonstrate that reporting lines are clearly articulated and operationally effective'.[50] This was a trend not confined to financial services, either, as noted in the paper *A Path to Integration: An Integrated Compliance Solution*,[51] the first of an annual series of surveys in non-financial firms by Deloitte. This describes a move 'to increased C-suite leadership for compliance' with 'over 45% of the functions surveyed reporting directly to the Executive Management'. And furthermore, in the regulatory survey *The compliance function in wholesale banks*,[52] considerations around independence, seniority of remit and so forth were reflected in another finding, that

> Compliance was commonly positioned as an independent unit with the Head of Compliance reporting to the CEO. A number of firms reported one layer away from the CEO, for example to the CRO, COO or Head of Legal, with the latter becoming less common.[53]

And also

> Responses to our questionnaire indicate that the compliance function is moving toward a pure, independent second line of defence risk function with a higher profile within firms. Compliance representatives have been added to boards and governance committees, and reporting lines of the function elevated.

This positioning will be explored further shortly.

Moving on from reporting lines in this sense, however, there needs to be consideration of practical reporting lines for the Compliance function more generally. To be effective, these should flow in a number of directions (Figure 5.2):

> Internally, this can include upwards to the board of directors, senior management and relevant committees, sideways to other oversight or assurance functions and business units, while

Figure 5.2 Reporting lines

outwards would include communications with the regulator and other relevant bodies. Less formal reporting channels should also be available if the Compliance function is to be effective. This is where the benefit of relationship management – as will be discussed in the latter part of this chapter – will really be felt, allowing the conveyance of issues informally. This has benefits both within the Compliance function itself and outside it directly – but still within the business – providing opportunity for adjustment in approach based on information provided or received.

The Compliance function, as with other assurance and internal control functions, must remain independent to provide an objective viewpoint that is not overly clouded by day-to-day business considerations. Remember, independent in this sense does not mean separate. Indeed, to be effective – as this text endorses throughout – such functions need to be at the very heart of business, rather than on the periphery.

Conflicts of Interest

Best practice guidance[54] recognises that the activities of the Compliance function and the roles of the Compliance professionals undertaking them may be undermined if there is an actual or potential conflict of interest between their Compliance responsibilities and other business roles. There is, however, recognition that complete separation of those working in business and Compliance roles may not be practical in smaller organisations. Therefore, caution is advised where Compliance staff may be conflicted – all activities must be performed in a way that avoids conflicts of interest. However, the general best practice recommendation is that there is separation, with Compliance personnel ideally performing only Compliance activities.

Practically, firms find different ways of structuring functions and agreeing reporting lines to promote efficacy within their own organisations. In *The compliance function in wholesale banks*[55] matters relating to the separation of duties across the Compliance field of responsibilities were reflected in the finding that 'Organisationally, some compliance functions were integrated with Operational Risk. One trend of note was the separation of financial crime from compliance into its own function, with separate reporting lines into senior management'.[56]

Of course, the existence of an agreed policy on this does not mean that there will not be conflicts and consideration needs to be given to how to handle these. What these might be and thoughts on how to handle them will be addressed in Chapter 8 when we explore Compliance challenges.

Compliance Plan

The Compliance plan is, essentially, a plan for scheduling and carrying out Compliance activities and checks to meet the objectives of the function. Taking a structured approach makes sure that these reflect the aims of the function, ensures effective utilisation of resource and allows firms to focus on specific issues in a timely manner.

Reflecting the two main aspects of the Compliance function's role (that is, watchdog and adviser) as will be explored later in this chapter, the inclusions within this plan, and considerations around these, can be broadly divided into those which are *proactive* and those which are *reactive*:

- *Proactive*: relate to activities that assist in the provision of advice and guidance, for example, together with education and training and the identification,'measurement and assessment of compliance risk.
- *Reactive*: involve monitoring and remedial activities (including testing and reporting), with of course each feeding into the other.

By its very nature, in terms of detail, the Compliance plan will tend to focus on *planned* activities, that is, those scheduled on a risk-assessed basis.[57] These take into consideration all the influencing factors previously discussed and in doing so a risk management approach is adopted to the frequency of scheduling and activity.

However, not all of the activities the Compliance function undertakes can be planned as the function will be regularly challenged by the conflicting needs of *cyclical* activities (that is, those that are scheduled or regular) versus *on-demand* activities (those arising on an ad hoc basis). On-demand activities, such as those emanating from within the business (a request for information from the board or an appeal from the business for action on a particular issue, for example), can have a notable impact on the resource available within the function. This has consequences for the existing plans of the staff required to address them and therefore on the overall plans for the department, and of course, the role it plays within the firm's overall risk management methodology. An effective

Compliance plan must make allowance for all of these types of activity, reflecting on them with appropriate consideration of risk management, and allocating resource (in terms of time and staffing) accordingly. It must do so with the certainty that there *will be* on-demand activities at some point in the year. In effect, this means either having a clear view of planned activities that are considered lower risk and can therefore be readily dropped to take on unplanned activities or, alternatively, include a contingency of unallocated time in the plan cycle that, if not required, can be easily filled from a pre-prepared list of lower risk activities. Not being flexible enough to support these demands will impact on both the credibility and standing of the function with the business, and it will therefore also impact on its overall effectiveness as many on demand activities may be of an immediate, higher risk nature (such as responding, for example, to actual or 'near misses' of breaches of regulations).

Systems and Controls

In the same way as the regulator needs to take into account a number of factors when considering appropriate levels of regulation and supervision, the business needs to consider what factors influence its own ability to achieve its business objectives in a compliant and timely manner. Systems and controls that are necessary to support the achievement of these therefore need to be implemented appropriately. Careful consideration needs to be given to the nature of controls to be put in place to support the systems.

The obligation is on the firm to determine the exact nature of the systems and controls that should be in place to allow them to meet the regulatory requirements. What is appropriate for one firm may not be appropriate for another – again, as with so many aspects of the Compliance role, there is no single standardised version of these that can be applied across the board. The firm must therefore consider what is necessary based on an understanding of the requirements and how these can be met given the specifics of the firm.

One of the main considerations of the Compliance function will be to ensure that the systems and controls that exist are appropriate. This constitutes one of the main activities undertaken by the Compliance function. Effective monitoring is key to ensuring this. In simple terms, effective systems and controls should:

- encourage compliance with requirements
- minimise opportunities for non-compliance
- allow assessment of adherence to the compliance policy and related procedures
- identify any issues arising.

In putting in place appropriate systems to support the controls that will help mitigate the manifestation of risk within the organisation, the types of points noted in Part I in relation to regulation and risk need to be considered.

What role should technology play in this? Consider RegTech (regulatory technology, a sub set of FinTech, financial technology) for example, the use of which is increasing.[58] An obvious benefit from the use of such is time and also allowing focus both of activity and output, potentially speeding up activity and decision making, while – albeit not immediately given the undoubted costs involved in initial set up – reducing costs. But it is important to keep in mind that, just as with manual activity, its *output* is only as good as its *input* and risks arising from this need to be addressed and managed. Information technology (IT) of whatever type is a tool, an enabler, and still requires appropriate knowledgeable human input. Nevertheless, the most recent *Cost of Compliance* survey indicates digital solutions are increasingly being used 'for compliance monitoring and anti-money laundering (AML) sanctions checking'. This will potentially free up resource for other types of Compliance activity for which technological solutions are not yet available, a point we will return to later on when we discuss the value added of the function.

Information technology (IT) of whatever type is a tool, an enabler, and still requires appropriate knowledgeable human input.

Monitoring and testing are an important element of the *Basel Principles* guidance, noted under *Principle 7*, and the recent MiFID legislation also makes clear that:

> firms should ensure that the compliance function establishes a monitoring programme that takes into consideration all areas of the investment firm's investment services, activities and any relevant ancillary services. The monitoring programme should establish priorities determined by the compliance risk assessment ensuring that compliance risk is comprehensively monitored.

From a practical perspective, practitioners in the *Future of Compliance* report recognise that 'Compliance monitoring is central to providing assurance to *senior management* that the business is adequately managing its regulatory risk exposure and that the controls and policies in place to manage these risks are effective'[59] and that 'A clearly defined programme of risk monitoring is vital and without this, the identification of risks, which is a core element of risk management, means little'.[60] The findings of *The compliance function in wholesale banks*[61] study also demonstrate the high level of consideration given to monitoring across the board.

In constructing Compliance systems and controls, again consideration must also be given to the activities of other relevant functions to avoid the emergence of gaps or unnecessary overlaps in coverage. It is also important for assurance functions to consider the impact on the operational areas of the business and avoid difficulties that could arise from a practical perspective. Consider the consequence of overload of focus at a particular time and the impact this may have on both the business being able to undertake its own day-to-day activities and the impact of possibly multiple remedial action plans received from different assurance functions at any one time. For example, the Compliance function undertaking a review of an area or particular product either at the same time, directly before or immediately after review by another assurance function would likely have a negative impact on business resources in terms of personnel and time, and should therefore, ideally, be avoided. Giving due consideration to the practical aspects of the procedures and systems to be implemented is important. There is also the danger of 'audit fatigue', where the attitudes of business areas may be negatively affected (and otherwise positive relationships damaged) by an ill-thought-out series of activities by assurance functions. We will expand on this point in the next chapter when we consider the importance of the Compliance function's approach.

Reporting

Reporting is another important element of the *Basel Principles* guidance and, as with monitoring, is noted under *Principle 7*. Consideration should be given to what information should be produced as an output of the various systems and controls put in place and the monitoring thereof. It is usually the responsibility of the firm to determine what and when information is required and to whom it should be conveyed; decisions as to the specifics of this should involve the input of all interested parties, so as to ensure that the information provided is appropriate for their needs. For example, consider the purpose and remit of some of the key assurance committees that exist within the organisation, such as audit or risk: they have an interest in the manner and means by which information generated from systems and controls are produced and disseminated, as their remits will require the use of the information arising. The Compliance function needs to participate in the development of these information systems to ensure they are able to provide guidance on relevant compliance issues, make recommendations on approaches and, most importantly, put the view of the Compliance function across. In doing so these views will be considered within the overall operational process and recognised as inherent to this, rather than being viewed as an afterthought.

It is also important to recognise that many of the reporting requirements will arise not solely from internally generated expectations, but from specific obligations set by regulators. For example, the MiFID legislation makes clear that:

> firms should ensure that the regular written compliance reports are sent to senior management. The reports should contain a description of the implementation and effectiveness of the overall control environment for investment services and activities and a summary of the risks that have been identified as well as remedies undertaken or to be undertaken. Reports must be prepared at appropriate intervals and at least annually. Where the compliance function makes significant findings, the compliance officer should, in addition, report these promptly to senior management. The supervisory function, if any, should also receive the reports.[62]

Regulatory firms subject to such legislation would therefore need to ensure that any report-producing systems took this into account.

As reporting requirements are considered, thought needs to be given to reporting around Key Risk Indicators (KRIs) and Performance Indicators (KPIs), which are essentially ways of objectively assessing activities and of measuring the output of the systems and controls. For example, information may be required on the type or level of business generated within a particular part of the firm, subdivided by product or division, or information could be required about problems arising, what they relate to and how quickly they are dealt with. Essentially, the reports around these KRIs and KPIs can be configured and scheduled in a variety of ways to reflect the information desired, expressing the needs and aims of the various interested parties.

KRIs and KPIs are also vital elements of control in that if they are set at an appropriate level, they can act as triggers to 'red flag' actual or potential issues requiring attention, thus allowing appropriate action to be taken. Such action could be remedial (for example, allowing problems to be addressed before they fully materialise) or reportable (for example, either as potential or actual breaches of procedure). What information is needed – and how KPIs can be incorporated to provide this – should be considered in the design of systems.

Within this, there should also be a clear link back to the aims and objectives of the Compliance function and the business overall. Merely meeting minimum legal and regulatory standards is unlikely to be sufficient to adequately fulfil the expectations of the regulator and other stakeholders; what should instead be the focus is to *move beyond merely complying* – essentially, keeping in mind the focus on outcomes previously referred to. With judgement considerations in supervision an ongoing feature of the regulatory landscape (and regulators looking at ongoing conduct both of individual firms and more widely within sectors and markets), there is a clear need for regulated firms to be able to evidence their own judgement and how this aligns with regulatory expectations. In terms of complying with requirements within the firm, the bar to be achieved should be set high enough in terms of the performance triggers to ensure information is available at an early stage, allowing action to be taken *proactively*, instead of only triggering after the event has taken place, thus requiring a *reactive* response. Doing so will help at both a practical level in terms of dealing with the situation at hand as issues arise but also in demonstrating to the board and to the regulator the robustness of the approach adopted overall.

> **The bar to be achieved should be set high enough in terms of the performance triggers to ensure information is available at an early stage.**

The information output of the systems and controls will provide the basis of the action subsequently taken; be this remedial, training, educational or simply reporting. For example, activities such as noting individual occurrences, dealing with these as appropriate and then recording these actions allows patterns to be tracked and addressed. This can then influence other activities, such as systems enhancement, policy review or training focus, over and above reporting to relevant committees. Reporting breaches to the regulator in accordance with requirements and internal reporting of such findings would also need to be factored in. All of this will be of benefit to the business overall, over and above being of benefit to the Compliance function itself. The provision of *effective* and *timely* information to all interested parties supports this, for example, that provided to the board and senior management helps ensure their focus is appropriate on an ongoing basis and that this focus can be adjusted where necessary. All aspects of the systems and supporting controls should provide an opportunity for checks to be made and for the Compliance function to recommend, take action and/or report on such action as necessary and in good time, so alerting the board and senior management as necessary – the board do not want surprises. In the view of *The Future of Compliance* report authors 'it is imperative that firms build a clear reporting structure into compliance monitoring plans in order that instances of non-compliance can be escalated to senior management once they are identified'.[63] The findings of *The compliance function in wholesale banks*,[64] previously highlighted in the Reporting Lines section, provide insight into developments in this regard.

Types of MI generated could include that such as: findings from compliance monitoring, risk assessment results, breaches of policy, notifiable events, key incidents, trends, information on fines, results of horizon scanning activity, feedback on training activity, staff issues, gaps in staffing, complaints, key compliance issues and so on. However, it is important to recognise that there are different audiences for MI and that content should be adjusted accordingly. Once again, a standardised approach will be very unlikely to work well: think of the different MI requirements for other assurance functions, business units or board committees for example. In the latter case, the version of the information provided will more usually be in summary format and cover a narrower range of topics (for example, significant or material compliance issues, risk assessment findings and confirmation of action, issues re monitoring, key matters noted during horizon scanning activities and so on). How the MI is presented is also important. Most firms (certainly larger firms) now adopt some form of 'dashboard'[65] system of presenting the output of monitoring and other activities, with findings and risks clearly presented, and including a form of 'traffic light' indication with risk categorised as Low, Medium or High/Green, Amber or Red, for example, allowing recipients to see clearly where particular concerns currently lie and the action being taken or recommended as a consequence.

Essentially, the more tailored the information is to the needs of the recipients, the more use it will be and the more likely it will be that it will utilised effectively. With that in mind, note that *The Future of Compliance* report points out that 'much criticism has been levelled at financial institutions following the financial crises to the effect that Compliance information was of insufficient detail and not escalated to *senior management* when appropriate'.[66] It is not only the amount of information that is generated, but it is also the quality and indeed what is then done with it that really counts: if the MI is poor or not reported properly or in a timely manner, it is next to useless. It is most important that the right information in the most usable format gets to the right people promptly.

It is important that the right information in the most usable format gets to the right people promptly.

Effective and timely information production and circulation is an important component in ensuring Compliance activities are effective and as such are not only beneficial to the business but are also clearly seen to be so. This is in itself an important element in ensuring the effectiveness of the overall framework. In terms of demonstrating an effective approach, firms

> which currently are best able to demonstrate this ... have clear mechanisms via which the head of Compliance reports to the Board. Where this reporting is a standing agenda item on the Board agenda this clarity in reporting to *senior management* will be further enhanced.[67]

This should be all the encouragement needed to focus on this aspect of the Compliance framework and, in so doing, improve the effectiveness of the Compliance function in achieving its overall aims.

Information Flow

Continuing many of the themes discussed in relation to reporting, information flow is another important component within the Compliance framework. The receipt and provision of information are the receipt and provision of *intelligence*, as discussed in Chapter 3. Those both within and without the company can benefit from it and utilise it to the greatest effect if it is appropriately risk focused. Relevant, focused and timely information is the lifeblood of business and the manner in which it is communicated greatly enhances its efficacy. In the previous section, we discussed MI in terms of Compliance reporting, which is essentially the *output* of the Compliance activities. But key to the effectiveness of these activities is the *input* of information that informs its efforts. This is dependent to a large degree upon the flow of information between the various parties involved, some examples of which are depicted in Figure 5.3.

Figure 5.3 **Information flow**

Note the manner of the information flow and observe its two-way nature, with information flowing both *to* and *from* the various parties. This is important if the activities undertaken and the reporting produced as a result are to be effective and able to support the Compliance function's overall objectives.

Information is necessary for all those working either directly within or in support of Compliance activities and is an important contributor to the Compliance environment, as should be apparent from all we have discussed in this regard. The effective flow of information plays a central role in supporting the Compliance function in its interactions with those with whom it has significant relationships. Two contrasting examples of the benefits to be gained from this, highlighting the need for *inward* and *outward* flow of information, are as follows:

- The Compliance function must remain aware of ongoing and planned regulatory developments to ensure its operations meet and continue to meet the regulator's requirements, so it is important that information about these topics flows *inwards* to the Compliance function.
- The board and senior management must be able to respond appropriately, taking all necessary decisions to ensure the organisation remains on track towards its objectives and address any issues that might challenge its success. Since they are reliant upon receipt of reliable and timely information, therefore, it is important that information flows *outwards* to them from the Compliance function.

This exchange of information is an essential component in the building of an effective risk assurance model for the business. An effective model needs to incorporate the actions and feedback from a range of sources (business units, key individuals, committees and so on), as well as information emanating from the various assurance functions, including the Compliance function. Information needs to flow well to ensure relevant data is received by the correct people within an appropriate time frame to allow them to act upon it effectively and, in doing so, make the right decisions for the business. As *The Future of Compliance* report comments, 'A board ability to oversee and manage regulatory compliance can only be as good as the information it receives'.[68] It is also important to note that the MI produced is open to challenge and may require additional clarification or be subject to debate. This is important, as it makes clear that the MI is being used and provides an opportunity for its production to be adjusted or refocused as required, ensuring it meets its aims. Furthermore, 'If MI is neither challenged nor acted on by the business then it is debatable whether the Compliance environment is subjected to sufficient *senior management* scrutiny'[69] – an important point to note in this age of evidencing action and demonstrating effective outcomes, and we will return to this subject again shortly.

The importance of information flowing proactively from business units into Compliance (for example about breaches or near misses, or escalation of issues) should not be underestimated. This helps Compliance be proactive themselves, enabling trend analysis to take place and allowing focused direction of resource on emerging or potential problem areas. This type of information flow relies heavily on good relations between business units and Compliance and a sound culture within the organisation, a point which we will return to in discussing the relevance of culture developments for our purposes in this text.

Promoting the Framework

Agreeing on the framework is one thing, communicating it to ensure everyone understands it is quite another; promoting awareness and understanding of the framework is an important next step. This usually takes multiple forms, but at its heart is the desire to ensure clarity of understanding regarding its purpose, together with setting out the relevance of this to respective stakeholders.

To be effective, the method of communication of any compliance message and the level/nature of the information provided should reflect a style and approach that is familiar within the particular workplace/organisation. For example, staff used to accessing information remotely as part of their day-to-day operational activity would be likely to find accessing such in relation to compliance requirements fairly straightforward, while those unfamiliar with doing so would require an alternative delivery channel or additional support to understand and access this. Essentially, what is needed here is consideration of the approach relative to context and adapting appropriately to reflect this.

A Compliance manual of some kind, detailing policies and procedures, produced and accessible via an appropriate format that reflects the approach within the business generally, is a useful means of communicating requirements. Such should also include details of compliance and Compliance objectives, responsibilities, personnel, reporting lines, systems and controls, procedures and activities. Distribution of this information as appropriate and relevant to the business should then ensure accessibility. For example, if the business utilises an internal web portal then those within it will be familiar with its use and therefore distribution of the Compliance manual via this format would likely be effective, while in an organisation more familiar with hard copy information distribution, this approach might be more effective. This type of action will provide the business with a clear overview of the Compliance operational framework.

Production and distribution of a Compliance manual that details the compliance requirements and approach does not, however, go far enough in promoting the Compliance framework and delivering an effective compliance message. There can be an unfortunate tendency amongst a busy workforce to leave such material unread until time of need. Consequently, the introduction of a framework needs to be followed by a robust embedding process, with notifications, guidance and training provided to support it. Focus within this should be on ensuring understanding not only of requirements but also of the applicability of those requirements in the context of the firm and the activities carried out within it. This is where effectively judged training and education activities within the business can really play their part in supporting an effective embedding process; we will return to focus on ensuring the efficacy of training and education in Chapter 6.

At this juncture it is worth re-emphasising the role of Compliance within the firm's risk assurance plans overall: while the first line of assurance controls is intended to result in compliance being genuinely embedded within the processes of the operations of the business, the Compliance function provides oversight on the effectiveness of these and is supported in this role by other risk management, control and assurance functions. Embedding of the Compliance framework within business operations is an important contributor to this, and in this, Compliance and risk management professionals have a key role to play in supporting the vision of the board.

ONGOING REVIEW

Once the framework has been agreed upon with all the various components in place and the function is operational, the various factors within it should remain under review on an ongoing basis. Regular adjustment of one or more components will be needed to ensure the framework remains current and appropriate while considering also any necessary adjustments to communications, relationship formation and management, supporting and strengthening as appropriate any of the factors that feed into the efficacy of the framework overall.

Developing the Compliance Framework

Development of the framework is vital if it is to remain up to date, fit for purpose and therefore effective in achieving its aims. While the output of the MI generated from Compliance activities should highlight 'hot spots' in relation to possible issues arising (potential breaches, complaints and so on, for example) and these should be responded to as necessary, there are also certain additional issues that the function should keep a regular and close eye on. Such will ensure the framework, and therefore the approach overall, remains appropriate given the functions remit and overall objectives, i.e. to help ensure the approach adopted is sufficiently up-to-date and current to effectively support the firm in the management of its compliance risk.

Although not an exhaustive list, topics such as those noted below should be regularly assessed with this in mind. As with most matters compliance-related, the specifics will differ from organisation to organisation and matters of particular relevance to each individual firm should be considered:

- *Regulatory change*: have there been or are there due to be developments in regulatory approach? Are new pieces of legislation being considered? What are the current issues on which the regulator is focusing? Are certain topics high on the regulator's agenda due to news stories or issues, for example? Perhaps issues are emerging in relation to a particular sector, product or service? Compliance should regularly look out for issues such as these and consider the potential for impact on the individually regulated firm in which they are located.
- *Changes within the regulated firm*: expansion, reduction, location, nature of products and services, alterations at board or senior management level, changes in strategy, joining or departure of key staff within the business: events of this type can have a significant impact on day-to-day operations within the firm, with risk considerations arising as a consequence and the approach of the Compliance function needs to adjust accordingly.
- *Availability of resource*: has this changed? Is it due to change? What will the impact be on the Compliance plan? Remember the Compliance plan is essentially a movable feast, subject to regular update and adaptation to ensure resource is appropriately risk focused.
- *Actual or perceived changes in how Compliance or compliance is viewed within the business*: Compliance should remain embedded within the day-to-day operations of the business – if not, why not? Has there been a change which has affected compliance operations or general operations within the firm? Regularly taking the temperature of attitudes towards compliance (and indeed Compliance) within the organisation will help ensure prompt adjustment of approach (if necessary) to ensure activities remain on track to achieve objectives.

Essentially, both in constructing the Compliance framework initially and subsequently adjusting it going forward, there must be consideration of all the issues that make up the Compliance environment and how these have in the past and currently impact upon it, plus a consideration of how this might change in the future. Such a base of understanding will continue to influence the structure of the function and the overall Compliance framework itself. Awareness of this, planning for imminent or future developments and adjusting the framework to better incorporate them is needed to ensure that the framework in place effectively manages the compliance risks the business faces.

Planning for imminent or future developments and adjusting the framework to better incorporate them is needed.

This is the responsibility of not only the Compliance function itself but of those with influence and responsibility around it, i.e. the board and senior management of the regulated firm. Documenting actions that evidence that reviews of this nature have been undertaken, enhancements or adjustments recommended, information challenged and so on, such as in the minutes of the committee or executive meetings for example, is an effective way of demonstrating activity in this respect. Regulators will be interested in such discussion and activity, for example as *The Future of Compliance* analysis notes that:

> if firms are unable to demonstrate ... examples of when Compliance MI presented has caused debate and challenge within executive level committees and the board, it is likely the (regulator) will view the MI as unfit for purpose or raise concerns over senior management oversight. Ensuring that MI is not only escalated but also actively debated is essential'.[70]

The actual frequency with which such a challenge takes place is also relevant, with the analysis also stating that it is

> a key determinant in assessing how well Compliance MI is used by senior management. We would expect board committees tasked with the oversight of regulatory compliance to meet at least four times per annum. This would be the minimum frequency required to demonstrate active and engaged senior management oversight of regulatory risks.[71]

Illustration of regulators' consistency in their expectations around the usage of MI can be found in a useful UK example, where a paper produced by the FSA in 2007[72] continues to be cited as remaining relevant by the FCA in aiding firms to 'develop their management information and includes hints and tips, along with examples of good and poor practice'. Within this, it is made clear that they wish to 'see evidence that the MI is used by the right people and in the right way', that it is 'seen ... challenged ... analysed and monitored ... acted on ... recorded', essentially to show that it has been actively engaged with.

Communication

Just as with promoting awareness and understanding of the Compliance framework and of the different elements within this, communication activities more broadly remain central to how effective the Compliance function will be. Whether oral or written, regular or periodic, the manner in which communication is undertaken by the function can strongly influence the way in which it is viewed (either internally within the business or externally amongst those with whom the function is fostering relationships). This in turn has an undoubted influence on the subsequent approach to, and view of, both compliance requirements and Compliance activities. Together with effective relationship management, which will be discussed in the next section, communication provides one of the best methods of embedding a positive attitude towards compliance and Compliance activities.

The various methods by which communication will be undertaken should be considered as part of the Compliance framework and regularly revisited to ensure they continue to achieve what is intended. An effective communication strategy should be structured to reflect the agreed communication aims, but should also be sufficiently adaptable to be able to adjust to the changing environment as, given the nature of the Compliance role, regular change is an intrinsic consideration within it. Too narrow or fixed an approach, considering only hard and fast factors as presented by the controls in place, could well result in some vital issues being overlooked. Continued vigilance and awareness through communication and interaction would make it more likely that *potential* issues would be flagged or noted before they become *actual* issues.

Initial communication of the Compliance message and the framework that supports this, through the production of the Compliance manual and the activities undertaken to embed understanding of it within the business, for example, should – as indicated above – not be a 'one-time' event. It must be ongoing if it is to be effective. Accordingly, dialogue between Compliance and the many stakeholders with whom it interacts should be regular, so as to maintain an effective level of awareness and understanding on one side and a clear appreciation of the impact of the Compliance requirements and any issues arising on the other. As with so many aspects of the Compliance approach therefore, communication should be two-way, with information flowing into the Compliance

Dialogue between Compliance and the many stakeholders with whom it interacts should be regular.

function just as it flows outward; there should be an open dialogue between key stakeholders, articulating what is required from all parties to ensure needs are met. There needs to be engagement between all those involved, both initially and on a regular basis thereafter.

Relationship Management

The Compliance function needs to foster a number of relationships and, be these internal or external, the effectiveness of the function will be strongly dependent upon this. Attention should be paid to such relationships right from the outset as issues can arise at any time and it would be problematic, to say the least, to have to introduce oneself for the first time only to have to swiftly follow this with an apology and the need to raise an issue! Time spent in advance of such an (hopefully rare) occurrence will undoubtedly be repaid should a problem occur. Ultimately, individuals are far more comfortable working to address problems with those they already have an established professional relationship with and with whom they will already (again, hopefully) have a reasonable level of trust in terms of both desire (and ability) to address a problem appropriately. Good relationships are invaluable – particularly when things go wrong. And, despite all good intent and endeavour, something invariably goes wrong at some point.

Whether internal or external, fostering of such relationships should be seen as a vital cog within the Compliance framework, oiling the wheels of activity and increasing the likelihood of effective, mutually acceptable outcomes to the challenges that will inevitably arise as a consequence of business activity. Let's consider these in a little more detail, beginning with the immediate internal relationships:

Internal

Compliance cannot work entirely separately from the rest of the business. Moreover, the Compliance function that does not have the support of other areas within the organisation will in all likelihood not be successful in their endeavours to help manage compliance risk. Establishing and continually developing effective working relationships within the business should therefore be an ongoing priority for those within the Compliance function. To ensure the activities undertaken by Compliance are relevant and appropriate, key members of the organisation should be involved in working with Compliance on their initial and ongoing development. The most important internal relationships to be nurtured include the following, summarised in Figure 5.4:

- *The executive board of directors*: this is possibly the most significant internal relationship the Compliance function has. The board strongly influences how Compliance is viewed and the tone the board sets in respect of this is invariably reflected throughout the business. How effective Compliance is will be shaped by how the board's view is perceived by those within the business: put simply, if the board is clearly seen to view Compliance as important, necessary and of benefit, this will be the view generally reflected throughout the organisation; conversely, if the board is known to view Compliance as a 'necessary evil', unimportant or a nuisance, this will likely be mirrored across the organisation. Though the formal approach of the board towards Compliance will have been evidenced, initially by their actions in terms of setting its structure, remit and so on, and all the other practical factors that provide the base of the Compliance framework, it is their ongoing attitude towards it that will truly demonstrate their *actual* approach to it. This is apparent in how they deal with issues flagged by the function, for example responding to issues raised, the respect shown to senior staff within the function, invitations to involvement in projects and so on. This attitude has very real practical consequences.

   The function can, however, positively contribute to how it is perceived by the board and, in doing so, shape and enhance its reputation within the business overall. They can do this by, for example, providing focused and timely information, contributing to relevant projects, keeping board members up to date on issues that might impact on their own activities and so forth – essentially ensuring that board members are made aware of everything they need to be made aware of from a compliance risk management perspective. All of this will contribute to a positive impression of the function and of those working within it. The individual who heads the function, the Compliance Officer, has a particularly important role to play in this respect, which will be discussed in detail in our next chapter.

The function can positively contribute to how it is perceived by the board and, in doing so, shape and enhance its reputation within the business overall.

- *Non-executive directors (NEDs)*: the importance of the role of NEDs has become increasingly recognised in recent years.[73] Ideally, they work as a 'critical friend' of the board of directors, critiquing the firm's performance and offering strategic input. Given their remit, NEDs will want to be assured that the activities and output of the Compliance function support their objectives and consequently those of the firm and they will better achieve this with a closer relationship with the function or key personnel within it. However, their role is actually much wider than this. For example, as a member of the board, they are responsible for an organisation's compliance and are liable when it is not. They hold roles of significant influence within firms (in the UK, for example, NED roles need to be considered in light of the SM&CR requirements). They are also often the Chairs of the various board sub-committees which are charged with over-seeing compliance and assurance activities in more detail.

- *Relevant committees*: due to the nature of the work carried out by the Compliance function and committees devoted to relevant areas such as Risk, Governance, Audit and Remuneration for example, it is likely that working relationships will be formed as a result; indeed, in many firms, Compliance will be an active member of these. Just as with the points noted earlier regarding the board, Compliance can positively contribute to how it is perceived by these committees through its interactions with them. For example, providing the right level of detail in reports presented, focusing their attention on the key issues, while providing an opportunity for further detail, all encourage a view of Compliance as pragmatic, aware of the role of those committees, their areas of focus and the many calls on their members' time.

- *Senior management*: senior management is accountable for effective management of compliance and therefore Compliance should foster relations with them to provide assurance of this. As well as the provision of the output of various monitoring activities, day-to-day interactions, formal and informal, between Compliance personnel and senior management present an opportunity to provide assurance of commitment in this area.

- *Operational business units*: Compliance personnel should be visible to operational business units (such as line managers of key delivery areas, including those involved in product and service developments, sales, HR, managers, training and so forth) as a recognised source of guidance and information, as well as being risk managers and monitors. This is more likely to be effective if successful relationships have been established. In the first instance, ensuring key personnel within the Compliance function are known and recognised, that they 'walk the floor' and are seen to be part of the business rather than being completely separate from it, is crucial in aiding understanding of the Compliance role and purpose. We hear often of the term 'tone from the top' in terms of the board's attitude towards compliance throughout the business and indeed we referred to this earlier in this text. As has been said previously, this is certainly important. However, on a day-to-day basis, in terms of swaying the opinion and influencing the attitude of staff within the business and their approach towards compliance requirements, the 'mood from the middle' (that is, the attitude of management and leaders – including informal leaders – within operational units) is just as important. It is these staff who will, day-to-day, over-see the practical implementation of business practices that either support, or detract from, the achievement of Compliance objectives. Concerted efforts by those within the Compliance function to foster the support of these staff, through clearly demonstrating the benefits to be gained by doing so, for example, will go a long way towards fostering an appropriate culture that successfully embeds a compliant approach across the business. This culture and the benefits of fostering it are explored in detail in Part III of this text.

- *Other business functions*: such as HR, marketing and others who are involved in supporting or developmental activities, including projects for example, so as to encourage engagement, awareness and understanding of respective roles and priorities and potential relevance from a Compliance perspective.

- *Other assurance functions*: those within the Compliance function should develop good working relationships with those in other oversight and assurance functions, such as internal audit, legal, risk and so on, not only from a routine practical perspective (to share information, cross-reference issues, prioritise and coordinate activities to reflect the organisation's risk management plan overall, ensure no gaps or overlaps in planned activities and so on), but also to help with the embedding of a positive attitude towards assurance activities and requirements within the organisation (such as the aforementioned scheduling timing of reviews to allow for business practicalities, for example).

- *Other Compliance functions*: if a Compliance function is part of a wider group of Compliance functions across the business, there should be close and ongoing relationship management between those who work within them.
- *Staff*: it is also important to consider the general staff within the business, supporting them and keeping them 'on side'. Offering an 'open door' policy, whereby business staff can bring issues to the attention of the Compliance function, and allowing open discussion on issues prior to them developing into problems, for example, will help in achieving this. Trust is an important component of this and nurturing of relationships helps foster this trust.

Strong relationships between Compliance and the rest of the business will encourage a greater understanding of what their role is and what it is seeking to achieve, and vice versa, allowing Compliance to better understand the workings and roles of others elsewhere in

Figure 5.4 Internal relationships

the business. Broadly speaking, effective working relationships provide the opportunity to encourage understanding of Compliance aims and objectives:

- Ensuring those working within the business appreciate why compliance is necessary so that compliance is considered an integral part of the bigger picture.
- Encouraging an improved appreciation of the wider business requirements.
- Helping both the Compliance function and the various units communicate developments or issues that need to be addressed.
- Providing the Compliance function with increased (and up-to-date) understanding of the business, as it will learn from the business experts and those at the frontline who are dealing with the organisation's products and services and the customers that consume them on a daily basis.

Looking at this from a wider perspective, numerous benefits can be achieved from taking time to nurture relationships both within and without the firm, and, indeed, taking such an approach undoubtedly helps with many of the Compliance challenges that will be explored later in this text.

External

The relationships the Compliance function has with external bodies will, like so many related matters, be dependent upon the particular organisation of which it is part. Some such relationships will involve frequent interaction, and others will be much less regular, but the benefits to be gained from these should not be underestimated. As with internal relationships, it is well worth spending time developing them, as they can be significant in helping the Compliance function, and indeed the business, achieve its objectives. Again, such relationships can also be beneficial should problems occur as it is much easier to discuss these or request help from someone external to the business with whom a relationship has already been established. Essentially, Compliance professionals should be pragmatic in their approach, establishing robust professional relationships with key bodies which, as well as bringing benefits to the Compliance professional, will enhance those bodies' perception of the firm and its Compliance function. In the event of problems, this will help them view any difficulties experienced more positively, as such bodies will have confidence in the firm's willingness and ability to rectify them via appropriate means. External relationships might usefully include the following, summarised in Figure 5.5:

- *Regulator(s)*: likely to be the most significant of the external relationships, the level of interaction with the regulator will be highly dependent upon the nature of the firm and its complexity. The head of the Compliance function is usually the main point of contact with the regulator, though others who take this role might include those such as the Chief Risk Officer or a member of the board or the Risk Committee. As such, this individual is responsible for relationship building with the regulator, influencing the regulator's view of the firm accordingly and, inevitably, influencing the firm's view of the regulator. It is recommended that firms have a clearly defined protocol for managing such liaison, with Compliance acting as the centre point, but involving all other areas of the firm that will have contact.

- *External assurance bodies*: such as lawyers and auditors. These can be really useful sources of external perspectives and provide insight into what other firms are doing as well as the firm itself. The Compliance Officer should always have a sound working relationship with key contacts in such firms.
- *Financial crime units and law enforcement agencies*: this would include effective working relationships with those with responsibility for dealing with Suspicious Activity Reports (SARs), for example (such as the National Crime Agency in the UK),[74] and other such bodies more generally, such as police and customs.
- *Professional bodies*: a number of these exist, such as compliance associations or industry bodies similar to trade associations and linked to products or services central to the business.[75] Membership of these can be beneficial both to the business and to the Compliance function in terms of keeping up-to-date with developments, providing a talking shop for the raising of concerns or issues relating to particular activities, or simply providing opportunities to interact with other professionals working in similar areas. From a Compliance professional perspective, development of a support network of fellow compliance professionals is perhaps the most important set of external relationships that they should build, as we will explore further in Part III.
- *Trade associations*: these are likely to be the producers of much information that will be relevant to the product and services of the firm (for example providing guidance on how issues arising from these should be managed). Alternatively, like professional bodies, such associations might provide a forum for the flagging and discussion of issues, attending events where intended or impending changes that will impact on the activities of the firm could be discussed and of course networking with individuals in similar organisations. All of these provide the Compliance function with opportunities to consider different approaches, views and opinions that might subsequently inform or challenge their own interpretation of requirements, allowing adjustment as necessary. Again, these will be discussed later in this text.

Development and maintenance of these and similar relationships help ensure the Compliance function remains abreast of developments arising from the areas of influence and the influencers that impact on the Compliance environment and, where appropriate, is able to contribute to these developments. Keeping up to date ensures the Compliance approach within the organisation remains current and appropriate, and does not stagnate or become unsupportive of business endeavours. It also helps ensure that any necessary action can be taken in good time to adjust to future developments, positively impacting upon the focus and approach within the Compliance role. Overall, the many benefits to be gained from developing such external relationships mirror the benefits of encouraging robust internal relationships: increased awareness, understanding and appreciation of each other's aims and objectives and the activities which are intended to support these, alongside the appreciation of how all of this contribute to the firm's overall business objectives.

Figure 5.5 **External relationships**

Supporting and Strengthening the Framework

As with all business activities where ongoing reflection on progress towards the achievement of aims pays dividends, regularly revisiting elements of the Compliance framework to ensure it continues to achieve its intended outcomes, adjusting the approach where required, will be beneficial to both the business more generally as well as the Compliance function specifically. For example, in considering how effective the output of the approach agreed upon has been in assisting with the strategic aims of the function, or reviewing related issues, such as the inter-relationships between those working within the framework. The entire process should be viewed as a continuous cycle, with the framework adapting to respond to findings that emerge from within it and also beyond it in terms of the general business strategy.

Its continuously evolving nature is – and indeed should be – one of its key strengths in achieving its intended aims.

ACTIVITIES AND APPROACH

The activities of the Compliance function take place within the Compliance framework. But of course, it is not only *what* the Compliance function does that contributes to achievement of its objectives, but also *how* it does this. Both the activities and the approach of the Compliance function are the subject of the next chapter.

NOTES

1 See *Compliance and the Compliance Function in Banks* 2005, as discussed in Part I.

2 The most recent of these can be accessed here: legal.thomsonreuters.com/content/dam/ewp-m/documents/legal/en/pdf/reports/cost-of-compliance-2022-competing-priorities.pdf. Produced since 2009 and proving useful annual insight into the activities and priorities of those working compliance roles, together with insightful commentary from the report authors, past reports can be located via a search at thomsonreuters.com.

3 KPMG (2012), *The Future of Compliance*. This analysis, drawing 'on research, insights and experiences of working with financial institutions to explore the current and potential impacts of their Compliance functions' provides insight into 'real-world' views on a host of Compliance practicalities relevant to this chapter.

4 Deloitte EMEA Centre for Regulatory Strategy titled *The changing role of compliance* 2015 deloitte-uk-financial-changing-role-compliance.pdf.

5 Thomson Reuters Cost of Compliance survey 2022 S Hammond and M Cowan.

6 Thomson Reuters Cost of Compliance Survey 2012 S English and S Hammond.

7 Thomson Reuters Cost of Compliance Survey 2015 S English and S Hammond.

8 Thomson Reuters Cost of Compliance Survey 2018 S English and S Hammond.

9 Thomson Reuters Cost of Compliance Survey 2021 S Hammond and M Cowan.

10 A view supported by *Basel Principle 1* which states: 'The bank's Board of directors is responsible for overseeing the management of the bank's Compliance risk. The Board should approve the bank's Compliance policy, including a formal document establishing a permanent and effective Compliance Function'.

11 *Basel Principle 2*: 'The bank's Senior management is responsible for the effective management of the bank's compliance risk'.

12 KPMG (2012, p. 17).

13 Deloitte EMEA Centre for Regulatory Strategy titled *The changing role of compliance* 2015 deloitte-uk-financial-changing-role-compliance.pdf.

14 Thomson Reuters Cost of Compliance Survey 2022.

15 BIS (2008).

16 guidelines_on_certain_aspects_of_mifid_ii_compliance_function_requirements.pdf (europa.eu).

17 ESMA Guidelines, point 57.

18 Ibid.

19 PRA, www.bankofengland.co.uk/-/media/boe/files/prudential-regulation/consultation-paper/2014/cp1414.

20 www.handbook.fca.org.uk/handbook/SYSC/6/1.html Note Senior Management Arrangements, Systems and Controls (SYSC).

21 *Basel Principles*, Introduction, point 7.

22 *Basel Principles*, Introduction, point 7.

23 *Basel Principles, Principle 7.*

24 BIS (2008, p. 3).

25 KPMG (2012, p. 19).

26 Ibid., p. 19.

27 Ibid.

28 Ibid.

29 FCA, *The compliance function in wholesale banks*, November 2017, www.fca.org.uk/publication/research/the-compliance-function-in-wholesale-banks.pdf.

30 *Basel Principles, Principle 7.*

31 Ibid., *Principle 7.*

32 BIS (2008, p. 3).

33 *Basel Principles, Principle 6.*

34 ESMA guidelines, www.esma.europa.eu/sites/default/files/library/guidelines_on_certain_aspects_of_mifid_ii_compliance_function_requirements.pdf point 14.

35 Ibid, point 47.

36 KPMG (2012, p. 22).

37 Ibid., p. 22.

38 FCA, *The compliance function in wholesale banks*, November 2017, www.fca.org.uk/publication/research/the-compliance-function-in-wholesale-banks.pdf.

39 Smith-Meyer (2013).

40 The *Journal of Business Compliance* was published for several years in the early 2010s. This article was published in volumes 02/2013 and 04/2013.

41 ESMA guidelines, www.esma.europa.eu/sites/default/files/library/guidelines_on_certain_aspects_of_mifid_ii_compliance_function_requirements.pdf, point 72.

42 Ibid., Point 78.

43 Thomson Reuters Cost of Compliance 2022.

44 Available at: www.fca.org.uk/firms/outsourcing-and-operational-resilience.

45 *Basel Principles*, p. 12.

46 *Basel Principles*, p. 11.

47 SYSC 6.1, www.handbook.fca.org.uk/handbook/SYSC/6/1.html.

48 Note www.fca.org.uk/firms/approved-persons.

49 Note www.fca.org.uk/firms/senior-managers-certification-regime.

50 KPMG (2012, p. 10).

51 Deloitte (2012b).

52 FCA, *The compliance function in wholesale banks*, November 2017, www.fca.org.uk/publication/research/the-compliance-function-in-wholesale-banks.pdf.

53 Ibid Point 6.

54 *Basel Principles*, Principle 5, for example.

55 FCA, *The compliance function in wholesale banks*, November 2017, www.fca.org.uk/publication/research/the-compliance-function-in-wholesale-banks.pdf.

56 Ibid.

57 Risk-based activities are discussed in further detail in the next chapter.

58 And is of increasing interest to regulators, note for example the recent output of the UK's FCA on this topic: www.fca.org.uk/firms/innovation/regtech.

59 Ibid., p. 20.

60 KPMG (2012, p. 20).

61 FCA, *The compliance function in wholesale banks*, November 2017, www.fca.org.uk/publication/research/the-compliance-function-in-wholesale-banks.pdf.

62 ESMA guidelines, www.esma.europa.eu/sites/default/files/library/guidelines_on_certain_aspects_of_mifid_ii_compliance_function_requirements.pdf, point 27.

63 KPMG (2012, p. 21).

64 FCA, *The compliance function in wholesale banks*, November 2017, www.fca.org.uk/publication/research/the-compliance-function-in-wholesale-banks.pdf.

65 There are many variations on this, with ample examples available via simple internet search (this one from Mckinsey.com for example www.mckinsey.com/capabilities/risk-and-resilience/our-insights/cyber-risk-measurement-and-the-holistic-cybersecurity-approach or alternatively note the UK's FCA Regulatory Initiatives Grid Dashboard www.fca.org.uk/publications/corporate-documents/regulatory-initiatives-grid/dashboard#overview). The key point to note however is that in this, as in so many other communication activities, the format adopted should be reflective of the presentational style appropriate for and familiar to the organisation.

66 KPMG (2012, p. 24).

67 KPMG (2012, p. 10).

68 KPMG (2012, p. 9).

69 Ibid., p. 25.

70 KPMG (2012, p. 25).

71 Ibid., p. 25.

72 *Treating customers fairly – guide to management information*, www.fca.org.uk/publication/archive/fca-tcf-mi-july2007.pdf.

73 There has been a good deal written on the role of NEDs over the past decade. See for example in the UK Parliamentary Commission on Banking Standards report *Changing Banking for Good* (UK Parliament 2013), the FCA's COCON Annex 1 Guidance on the role and responsibilities of non-executive directors of SMR firms (2016, updated 2018) www.handbook.fca.org.uk/handbook/COCON/1/Annex1.html. The more general output on this topic from the Institute of Directors also provides an interesting read www.iod.com/resources/factsheets/company-structure/what-is-the-role-of-the-non-executive-director.

74 Further information is available at: www.nationalcrimeagency.gov.uk.

75 Examples are included in Appendix 2.

6

Compliance Activities and Approach

A POINT TO KEEP IN MIND

It is important to emphasise once again that just as compliance is not an end in itself but rather a means to an end, so too is the Compliance framework. Its whole purpose is to provide a structure, tailored to the requirements of the regulated business, in which to conduct the activities of the function. Within this, it aims to shape and determine how those activities are carried out. In this chapter, we focus on a crucial element of the Compliance framework: the role of those who work within the function and the activities of which this work comprises, together with the skills and attributes required of Compliance personnel to be effective in their approach.

ACTIVITIES VERSUS APPROACH

The general view of the Compliance role tends to place great emphasis on the activities it undertakes in pursuit of its objectives and it is obviously important to have a clear understanding of what these involve. However, if they are to be effective, how these activities are performed is of equal importance. In this sense, it is not just *what* Compliance does that is relevant, but *how* they go about it. For example, as was discussed in the previous chapter, relationship management – both internal and external – is an essential practical consideration for the function, given the role it plays in ensuring the effectiveness of the Compliance framework in achieving its aims. In this chapter we will begin our reflections around this by examining the actual activities the Compliance function undertakes together with how these are planned and executed. We will then consider how the behaviours and skills of Compliance professionals (that is, their approach to those activities) can positively contribute to effective relationship management and so increase the effectiveness of all the activities undertaken in pursuit of the Compliance function's goals, and its support of risk management objectives more widely. Once again this chapter draws on information provided in a series of reports, reviews, studies and pieces of analysis based on the experiences and views expressed by practitioners, together with information garnered from formal and informal interviews with them, in order to benefit from their insights.

DOI: 10.4324/9781003431305-9

ACTIVITIES OVERVIEW

When thinking about the activities carried out by the Compliance function, consideration must be given to their scope, that is, what these activities are to cover within the context of the function's overall remit. The type of activity carried out by the Compliance function can be broadly categorised along the lines of those set out in *Principle 7* of the *Basel Principles*, which provides a useful high-level summary. The previously highlighted IOSCO[1] guidance provides a more detailed list, drilling further into the specifics of the activities. Detail from these is set out in Table 6.1 for ease of reference.

A further output from IOSCO sets out additional examples of activities and responsibilities, included here for illustrative purposes:

Extracted from Appendix C of IOSCO's *Compliance Function at Market Intermediaries –* March 2006[2]

TABLE 6.1
Compliance function activities

Basel principles	*IOSCO*
• Advice • Compliance programme • Identification and assessment of compliance risk • Monitoring, testing and reporting • Statutory responsibilities and liaison	• Business review • Compliance-related projects • Dealing with complaints and investigations • Developing the Compliance plan • Education and Training • Internal and external liaison • Monitoring • Provision of advice • Risk Assessment • Setting policy and communicating and providing advice on the same • Training

---

Examples of the Main Responsibilities and Tasks of the Compliance Function

The following is a list of tasks and responsibilities that may be within the compliance function, created by a combination of tasks indicated by regulators and of tasks indicated by commentators. Firms are not necessarily expected to include all of these in their compliance function.

- Identifying regulatory risks;
- Advice to management, including during the design of internal controls in respect of regulatory risks;
- Ensuring that a business supervisory structure is in place;
- Detection, prevention and management of conflicts of interest;
- Defining and monitoring information barriers;
- Monitoring of areas of potential market manipulation/insider trading monitoring;
- Industry surveillance;

- Anti-money laundering functions including advising on and developing of a firm's money laundering deterrence programme;
- Data privacy, net capital and financial responsibility compliance;
- Monitoring (or ensuring that an internal audit function undertakes such monitoring) of a firm's activities, using a risk-based approach, to confirm, or otherwise, adhere to the policies and procedures designed by the firm to address securities regulatory requirements. As a consequence of this monitoring, the compliance function should present a status report to management;
- Cooperation with the operational risk function and legal service to provide a specific model for the management of the intermediary's liability for specific crimes committed by employees on behalf of the intermediary;
- Provide systems, structures and behaviours that engender compliance without undue emphasis on the narrow legal requirements, but rather the broader issues included in codes of conduct, internal policies and procedures etc.;
- Dealing with customer complaints;
- Identification and monitoring of data or privacy security and protection;
- Prevention of undue disclosure of confidential information;
- Records and documentation, including safeguards for the privacy protection of client records and information;
- Licensing and registration of the firm and its registered personnel;
- Internal inquiries and investigations, a role that can be played by any or a combination of several control functions within a firm, and may involve the use of third parties;
- Monitoring and surveillance of business units to identify potential issues, including, *inter alia* the handling of customer accounts, including the opening of new client accounts, proprietary trading, and employee-related trading and communications;
- Oversight of risk function and business contingency planning;
- Participating in the rule commenting process, e.g. consultation process, in particular by collating business management comments;
- Participating in industry committees and working groups;
- Measures to identify and document qualifications of individual employees to provide regulated services;
- Compliance with the conduct of business rules by the firm and its staff;
- Supervision of advice provided to clients;
- Supervision of the various duties relating to information to clients and marketing information;
- Education and training to keep business personnel and other employees apprised of policies, procedures, regulatory requirements and how to comply with such requirements;
- Staff education programme that should also include the explanation of weaknesses or non-compliance noted during any audits or inspection;

- Promotion of ethical behaviour among staff and colleagues;
- Advice to senior management on disciplinary issues, including terminations;
- Escalating compliance issues to management (and if this is to no avail, to an audit/compliance committee or independent directors);
- Periodic reporting to regulatory authorities;
- Acting as the liaison for the regulators with the firm.

In 2021, an update to another piece of guidance – the ESMA guidelines on the MiFID legislation (originally published in 2012) – was issued,[3] building on the original guidelines which covered risk assessment, monitoring, reporting and advisory activities in terms of compliance function responsibilities specifically. It is evident that these are seen as the main activities in which the function is involved, although within the guidance there are references to numerous others in support of these. The *Cost of Compliance* surveys have provided useful insight into areas of activity and priority amongst these and we will explore some of these a little further in the Changing Priorities section later in this Chapter. However, the sheer variety of activities that may be undertaken by the Compliance function should now be apparent and this is the main point to keep in mind at this stage. From a practical perspective, these activities can be broadly grouped into four areas (Figure 6.1).

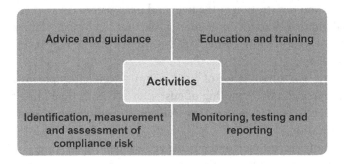

Figure 6.1 **Compliance activities**

Note how these comprise a mix of 'monitoring' and 'supporting' activities. Essentially, however, all activities reinforce the overriding purpose of the Compliance function: to assist the firm in the management of its compliance risk and, consequently, avoid realisation of regulatory risk. Remember, given its compliance risk management focus, decisions about the level of risk a business is willing to accept are helped by the Compliance function's involvement. Consequently, Compliance activities can also provide the relevant regulator or regulators for the firm with an assurance that such risks are recognised and are being actively managed. A reasonable 'comfort level' is what the board is looking for, as are the regulator(s).[4]

The importance attributed to certain activities can be judged from how frequently they appear in specific legislation and requirements. For example, responses to the BCBS survey on the implementation of the *Basel Principles* discussed in the previous chapter showed that the tasks: 'most frequently defined in laws, regulations or binding guidance are 'monitoring and testing compliance' as well as 'reporting on a regular basis to senior management'. Three other tasks, namely 'advising senior management on compliance laws, rules and standards', 'providing guidance and educating staff', and 'identifying, measuring and assessing compliance risk' are also frequently defined through enforceable means.[5]

As a consequence of this seeming focus on the clearly visible and definite aspects of the Compliance role, the relationship management aspect as discussed in the previous chapter can sometimes be viewed as a rather 'invisible' Compliance activity. Yet it is extremely important in a practical sense. We will return to this point shortly when we examine the Compliance approach specifically. Before doing so, it is helpful to explore each area of visible activity to appreciate its purpose and what it consists of.

Advice and Guidance

An ongoing part of the Compliance role is the provision of advice and guidance on a whole variety of compliance and regulatory matters. For example, the staff within the function generally:

- Advise the board and senior management, providing updates on impending change within the regulatory sphere that may impact on the firm and thus influence their business decisions.
- Provide advice to staff within the business on the interpretation and application of requirements and particular laws, rules, policies and so on.
- Assist business managers to understand what is required to formulate appropriate policies and then implement sufficiently robust procedures to support and maintain them.
- Act as the main point of contact with the regulator in all their dealings with the firm, assisting in the development and subsequent support of relationships between senior management and relevant board members and the regulator.

Under this heading might also fall provision of external advice, guidance and feedback about the firm's activities, approach and views. For example, this might include liaison with regulators and other relevant bodies in respect of queries or enquiries about business priorities, issues arising and so on, or responding to consultations by providing the view of the firm on proposed developments that will impact upon the Compliance environment.

The provision of advice and guidance will form a regular and ongoing aspect of the Compliance role and be provided on both a formal and informal basis, depending upon the nature of the issue at hand.

Education and Training

In support of the provision of advice and guidance, Compliance staff are increasingly involved in education and training activities relating to compliance matters. Whether developing and delivering training directly or working via dedicated training teams or with relevant members of the business units, the work of Compliance in this area does a great deal to support its overall objectives. The types of activity that might be undertaken include:

- Development of educational programmes aimed at helping those within different areas of the business understand compliance requirements, showing how these relate to the laws and rules from which they derive and how these apply to the regulated business (for example, input to or delivery of induction training for those who have newly joined the business, training activities in respect of new or revised products or services or remedial training where issues have been identified and rectification is required to prevent any recurrence, education activities for executive and/or non-executive board members in respect of an updated regulatory requirement to ensure clarity of understanding).
- Training for staff on compliance and regulation-related topics as these apply specifically to the business (such as complaints handling, conflicts of interest, fraud prevention and so on).
- Education relating to particular compliance requirements (arising from new or enhanced regulations, for example, or new areas of business activity).

While not necessarily an activity that may have immediately come to mind when considering the role of the Compliance function, training is nevertheless one of the most influential and thus important that it is involved in. Whether conducting training directly, contributing to it or simply influencing it, education is perhaps one of the most significant ways in which Compliance can inform the business about compliance requirements. In turn, it is also one of the key routes through which those within the business are able to appreciate what compliance-related requirements are and why they are necessary, and are hopefully then able to appreciate why their input in relation to these is needed.

As well as addressing specific issues, education and training activities help encourage the development of a culture within the organisation that is supportive of the Compliance role and of compliance-related activity generally. More widely still, this helps with the development of an appropriate ethical culture. This is an important point which we shall return to.

Education and training activities help encourage the development of a culture within the organisation that is supportive of the Compliance role and of compliance-related activity generally.

Education and training activities provide excellent opportunities for the Compliance function to communicate, so should always be imbued with a sense of the function's aims in addition to focusing on the needs of the recipients. If it is to be effective, a generically styled, formulaic approach to training should be avoided, although these have certainly been common in the past[6]. Training is the medium through which the Compliance 'message' can be delivered while increasing staff knowledge and enhancing relationships. The training provided should be underpinned by the Compliance function's knowledge and appreciation of the business (issues relating to products and services, business priorities and so on), demonstrating that Compliance is able to align its training focus to incorporate the business' needs alongside regulatory requirements. In doing so, the training will have more relevance and will therefore be of greater practical benefit. Linking training issues to topics with which recipients have actual experience is an effective means of helping to ensure understanding. As such, Compliance training that bears this in mind will likely be more effective for both its target audience and the Compliance function itself.

Identification, Measurement and Assessment of Compliance Risk

The function's primary purpose of assisting the firm in managing compliance risk is not one that can effectively be undertaken in isolation from its other activities, nor indeed the activities of other functions within the firm. The role of Compliance in managing compliance risk is closely related to the activities of other oversight, control and assurance functions and, therefore, the assessment and management of compliance risk should be considered in this context. In Part I, we discussed how decisions on approach need to be taken within the agreed risk framework of the firm and this is also a point relevant here. This is an approach that has been agreed by the board on the basis of relevant, appropriate and timely information from within the business and factoring in the activities of other relevant functions to avoid unnecessary overlaps or gaps in the process. The Ernst & Young paper *Maximizing Value from Your Lines of Defense: A Pragmatic Approach to Establishing and Optimizing Your LOD Model*[7] is a useful example of focus on this process in action, while the content and guidance available in respect of the IIA's updated 'Three Lines Model'[8] highlighted in Part I will also provide some useful insight into practical considerations.

While there is much to be taken into account in assessing any type of risk within an organisation (and then subsequently taking action to manage it), with compliance risk there are particular issues that need to be factored in, both in respect of the nature of this risk itself, but also in what is required to increase the likelihood of effective management. Obviously, the approach taken can reflect and be part of general risk management, but because of the specialised nature of compliance risk (and, in the context of our discussions in text, its link to regulatory risk), there is a particular significance for the firm if the impact of issues arising from it are not contained or addressed. Points to consider include ensuring that:

- Identification, measurement and assessment of the risk are fully informed, that is, that *all* relevant stakeholders are involved in development of the assessment and management process, for example not only direct Compliance stakeholders but also those elsewhere within the business. One way of supporting this is ensuring that, as discussed in the previous chapter, information flows *into* the Compliance function as well as *from* it (for example, ensuring that issues arising from the interactions between the front and back office are identified, allowing matters to be flagged and addressed promptly).
- The methodology for identification, measurement and assessment is fully documented and incorporates a cyclical review process that facilitates adjustments if the intended outcomes are not being achieved (for example having a compliance trail built into activities – both business and any assurance assessment – so that relevant

actions can be tracked) and that the success or otherwise of breach rectification activities can be noted, which in turn can inform future action.

- There is flexibility and continuous improvement in the approach being taken, that is, awareness of issues emerging from within the existing methodology or there being a method of incorporating additional issues into it if necessary. These might arise from within the firm or externally from it and where these impact upon the approach currently taken there should be a mechanism in place to allow adjustment of the process going forward. Flexibility is required to reflect issues identified and changing needs, arising from a myriad of different sources. As we have noted in respect of other areas, a static, unchanging approach will be unlikely to lead to effective outcomes.
- The output of the findings resulting from the process at each stage is timely, appropriate and presented clearly (for example, preparation of something along the lines of the aforementioned 'dashboard' to highlight areas of concern requiring attention). There should be clear signalling of risks for focus and action, prompt reports of findings to relevant parties, together with details of the recommended activity, liaison with key stakeholders and flagging of subsequent planned actions to improve the risk management process where needed.

Embedded within the process should be the clear acceptance of ownership of compliance issues across the organisation and that this is not solely the preserve of the Compliance function. As a consequence, responsibility for the management of risk should also be embedded across the organisation, with individual accountability for its management in relation to each individual activity.

Finally, the identification, measurement and assessment of compliance risk should not be a one-time event: risk management is an ongoing process and activities in relation to it (whether focusing on identification, measurement, assessment or reporting elements) should be organised with this in mind. Risk management is a continuous cycle and the management of compliance risk should reflect that. Compliance risk priorities – and consequently activities – should not deviate from business priorities in this respect; both should be aligned and reflected in the approach taken, be this in the activities themselves, their scheduling or whatever is done with their output.

Monitoring, Testing and Reporting

With the identification, measurement and management of compliance risk in mind, the construction of an appropriate monitoring programme will be one of the main undertakings of the Compliance function. In most jurisdictions, it is usually a mandatory regulatory requirement.[9] In addition, boards will of course expect monitoring of agreed procedures, systems and controls to be undertaken so as to give assurance that these requirements are being adhered to: a primary aim of any assurance function. Monitoring must therefore encompass the necessary elements of the Compliance policy and approach. Implementation and subsequent maintenance of these are key to providing the level of assurance desired internally by the board and externally by the regulator.

It is also worth highlighting the fact that the provision of feedback by the Compliance function about Compliance activities to the board not only provides them with the information per se, but also serves a wider purpose in emphasising its benefits, providing assurance to the board that the function is acting as required. Communication of this message effectively (through ensuring reporting is appropriate, targeted and meets their expectations by providing necessary and valuable information in a succinct and timely manner) is an effective means of subtly emphasising the function's worth and helps to further embed the desired Compliance message.

Monitoring provides the opportunity for the identification of actual or potential breaches of the systems and to assess the procedures put in place to support the compliance policy. If conducted correctly it should identify actual or potential risks to the achievement of Compliance objectives, allowing action to be taken to address these in a timely fashion, as discussed in the previous chapter, that reflects the needs of the business. There is therefore a need to set the bar within the monitoring approach appropriately. Within this, it is important to consider the risk appetite and tolerance of each element that feeds into it and of the firm overall, and then build that information into the approach, with appropriate flagging of issues at each stage. For example, consider breaches of requirements, intentional or inadvertent: do they need to be reported or not? If so, to whom and what action is to be taken? What form of redress is required? Has the issue occurred before? Is there a pattern emerging? What action will be taken to prevent any recurrence? Is training necessary? Or sanction? Given that actual regulatory breaches are unacceptable, what action is being taken to mitigate them? If they occur, what action is taken as a result? Points of this nature need to be factored into the monitoring methodology and checks made to ensure appropriate 'trigger' mechanisms are included within the systems, controls and procedures so that the information that informs monitoring is available at the right time and in the requisite format.

All activities are connected. Information arising from each activity should ideally inform the others. Flagging issues for rectification (for example compliance procedural risks) and information flow between each (Compliance to business, business to Compliance) plays a role in supporting this approach. Reporting output from the Compliance function is not restricted to that arising from monitoring, however. Reports produced might link into the guidance and education aspects of the Compliance role, such as when providing an overview of impending regulatory developments, reporting on relevant industry cases that might be of interest and so on. A mechanism should exist to glean information during the performance of each and every Compliance activity, which can then be reflected upon within the context of the Compliance function's aims, thereby providing the opportunity to propose improvements and further enhancement.

The level of overlap in all these Compliance activities with the activities of business functions should be apparent and this needs to be borne in mind when building these into the plan of action for the function, i.e. the Compliance plan.

Developing the Compliance Plan

The drawing up of the Compliance plan (that is, the setting out of the intention and activities of the function, collectively the means by which the Compliance function will achieve its objectives) makes a key contribution to how effective the function will be and how it is perceived. The plan includes not only *what* specific activities the function will be responsible for, but *how* and *when* it will focus on these in pursuit of its objectives (over the course of a year or part of year, for example) and how the activities will meet the strategic and policy requirements of the function. In developing the plan, there needs to be a balance between:

- *over-compliance* (that is, the imposition of too great a set of requirements, such as might needlessly inhibit business transactions), and
- *under-compliance* (that is, not doing enough to meet the compliance objectives of the firm and the regulator, so as to avoid wasting resources or creating the potential for gaps).

How the intended activities relate to intended benefits (such as the objectives of the firm in particular areas, for example, or to reflect current areas of focus for the regulator) is a useful means of justifying the compliance requirements that are in place and thus gaining support from the many stakeholders involved. Given the level of Compliance impact on such a wide range of business factors (reputation, strategy, operations, finance and so on), securing buy-in from stakeholders contributes to the effectiveness and therefore the more clearly the function is able to articulate its balanced and appropriate approach, the better. The Compliance plan then becomes in itself a useful mechanism for communicating this.

In planning activities, there needs to be consideration of the structure of the Compliance function. Consider the differences between large organisations (where multiple Compliance functions might exist, for example, possibly within different jurisdictions and where the specific day-to-day activities within each will inevitably differ from each other) versus the activities carried out in a smaller firm (which might possibly have a wider remit or fewer staff). A useful example of this relates to money laundering or fraud prevention – larger firms often have designated departments or teams within departments focusing solely on these topics, while in smaller firms, these might be located directly within the Compliance function itself.[10] Similarly, depending on the overall structure of the Compliance function across multiple jurisdictions, a team within a particular jurisdiction might not deal with a particular activity and simply pass anything related to that activity over to another team elsewhere.

Howsoever the Compliance plan is formed, what is important is that, operationally:

- it is conducted in a manner which most suits the individual firm
- is developed to reflect the business requirements and in consideration of the various business systems that are in place.

The risk assessment and action process around this needs to be practical if it is to be of benefit: there is little to be gained by developing a methodology which looks perfect on paper, but when translated to the real world does not work. To be effective, the approach taken needs to reflect its environment and, therefore, in its development it is important that all relevant stakeholders are involved. Who these might be will be as is appropriate for each firm, though examples of these might include not only, as would be expected, the board and relevant business units, but also those from related functions such as project management, new business/product development[11] and so on. Essentially, what is important here is that thought is given to what the business does, the risks arising from that and how the range

> **There is little to be gained by developing a methodology which looks perfect on paper, but when translated to the real world does not work.**

of Compliance activities can be utilised in mitigation. Such issues are best informed by those who are involved in dealing with them on a day-to-day basis, wherever in the business such responsibility lies.

In terms of developing this plan of activities, consideration also needs to be given to how aspects of it are prioritised. As with other areas of business, the resources of the Compliance function are not limitless and therefore need to be applied judiciously, being focused as appropriate using an appropriate risk-based methodology. As *The Future of Compliance* report makes clear in commenting on the need for balance between elements such as monitoring and advice:

> Ensuring the correct split of resources between these two teams will permit more rigorous testing and additional reviews to be undertaken to provide assurance to stakeholders (backward looking – 'reactive') and to ensure potential issues are dealt with proactively (forward looking – 'pro-active').[12]

Allocation of resource needs to reflect priorities and activities linked to the achievement of overall objectives and will therefore likely be subject to regular adjustment to ensure it remains appropriate.

Prioritisation within a Risk-Based Methodology

Some ten years ago a *Cost of Compliance* survey[13] suggested that approximately half of the typical Compliance Officer's week was spent dealing with the type of on-demand activities discussed in the previous chapter, that is, those that were not able to be specifically scheduled into the compliance plan, such as:

- The provision of ad hoc advice.
- Responding to general queries and the provision of advice or training arising therefrom.
- Carrying out training following the identification of problems.
- Investigations.

Subsequent surveys and liaison with compliance practitioners support this finding; clearly, a good deal of the Compliance role comprises activity in response to unfolding and emerging requirements, rather than those that have been planned and scheduled. Consider the practical consequences for the Compliance function of requirements such as these needing to be dealt with on a daily basis. To mitigate these, the Compliance plan must allow for these on-demand activities, providing sufficient flexibility and sufficient resource.

Within any organisation the level of accepted risk will be weighed against the potential for reward, as explored in detail in Chapter 3. In the scales when considering regulatory risk are the possibilities of regulatory censure and all the related risks that flow from it (reputational, financial and so on). Any risk has to be managed and consideration of how it will be managed will have formed part of the overall decision of the business regarding what level of risk to allow. This then informs the systems and controls that are in place in support of this decision, which in turn should be built into the Compliance function's policy. As noted when we discussed monitoring activities earlier in this chapter, the agreed 'red flags' (that is, signals that a breach of procedure has occurred or is imminent or potential), triggered at predetermined points, can then allow risks identified to be considered in the context of what is expected from the Compliance function.

In drawing up the Compliance plan, a robust *probability and impact assessment* needs to be carried out on the various factors that lie under the Compliance function's span of responsibility; as highlighted in the previous chapter, these need to consider cyclical and on-demand activities. Which should be prioritised: cyclical activities scheduled as per the Compliance plan or immediate on-demand activities?

The key to being effective in this decision-making is to consider *all* activities, irrespective of whether planned or not, from a risk perspective. Staff within the Compliance function need to manage often conflicting demands effectively. Taking a risk-based approach will help with this enormously: a risk rating will help clarify the importance of the activity and allow it to be appropriately prioritised. For example, would a request for clarification on whether or not to continue with a closure request on an account that has been flagged as 'potentially of concern' from a financial crime perspective take precedence over the need to prepare for a board meeting? Would attendance at a meeting on the development of a new product take precedence over providing guidance on dealing with a customer complaint?

Of course, given the overall Compliance role, it's not only what is done here that is important, but also *how* it's done. For example, in each of the above scenarios the possibility of delegation of the activity to another might be considered, but that will of course be dependent upon the specific nature of the concern that has been flagged on the account and the specific nature of the customer complaint. The manner in which the individual approaches this weighing up of information will be strongly influenced by their understanding of the issues, their experience and their overall skill set, an important set of factors that we will return to shortly. However, taking a measured and considered approach in this way will ensure the function is able to deal with on-demand activities in an appropriate manner that not only supports the overall aims of the function but is also seen as doing so while ensuring that the planned activities intended to ensure achievement of the function's overall aims are not compromised.

CHANGING PRIORITIES

When priorities change within the Compliance environment, so too does the amount of resources that the Compliance function devotes to its various activities. Surveys over recent years[14] have highlighted shifts in the amount of time spent on different activities by Compliance personnel, due largely to changes in focus and prioritisation of different issues. Findings of the *Cost of Compliance* surveys of recent years demonstrate that trends and priorities vary over time and that the specific focus of activities also varies:

- For example, in summarising the typical week of a Compliance Officer as discussed in the previous section, the survey previously referred to[15] separated the activities into five sections: tracking and analysing regulatory developments, board reporting, amending policies and procedures, liaison with control functions and other compliance tasks. Note that this 'Other Compliance Tasks' included monitoring activities, training and the provision of guidance and advice. By far the greater amount of time (56% of a typical week) was spent on this latter category. The most recent of these surveys[16] provided insight into practitioner's views on areas in which compliance would be involved over the coming year. Notable amongst these were a number spanning the compliance activity range previously referred to, albeit with a more current focus in relation to certain topics, not least in respect of 'assessing cyber resilience, implementation of a demonstrably compliant culture and post-pandemic review/planning', an interesting insight into more recent and ongoing priorities for the function.

- Other findings that stood out in the earlier survey included that 'On average, just over one day per week was spent tracking and analysing regulatory developments and amending policies and procedures to reflect this'. This was a similar figure to that for the previous year, though one might expect it to be higher given that the implementation of regulatory change and tracking regulatory change were in the number one and two spots of the greatest compliance challenges anticipated for the coming year at that point. This was a shift from the previous year where although the amount of regulatory change was highlighted as one of the main challenges, the second was noted specifically as 'the perennial issue of resources'. In the words of the report authors, 'it appears that compliance officers are unable to squeeze any more time out of an already packed week to consider these developments'. The authors of the survey reflected on this finding and made a recommendation that resonates with the methodology, approach and focus of the Compliance function as addressed within this and the previous chapter, stating that it would be useful for Compliance personnel to consider changing their approach to this activity:

> Compliance staff may wish to assess whether they are the right people to be updating policies and procedures. The role of compliance is to advise and assist the business, and the business itself should own its policies and procedures. It may be that it is quicker and more straightforward for compliance to do the work, rather than advising the business and then checking that the business has implemented the advice correctly in a redrafted policy, but in the current environment, where compliance resource is stretched, it could be worth compliance asking the business to do more.

This latter point is particularly relevant, but not only to this particular activity: time is not the only consideration here, but also developing a culture within the organisation that clearly sees the business as the "owner" of these requirements, rather than the Compliance function.

Clearly, there has been progress in the specifics of Compliance activity as it has developed over the interim period, with the most recent survey indicating Compliance involvement in an array of higher-level activities such as the aforementioned 'assessing cyber resilience, implementation of a demonstrably compliant culture and post-pandemic review/planning' together with

> addressing effectiveness of corporate governance arrangements, setting of compliance budget and other risk management resources, setting of risk appetite,

liaison with and up-skilling of senior managers and the board, assessing fin tech/reg tech solutions, assessing climate change risk, assessing geo-political risk.

The survey provides a useful highlighting of differentiation between activity in large firms (G-SIBS[17]) and others, with topics such as the implementation of a demonstrably compliant culture, assessing fin tech/reg tech solutions and assessing climate change risk a higher priority for these.

- In the earlier survey 'Just over one other day was spent communicating with those outside the compliance function (6 per cent spent reporting to the board, and 16 per cent of time spent liaising with control functions)'. This raised interesting questions regarding the interactions of Compliance with other parts of the firm: is the Compliance function in some organisations being rather insular in their approach? Or perhaps so overburdened with tasks that anything that is not of immediate concern is not prioritised? This is an important point given the significance of how the way in which the function approaches its role can have such a significant impact on how effective it is in achieving its goals, as asserted throughout this chapter. Regional differences were noted, however, that suggest there may be other explanations:

  The survey results in this area highlighted stark regional differences in internal communications between compliance and the other control functions. In the UK, 21 per cent of respondents spent more than 10 hours per week consulting with the risk function; this was a marked increase from last year's figure of 14 per cent. In the U.S. and Asia, however, firms spent less time talking to risk than last year. Just over 5 per cent of US respondents said that they gave risk over 10 hours of their time on a weekly basis (a decline of 5 per cent from last year's figure of 10 per cent). In Asia, this year's survey showed that 42 per cent of firms spent less than an hour a week speaking to risk (up from 32 per cent last year), and in 2012 over 10 per cent spent more than 10 hours a week speaking to risk, compared with a mere 2 per cent this year.

- This information is quoted in detail here as the contrasts raise some interesting points that bear reflection upon in the context of the focus within this chapter. Essentially, why might the situation as described in this excerpt have been? It is at least to some degree likely to have been influenced by the culture that exists within different organisations in different jurisdictions. In the intervening years since that time there has been an increased focus on supporting the development of an appropriate compliance culture within regulated organisations, with an increasing focus on conduct more generally; all of these developments the compliance function have, or should have, been closely involved in. The most recent of these surveys, interestingly, highlights communication skills as amongst the top three requirements for an ideal Compliance Officer, while 'implementation of a demonstrably compliant culture' is an anticipated ongoing area of Compliance involvement, suggesting these two requirements remain a continued area of focus for the function as well as the regulated firms and industry more widely.

- At the time of the earlier survey, regional differences were also noted in the amount of time spent on preparing reports for the board. Although globally 38% were spending between one and three hours on this and 36% more than four hours, in the US '42 per cent of firms reported spending less than one hour creating and amending reports for the board', significantly higher than any other region although a slight drop on the figure for the previous year (50%). The survey report made an observation on this point, one which would appear to reflect prevailing trends in the regulatory sphere as discussed in the previous chapter:

> Compliance teams who find themselves doing very little work on preparing reports for their board should be asking questions. Boards need to be proactive in gathering effective management information that provides them with adequate oversight and control of the firm's activities, but where this is lacking compliance can take the initiative and submit reports nevertheless. Those compliance teams which reported spending less than an hour per week on this important task may need to reconsider their approach to, and their relationship with, the board. It is critical that boards are aware of the risks faced by the firms they govern and understand that detailed board reporting forms an essential component of effective corporate governance.

Certainly, a point to ponder on, while emphasising the word 'may' in this finding and bearing in mind that if board reports are considered particularly significant within a firm, their production may well have benefited from substantial IT or other support, allowing them to be produced in an efficient way. For example, the board may reasonably have wished the Compliance function to be focused on actually doing the work rather than be bogged down with preparing reports about it and might therefore have quite reasonably invested in systems to support the production of MI wherever possible that can be fed seamlessly into the reports required.

Similarly, what is the nature of the reporting being prepared? If it is simply a 'dashboard' indication that all is well with nothing more required then that is straightforward; however, if problems are highlighted does that in turn generate a demand for more detailed reporting? It could potentially be misleading to view the amount of time spent preparing board reports as a positive of report effectiveness and/or the how seriously the board takes Compliance. Instead, time and effort in this regard needs to be viewed in context; might it perhaps be more telling to reflect on the amount of time spent discussing, auctioning or challenging the content of the reports presented, such as discussed in the previous chapter in respect of action around MI?

Consideration of the amount of time spent liaising with regulators provoked another pertinent finding, particularly relevant to our discussions in this text. The survey reported that some 65% of firms believed there would be either a slight or significant increase in the coming year. Reasons why were varied, but generally reflected the demands placed upon them by the continuously shifting regulatory environment. Interestingly, it was believed that the increasing contact would 'be driven by the regulators themselves, as they become more intrusive and attempted to control the activities of firms, particularly larger ones, more closely', a view shared by 'the vast majority' of firms that responded. On a related note, a further thought-provoking finding related to the impact on firms dealing with multiple regulators and:

> Significant numbers of respondents also said that regulatory liaison would increase due to the need to liaise with multiple global regulators. But firms should not assume that regulators themselves will effectively co-ordinate their efforts. It is essential that firms which operate across multiple jurisdictions ensure that their internal communications keep track of what is being said to regulators in different areas, and also what those regulators are requesting. Firms may find themselves under a duty to share information with different regulators, or to tell one regulator what another regulator is looking at. The consequences of not liaising effectively can be severe ....

Clearly this was anticipated as a potential area of challenge for firms and consequently for the Compliance function which could have become ever more significant over time. With 'liaison with and up-skilling of senior managers' a continued priority for the respondents to the most recent survey, alongside a significant amount of time spent 'liaising and communicating with regulators and exchanges' it appears gathering of information and presenting this in an appropriate manner to ensure effective reporting constitutes a notable ongoing feature of compliance activity.

All this said, it should be clear that regular re-evaluation of priorities, and the necessary response required in terms of the different activity areas to be focused on as a result, is an essential requisite of the Compliance plan. Issues arising both internally and externally will have an impact in some form or another and will need to be factored in (for example, Compliance and business-orientated training requirements should continue to be reviewed to ensure they remain relevant and up to date). Armed with this type of input on a regular basis, the Compliance plan can be adapted as necessary to ensure an appropriate focus is maintained.

THE COMPLIANCE FUNCTIONS APPROACH

As we have seen, the Compliance function's remit is multifaceted. The sheer variety of potential activities requires a lot from the function and therefore of the individuals working within it. Earlier it was stated that *how* Compliance activities are carried out, that is, the Compliance *approach*, is as important as the range of the activities themselves. It was also observed that the less visible activities undertaken by the Compliance function are often some of the most important. This relates to both the actual performance of activities and the approach taken in doing so:

- *Performance of activities*: activities should be carried out in a manner which is familiar to the firm so as to be recognisable to the various stakeholders involved. This is likely to encourage a more receptive environment within which Compliance-focused efforts can be undertaken. Adopting similar approaches and methods[18] (such as in terms of language, style, communication or training practices, for example) would make it more likely that the Compliance matters that were the focus of such activities were seen as familiar and recognisably 'part' of the business, rather than being seen as in any way 'other' or 'alien'. Such a positioning improves the likelihood of acceptance by those within the business, increasing the chance of success for the function. There is little to be gained by the Compliance function adopting a set of aims and practices that are demonstrably contrary to those of the business or indeed in generally adopting an approach to these that is at odds with the approach of the firm (recognising that an important part of the Compliance function's role is to support developments in this regard, for example, the embedding of a more effective view of compliance, and with consideration around matters of ethics and integrity); the better the 'fit' of the Compliance approach (the previous point not withstanding) with the firm overall, the more effective it will be. This will increase the likelihood of it becoming embedded, i.e. seen as part of the way things are done day-to-day.

- *Approach to how activities are conducted*: the attitude of Compliance staff towards the performance of Compliance activities and the approach taken to them plays a significant role in their effectiveness. This is apparent none more so than in the attitude and approach of the head of the function, the designated Compliance Officer. We will focus specifically on this role shortly. Ahead of doing so, recognising that an appropriate attitude towards the performance of Compliance activities and that this should be reflected in the manner in which these are performed by *all* staff within the function is important. Such recognition denotes a competency in the role that is a step beyond merely achieving specific measurable aims, which is an important point to note. How Compliance is viewed both within the business and more generally is an ongoing consideration for the function; competent staff will acknowledge this and position their approach accordingly. This lends itself to consideration not only of *knowledge* but also of *behaviours*, both of which will be addressed in the following sections in so far as they affect the performance of the Compliance role.

In terms of both performance and approach, of course, those who work within Compliance play an essential role in ensuring the function is effective and, ultimately, achieves its aims. The Compliance function needs to have the respect of the board, of the business and of stakeholders more widely, maintaining effective relationships with each. Note that the focus here is not on being liked and developing an approach and relationships with this in mind, but on being respected. As we know, this is strongly influenced by the attitude of the board who essentially need to be able to view the Compliance function – and the Compliance Officer in particular – in the same way as the regulator needs to be able to view the board of a regulated business: that is, as being competent in their role, aware of requirements and keen to work effectively to ensure these are met. If the board has confidence in the Compliance function, this in turn will foster growth in the positive perception of the benefits Compliance brings to the business as a whole.

Compliance Skills, Abilities and Behaviours

The regulatory environment in which the business – and by definition the Compliance function – is located will, broadly speaking, play an important part in influencing the different attributes and behaviours necessary to achieve success within the Compliance role.

For example, rules-based and principles-based regulatory approaches generally require different skill sets, although of course there are areas of overlap:

- Under a rules-based regulatory system, a good memory of all the specific rules and requirements would be one of the primary skills required.
- Under a principles-based system, a greater emphasis on interpretative skills would be required in order to arrive at a particular position.

Effectively, one regime leans more towards *knowledge and understanding*, while the other leans more towards *behaviours and abilities*. Therefore, while both require many of the attributes to be discussed shortly, the way in which these are utilised and implemented to support the effectiveness of the Compliance function would need to be different. In setting up and populating the function, as part of constructing the Compliance framework, this type of issue too needs to be borne in mind, particularly when recruiting the head of the Compliance function.

Requirements in respect of what regulators expect of Compliance personnel, specifically the Compliance Officer who leads the team, are relatively straightforward in many ways in that they generally reflect what is required of any competent professional. They are expected to act with integrity and they are expected to have the necessary skills and abilities to perform their role effectively. In addition, most regulators also require that individuals who have overall responsibility for the Compliance function need to be individually authorised. Accordingly, they would also need to meet the specific requirements of the regulator for authorisation. However, these have tended to be fairly generic in nature and specific guidance on how these requirements are to be met has been fairly limited as a result. In the past, there has been a tendency at both an international and national level to leave it to individual firms to interpret the requirements, apply them to their own circumstances and then make a decision as to whether the Compliance professional is suitable. Examples include:

- *Basel Principles* highlight the qualities required in compliance personnel under *Principle 6*: Resources, stating:

  > compliance function staff should have the necessary qualifications, experience and professional and personal qualities to enable them to carry out their specific duties. Compliance function staff should have a sound understanding of compliance laws, rules and standards and their practical impact on the bank's operations. The professional skills of compliance function staff, especially with respect to keeping up to date with developments in compliance laws, rules and standards, should be maintained through regular and systematic education and training.

- *The Compliance Function at Market Intermediaries*[19] paper, under Topic 4: Qualification of Compliance Personnel, stating: 'Principle: Staff exercising compliance responsibilities should have integrity, an understanding of relevant rules, the necessary qualifications, industry experience and professional and personal qualities to enable them to carry out their duties effectively'. In support of this it notes:

  > Staff exercising compliance responsibilities should have the skills, knowledge and expertise necessary for the discharge of their responsibilities or tasks. In

addition to formal qualifications, the main requirement should be the ability of compliance staff to perform their role, which may be gained by reason of experience rather than through only study. In addition to technical knowledge of relevant rules, compliance staff should understand the nature of the business within which they operate. Certain personal qualities and soft skills are also important, examples of these include analytical skills, communication skills and problem solving skills. The requisite competency for compliance staff will depend on the range of regulation and business activities that are their responsibility.

In the years since the global financial crisis, there was an increase in focus on expectations of individuals in key functions and this has extended to the Compliance Officer. In the UK, for example, there was a revision of the regime in place following the identification of significant conduct failings[20] and recommendations for a new accountability framework focused on senior management.[21] This is broadly intended to ensure firms are appropriately governed and that only persons with the appropriate skills, capabilities and behaviours should be in place in certain positions. The UK regulators consider the appropriateness of an individual's appointment to a board within the context of the board's overall composition. They take a risk-based approach to approving individuals who perform controlled functions, adjusting their approach accordingly. In higher-impact firms or where roles are particularly significant, for example, they interview these individuals. The types of issues considered in assessing how appropriate the individual is for appointment reflect those that demonstrate the individual's ability to ensure the business is organised, controlled and monitored effectively. The assessment is also judged in the context of the individual's awareness and understanding of a range of matters including 'the market in which the firm operates; Business strategy and model of the firm; Risk management and control; Governance, oversight and controls and Regulatory framework and (the regulator's) requirements and expectations'.[22] If the regulator is not satisfied that a candidate is fit and proper, a recommendation can be made to refuse the application. Though on paper this approach appeared robust, as ever it is down to implementation and certainly the prevailing view prior to the more recent changes was that implementation was perhaps not as strong as it should have been. There had been criticism of it over a number of years, even during the period where concerns in this regard were high on the regulatory agenda – an example of which was a particular case in 2013[23] where it emerged that an individual, patently unsuitable for such a role, had nevertheless been authorised to perform it. This fuelled the ever-present concerns around this issue. The entire regime has consequently been the subject of an overhaul within the past decade, and subject to periodic updates/expansions in remit/focus when deemed necessary in support of its overarching aims.

The Senior Managers and Certification Regime (SM&CR),[24] which replaced the initial Approved Persons Regime, is the current accountability framework for senior management, applying to the banking sector in the UK since March 2016 and expanded since. There are three parts to it: Senior Managers Regime, Certification regime, conduct rules. In the context of our discussions within this text, it is the first of these which particularly interests us. Note the following, drawing on FCA content[25]:

Senior Management Regime – Most senior people who perform key roles (senior management functions) need PRA or FCA approval before commencing. Every senior manager must have a 'statement of responsibilities' which should clearly set out what they are responsible and accountable for. Some specific responsibilities are known as 'prescribed responsibilities', plus business functions and activities for which senior managers are responsible, known as 'overall responsibilities'. Certain firms have to provide 'responsibilities maps' which outline the responsibilities of senior management plus their management/governance arrangements. There is a requirement that once a year firms need to certify senior managers are suitable for their roles.

In 2020 the PRA published an *Evaluation of the Senior Managers and Certification Regime (SM&CR)*[26] which concluded that 'introduction of the SM&CR has helped ensure that senior individuals in PRA-regulated firms take greater responsibility for their actions, and has made it easier for both firms and the PRA to hold individuals to account'. Findings underpin achievement in respect of improving clarity around individual accountability, while also identifying areas for further action and recommendations arising from this.

Overall, there has been an increased focus on those who have a significant influence on the conduct of a firm's affairs. Those that fall into this category are subject to specific scrutiny. The Compliance Oversight role is one such function.[27] A required Senior Management Function, the Compliance Oversight function (SMF16) is 'the function of acting in the capacity of a person who is allocated the function'.[28] Persons acting in such capacity are required to meet the 'fit and proper' benchmark to evidence suitability, with matters such as honesty, competence and capability, as well as financial soundness, being considered. Applicants also need to supply regulatory references from other firms, i.e. past employers, if applicable. Information setting out requirements and guidance on how to comply with these is extensive on the regulator's website, and is regularly updated. For example, in 2022 the FCA issued additional guidance related to heads of compliance and MLRO applicant competency and capability.[29] Emphasising that 'authorised and registered firms should have heads of compliance and money laundering reporting officers (MLROs) who are suitably competent and capable of effectively performing the roles'. the guidance made clear that 'firms should carefully consider how individuals can demonstrate this ahead of seeking regulatory approval', setting out expectations of effective practice around this spanning Training and Experience.

Setting specifics in terms of regulatory requirements for authorisation and evidence of competency overall aside (for now), as a minimum proficient senior Compliance personnel – in particular the Compliance Officer, the head of the function – should demonstrate the same range of characteristics as an effective business manager. This includes appropriate knowledge, communication skills, decision-making abilities, risk awareness and so forth. In addition to this, Compliance professionals, in order to be truly effective within their roles, must also add an approach in terms of skills, abilities and behaviours that supports the aims of the Compliance function, imbuing each character-istic with the emphasis necessary for their achievement. For example:

- *Business intelligence*: understand how the business operates and able to carry out Compliance activities with an awareness of business objectives.
- *Communication*: given the day-to-day interactions of Compliance professionals across the business and the wide range of activities undertaken, effective communi-cation skills are imperative.
- *Decision-making*: there is a need to be able to respond in a timely and decisive man-ner to a host of situations and issues as and when they occur.
- *Influencing abilities*: the ability to influence others of the need for a particular approach or of the validity of a particular view is an inherent part of the Com-pliance role.
- *Inter-personal skills*: supporting 'hard' skills such as those listed here are many so-called 'softer' skills, such as empathy, diplomacy, tact and so forth, all of which help with the development of relationships and the smooth running of Compliance oper-ations on a day-to-day basis.
- *Risk awareness*: understanding the wider risks faced by the business and how they in turn affect the Compliance environment.
- *Subject knowledge*: understanding the relevant regulatory rules and requirements and how they impact on the firm and practices within it.

Note how these comprise a range of requirements in terms of understanding, skills, abili-ties and behaviours. Within these, emphasis will be placed on the following in particular:

- *Understanding, knowledge and skills*: a variety of skill sets are needed by the Compli-ance function and the requisite mix of these, including levels of knowledge and abil-ities, will vary depending on how they fit with the overall structure of the function within a particular business. Nevertheless, a Compliance department would reason-ably comprise individuals with a variety of skills linked to the roles they perform. For example, those with a responsibility for training would, in addition to a certain level of compliance and business-related knowledge, also need to demonstrate knowledge and understanding of suitable training methods, while alternatively those whose role is concerned with ensuring the function remains up-to-date with relevant develop-ments and/or communicating change to the business would be expected not only to have a thorough understanding of how such regulation affects their organisation, but also have strong communication skills in order to disseminate this information effectively. The most recent of the *Cost of Compliance*[30] surveys highlighted Subject Matter Expertise as the main key skill of an ideal Compliance Officer identified by its respondents, closely followed by attention to detail and communication skills, un-doubtedly reflecting the challenges faced by professionals working in this field as dis-cussed previously in this text. Such will be explored in a practical sense in Chapter 8.
- *Attributes, abilities and behaviours*: the seniority of the Compliance professional necessarily impacts on the prioritisation of some attributes over others. Clearly the actual Compliance Officer, in leading the function, should demonstrate superior

skills in each of these areas and indeed more if they are to be seen as effective in their role. The manner in which particular abilities and behaviours are attributed to Compliance personnel will again depend to a large extent upon the role they are to perform within the function. Senior roles will require high levels of communication, decision-making, influencing and problem-solving skills, especially when working directly with business units.

Appropriate skills, abilities and behaviours not only help with the performance of day-to-day Compliance activities and enhance inter-personal interactions (both within the business and externally) but they also help 'sell' the benefits of compliance, which is helpful in reinforcing the belief that Compliance adds value. Accordingly, how the Compliance function should be staffed, how the initial competence of those staff should be assessed and how this should be developed on an ongoing basis is an important aspect of the overall Compliance framework. It therefore merits careful consideration.

ROLE OF THE COMPLIANCE OFFICER

The Compliance Officer: expert, diplomat, counsellor, investigator, strategist, teacher – philosopher even? The Compliance Officer is, at one time or another, all of these archetypes and others besides, as they work within the business to achieve the objectives of their function. The activities in which they are involved on a daily basis makes them ideally placed to directly influence the attitude towards compliance requirements within the firm and the culture that supports this attitude. The Compliance Officer is the architect of the Compliance approach within the firm: overseeing, implementing and shaping it, establishing standards and implementing procedures in support of it. They influence, through the approach they take and the example they set, how Compliance staff carry out their roles and thus how compliance and Compliance are viewed by the business. The regulatory requirements of the appointment aside, the decision as to who to appoint to this pivotal role is an important one for any business.

The Compliance Officer is the architect of the Compliance approach within the firm.

A useful summary of the knowledge, understanding, behaviours and abilities usually expected of compliance professionals, specifically the individual with overall responsibility for the function, is set out in the *National Occupation Standards (NOS) for Compliance*.[31] These represent the areas identified by industry practitioners as underpinning effective performance in Compliance roles, and span activities such as 'Develop yourself to improve and maintain workplace competence in a financial services environment' and 'Comply with regulations in your financial services environment'.

The level of knowledge and the capacity to apply this effectively in order to be effective in this role, spanning the range of issues that impact on the Compliance environment, should be continuously updated, reflecting developments within the Compliance environment and wider regulatory environment. The core knowledge underpinning the compliance role should reflect the type of issues summarised in Figure 6.1 earlier in the chapter, but it should be recognised that the flavour of these will be heavily influenced by the business area of operations.

It is not, of course, necessary for an effective Compliance Officer in all businesses to have intimate knowledge spanning *all* these areas. This would be next to impossible given their broad range of responsibilities, particularly in larger firms. Instead, responsibilities for certain areas will ideally be assigned to specific individuals or teams of people within the Compliance function, with the Compliance Officer maintaining a more high-level awareness and level of knowledge, ensuring they are familiar with key developments and issues.

The skills, abilities and behaviours demonstrated by the head of the Compliance function provide the foundation on which the Compliance Officer can build his or her approach, creating the structure within which they are able to affect their goals and achieve their objectives. Given the nature of this particular role, the Compliance Officer should be able to challenge the business and to ask difficult questions, including to those right at the top of the organisation, and expect that their challenge, queries or concerns will be accorded due respect and will be effectively addressed. They need to have sufficient authority to do so and this derives not only from the formal status they hold as the head of Compliance but also the attitude of stakeholders with the firm towards them, attitudes that will be influenced by the Compliance Officer's own personal abilities and the respect they inspire as a consequence.

The Compliance Officer should be able to challenge the business and to ask difficult questions.

Even more than specific knowledge, the way in which a Compliance Officer, or indeed any member of the Compliance team, performs their role has a direct impact on the effective achievement of the function's goals, those of the business and ultimately those of the regulator. To be effective, Compliance must be seen as relevant and necessary, not only because of the possibility of regulatory censure or senior management sanction if requirements are not adhered to, but because those within the operational areas of the business recognise the value of the Compliance function's contribution to the business. Although the status afforded to the Compliance Officer and function, by both the board and the regulator, initially provide a strong foundation for the function and while the ongoing support of the board helps support this status, the function will not be effective if its behaviours, as exemplified by the Compliance personnel working within it, are not as they should be. Just as the best procedures in the world will not be effective if they are not followed, the most effectively structured and outwardly supported Compliance function will be ineffective if the behaviours of the Compliance personnel are not appropriate.

The most effectively structured and outwardly supported Compliance function will be ineffective if the behaviours of the Compliance personnel are not appropriate.

What do we mean by this? Reflect on the perceived view of the Compliance function of the past, as discussed in Part I of this text: an entirely separate entity, an 'add on' to day-to-day operations within the business, taking a mechanical approach to their role with a tick-box mentality, considered the 'business prevention unit'. In many ways, the Compliance function was seen – and indeed is still seen, by some – as more of an administrative 'policing' function, rather than a part of the business with *real* day-to-day relevance, although fortunately that view is far less in evidence nowadays. Inevitably, this impression of the Compliance function will largely have been derived from experience and observation of the Compliance function's activities and the behaviours of the individuals working within it, together with the attitude of influential others towards these.

Incorrect beliefs as to where responsibility for compliance lies, uncertainty as to the value added by Compliance, staff remuneration failing to consider compliance matters, Compliance taking a mechanical approach to their activities, confusion over reporting lines, poor communication, the existence of a 'blame' culture – the presence of any single one of these fairly common scenarios and others like them would have a distinct, likely negative, impact on how Compliance is perceived within the organisation and thus on its likelihood to be effective in the achievement of its aims. For example, in the final point, where there exists a culture which seeks to apportion blame, this could potentially lead to business staff being both suspicious of Compliance and unwilling to engage with them in case they find something wrong, with a resulting negative impact for the business staff.

Note the contrasting Compliance function views and approaches in the following two scenarios[32] and consider the consequences for the function that might result. Reflect on the implications of these for the perception of both compliance generally and the Compliance function specifically:

Scenario 1 – The Compliance Officer is autocratic in manner, taking a harsh approach to compliance matters, issuing directives to staff within the compliance team and within the business without discussion or explanation. The Compliance function, responding to the approach of the Compliance Officer, takes a similar hard-line approach, brooking no discussion with the business over how regulatory requirements should be met, only that they should be. The business has a general reluctance to contact the Compliance Function and communication tends to be one way.

Scenario 2 – The Compliance Officer takes an open and consultative approach to compliance, encouraging his/her team to do likewise. Setting appropriate guidelines that reflect regulatory requirements, staff within the Compliance function recognise the positive benefits their role brings to the business and are keen to work collaboratively to achieve results that reflect both regulatory and business needs. When speaking with business units, they take care to explain the reason for the compliance position on particular matters and ensure that they provide regular feedback and guidance. Communication is two-way, as the business actively brings their concerns to Compliance and knows they will get a sensible response.

The likely outcomes of each style of approach are as follows – simplistic, yes, but certainly most firms would wish to err towards the second style, given all the benefits it brings and the potential issues it mitigates against:

Scenario 1 – The business approaches the compliance function only when absolutely necessary, keeping their interactions to a minimum. A request from the compliance team to members of the business units to attend training sessions on compliance matters is viewed with trepidation. If problems occur, or mistakes are made, these are not brought to the attention of compliance, unless there is no alternative. Members of the compliance function are not invited to attend product or service development meetings.

Scenario 2 – Members of the compliance function regularly attend meetings with different business areas and are encouraged to provide feedback on developments at an early stage. Where problems occur, business staff feel comfortable raising them with compliance to obtain guidance on the action to be taken to address them.

Essentially, those who have experienced a hands-off, dictatorial approach to Compliance are unlikely to view it as helpful and responsive to the needs of the business, which in turn is likely to breed a potentially negative attitude towards compliance requirements themselves. Given that the business as a whole is responsible for compliance, to embed such a negative view based on the approach and behaviours of the Compliance personnel appears not only unhelpful but also an opportunity lost in the organisation's (and the regulator's) pursuit of their risk management goals. Hence the developments in this area and the desire to embed a more enlightened and cooperative view of the Compliance role.

How Compliance can influence and enhance the development of an appropriate culture within an organisation is an important consideration for any firm in its pursuit of effective regulatory risk management, indeed of all risk management. Investment by the firm in the approach taken to ensure both initial and ongoing competence of Compliance personnel is worthwhile: competent, knowledgeable and skilled personnel working in this area are necessary if the aims of the function – and, as a consequence, the aims of the firm as regards effective management of regulatory risk – are to be achieved.

COMPLIANCE DEVELOPMENT

Remember, irrespective of the preventative measures in place, 100% protection from error cannot be guaranteed. Things go wrong: people are imperfect, and procedures are fallible. Taking time to consider measures that counter these shortcomings through appointing the right people and engendering the right culture can go a long way towards minimising errors and their impact on the business; compliance matters are, and should be, on the radar of the board. Compliance should be at the heart of business in supporting this activity, having an impact in a visible way. In the final Part of this text, we reflect on progress in this regard, making clear why Compliance matters whilst also highlighting challenges and posing questions for consideration, as we consider what next for the function in 'Compliance Development'.

NOTES

1   *The Function of Compliance Officer* IOSCO (2003).
2   As referred to in Chapter 4: www.fsa.go.jp/inter/ios/20060510/02.pdf.
3   Guidelines_On_Certain_Aspects_Of_Mifid_Ii_Compliance_Function_Requirements.Pdf (Europa.Eu).
4   Discussions on the use and challenge around Management Information in the previous chapter refers.
5   BIS (2008).
6   And no doubt many of us have suffered through periodic exercises of this nature that seemingly bore little relation to our own area of activity within the business. These were thus not only fairly tedious, but also of little practical benefit, other than allowing the trainer (and the firm) to confirm that yes, 'training' on a particular topic had verifiably been carried out.
7   Ernst and Young (2013b).
8   www.iia.org.uk/resources/corporate-governance-basic-overview/application-of-the-three-lines-model.
9   Note the Austria, Australia, Canada, Ireland, the Netherlands and UK examples referred to earlier in this text.
10 Or indeed, in very small firms where the Compliance function might comprise a single individual.
11 The enforcement action against Citibank by the US Office of the Comptroller of the Currency (OCC 2012) in 2012 provides a pertinent example of how important this is.
12 KPMG (2012, p. 23).
13 Cost of Compliance Hammond and Walshe (2012).
14 The Thomson Reuters Cost of Compliance Surveys 2012–2022, with the 2012 Survey contrasted with the 2022 Survey for comparative purposes.
15 Cost of Compliance 2012 English and Hammond.
16 Cost of Compliance 2022 Hammond and Cowan.
17 Global Systemically Important Banks.
18 Accepting of course that the firm and the Executive board at its head extol the virtues of a compliant approach in their own day-to-day approach.
19 Note Appendix 3 references.
20 Note the PCBS recommendations discussed in Part I.
21 Note www.fca.org.uk/publications/consultation-papers/cp14-13-strengthening-accountability-banking-new-regulatory.
22 Refer to fca.org.uk.
23 Mr Paul Flowers of The Co-operative Bank, fortunately not in a Compliance role.
24 www.fca.org.uk/firms/senior-managers-certification-regime/dual-regulated-firms.
25 To complete the information on the three parts within SM&CR note the following from the FCA website: *Certification regime* – Relates to employees whose role 'means it's possible for them to cause significant harm to the firm or its customers'. These are known as certification functions. No requirement for approval by FCA or PRA but annually firms must check and certify they are fit and proper. *Conduct rules* – Minimum standard of individual behaviour in financial services. Aim is to 'improve individual accountability and awareness of conduct issues across firms'. Note alsowww.fca.org.uk/firms/senior-managers-certification-regime/dual-regulated-firms. www.fca.org.uk/firms/senior-managers-certification-regime/dual-regulated-firms.
26 www.bankofengland.co.uk/prudential-regulation/publication/2020/evaluation-of-the-senior-managers-and-certification-regime.
27 Note www.handbook.fca.org.uk/handbook/SUP/10C/6.html?date=2020-10-01.
28 Again, note www.handbook.fca.org.uk/handbook/SUP/10C/6.html?date=2020-10-01.
29 www.fca.org.uk/firms/approved-persons/heads-compliance-mlro-applicant-competency-capability.
30 Thomson Reuters Cost of Compliance 2022.
31 Accessible at: www.ukstandards.org.uk.
32 Extracted from S. Ward, *Financial Services Compliance Elective Module 2011–2020, CBMBA*.

Part III

Compliance Development

Building on the practical content within Part II, Part III considers why, specifically, Compliance matters and to whom, and why the activities of this role are now more important than ever before, addressing challenges arising in performance of the role and providing recommendations for its future development:

- In Chapter 7 we consider the role Compliance plays and why, as a consequence, Compliance matters: not only to regulated firms but more widely. We will examine efforts currently under way to address the problems of the past, which are intended to support the shift in societal and business culture to one which is more ethically robust, and reflect on progress in these areas. In doing so we will look at how Compliance activities can effectively support activity in this area for the benefit of the regulatory environment overall.
- In Chapter 8, as a means of further demonstrating why Compliance matters, examples of the ongoing challenges faced by the function and those working within it are explored. The consequences of these for different stakeholders are also considered and practical solutions to most effectively addressing them are put forward.
- In Chapter 9 we look at ways in which the Compliance function and those professionals working within it can be further enabled to better perform and achieve the objectives of their roles. We highlight ways in which their activities and approach could be leveraged to good and better effect allowing both businesses and regulators to more effectively harness the available skills and expertise of these professionals. In doing so, we will consider how the operational Compliance function and Compliance professionals themselves can provide more value in their roles, allowing them to contribute even more effectively to the management of risk within organisations and within the wider business environment, demonstrating that it is to the advantage not only of those organisations to do so, but beyond.

The three chapters that form this third and final Part of the text seek to act as fulcrum for development of this growing profession, with ideas for reflection and consideration applying at multiple stakeholder levels: personal, organisational, sectoral, jurisdictional and global.

DOI: 10.4324/9781003431305-10

7

Why Compliance Matters Now

WHY NOW?

Notwithstanding those that occurred before then, the series of scandals within financial services throughout the latter part of the twentieth century, into the twenty-first and right up to the present day – varying in form but with many similarities – stand as a recent testament to the recurring regularity with which the regulatory environment, and the efforts of those tasked with regulating and ensuring compliance within it, are challenged. As may be seen from what we have discussed so far, some might argue that regulatory attention and thus compliance attention was perhaps not focused as it should be as such scandals unfolded, not least during the period leading up to the Global Financial Crisis of the late 2000s. This allowed all manner of complex products to be developed, confusing approaches to be accepted and questionable cultures to proliferate, seemingly without challenge. The resulting fallout, however, ensured that in the subsequent period, attention was firmly focused on the industry, with challenges clearly under the spotlight. Under this illumination, business culture was publicly 'outed' as flawed in a number of respects: integrity, behaviours, ethics, regulation and regulatory action, to name but a few. As we discussed at the outset of this text, credibility in the industry has been seriously undermined and despite stringent efforts made to address the weaknesses identified it will take much to restore any robust form of faith in it or indeed in many of those who work within it. Given that the role of the industry and of certain key institutions in particular, such as banks, is so central to our society, it is difficult to contemplate a more onerous challenge than the task faced by those who have been, and continue to be, working to restore that credibility.

Prominent amongst the actions being taken and ideas mooted for consideration are those relating to ethics and integrity, considered integral to any possibility of restoring trust and confidence in this arena. Cited as one of the main areas of focus, calls for the improvement of the culture of the industry through efforts to improve the integrity of both the systems and those working within them are heard from all quarters. However, as with so many matters in life, there is a distinct difference between *talking* about something, *intending* to do it and then *actually* doing it. It is in the practical implementation of actions to address the generally agreed ethics and integrity-related vacuum that the industry has yet to genuinely find its feet and to be seen to do so. If this is to be achieved

DOI: 10.4324/9781003431305-11

There is a distinct difference between *talking* about something, *intending* to do it and then *actually* doing it.

and the desired outcomes met, the sector will need to draw on all available resources, working collectively to achieve this common goal.

WHY WE DO WHAT WE DO

It is worth pondering for a moment why we do what we do. We – that is, we humans – are more usually drawn towards actions that lead to our perceived betterment. As a result, humans respond well to incentive and our approach within business has tended to evolve to reflect this, more often than not focusing on reward in one form or another. This impacts on our attitude towards regulation and compliance with it. Hitherto the incentive for compliance had largely tended towards the 'stick': comply or be subject to regulatory censure, though for a number of years now there has been increased attention paid by some to a 'carrot' option, recognising the benefits to be gained from this.

Reflecting on past actions in this regard and on the business/individual approach to this, during the 'good' years financially, this might have been adapted thus:

> comply or be subject to regulatory censure – or maybe not, depending upon whether a "light touch" approach to regulation is being adopted or whether there is genuine regulatory focus on more of a 'stick' approach in which there is therefore increased likelihood of challenge arising – so, essentially, weigh up how much complying is going to cost against how much not complying will (and whether or not you will be caught) and make a decision on that basis.

More recently there has been a not-so-subtle change in focus – albeit we could argue, still with overtones of the second approach for many firms – to something more akin to 'comply and be seen to comply or face not only regulatory censure (well, perhaps) but certainly face the court of public disapproval'. Putting aside whether you agree or disagree with the sentiments expressed here (these are included for provocative purposes anyway, to make you think!) do you notice the links here? All are very negative, albeit reasonable, reasons for complying that apply whether we are speaking of rules and regulations per se or those of the Compliance function itself. But what of the positives we have alluded to? And how might these act as an incentive?

Firms, like people, will do what is in their best interest and if it can be made clear that this interest aligns with that of the Compliance function and the regulator, so achieving regulatory objectives overall, then all the better. Raising awareness of and promoting these benefits is one of the reasons why Compliance matters and why its activities can be of benefit to all of us as stakeholders in the financial services environment.

The Past Is the Past Is the Past – Or Is It?

Historically, regulation of the financial services industry has seen a frequently occurring pattern of events then reaction, events then reaction, and so on, as discussed earlier in this text, and so we continue on, addressing some issues while others – which are not currently on our immediate radar – emerge elsewhere. Mentally, it conjures an image of the children's game of 'whack a mole' – though unfortunately with greater consequences for all concerned (with that in mind it might be argued that it is the taxpayers providing state support to banks and customers mis-sold products who are the moles, rather than the various crises themselves …). 'Lessons will be learned' is the inevitable response to the uncovering of major wrongdoing, but are they really? The tsunami of cases in the more than a decade since the global financial crisis would suggest not, for though some of these have their origins pre-crisis,[1] in many instances, it would appear that some of the worst of the activity or behaviours occurred *post*-crisis, during the period of alleged atonement and heightened focus on righting the wrongs of the past and improving the perception of the industry.

> **'Lessons will be learned' is the inevitable response to the uncovering of major wrongdoing, but are they really?**

This is deeply troubling, not least because as the old saying goes, 'do what you have always done and get what you have always got'. And the wider ramifications of this continue, with echoes of past scandals such as Enron, for example, with the ongoing FTX crypto case being a current example that suggests lessons have *not* actually been learned. And so another scandal emerges… Ostensibly, efforts to remedy past failings continue apace, spanning a broad range of activities such as those discussed earlier in this text, including the revision of regulatory structures, new appointments in key roles, focused initiatives on ethics and conduct, action at international level and so on. There are some notable gaps in types of effort, however, some of which many believe would go a long way to genuinely reinforce the stated intention to 'clean up' the industry and set the tone for a cultural shift. While there has been the pursuit of firms through enforcement action and much publicity surrounding this,[2] as we will discuss further in a moment, in many jurisdictions direct focus on individual culpability has only fairly recently been an area of attention.[3] The actions of some of those involved in the scandals of recent years are viewed by many as tantamount to illegal and many would support stronger pursuit of individuals on such charges.

In the UK, for example, there have been rumblings in the background to this affect for some time and we have seen some specific actions, such as:

- Serious Fraud Office (SFO) investigations and charges in relation to LIBOR rigging, changes to LIBOR and announcements on the end of LIBOR.[4]
- *Parliamentary Commission on Banking Standards* recommendations, the introduction of SM&CR.[5]

Continued and stronger action in this area, with an increased focus on individual sanction, would be warmly welcomed by many and send a strong message that not only is such action unacceptable, it will have *personal* consequences – there can be no hiding behind collective responsibility for individual actions. In addition to more widely recognising the push in this direction at a global level, it is to be hoped that the output of national initiatives such as the *Parliamentary Commission* will be genuinely acted upon. The generally positive responses to its initial recommendations from stakeholders within the industry were encouraging[6] and the ongoing embedding of the SM&CR which arose from this (as highlighted in the PRA evaluation of its implementation[7]) are similarly pleasing to note in the context of our discussions across this text. It is hoped that together continued highlighting of the consequences of non-compliance for both firms and individuals (not least in the form of fines following regulatory sanction) will concentrate the minds of future individuals contemplating such action as well as giving existing proponents pause for thought.

With that in mind, it is interesting to look beyond the surface headlines of some of those scandals that have emerged and consider, practically, what lessons there are to be gleaned from these so that we can genuinely make efforts to learn. As well as reflecting on pertinent findings and themes from these in this chapter, in Appendix 4 we examine the detail of a selection of real-life cases from a particular jurisdiction to illustrate this point, highlighting findings/failings relevant to the Compliance role. In Appendix 5 we look at particular examples of incidents where the Compliance Officer themselves has been sanctioned. Key aspects and useful sources of information relating to them are included; however, it is well worth spending time exploring each of these further and reflecting on their relevance for Compliance developments by accessing the source material.

In examining these, some of the high-profile cases that fed into key reforms within the financial services industry of a particular jurisdiction over the past decade and considering the activities of different stakeholders involved in relation to these both before, during and after details of the scandals emerged, we can identify a number of common threads. Many of these provide useful lessons for Compliance professionals to ponder on, irrespective of sector or jurisdiction. These include, in broad terms:

- Creation of a culture that made the unacceptable 'acceptable'.
- Lack of challenge on part of regulators and Compliance.
- Where challenge was made, the approach to enforcement was weak.
- Attitude of the firm and Compliance toward compliance in the firm.
- Attitude towards Compliance of the firm and regulators.
- Standing and seniority of the Compliance function.
- Consequences of 'group think' by different sets of stakeholders.
- Little action taken following escalation of issues.

Such failings provide an insight into how the application or absence of effective compliance requirements, such as detailed in Part II, can have consequences for all stakeholders involved and contribute to problematic outcomes for us all. It is therefore useful to consider their practical implications for the Compliance function and how we might address challenges within the workplace environment to avoid or mitigate the impact of these from a regulatory risk perspective arising in our spheres of influence; this will be the subject of our next chapter.

Ongoing Issues

Alongside this, other than the specifics of each of these examples, what is rather depressing about such cases is the regularity with which issues occurred, over how long a period and, in some, how recently there is evidence of their proliferation; that actions taken to address problems that contributed to a previous scandal appear in the next and then in the next. We can go back even further and see that many of the notable issues in recent cases echo those of past high-profile cases, where the efforts expended subsequently by all stakeholders were intended to ensure *that lessons were learned*, that identified weaknesses would be addressed and that there would be no recurrence. The following examples illustrate this point:

- In the UK, the Barings scandal[8] contributed to a complete overhaul of the regime under which key personnel were authorised to act in certain key positions (Significant Influence positions). The 'Approved Persons' regime was introduced with great fanfare and much effort, intended to really focus the minds of the individuals who held these posts on their own personal responsibility and their role in preventing such rogue activity.
- The fallout from the Enron[9] accounting scandal and audit failure was significant in many ways, not least for the scale of the fraud and activities within the firm and in the immediate aftermath of the collapse of its auditing firm Arthur Anderson. It led to a heightened focus on a number of key areas, leading to the passage of the US Sarbanes–Oxley Act in July 2002 (SOX), as a result of which senior management must now individually certify the accuracy of financial information, penalties for fraudulent financial activity are much more severe, it also increased the oversight role of boards of directors and increased the independence of the outside auditors who review the accuracy of corporate financial statements. This case had significant implications for accounting and corporate governance issues around the world.

In both instances, as well as addressing specific tangible 'definite' issues arising from each case, concerted efforts were apparently made more generally to address the rather less tangible matters that were apparent, such as cultural issues for example. In the aftermath of each case, there was heightened focus aimed at getting to the heart of what went wrong, widespread calls for action and prominent reporting of issues and actions.[10] Problems still occurred in the subsequent period, however, as the following examples illustrate:

- Despite the robust warnings provided by the Barings case, around the globe scandals continued to occur that involved other so-called 'rogue traders', including such infamous cases as: John Rusnack (a currency trader at US Bank Allfirst, pleaded guilty to $691 million fraud in 2002: jailed for seven-and-a-half years). In November 2012 UBS was fined £30 million by Britain's financial watchdog and put under extra scrutiny by its Swiss counterpart over failings that allowed a rogue trader to lose $2.3 billion (Kweku Adoboli, a trader on UBS's Exchange Traded Funds desk in London, subsequently jailed for seven years after admitting trading far in excess of authorised limits in the biggest fraud in British history).
- As to the much-lauded UK Approved Persons regime, there were rumblings as to its efficacy for some time, not least following the 2013 revelations about the then chairman of the Co-operative Bank who had been approved to that position despite having little banking experience (and during the post-financial crisis period when

supposedly there were tighter controls in this regard). The regime was roundly criticised in the Banking Commission report referred to previously and recommendations made for it to be overhauled, leading to the SM&CR regime, developments in relation to which have been touched on throughout this text. The focus within the more recent of these – clarifying expectations in some areas following the FCA's stocktake of the embedding of the regime,[11] for example, and those relating matters such as the training and experience of Heads of compliance and MLRO's[12] – suggest that the need for ongoing work in this area is recognised.

Cases can take a good deal of time to work their way through the investigation process, as some of the examples in Appendix 4 attest. By the mid-2010s what could be seen, writ large in the evidence of the multitude of scandals that had arisen in recent years[13] was a litany of failure to achieve what was intended in our past responses to scandals, regulatory and otherwise. Have matters improved significantly since then? The aforementioned reference to actions of the UK regulator the FCA in recent years would suggest ongoing work in this area, with its structure and resource focus showing the direction of travel, and it can also be useful to note the actions of other regulators, such as in the US for example, who have been particularly active in this area.[14]

As an aside, however, whether all the events in connection with the emergence of such scandals should be viewed simply as failings is an interesting point. Of course, it would be better had such events not occurred in the first place and certainly the fact that they did so is to be decried. But should their identification (albeit, unfortunately, not until after some time had passed in several cases) not be viewed as a success in some ways: the fact that details of each scandal emerged, rather than remaining undetected, that there appear to be genuine efforts on the part of stakeholders to bring these matters to light? Perhaps the very fact that contributory factors have been identified and are now open to public scrutiny and widespread censure is an indication of a genuine desire to address these problems, rather than bury them out of sight. Surely such behaviour could be seen as indicative of an underlying, more positive and ethical approach to matters than previously existed? A positive change in culture perhaps? Or, more negatively viewed, might such findings simply be awareness of the tip of the iceberg, with far more going on beneath the surface than is identified?[15] Either way, this gives those of working in this area much to reflect on.

PROMOTING THE LINK BETWEEN COMPLIANCE, ETHICS AND CULTURE

'Culture' is often referred to, not only in respect of financial services[16] but also more widely to encapsulate the general attitudes or behaviours of the particular group in question. But what, exactly, is meant by this in the context it is being used? The term 'culture' frequently appears to be used as a shorthand, in order to avoid the need for a more detailed explanation about what is actually being referred to. While that is reasonable in a wider-ranging conversation as it is a term that is generally understood, when we discuss 'culture' in relation to that which exists within financial services, we need to be more specific. In this sense, we are using 'culture' as it reflects the beliefs and attitudes of a particular group, reflected in their collective behaviour, as demonstrated by their approach to and pattern of working. If we are to create and maintain an environment that is supportive of activities to manage regulatory risk, we need to cultivate the right type of culture. This cultivation applies not only to regulated organisations, where the term 'compliance culture' is, to a degree, already embedded, though the focus in more recent years has been to move beyond this, as discussed in earlier parts of this text. Nor is it restricted to that emanating from the regulator and the strength of the position they take.[17] It applies even more widely still. The compliance and regulatory environments, as with all working environments, are in many ways nothing if not reflective of the attitudes that exist within society itself.

> **We are using 'culture' as it reflects the beliefs and attitudes of a particular group, reflected in their collective behaviour, as demonstrated by their approach to and pattern of working.**

At the moment there is a growing and concerted focus on encouraging compliant and ethical behaviours; how effective this focus is will be dependent upon the degree to which this becomes embedded within the general psyche of the populace and whether there is a genuine will to address perceived shortcomings. Whether the current popularity of such topics is based on a genuine desire for change and to address these problems, accepting all the potentially negative issues arising from them, or whether instead it is more concerned with being *seen* to be doing something – a form of window-dressing if you will, while behind the curtains business as usual continues as before – is a matter for debate.

Although our focus in this text is on one industry in particular, given that those who work within it are drawn from wider society, might the prevailing culture within that wider society not be something that needs to be borne in mind? For example, those in other areas of business? Consider the non-financial services scandals that abound: misconduct in the automotive sector with the Volkswagen/Audi emissions rigging; the cycling drugs scandal surrounding Lance Armstrong; wide-scale match fixing at football matches across Europe; the Theranos case in respect of blood-testing; cultural failures at Uber; tech failings such as Apple adjusting the processors on older generation iPhones and Facebook negligence concerning Privacy; the awarding of PPE contracts during Covid-19; and the ongoing Bulb Energy situation, to name but a very few. Many of these also call into question matters of regulation around them. Irrespective of the particulars in each instance, what could be said to underpin each of these in broader terms though is the question of standards, of ethics, of the degree of adherence to good and fair practice, these and the actions taken where failings were found, combined with matters relating to skills, incentives, and effectiveness, or otherwise, of leadership/management. These are the very same issues we are challenged within financial services. As discussed earlier in this text, people are said to be at the heart of business, but in effect, they are not just at the heart of it, they actually *are* it: people are business. They are the ones that drive it, manage it and shape it. Therefore, in considering culture, we need to think about people, why they do what they do, what motivates them, what turns them off and what causes them to act in particular ways. And in doing so we need to consider not just the micro-cosm of culture that exists within our own little frame of reference, but also how this is influenced by wider factors. In the context of prevailing culture generally, are people really less ethical nowadays than in the past?

People are business. They are the ones that drive it, manage it shape it.

Given the range and frequency of scandals within the industry over the years as we have seen, it could be concluded that not much has changed. And nothing *will* really change until the culture changes and that change becomes embedded. Before we look into that point further, let us pause for a moment and ponder on a potentially con-troversial point: do we, all the stakeholders within the industry collectively, really and genuinely *want* it to change? What might the ramifications of that be? Yes, there is a clear upside: all the positive objectives of regulation we have discussed so far would create the hoped-for world of sunny opportunity for all in engagement in financial services activ-ity. It would also be interesting to consider what really fundamental change might look like – consider the current discussions in respect of sustainability matters, for example. But recall our brief discussion on the purpose of business earlier in this text, specifically the prime motivation: the creation of profit. If this is the prime motivator for business, then curbs upon it will not be welcomed by all. There will be resistance; even if that re-sistance is not overt, because to be *seen* to be primarily in pursuit of profit does not, in today's climate, reflect the prevailing mood. But given the nature of business and indeed, the nature of human beings, covert resistance to potential curbs on profit (both collective and personal) will undoubtedly be present throughout the majority of business indus-tries,[18] even in a small way, even if it remains unacknowledged. Think about this: if all stakeholders were genuinely committed, collectively, to 'cleaning up', 'addressing the ills of the past', 'embedding integrity and ethics', wouldn't

If all stakeholders were genuinely committed, collectively, to 'cleaning up', 'addressing the ills of the past' and 'embedding integrity and ethics', wouldn't we have achieved that already, or certainly be far further forward?

we have achieved that already, or certainly be far further forward? Are there some stakeholders who in reality are actually keen to maintain the status quote as it currently stands because this supports their own – comfortable from their perspective – position?[19] The truth of such uncomfortable and generally unacknowledged resist-ance to a fundamental change in our ethical approach is evidenced in what we see around us. If we genuinely wish to address issues, we do ourselves no favours by not acknowledging this resistance and including considera-tion of its consequences in our efforts at improvement.

Accordingly, there has to be a realisation that there will be consequences from focusing on these issues and that there is a need to balance ideology with commercial reality. If, when balanced against each other, an ethical investment or action will result in performing poorly in comparison to the less-ethical alternative, will shareholders (us) be willing to accept this? And what of everyone else? Consider the impact if one company chose to take a particular position while everyone else did not: would the increase in customers cover the increase in costs? Now consider this in the context not of businesses, but of sectors, of jurisdictions: what would the impact be then? These are weighty matters for consideration and the detailed analysis is outside the scope of this text,[20] but they do provide an indicator of some of challenges contributing to the background within which the Compliance function operates.

Essentially, in any environment, we have the culture we have developed or allowed to develop. This is reflected in the wider world, but also, more unforgivably, in many of our workplaces, where we have more control over what is considered acceptable and what is not. Much work has been done on the development of cultures within business organisations and considering the consequences for individuals and for firms. The detail of this too is outside the scope of this text, but in broad terms this warrants further consideration in the context of the role Compliance can play in its improvement. Consider the Goldman Sachs resignation case,[21] where the departing individual produced a resignation letter that prompted widespread discussion in which he spoke of the culture that existed which resulted in new members of staff, arriving wide-eyed and ready to soak up the guidance of their more experienced 'professional' colleagues, hearing clients referred to disparagingly and certainly disrespected in the context of 'cash cows' from whom more income needs to be squeezed. As the author said: 'You don't have to be a rocket scientist to figure out that the junior analyst sitting quietly in the corner of the room hearing about "muppets", "ripping eyeballs out" and "getting paid" doesn't exactly turn into a model citizen'.

Whatever the truth of the situation at this firm, the level of a wider discussion of the letter and the points made within it, coming at a time when scandals such as those discussed previously were emerging, certainly fed the view that behaviour such as this was endemic within some of our major institutions. Are we confident such examples are no longer to be found in any of our organisations?[22] In such instances, individuals have been encouraged, through the culture that existed within such organisations and the 'group think' mentality that flows from that, to act in ways that, prior to arrival at the firm, would have certainly caused many to have paused to consider whether what they were doing was right, was ethical. But in being initiated into the culture within an organisation, they moved away from what may well have been a personal sense of right and wrong and adopted the established approach of their new colleagues. So, as they proceed through the ranks, surrounded by others whose actions and approaches reflect their own, is it surprising that their 'ethical radar' dims or narrows its view, that they don't see what they do as in any way 'wrong', as it has in fact become 'normal'? We've all heard the urban legends about famous celebrities demonstrating all sorts of excessive behaviour that to most of us seems bizarre and faintly disturbing, but to them, surrounded as they are by others either acting as they do or sycophants responding to their every increasingly outlandish request, what to us seems odd, to them becomes 'normal'. And so it is in the case of the culture we allow to develop within our organisations, with what is allowed and condoned day-to-day being seen as acceptable, whether or not it is in fact so.

Has much changed over the intervening years since the events depicted in the example highlighted above took place? It is certainly to be hoped so, and as we have discussed in this text many initiatives have been undertaken both within individual firms and more broadly to address matters around culture and conduct.

But why are attempts to address this even necessary? Why not let businesses be run as they wish and never mind what the culture is? Of course, this comes back to the purpose of regulation in the first place and the objectives of financial services regulation in particular. As discussed right at the outset of this text, if we are to maintain a financial services marketplace that is fair and seen to be so, that is open to all on an equal footing, that is not the preserve of the unscrupulous or of criminals and so on, entry to the market place should be restricted to those who meet certain standards, are confirmed as having done so and of continuing to do so. Regulated firms must adhere to these standards on an ongoing basis, putting in place the necessary policy, procedures, systems and controls to do so and supporting these through their actions. Put simply, if we take the collective view that regulation of the markets is 'a good thing', an effective culture within regulated organisations is necessary to support this: all the policy, procedures, systems and controls in the world will not be effective if considerations about human behaviour are not woven into them.[23] It is, ultimately, human behaviour that either supports or undermines this.

> **All the policy, procedures, systems and controls in the world will not be effective if considerations about human behaviour are not woven into them.**

But how best to achieve the type of culture we agree is necessary for the desired betterment of the industry? In an article that addressed how organisations can encourage a culture of integrity,[24] Professor Roger Steare addresses human behaviour and argues for a better understanding of the culture this fosters within organisations. He acknowledges the need for cultural change within the industry and cites two distinct types of culture: 'command-and-control, which reinforces a climate of fear, or a culture of integrity, in which individuals are encouraged to be the best that they can be'. The consequences of such different cultural types can have huge significance for the environment in which they proliferate, with the former being more 'do because you have to – or else', the latter being more 'do because you believe it's the right thing to do'. Essentially, this latter approach echoes the type of culture the Compliance function seeks to foster within an organisation.

> **Different types of culture can have huge significance for the environment in which they proliferate.**

As many have come to recognise, a command-and-control-style approach to managing does not necessarily achieve the desired results in terms of cultural development. Instead, a values-led and lead-by-example approach would be more successful. Furthermore, firms need to recognise that there are elements within their organisation that they cannot control or manage simply through systems and procedures and the implications of this for risk assessment and management are significant. Such elements must be more subtly managed to reflect business expectations.

Recognising that focus on embedding an appropriate culture within the organisation through the embedding of appropriate values will help with this is a key step. In doing so, this will entrench behaviours that will be apparent *all of the time*, not just when disallowed by a stream of rules or restrictions or undertaken when no one is looking.

Entrench behaviours that will be apparent *all of the time*, not just when disallowed by a stream of rules or restrictions or undertaken when no one is looking.

Promoting the all-round benefits to be achieved from doing so, and the individual's rights and responsibilities in respect of this, supports this type of culture. This has the integrity as its overriding aim; a culture which supports the aims of regulation far more effectively.

A paper produced by The G30 group ten years after the global financial crisis echoes many of the themes touched on by Steare, and progress – or otherwise – made in this regard. In the *Banking Conduct and Culture: A Permanent Mindset Change*[25] the authors emphasised the aim of supporting 'the process of reform in banking culture and conduct that is underway across the industry'. Highlighting that 'sources and scope of culture issues will continue to evolve, and so too must oversight and monitoring of bank culture and conduct', the report found that though a great deal of work had been carried out in this area across the industry it 'still suffers from negative reputation, and trust still needs repairing because serious conduct and culture failures continue to occur in many markets'. It emphasised that on the topics of conduct and culture 'boards and senior management must lead by example'. In order to ensure a genuine change of a permanent nature

banks now need to focus on embedding culture awareness and stewardship at all levels of the organisation … only by making culture stewardship a permanent and integral part of how business is conducted will organisations avoid culture fatigue and backsliding.

These points on 'culture fatigue' and the need to avoid 'backsliding' are particularly interesting in the context of our discussions.

A setting within which the importance of regulatory compliance, both to the firm and to the wider industry, is known and understood, together with an appreciation of the consequences for all of non-adherence, exemplifies the existence of an effective 'Compliance' culture.

THE LINKS BETWEEN ETHICS, REGULATION, GOVERNANCE AND COMPLIANCE

Following through on this train of thought, there is a clear link between ethics, regulation, governance and compliance. In contemplating the development of an appropriate, effective and ethical culture within the regulatory environment generally and within regulated business specifically, this is an important point to keep in mind. A setting within which the importance of regulatory compliance, both to the firm and to the wider industry, is known and understood, together with an appreciation of the consequences for all of non-adherence, exemplifies the existence of an effective 'Compliance' culture. This in turn positively supports the more general culture that exists. Such a culture is able to support the activities of the Compliance function and, through this, the aims and objectives of the Board and Senior Management, set out through a clear vision and set of values.

In order to be seen to be focusing on issues of ethics and integrity, there is an increasing emphasis on transparency and openness in business practice; not simply actual transparency and openness, but that which is *clearly seen to be so*. So not only is there an apparent increase in attention to be paid to these issues, but also, in order to reflect the current business context and, more widely, the spirit of the age in which we live, to be *visible* in so doing. However, in pursuit of establishing and maintaining an effective culture within the firm, it is important to ensure that any work undertaken is in accordance with the 'spirit' of the requirements set, not just in working to the 'letter' of them. Focusing only on how things appear would tend to lean towards this latter approach and, in many ways, is unfortunately where some of us might be said to be currently in terms of our general attitude.[26] Essentially, working to the 'spirit' means working in a manner that reflects what was *intended* by the requirements, what underpins them, adapting the business approach to reflect this, rather than working in a way which is only in line with the *specific* wording of these. This requires a more holistic approach to compliance.

As a result of its constituent parts as discussed in Parts I and II of this text (such as market conventions, legislation, rules and standards, guidance, codes of practice, internal codes of conduct and so on) the elements that make up the Compliance environment are 'likely to go beyond what is legally binding and embrace broader standards of integrity and ethical conduct'.[27] Entwining the aims and objectives of Compliance with the concepts of ethics and integrity, and consistently emphasising these within the accepted approach in the firm, positively influences the firm's culture and becomes an accepted position on how things are to be done. This echoes and supports the aims of good internal governance, incorporating the objectives of corporate governance initiatives and the requirements that stem from them. It is also to the firm's benefit in a wider sense, reflecting the generally agreed fundamental objectives of financial services regulation and the statutory objectives of the industry regulator arising from these. Essentially, the concepts of integrity and ethics sit at the core of financial services regulation; legal requirements are a codification of these concepts. But there does of course need to be consideration of whether these alone would be the most effective approach to the achievement of stated aims; in this context, support for specific rules might be viewed as akin to that of backing for systems and processes within businesses: as we have discussed these are not sufficient on their own for the achievement of ethical and effective compliance. Therefore, would codification alone be the right solution? Indeed, does specific legislation help to achieve the objectives of financial services regulation if there is actually no wider impetus, at a political or cultural level for example, to do so?

In this context, therefore, there is an important point to take into consideration: it is still possible to be *technically* in compliance with the regulation, but still be unethical and without integrity. Conversely, if a firm is essentially ethical and acts with integrity, it will also be compliant. Compliance activities, regulatory expectations, governance endeavours and ethical considerations within regulated businesses share many a common purpose and in supporting the objectives of regulation more widely, they work side by side.

Finally, in considering this particular set of issues, it is useful to note related initiatives by some of the influential international bodies discussed earlier in this text (note Appendix 1). These provide insight into thinking at a global level around matters linking ethics, regulation, governance and culture and the role of regulators, boards and Compliance in supporting their embedding and endorsing the points highlighted above. Note the range of activities referred to:

- *Good Practice Guidance on Internal Controls, Ethics and Compliance*[28]:

> This Good Practice Guidance … is addressed to companies for establishing and ensuring the effectiveness of internal controls, ethics, and compliance programmes or measures for preventing and detecting the bribery of foreign public officials in their international business transactions (hereinafter "foreign bribery"), and to business organisations and professional associations, which play an essential role in assisting companies in these efforts. It recognises that to be effective, such programmes or measures should be interconnected with a company's overall compliance framework. It is intended to serve as non-legally binding guidance to companies in establishing effective internal controls, ethics, and compliance programmes or measures for preventing and detecting foreign bribery.

Updated in 2021,[29] the revisions include additional guidance on improving anti-corruption compliance programmes and internal controls (expanding factors for evaluating foreign bribery risk, for example, revised good practice in respect of high-level commitment to the compliance programme i.e. by the board, and a number of other developments).

- European Banking Authority (EBA) *Guidelines on Internal Governance (GL 44)*,[30] most recently updated in 2021, highlighted some interesting points about the compliance functions' role in respect of the internal governance framework, for example:

> '30. The risk management function and compliance function form the second line of defence. The risk management function (referred to in the previous guidelines as the 'risk control function') facilitates the implementation of a sound risk management framework throughout the institution and has responsibility for further identifying, monitoring, analysing, measuring, managing and reporting on risks and forming a holistic view on all risks on an individual and consolidated basis. It challenges and assists in the implementation of risk management measures by the business lines in order to ensure that the process and controls in place at the first line of defence are properly designed and effective. The compliance function monitors compliance with legal and regulatory requirements and internal policies, provides advice on compliance to the management body and other relevant staff, and establishes policies and processes to manage compliance risks and to ensure compliance. Both functions may intervene to ensure the modification of internal control and risk management systems within the first line of defence where necessary'

and

> 35 … The risk management function and compliance function should be involved in the establishment of the framework and the approval of such changes

to ensure that all material risks are taken into account and that the institution complies with all internal and external requirements.

- International Standards Organisation ISO 37301:2021 Compliance management systems[31] which 'specifies requirements and provides guidelines for establishing, developing, implementing, evaluating, maintaining and improving an effective compliance management system within an organization'.

HOW COMPLIANCE (AND THE COMPLIANCE FUNCTION) BENEFITS THE BOARD, THE BUSINESS, THE REGULATOR AND FINANCIAL SERVICES AS A WHOLE

Better relations between the firm and the regulator bring numerous benefits to both parties and are undoubtedly worth investing in:

- from the regulator's perspective, increasing the regulator's confidence in the firm and thus, from a risk-assessed perspective, reducing the need for regulatory focus or involvement; and
- from the firm's perspective, reducing the likelihood of regulatory censure in the form of enforcement action leading to fines, reputational issues and loss of business as a result.

The Compliance function, in acting as the bridge between both parties, can be significant in the development of this relationship and this is yet another example of why Compliance matters and the contribution it can make. Almost inevitably when considering what benefit compliance brings, for many the first points that come to mind are linked to regulatory matters. This view on what compliance and Compliance have to offer is an understandable consequence of the way in which the role of Compliance within business has been viewed and carried out in the past. Important though regulatory benefits are, however, the benefits of regulatory compliance should be viewed in a far broader fashion than these alone. That said, within the firm environment we can begin by taking this established narrow viewpoint and use it to our advantage in driving home to all stakeholders the advantages to be gained from compliance and Compliance.

As the role of the Compliance function has developed, its activities and its approach have expanded into many facets of business activity. As a consequence, there has been a shift in how it is perceived. The function now recognisably works to actively support business objectives and add value to them; their focus is not simply on monitoring and reporting on adherence to sets of rules. From the board's perspective, it is not just about the mechanics of compliance – of course risk assessment and dashboards flagging risks and so on are important, as we have already discussed, but those alone are not sufficient. Corporate culture plays a vital role in embedding compliance into the organisation. Nurturing that culture provides the best means of steering a safe course through the regulatory and compliance environments. Not only that, however, but studies[32] show that firms adopting such an approach have advantages over their competition.

As such, having in place a strong and effective Compliance function can be advantageous in a business sense, a demonstrable provider of business value. An integrated holistic approach to the Compliance function's activities supports the embedding of an effective corporate culture. The Compliance role in its broadest sense is the lynchpin that ties together matters as wide-ranging as reputation, responsibility, profit and value, not just for the business, but the wider regulatory environment. Compliance requirements are a fact of life and with that in mind, businesses should maximise the benefits to be gained from them.

The benefits of compliance can be clouded, however, by the fact that many of them are seemingly intangible and as such can be problematic to objectively measure. With technological developments allowing for an additional level of data available through multiple sources both external and internal to an organisation, however, alongside an increased recognition of the need for effective compliance in a practical business context, it may be that such can be measured more effectively than in the past. This will provide further opportunities to demonstrate compliance benefits. Efforts need to be made by the personnel within Compliance function (particularly the Compliance officer) and those within the business who are able to shape organisational culture (particularly the board, senior management and other internal influencers, both formally and informally) to effectively 'sell' the benefits (both internal and external) of regulatory compliance and of the activities of the Compliance function and personnel.

The relationship management endeavours discussed in Part II go a long way towards supporting this aim, helping to ensure that Compliance is seen as a contributor to the business, rather than a business hindrance or solely as a cost. Alongside this, Compliance should demonstrate how their role and activities benefit the firm's relationship with its regulator, showing how the culture within a firm (and its values, as evidenced by its behaviour, and supported by Compliance activities) influence that relationship. The relationship between firms and those that regulate them is not always the best (simply refer back to the cases discussed earlier in this chapter for apposite examples), but enhancing this is widely acknowledged as important. At a global level, for example, the benefits of this were flagged in *A New Paradigm: Financial Institution Boards and Supervisors*.[33] Published in 2013 this report was an update on the findings of a previous study,[34] which showed how weak and ineffective governance in systemically important financial institutions (SIFIs) contributed to what the report called 'the massive failure of financial sector decision making that led to the global financial crisis'.[35] There was a request from the supervisory and Financial Stability Board community to 'provide additional insights into how interactions between boards and supervisors could be enhanced, and how the issue of strengthening and assessing risk culture could be tackled, particularly for SIFIs'. The latest report considered 'insights into how interactions between boards and supervisors could be enhanced, and how the issue of strengthening and assessing risk culture could be tackled', noting that 'Research conducted for this report confirmed that current relations between boards and supervisors generally are not optimum' before going on to highlight that 'Supervisors need to know that boards are doing an effective job and to act appropriately if they are not'. They observed that

> What is needed is not more of the same, rather it is a step change in the level and quality of the interaction between boards and supervisors, and having the right people who take the time to make that happen.

In making some useful points on what relations between boards and supervisors should look like, what boards can contribute and the role of culture and ethical standards in relation to this, the content of this paper is very pertinent for our discussions in this text.[36] It might therefore be helpful to reflect on the matters implicit within this, for example thinking beyond the more obvious issues such as where board oversight fails overall, instead considering where and how it is ineffective in particular situations. For example, where board members fail to restrain the drive for short-term profits from CEOs, who themselves may be focusing on quarterly results and the content of the annual report, rather than on longer-term strategic aims. It is these types of issues, and the actions taken in respect of them by the various parties involved, that will have material impact on the efficacy of the relationship and achievement of stakeholder objectives.

In terms of demonstrating how different values and cultures impact on the regulatory relationship and the consequences for the firm, a discussion paper published as long ago as 2002, *An Ethical Framework for Financial Services*,[37] provides a useful overview. It explores how, as the values and cultures of a firm move from minimum standards through to a values-led business, via a compliance culture and one described as 'beyond compliance', this has a positive impact on the regulatory relationship and thus the regulatory approach, as this moves from policing through to a mature relationship. In considering this it is useful to note the benefits for each party as the relationship moves through the various stages of development, with the regulatory relationship developing from one of policing to maturity/benchmarking via supervising/educating and educating/consulting.

In many businesses, the focus is inevitably on 'the bottom line', that is, the profit. While accepting this of course is extremely important – after all, as we discussed earlier in this text, without profit there would be no business – there are many other considerations for firms and for the wider environment in which they operate. Nonetheless, with focus on the bottom line being ever evident, it can often be difficult to see the benefits of a function that is not clearly profit-producing. It is possible, however, to link the benefits of being compliant to the bottom line by showing what can happen to that bottom line in the event the business is found to be non-compliant, with the latter resulting in increased likelihood of:

- financial loss from regulatory censure and fines
- which inevitably leads to reputational damage
- followed by further financial loss from the reduction in business arising from the reputational damage
- the staff costs, comprising direct costs where additional staff have to be employed and opportunity costs where existing staff have to be redirected to undertake internal reviews and remedial action.

Clearly, the true cost of a regulatory fine to a business is significantly more than the cost of the fine itself. The costs of compliance in terms of staffing, training, provision of workspace and technology can more than hold their own against the real costs of non-compliance including reputational loss, remediation costs if required, increased costs of compliance arising from additional regulatory scrutiny such as with deferred prosecutions for example, impacts on the cost of market share arising from reputational issues and impact on the marketplace more widely, for example, not to mention the potential for business interruption or possible business suspension.

Although ensuring awareness and understanding of the impact of non-compliance is necessary and tying this to bottom-line interests a useful mechanism to concentrate minds, rather than prioritising focus on this negative type of issue (i.e. what could happen if requirements aren't followed) the Compliance function is better served by focusing just as often on embedding an awareness of the positives of compliant behaviour for the business, over and above the regulatory pay-off. There is a strong case to be made for these, including:

- reducing costs
- embedding more effective control measures
- protecting brand values
- providing opportunities for growth
- improving customer satisfaction

Statistical information can support efforts in this regard, with focused MI helping to demonstrate the contribution that Compliance can make. For example, identifying categories of activity and output which impacts compliance culture related to the aims and activities of different stakeholders and/or different areas of responsibility, breaking this down as fully as possible to reflect how a company *actually* views compliance and governance structures, procedures and systems, within the clear context of culture embodying the values of the organisation and the senior management, defining the purpose, role and impact of its operations *in reality*.

Drawing out variables from the various different types of procedural output that feeds into the operational MI produced should help to provide an overview of the ethics and principles that are embedded within its firm, evident from its culture, and thereby help with more focused and effective decision-making capability linked to this across the business. Essentially, we consider the key factors that contribute to the culture within that firm. Improvements in this area can have widespread benefits for the firm. This translates to a real qualitative difference for the business too in terms of the performance: supporting a values-based culture through a values-based compliance approach can have clear tangible benefits for the firm and also practical benefits in embedding this throughout.

Let us now look at some of these practical, visible and certainly tangible internal benefits, with consequences for both strategic and general business activities:

- A dedicated oversight and assurance function focusing on such issues means that compliance risks will be managed more effectively.
- Speedier awareness of regulatory developments providing potential to access additional business opportunities.
- Enhanced management information provided to the Board to assist in their strategic decisions.
- Better understanding achieved via improved information leading to better decision-making throughout the business generally.

- Better and more targeted information produced, which, as a result, is more accurate and specific, helps improve management decisions in both related and unrelated areas.
- Supporting the business helps ensure risks are managed more effectively, resulting in fewer errors or breaches of requirements and a reduced need for revision of work undertaken, thus reducing overall costs.
- Alertness to regulatory developments, allowing early change in approach or internal focus, thereby reducing the likelihood of costs resulting from last-minute alterations.
- Involvement with product or service development at an early stage will help ensure any issues arising are either avoided or addressed promptly, improving productivity and potentially increasing the speed at which products can be marketed.
- Less time wasted investigating errors, due to fewer breaches arising.
- Resource savings as decreased need for rework due to fewer errors.
- Reducing the cost of centralised compliance – a more collective approach arising from the embedding of a positive attitude towards compliance requirements with the business taking ownership for compliance.
- If problems do occur, confidence that these will be identified and managed.

And what of the impact on staff? As a consequence of having both a robust Compliance function and culture in place, there will inevitably be behavioural improvements. This is because staff know the company takes these issues seriously, and that there are benefits to be gained from complying with requirements and unfavourable consequences if not. There is also, of course, the impact of general improvement in staff attitudes and behaviours arising from the understanding that the organisation within which they work takes a compliant and ethical approach to their activities. Studies[38] have also shown that there are benefits for the firm in having staff work in such an environment, an important consideration not least from a recruitment and retention perspective.[39]

Benefits to the firm are not limited to those within the organisation itself. More widely, how does the opinion of the firm change as a consequence of gaining a reputation for having a compliant approach and undertaking effective Compliance activity? This leads to improved customer trust and improved peer trust, contributing to reputational enhancements and benefits along the lines of the following, for example:

- Using compliance to help the business seek competitive advantage – benefit from being seen as caring about these issues, particularly now in light of recent events in the industry.
- Greater trust in a firm that is known to be ethical and compliant, enhancing the firm's reputation, increasing likelihood of customer retention and growth.
- This improved trust having a positive impact on consumer decisions as to which firm to do business with.
- Positive influence on the impression gained by other firms wishing to do business and who they select to do business with.
- Decrease in the likelihood of a firm being targeted for financial crime purposes, as its ethical and compliant reputation will create an awareness of the likelihood that appropriate systems and controls will be in place to deflect this.

All of these benefits, though ostensibly of direct benefit to the regulated firm in which the Compliance function is located, are not confined to that firm alone. The activities and approach of the function, and the benefits arising as a consequence, have a 'spill-over' effect beyond the business itself, with positive impact for the regulatory environment as a whole, as for example:

- A greater number of demonstrably robust firms improved the reputation of the regulator and sector/jurisdiction.
- Greater trust in a sector/jurisdiction that is recognised as ethical and compliant.
- This trust attracts additional business to the sector/jurisdiction, as businesses feel confident to participate within that regulatory environment.
- Just as with firms themselves, a robust reputation will decrease the likelihood of a sector/jurisdiction being targeted for financial crime purposes, as potential criminals and wrongdoers will recognise that the sector/jurisdiction takes such matters seriously and will robustly defend attempts at crime and prosecute wrongdoers, so will be more likely to seek easier targets elsewhere.

The role of Compliance in developing and supporting the culture within each firm, Compliance acting as steward, overseeing the embedding of the compliance culture and helping everyone to understand why compliance matters, has favourable consequences far beyond that one firm. The positive 'ripple effect' ensures that.

POSITIVE COMPLIANCE

Challenging events over many years in the financial services industry have left rather a negative impression, not only on those of us who work within the regulatory field but on all stakeholders impacted by it. This illustrates the consequences if poor practice is allowed free rein and appreciation of this fact provides further encouragement to do something about it. It is accepted that the actions that gave rise to the situation we currently find the financial services industry in occurred over time. In part, it was in order to limit the occurrence of such situations that regulation was implemented in the first place. However, the fact that there is a great deal of focus on rectifying the problems in this important industry – with interest in highlighting and investigating wrongdoing, with compliance and ethics being increasingly seen as central to effective performance – should be viewed as at least a partial success of these aims, albeit recognising there is still with a long way to go to fully achieve them. As any good student of history knows, if we do not genuinely learn from the past, we will inevitably repeat the same mistakes in the future. We need to find better ways of addressing the challenges we face, rather than attempting to achieve something different by simply doing the same thing, as to do so dooms us to disappointment and an inevitable repeat of past failures.

As to the role that Compliance can play in this, it is through focusing on the positives of compliance rather than compliance for negative reasons that the activities and approach of the Compliance function can add particular value. Key influencers, such as the boards of regulated businesses and the regulators themselves, can support them in this to the benefit of all. We will return to this point later in this text. Before that, however, we need to consider some of the specific challenges the function faces as it carries out its role and how such challenges might be addressed. This is the subject of our next chapter.

NOTES

1 As per the example cases highlighted in Chapter 1.

2 For example, in 2012–2013, the FCA took action against 55 individuals, imposing in the process £5m in fines and 43 prohibitions, and obtaining 13 criminal convictions. As the Director of Enforcement and Financial crime Tracey McDermott pointed out, 'That is more action than we took against firms'. Available at: www.fca.org.uk/news/speeches/financial-services-regulation-enforcement/. More recently, as noted here www.fca.org.uk/news/press-releases/highlights-fca-new-approach-2021. 'The FCA has continued to act to protect and enhance the integrity of the UK financial system, early this month NatWest was fined £264m, in the FCA's first ever criminal prosecution under anti-money laundering legislation. In total FCA actions has resulted in financial organisations in the UK being fined £568m in 2021, including £147m against Credit Suisse and £63.9m against HSBC. The FCA has also taken action against individuals for insider dealing, non-financial misconduct and carrying out regulated activities without authorisation. Beside enforcement cases, the FCA has also varied a firm or individuals' permissions over 100 times in 2021'.

3 In the US, action appears slightly further advanced in this regard, having clearly signalled back in 2012 a heighted focus on individual culpability, particularly in respect of insider trading and related cases. More information can be found at: www.lexisnexis.com/legalnewsroom/securities/b/securities/archive/2012/07/06/trends-in-sec-enforcement-actions-focus-on-individuals-insider-trading.aspx/. More recently, as noted here, www.sec.gov/news/press-release/2021-238. 'The Securities and Exchange Commission today announced that it filed 434 new enforcement actions in fiscal year 2021, representing a 7% increase over the prior year. Seventy percent of these new or "stand-alone" actions involved at least one individual defendant or respondent. The new actions spanned the entire securities waterfront, including against emerging threats in the crypto and SPAC spaces. For example, the SEC charged a company for operating an unregistered online digital asset exchange, charged a crypto lending platform and top executives alleging a $2 billion fraud, and brought an action against a special purpose acquisition company, its merger target, top executives, and others for alleged misconduct in a SPAC transaction. The SEC's whistleblower program was critical to these efforts and had a record-breaking year'.

4 UK Government (2014a) and also in 2021 the FCA confirmed that 'all LIBOR settings will either cease to be provided by any administrator or no longer be representative', with allowance for transition. The Bank of England Governor Andrew Bailey stated 'Today's announcements mark the final chapter in the process that began in 2017, to remove reliance on unsustainable LIBOR rates and build a more robust foundation for the financial system. With limited time remaining, my message to firms is clear – act now and complete your transition by the end of 2021'.

5 As discussed in Part I of this text. This criticised the existing enforcement sanctions regime against individuals, recommended an overhaul of this and said that 'a criminal offence will be established applying to Senior Persons carrying out their professional responsibilities in a reckless manner, which may carry a prison sentence; following a conviction, the remuneration received by an individual during the period of reckless behaviour should be recoverable through separate civil proceedings'.

6 Note also the formal FCA response to this which was issued in October 2013 (FCA 2013d), for example.

7 www.bankofengland.co.uk/prudential-regulation/publication/2020/evaluation-of-the-senior-managers-and-certification-regime.

8 Much has been written about this and the rogue trader at the centre of the scandal, this link provides a useful summary: http://news.bbc.co.uk/1/hi/business/375259.stm. For an insight into the events that surrounded the emergence, Gapper and Denton (1996) provide a very readable text.

9 Again, much has been written on the subject of Enron, but the following website provides a useful overview of events: http://news.bbc.co.uk/1/hi/business/1780075.stm. For those interested in reading more about this *The Smartest Guys in the Room* by Bethany McLean and Peter Elkind in 2003 is recommended as a straightforward, interesting and highly readable text.

10 Including the memorable *Time* magazine Person of the Year cover of 30 December 2002 emblazoned 'The Whistleblowers' and showing Cynthia Cooper of Worldcom, Coleen Rowley of the FBI and Sherron Watkins of Enron.

11 www.fca.org.uk/firms/senior-managers-certification-regime.

12 www.fca.org.uk/firms/approved-persons/heads-compliance-mlros.

13 Note www.fca.org.uk and search on Fines for example.

14 Note www.reuters.com/business/us-sec-levies-39-bln-fines-fiscal-2021-2021-11-18/.

15 As is perhaps suggested by the continued flow of proceeds of crime through London, for example. For reada-ble insight into a related topic, note *Butler to the World*, Oliver Bullough, 2022.

16 Where it has, unfortunately, often been accompanied by words such as 'greed', 'self-serving' or 'toxic'.

17 An ongoing priority for regulators focus with regulator output at jurisdictional level on this as well as the global output previously highlighted. For example, note *Culture in financial services – a regulators perspec-tive*, www.bankofengland.co.uk/speech/2016/culture-in-financial-services-a-regulators-perspective and the FCA's 'Culture and governance' page: www.fca.org.uk/firms/culture-and-governance with its links to numer-ous related topics and output.

18 Ongoing challenges in respect of climate change and the need for fundamental shifts in approach to achieve stated objectives versus reluctance on the part of stakeholders to make those changes where these impact on an established way of doing things provides a pertinent example of this.

19 We also see examples of what could be deemed 'work arounds' being found for certain rules or restrictions put in place, technically abiding by the rules but not necessarily the 'spirit' of them, what does this imply about commitment in this regard? Might the approach to capping of banker's bonuses and the subsequent increase in bankers' salaries in the UK be an example of this? See www.bbc.co.uk/news/business-12238763 and then, more recently, calls for a removal on the cap www.ft.com/content/d3fc81d8-0f29–4069-9f51–9eb9605c24f0.

20 Interested parties may therefore wish to research further and there are ample sources available via an internet search on this topic.

21 Greg Smith (2012). Note www.bbc.co.uk/news/magazine-17380418 for background and links.

22 A recent publication from a former employee of the Goldman Sachs *Bully Market: My Story of Misogyny at Goldman Sachs* highlights issues of harassment, greed and bullying that suggest ongoing challenges in the culture of this particular organisation.

23 The often-quoted assertion attributed to Peter Drucker (author, consultant and considered the father of mod-ern business management) that 'Culture eats strategy for breakfast', although a slight misquote (refer to www.drucker.institute for clarification around this) neatly encapsulates this point.

24 'Beyond the fear factor …', in *inCompliance – Quarterly Journal of the International Compliance Association*, summer 2013.

25 Note group30.org/images/uploads/publications/G30_Culture2018_FNL3lo-compressed.pdf.

26 The current emphasis on ESG matters (Environmental, Social, Governance) and concerns around 'Green-washing' (see www.fca.org.uk/news/press-releases/fca-proposes-new-rules-tackle-greenwashing for exam-ple) provides a practical illustration of what can happen when endeavours to *appear* to be acting in accordance with certain expectations such as to enhance reputation can be in sharp contrast with reality, highlighting concerns around this.

27 *Compliance and the Compliance Function in Banks*, Introduction point 5, note Appendix 3, as discussed in Chapter 4.

28 OECD (2010a), adopted 18 February 2010.

29 legalinstruments.oecd.org/en/instruments/OECD-LEGAL-0378#mainText.

30 European Banking Authority (EBA) 2011–2021, www.eba.europa.eu/sites/default/documents/files.

31 www.iso.org/standard/75080.html.

32 Numerous commentaries on this, note *The Advantage: Why Organisational Health Trumps Everything Else in Business*, P M Lencioni, and also www.thecorporategovernanceinstitute.com/insights/guides/examples-of-good-company-cultures-and-why-culture-matters/ for example.

33 G30, October 2013.

34 Group of Thirty (G30) 2012.

35 Ibid, p. 5.

36 Interestingly, however, throughout this document the term Compliance Officer or similar is not used at all. Reference is instead made to the Chief Risk Officer, though it does acknowledge that 'Compliance functions in certain major institutions are going beyond their traditional role to form judgments on internal attitudes and standards'.

37 FSA (2002). In this many of the topics that became the focus of UK financial services regulators priorities during the post-global financial crisis overhaul can be clearly seen.

38 Numerous commentaries to this effect over recent years, but note www.bbc.com/worklife/article/20220223-are-workers-really-quitting-over-company-values and hbr.org/2021/05/what-your-future-employees-want-most, for example, plus also a more general study highlighting related points: www.greatplacetowork.co.uk/assets/Affiliate-UnitedKingdom/UKs-Best-Workplaces-22-Publication.pdf.

39 An ongoing consideration in the Compliance & Risk space, for example, as evidenced by the Thomson Reu-ters *Cost of Compliance* Surveys referred to in this text.

8

Compliance Challenges

CHALLENGES TO EFFICACY

The efficacy of the approach to compliance management within a firm will be evidenced by the results achieved. However, both in the actual conducting of activities in pursuit of such goals and in its approach to them, the Compliance function and the Compliance professionals working within it face challenges. These range from the practical (such as those involving resource and areas of focus, for example) through to those of a more behavioural nature (such as involving personnel and their approach to their role), together with many others in between. How effective the function is will ultimately be determined by how it overcomes the challenges it will invariably face.

CHALLENGE AREAS

The challenges faced by Compliance (both the function and the personnel who work within it), though varied in their specifics, can broadly be grouped into three categories derived from the main elements of the role as discussed in Part II, though of course there will likely be some overlap:

- practicalities;
- activities;
- approach.

This categorisation impacts not only on understanding of the implications of such challenges but also on practical methods of addressing them, as these tend to follow similar patterns. In order to appreciate them more fully, we will consider examples within each category, discussing the potential consequences when they arise and how these might broadly be addressed. Inevitably, not all challenges experienced by Compliance professionals will be covered here, for the Compliance role and the experience of those working within this arena will vary from individual to individual, firm to firm, sector to sector, jurisdiction to jurisdiction, with each as varying in specifics as the regulatory and compliance environments themselves. Nevertheless, the inclusions within this chapter are indicative of the type of issues that are likely to present themselves at one time or another and should provide food for thought regarding mechanisms to assist in addressing them

DOI: 10.4324/9781003431305-12

as we reflect on why Compliance matters, as discussed in the previous chapter. Throughout our consideration of those we do select though, as before we will draw on sources emanating from the many stakeholders involved in the regulatory and compliance environments, utilising published reports, the output of a range of studies and interviews, speeches from key individuals, surveys and statistics.

As we examine how practicalities impact on both the initial formation and the ongoing development of the Compliance function and framework, and on the function's activities and approach, there can be little surprise that challenges will arise in relation to both. Not only that, but some of them in particular will probably arise fairly frequently. In simple terms, the key to dealing with issues around practicalities, activities and approach, of whatever nature, is to:

- focus on their purpose in the context of the Compliance framework
- consider how and why an issue has arisen which challenges this
- link rectification back to their purpose in the overall Compliance framework
- address them on that basis, working with relevant stakeholders accordingly.

Let's now look at some example challenge areas under each of the three categories so that we might work through this approach in context.

Practicalities

These types of challenges are ever present and by their nature can be extremely wide-ranging, incorporating many aspects of the Compliance role.

Resource
Think of the challenges that might arise in relation to resource. Even in those firms which positively support the role of Compliance, the function may experience difficulties in securing sufficient resources to carry out the multitude of activities necessary to meet its many aims and objectives. Just as with any other business unit, the Compliance function is vying for a share from a finite supply. In the previously discussed *Cost of Compliance* surveys,[1] a decade ago approximately 50% of respondents anticipated a marginal increase in the budget during the year, but 33% anticipated their budget being the same or less than the previous year. The survey authors suggested that this might 'indicate that, in around a third of firms, budgetary constraints will lead to increased pressure on existing resource to do more'.[2] In 2022 'Lack of budget and resources' was highlighted as the second of the top five challenges by compliance practitioners, and it has regularly featured in the survey responses over the past decade, indicating this as an ongoing challenge. The Compliance function should recognise that resource and the securing thereof needs to be a regular consideration and should be active in supporting their case for the apportionment of adequate amounts. Activities as per the Compliance plan should be considered, including day-to-day on-demand requirements that arise, together with the resource required to address significant issues that (hopefully!) occur less frequently such as major problems, regulatory visits and so on.

The function should regularly reinforce the value to be gained from having effective compliance programmes and how this benefits the firm overall. In this regard, as focused on in Chapter 6, it is not only *what* is said that is important, but *how* it is said. This view is supported by the previously highlighted study in the *Journal of Business Compliance*,[3] focusing on mechanisms for the effective communication of the value to be gained from investment in compliance programmes and how these influence-related budget decisions.[4] As discussed in Chapter 5, this study sought to consider means by which the value of such programmes could more effectively be communicated, thus easing the process for all concerned and increasing the likelihood of securing appropriate resources to meet the requirements of all interested parties. Wider considerations need also be factored in, such as the allowances being made by regulators for having compliance programmes in place.[5]

> **Wider considerations need also be factored in, such as the allowances being made by regulators for having compliance programmes in place.**

Allocation of appropriate Compliance resource is a clear recognition of the integral role the function plays within the organisation. Not allocating sufficient resources to Compliance undermines the effectiveness of the business overall, with an impact on the immediate bottom line and longer-term reputation. Where challenges arise in this area, therefore, it behoves the function to address them promptly. This might include, for example developing standard operating procedures (SOPs) that take compliance matters into account, or ensuring business proposals consider pertinent resourcing requirements as an opportunity to reduce compliance risk. Approaching this with awareness of developments and research into best practices and recommending alternative solutions can be extremely helpful in doing so.

Workload

Issues of resource invariably impact on what the function does and indeed on what it is able to do. This gives rise to another challenge area: that of simply having too much to do. Remember, the Compliance function exists for a purpose: it has a set of objectives which its activities are intended to achieve on behalf of the firm in which it is located. If workload has reached a level where there is genuinely far too much to do to the point where the attainment of these objectives is compromised, then it is the responsibility of the function to flag this as an issue to the board and senior management. Not to do so would leave the function exposed in several ways: that is, not doing what it is mandated to do, but even more importantly than that, not ensuring that the board and senior management are aware of the fact so that they can factor the issue into their decision-making for the business overall. A recommendation of what action can be taken and the consequences of not addressing the resourcing issue should be made clear. For example, a request could be submitted for additional resources, to defer a particular activity/project or set of activities, to prioritise certain actions over others and so on and so forth, depending upon the situation. Essentially, it is all about managing expectations and keeping in mind the keyboard requirement we have highlighted previously: no surprises. If the function has undertaken to achieve certain objectives unless the board has been advised to the contrary, then that is what they will – quite reasonably – expect. In this context, it is the function's role to keep them appraised of issues arising and it is the board's role to address these as necessary.

Remember, the Compliance function exists for a purpose: it has a set of objectives which its activities are intended to achieve on behalf of the firm in which it is located.

Staffing

Resource is not, of course, confined only to funding, but also to actual staffing. Unfortunately, securing a sufficient budget to appoint staff is no guarantee of being able to do so or at least being able to appoint the *right* staff. Difficulties in this regard arise from a number of factors, including there being no single or longstanding established career or development pathway for individuals wishing to work in these roles as there would be in other professions, although developments in this area are ongoing. Most are recruited via multiple different routes and drawn from a variety of backgrounds, from the business, from internal audit, legal or accountancy roles, for example.[6]

Furthermore, though there will be some commonality in the range of knowledge and skills required to be effective in these roles (these being generally those as discussed in Chapter 6), individual Compliance functions will require specific expertise in different areas. Recruiting and retaining suitable individuals can therefore prove challenging. Of course, once in a role, staff can be developed, but, nevertheless, the appointment of the right staff in the first place is crucial. It is also important to note that (again as discussed in Chapter 6) it is not just about 'right' in the sense of an appropriate knowledge and skills set, but also about behaviours and approach to the role.

The lack of availability of suitable staff is an ongoing area of concern, as touched on in Part II. For example, while a recent survey[7] indicated 94% of candidates were confident in the current job market, 93% of employers flagged finding it 'challenging to find skilled talent today'. The reasons for this will vary but might reflect wider issues such as the attractiveness of working in this and related professions when compared to other areas of business, experienced practitioners growing older and electing to retire, insufficient pipeline of new practitioners, all of which may well reflect wider societal issues such as shifting work patterns, or increasingly aging populations, for example. Horizon scanning, considering requirements across the function, balancing skills sets, anticipating the need and planning accordingly will all help with managing requirements in these areas.

Retention post-appointment is another issue for consideration. The expertise and skills developed in a Compliance setting are highly sought after[8] and as a consequence, staff can be open to transfers to other departments or departures to rival firms. There is also the fact that these are challenging roles, particularly at higher levels, make no mistake about that. As a consequence, although this is a professional area that is in the ascendance, providing an interesting and challenging working environment that is attractive to many and with increasingly good remuneration packages,[9] the many difficulties that accompany it can pose challenges for individuals to the point where some opt for alternative careers or consider doing so.[10]

Lastly, it's important to recognise the changes taking place in the wider working environment, with staff increasingly seeking more than simply higher salaries. Factors such as work/life balance, the opportunity to work from home, career development and improved benefits regularly feature in terms of what staff are looking for, while generational shifts in terms of what is being prioritised by individuals will also play their part.[11] For those tasked with resourcing and developing the function and those who work within it, recruitment and development of staff poses some significant challenges, not least because to do so effectively can be extremely time-consuming. Other functions within business will necessarily be involved in such matters (such as Human Resources departments[12] which will often take the lead in recruitment, particularly in larger firms) and developing effective working relationships with such will be helpful in ensuring a sufficiently rounded approach is adopted within the business to ensure desired objectives are met.

Change
Tangible considerations such as resources aside, another significant challenge area for Compliance is change, not least because of the consequences it has for the Compliance framework overall. Being aware of changes, both internally and externally and particularly in key areas such as regulation, is vital if the Compliance function's approach and activities are to remain current and relevant. Key stakeholders within the firm rely on the function to appraise them of current or anticipated changes that will impact on the firm, so that they can adjust their own approach accordingly. External parties want to be confident that regulated firms, and thus the Compliance functions within them, are on top of these. Being aware of relevant changes in the Compliance environment that will affect compliance activities and approach is certainly challenging, mainly because of the sheer volume of change. An area of much concern to Compliance officers as flagged in the *Cost of Compliance* surveys relates to regulatory change and implementation thereof. Indeed, many of the challenges for Compliance highlighted by respondents related to change in one form or another.[13] The function should ensure adequate plans are in place to monitor relevant sources for information on the impending and imminent change. Consideration can then be given to consequences for the business arising as a result, and to then disseminate this information to interested parties, so that the appropriate action can be taken.

In larger Compliance functions, there may be specific individuals or indeed teams of individuals with responsibility for this undertaking. In smaller firms, this might be just one responsibility amongst many for the few staff in situ. Either way, it is incumbent upon the function to prioritise this activity on an ongoing basis. Keeping up to date, not only with a focus on specific changes but also in relation to consultations, projects, studies, reports and so on, essentially anything that could impact on the function's purpose, is crucial for the effective performance of the Compliance role for all the reasons previously outlined. Because this too is invariably time-consuming, it also can be challenging. As with any changes, however, key stakeholders within the firm rely on the function to appraise them of relevant developments, so they can factor these into their own approach, it is also important for all stakeholders to be confident of the Compliance function's relevance and abilities and being seen to be up to date with developments is an effective means of demonstrating this. With that in mind, Compliance keeping up to date with the activities and output of all the relevant influencers highlighted in Part I and discussed in the context of the Compliance environment in Part II should be seen as a prime necessity.[14]

A useful practical example of how important this is are those challenges that arise from the practical implementation of either new requirements or those which are receiving heightened focus. 'Extra-territoriality' provides a useful illustration of this. This is a serious topic for many, requiring specific focus and resource. Essentially, its premise is that it is not enough for firms to concern themselves only with the relevant laws of the land in their own jurisdiction and those of their overseas subsidiaries and so on, the extra-territorial laws[15] that exist require far more than that. In an illuminating article in the *Journal of Business Compliance*,[16] the reach of extra-territorial laws was highlighted, as was the fact that so few companies were aware of the threats facing their business as a result of these, with a number fined at significant levels for violations as a consequence.[17] The Compliance function should make it their business to familiarise themselves with the requirements of these laws as they apply to their individual firm. They should seek assistance from legal experts as necessary, and ensure measures are in place to address these or, at the very least, that consideration of these issues is on the board's agenda.

Alongside this, for the individual Compliance professional themselves, maintaining a good current awareness of issues that may impact on the role and thus the profession is also desirous, as there may be personal consequences in terms of new areas of focus within their current role. Increasingly, we are seeing that ongoing and interrelated changes are part of our operational landscape, rather than one-offs, with an increased need in capacity to accommodate and adjust, both at the firm and individual level. This might prompt the need for specific training or involvement in a different aspect of the role, or alternatively flagging opportunities for development or career advancement. We will return to this point in the final chapter.

Lack of Experience

In a constantly shifting operational environment and with the challenge of keeping up to date in all its many forms, lack of experience will prove a challenge for many. Unfortunately, experience only comes with familiarity and it is not possible to fully appreciate what a Compliance role involves until it has actually been experienced! This is where the support (of peers, perhaps, or that of a mentor: topics that will be discussed in detail in the last chapter of this text) can be particularly useful. However, remember that many of the skills needed to be effective in a Compliance role mirror those of a successful senior manager and individual Compliance professionals will undoubtedly have displayed many of these or they likely would not have been appointed. As to dealing with a particular challenge where there is the potential to feel overwhelmed, obtaining information, guidance and support from relevant sources should be seen as a priority (followed by taking a deep breath and getting on with it: it probably won't have been the first challenge faced, it certainly won't be the last!).

Isolation

Isolation can present challenges for those in the Compliance function. Physical isolation should be addressed by liaison with key stakeholders regarding the location of the Compliance function within the firm (as discussed in Part II). Information on the likely benefits of the function being located closer to the business should be provided together with an indication of the potential dangers of not doing so (such as those noted in some of the scandal-focused cases highlighted in Appendix 4, for example). Alternatively, if that is not possible due to issues of a practical nature (such as building constraints, for example, or the increase in remote working over recent years) then those within the Compliance function should make an even greater commitment to ensuring visibility. Walking the building, attending formal and informal meetings and get-togethers, seeing and being seen, speaking to staff, being part of discussions and so on – all as would usually be done (and as discussed in Part II), but with a necessary additional effort to overcome the physical isolation. As to personal isolation, which might more often occur in smaller businesses with consequently few or indeed potentially only a single member of Compliance staff, this can be addressed predominantly by 'getting out there' externally to the firm: mixing with others who are in the same or similar roles. In the early days, many Compliance officers struggled in this regard. To address this many of us made efforts over the years to develop both individual and then wider networks of fellow professionals working in similar areas. Compliance professionals of today can benefit hugely from those efforts. Membership of such groups and the ability to liaise with others really help address feelings of isolation in this challenging role. Suggestions as to associations and bodies that might be of interest are set out in Appendix 2. The final chapter of this text, with its focus on further enabling the Compliance function's role, provides a number of additional mechanisms which would also be of benefit in this regard.

Support (or Lack Thereof)

An obvious mechanism for addressing the challenge of any form of isolation lies in the quality of the support available, not only from the board and senior management (although obviously their endorsement of the function is important), but within the business itself. Linked to poor understanding and perception of the Compliance role this should be addressed through liaison with key stakeholders to ensure that there is *practical* support in place. This includes that such as sufficient resource, appropriate reporting lines, mechanisms for communication of compliance findings, fora for discussions of compliance-related issues and so on. This should be followed by, as discussed in Part II, addressing more general issues that contribute to supporting the activities of the function, the general attitude towards the function and its activities, looking at what the culture within the firm is like, how the attitude of key stakeholders towards compliance manifests, for example. An objective assessment of all such issues should be made and, once weaknesses are identified that impact upon how supported Compliance is within the firm, efforts made to address these. Considering how best to do this will vary depending upon circumstances, but as well as those previously cited internal activities within the firm, might also extend to external activities such as increased engagement with peers through membership of professional bodies, liaison with an appropriately experienced mentor, or work with professional business coaches.

Compliance Structure/Location

Other practical Compliance challenges might occur as a consequence of how the function is structured, such as in terms of location and reporting lines, or whether aspects of the function are outsourced. For example:

- If all Compliance activities are confined to a central hub (that is, within a centralised function), but business activities take place in satellite or divisional areas, there is a danger that the function will not be able to respond promptly to issues occurring or emerging. This might be because they were not aware of them as quickly as they should have been (if at all). Alternatively, potential issues might be overlooked for similar reasons. These and other such concerns could lead to the Compliance function not achieving its aims. Essentially, Compliance could end up being too remote from the actual business and so being distanced from the practical consequences of their activities and approach. This may give rise to problems and perpetuate those problematic historical perceptions of the function previously discussed. Conversely, those working in decentralised functions might find that, though this approach might have addressed some of the potential challenges arising under the centralised structure, they are faced with a new set of challenges. For example, there is the danger of individual Compliance functions in the satellite sites developing their own set of approaches, their own 'culture' almost, or potentially seeing themselves only as part of the business in which they are situated, rather than part of the Compliance function as a whole. Being mindful of such possibilities would go a long way towards preventing them, especially so in organisations operating in multiple jurisdictions.

- As to reporting lines, even if ostensibly appropriate and reflecting best practices (as discussed in Part II), challenges can still occur. Reporting lines should be regularly assessed to ensure they work well. For example, though Compliance reporting to the board is recommended, the practical consequence of that might be that the function faces difficulties in actually being able to arrange a meeting with relevant board members, because of their busy schedules and many commitments. Mechanisms should be put in place to address this, a practical workaround adopted if necessary.

- Structure/location challenges in respect of outsourcing, as is increasingly taking place. These might arise in relation to the performance of the third party to whom responsibilities have been outsourced. However, it is to be hoped that through thorough vetting at the outset and ongoing review throughout, such issues would be mitigated (or at the least identified promptly) then swiftly resolved. If issues occur, once they have been addressed, a review of what happened should always take place. This should include revisiting procedures, systems and controls and so on to identify where enhancements can be made to ensure a better outcome next time. There has been a flagging of concerns regarding outsourcing in some sectors,[18] particularly in relation to 'recovery and resolution plans', and additional useful guidance has been issued as a result.[19]

  - The practicality of structures also needs to be considered in the context of resource, as discussed previously. For example, limitations in this regard might dictate structure at a particular time, while lack of staff (due to recruitment availability challenges perhaps, or absence due to illness, and so on) might necessitate re-organisation on a temporary basis.

Technology

Practical challenges arise from technology. The ever-increasing use of such for all manner of activities has become an accepted norm across the world and improvements in its efficiency have enriched the interconnectivity of all parties and processes involved. There has been a resulting explosion in the speed and opportunity of delivery mechanisms for financial services that have arisen from it. Alongside this, the increasing immediacy of transaction and information exchange has had a notable impact on the activities of both consumers and firms, indeed on the operations and approach of all stakeholders within financial services.

Technological advances have contributed to the expansion of product and service innovations, which in turn have significantly impacted on the Compliance environment.[20] The development of more complex activities has consequences for the development of regulation because, as the level of complexity has increased, so too has the level of regulation intended to support these activities and the challenges, including risks, arising therefrom. Fortunately, the technological advances that give rise to these in respect of timeliness and complexity also provide the means for addressing them. There have been some excellent advances in technology designed to assist in assessment and monitoring. Many firms are investing in these. Compliance functions should familiarise themselves with what is out there and consider this in the context of the business conducted in their own firm.[21] Expansion of hybrid-working type approaches to working style, including an increased level of working from home for many roles, brings with it a number of challenges that need to be carefully considered, such as data security implications for example. Essentially, investment to the degree necessary to meet the challenges presented by the location, nature, scale and complexity of business conducted by the organisation should be taken as a given. If not, then recommendations (supported as always by evidence of benefits to be gained and likely dangers if not), should be made to those with funding responsibilities.

Credibility

Our final example area of practical challenges relates directly to Compliance personnel themselves, i.e. the standing of Compliance professionals and their credibility. First, let's consider the standing issue. Although the Compliance role is increasingly recognised as one that in many ways is on par with other professional roles such as those performed by in-house lawyers, it is not always seen as such and some within the business may simply not understand what it is all about. This lack of understanding might manifest in a number of ways. For example, there may be some, perhaps those working in roles that do not have direct interaction with the function, who do not appreciate what the purpose of the Compliance role is and thus why they need to interact with the function. Alternatively, there may be others who have an outmoded or inaccurate understanding of the role and its purpose, perhaps seeing it simply as an 'insurance policy' for the business against the possibility of regulatory censure. Addressing a lack of understanding through education and training should be a prime activity for the Compliance function: you will recall this was one of the four main areas of Compliance activity and approach discussed in Part II. Such endeavours should focus not only on providing information on the Compliance role and the activities undertaken in pursuit of this but also addressing issues relating to culture, expectations and so forth.

To a large degree, the standing of an individual Compliance officer within a firm is shaped by practical issues. These include their position with the company (whether they are a member of the senior management team, a director, at the general management level and so on), reporting lines and the prevailing attitude of senior staff. Where challenges arise in this regard, questions have to be asked regarding the approach to compliance requirements within the firm. Are they embedded within business practice and undertaken as a matter of routine within general operations, so that it is routine to all those involved? Or are they an additional consideration, an 'extra' requirement that necessitates separate thought? What is the culture within the firm like? What is the attitude of key stakeholders towards compliance? How does this manifest? An objective assessment of all such issues should be made, and weakness that can impact on the embedding of compliance requirements identified and then addressed. Consider again the scenarios highlighted in Chapter 6. Think about how these might provide challenges for Compliance and Compliance professionals and how these might be tackled. Look again at the real-life cases in Chapters 1 and 7; consider how compliance and indeed Compliance was viewed in these organisations and how this contributed to the events described.

Externally, how Compliance is viewed will differ, dependent on the eye of the beholder. In being increasingly accepted as a vital component in the risk management framework, in some jurisdictions and sectors this has resulted in an overall uplift in the standing of Compliance professionals, with an enhanced view of the role as a profession akin to other professions. The growth in related professional bodies and associations at both international and national levels[22] provides a focus for individuals working in this area. Opportunities to network and develop are available, while Compliance qualifications are becoming far more prevalent and indeed increasingly becoming necessary. This is because they are either mandatory or desired by regulators as a requirement of authorisation for appointment in such roles.[23] Those working in Compliance can enhance their standing internally through attention to practical issues such as addressing their formal position within the organisation, reporting lines and so forth. In addition, they can enhance how they are perceived generally within their role through the way in which they approach it and the results achieved, as discussed in Part II.

Individuals can work to develop the perception of Compliance more widely through activities as varied as involvement in industry initiatives – for example, being members of working parties on key topics, responding to discussion papers, attending conferences, developing relationships with key third parties and so on. They can also obtain recognised qualifications in this area and join professional associations, teaming up with fellow compliance professionals, forming professional relationships with others with whom they can share views and opinion, exchange ideas, developing a web of networks at both a national and international level of others working in similar roles and having similar experiences. Essentially, by developing the standing of the profession in the same way other professions have developed in the past. Means by which the Compliance role can be further enabled are explored in Chapter 9, recommending a variety of ways in which the standing of Compliance professionals can be further improved.

Alongside this enhancement in the standing of the Compliance role sits the issue of credibility, which has undoubtedly been called into question in the years since the global financial crisis, as have most regulatory risk and regulation-related roles. Simply put, Compliance programmes were in place and yet scandals still occurred. Compliance officers themselves played a role in those firms involved in scandals over recent years (refer again to the cases discussed in Chapter 7). It may therefore be asked why didn't the programmes have any effect, where were the Compliance officers and why weren't they able to prevent the wrongdoing? Some might agree this is a fair enough point, and some might say this very question indicates a lack of knowledge about the Compliance role, but there is much to be learned from examination of such cases and considering what the actual role of Compliance and the Compliance Officer in such firms was: did they genuinely have a role which exemplified the central tenets of the Compliance function as discussed in Part II (Independence, Adequate resources, Clear areas of responsibility – three key features considered vital to the effective performance of the Compliance role)? What were their reporting lines? Were they taken seriously in their role? What within the culture of the firm allowed such activity to flourish unchecked? What role did Compliance have in influencing this? These and many more such questions can usefully be asked in relation to scandals that emerge, in considering the efficacy of the Compliance role and what can be learned from this. The examples included in Appendix 4 are useful in reflecting on this, alongside those in Appendix 5 where the Compliance officers themselves were specifically flagged as being at fault and being sanctioned by the regulator as a result. Key stakeholders within business can learn much from such examples which will no doubt be studied intensively over the coming years, and Compliance officers would do well to learn from the perceived inaction or ineffectiveness of their peers in the past. In doing so, they can then reflect on their own approach to and their role within Compliance and how this might usefully be adjusted. Examples of where things have gone wrong are a valuable tool for learning and for identifying mechanisms for addressing challenges as they arise.

Activities

Ongoing, exceptional, planned or on-demand, the activities of the function can give rise to any number of challenges – challenges arising both during their actual conduct and also those surfacing thereafter.

Training and Education

Let's begin by considering one of the four main areas of Compliance activity (as discussed in Part II). The impact of training and education activities has a wide reach. Effective training, tailored to the desired objectives and working to embed lasting behavioural change, will reverberate throughout the firm, contributing positively to Compliance goals. For it to be valuable, Compliance should consider training in all its many guises: for example, not necessarily just directly focused compliance training but feeding Compliance requirements into other forms of training. They should see every interaction as a training and education opportunity, howsoever subtle this might be.

Where vital training and education activities are challenged by resource in terms of time and expertise, it is the responsibility of the function to flag this as an issue to the board and senior management. This should be accompanied by a recommendation of what action can be taken to mitigate this and the consequences of not doing so. For example, just as with some of the practical issues discussed earlier in this chapter, submit a request for additional resource, defer a particular activity/project or set of activities and so on and so forth, depending upon the situation.

Communication

Another challenging area linked to activities is communication. Like training and education, this plays a vital role in supporting the Compliance message. Clear, concise and appropriately worded communications that meet the needs of the target audience are essential. For example, the tone and language appropriate for communication in a board report differ from that appropriate for communication of a regulatory update to business management or a guidance note for new sales staff. Compliance personnel need to ensure they tailor their communications appropriately. Likewise, consideration should be given to verbal communication and the skills discussed in Part II. Drawing on these skills to ensure any communication, in whatever format, is appropriate will go a long way towards enhancing the Compliance message and overcoming any potential hurdles.

Monitoring, Testing and Reporting

Turning now to another of the four primary areas of Compliance activity, monitoring, testing and reporting activities could give rise to a host of challenge areas. Take, for example, the handling of breaches (either of regulatory or compliance requirements) – how effectively these are managed will to a large degree influence the consequences arising from the breach. While never desirable, 'near misses' can provide valuable lessons which if taken on board can help prevent an actual breach. In this sense, they should be regarded reasonably positively and as an indication that the firm's 'early warning system' is working. See them as a learning opportunity and work with the business to ensure there is no recurrence. Look out for patterns – does this look to be an isolated near miss or is it part of a developing theme? Which part of the business does it relate to? Essentially, undertake an objective assessment of all the issues around the breach and weaknesses identified that have contributed to and could lead to a recurrence.

As to actual breaches of regulatory requirements, the systems and controls put in place and the various procedural mechanisms that support these should have ensured that a regulatory breach was identified promptly. If not, then the system for flagging these should certainly be revisited. However, the primary concern should be dealing with the breach itself (in terms of taking prompt action to prevent further occurrences, minimising consequences arising from it, for example) and reporting it (both internally and externally), only then followed by handling the fallout from it. This should include considering issues such as: how was a breach allowed to occur without triggering the firm's early warning system? This should then be revisited. Were all procedures followed in the lead-up to the occurrence of the breach? If so, how was the breach able to occur? Does the breach appear to be an isolated incident or indicative of a bigger problem? Is it linked to breaches occurring elsewhere and if so how are these related? And so on.

Raising Issues/Flagging Concerns

Inevitably, as a result of what is involved in the Compliance role and the output of its activities, there may be occasions on which its personnel will be the bearers of bad news, be this to the board, to the business units or whomever. This can give rise to another area of challenges. In addressing them, however, it is important to remember that whatever the issue or response *it's not personal*. Keep in mind the purpose of the Compliance role, the vital service it provides to the business and approach discussions relating to 'bad news' from that perspective.

As a result of monitoring, testing and reporting there may arise additional challenges, possibly involving potentially difficult interactions with stakeholders both within and without the business. For example, it may be necessary to challenge the actions of others: the board, the business, possibly even the regulator. The focus throughout all of these interactions should be on clarity and focusing on the benefit the function is providing in identifying and flagging these issues, all linked to the purpose of the role:

- Challenging a board decision or idea is never going to be an easy task but the challenge is important to ensure that their decisions are made with the fullest available knowledge of the potential consequences. As with so many Compliance activities, the way in which these are approached is key to their efficacy. This is also where efforts to establish a helpful and supportive reputation and to nurture effective professional relationships with all key personnel (as discussed in Part II) will help.
- A challenge might arise whereby it is necessary to present business units or key personnel within them of findings which indicate they are not acting as they should be. Just as with the board, it will be on such occasions that efforts to establish and nurture effective professional relationships with all key personnel will prove invaluable. In addition, efforts made to genuinely involve Compliance in relevant business activities (such as project planning or product/service development, for example, in addition to specific 'compliance'-related activities) will have reinforced the Compliance role within and as part of the business. Therefore, suggestions, requests for clarification or challenges are likely to be viewed more positively, as they will be seen as intended for the good of the firm and all stakeholders as a consequence.

Be sure of your facts, supporting your points with evidence. Be clear on the implications of proceeding in the same manner or as intended: what the implications will be and for whom, what the consequences are and for which of the various stakeholders. If possible, provide alternative solutions. Employ your skills and attributes to positively support discussions.

Of course, the board or the business areas may not accept the challenges raised and may challenge right back! There may be one (or more) of a number of reasons for this. For example, where the challenge relates to issues identified in current practice through Compliance-monitoring activities there can sometimes be a tendency for those on the receiving end to take a defensive stance, perhaps because they are feeling threatened. Or perhaps there might be a reason for a particular occurrence that Compliance simply weren't aware of, which might have implications for current or future practice and plans. In the first instance, you should always be sure of your ground. Check, check and check again, ask questions, and clarify any areas of uncertainty, *before* you challenge. If, having done so, you become aware of a mitigating issue that changes the position, acknowledge this, again employing your skills and attributes to assist. But also take time to look again at your procedures so you can ensure if at all possible that there is no repeat of such an incident: it is an important part of building Compliance credibility that there can be confidence in your approach.

Depending on the type of business undertaken within a firm, interaction with regulators can be fairly frequent and much can be required of firms to provide the necessary reassurance that the regulator is seeking. Most of this will be routine and should not prove too onerous if approached appropriately. However, there may arise occasions where it will be necessary to challenge the approach or actions of the regulator – it does happen! There is a useful historic example of a particularly challenging case of note in the UK which had an impact on the perception of the then regulator (the FSA). This was the landmark case of *L&G v. the FSA*.[24] The case had notable repercussions for the regulator and raised many pertinent issues about the regulatory approach. It also focused attention on the role of the Compliance Officer in challenging the regulator. In this case, dissatisfied with the FSA's enforcement methods, which resulted in a fine, L&G took the case to the Financial Services & Markets Tribunal. The tribunal reduced the fine imposed and was critical of the FSA's approach.[25] From a positive perspective, this case showed that where regulated firms are unhappy with the manner in which they are being regulated, they do have a means of challenge. From the firm's perspective, this was a positive result. However, from the regulator's perspective and that of the wider regulatory community, there are downsides. Criticisms of the regulator reflected poorly on it overall, questioning the validity of their supervisory and enforcement process. Subsequently, although ostensibly not as a direct result of this case, the FSA fully reviewed its enforcement process and enhanced its enforcement guidance.

More recently, the findings of the Gloster report into the collapse of London Capital & Finance Plc made uncomfortable reading for the FSA's successor, the FCA, making it clear that failures in the regulator's regulatory action contributed to the outcome: 'The report concludes the FCA did not effectively supervise and regulate LCF during the relevant period, and makes nine recommendations for the FCA, focusing on how they should improve their internal authorisation and supervision processes'.[26] Publication of the report led to an apology from Andrew Bailey, head of the FCA throughout much of the relevant period,[27] and prompted further action.[28]

The ongoing focus on more judgement-led supervision amidst outcome-focused regulation will inevitably lead to a greater challenge by firms and senior management. As this beds in we await indication of the practical consequences of this shift in approach. More usually, however, the challenge of the regulator would be of a more low-key nature. While querying what the regulator is asking of the firm or the way in which they are looking for something to be done is straightforward, pushing back on regulatory demands can be daunting. However, provided such requests are reasonable and well-grounded, there is no reason to be concerned. Remember, the regulators want to view you positively unless given a reason not to. This is another area where efforts made to develop a reasonable relationship with them will be of benefit. Furthermore, if the reputation of the firm is positive (enhanced undoubtedly by your good work within the Compliance function) and the reasons for your request well-grounded, there should be few issues with this. As with internal challenges, take care to position your request appropriately, supporting this with evidence of impact and offering an alternative approach, while employing your skills and attributes to positively support communication and subsequent discussions.

The Regulatory Visit

A singular challenge for the Compliance function will be the notification of an impending visit by the regulator. Whether a visit to a particular organisation in isolation, part of a thematic review or similar, such can be time and resource intensive. The Compliance function would need to be at the centre of preparations for the review or visit beforehand, then closely involved and coordinating activities both while it is taking place and again thereafter. Accordingly, there would be challenges arising in terms of a whole host of activities and practicalities. Factors that would need to be considered here would include practical measures such as gathering requested/required information and ensuring physical space available for the duration, as well as ensuring the availability of key staff and preparing them as necessary. An activity such as this is an important periodic undertaking and is a real test of the Compliance function and the personnel within it.

Balancing Commercial Reality v. Regulatory Requirements
Throughout the conduct of Compliance activities, challenges will arise in balancing commercial reality with regulatory requirements. An inevitable part of business life, this is all about getting the balance right. In many ways, taking into account the aims and objectives of all parties will help find common ground and therefore go a long way towards achieving a balance. There are of course certain boundaries that cannot be crossed: certain regulatory requirements that are a must, not simply desirous. Educate the business about what these are, ensure they know what is permissible and what is not, so that all approaches and activities can be developed with these in mind right from the outset. Where errors are noted, it is not just a question of identifying and flagging but also going back to find out why these occurred. It is perfectly possible to balance commercial reality with regulatory requirements though it is not always easy. However, reminding relevant stakeholders of the potential consequences of overstepping the mark can often do the trick.

Unexpected Events
Being alert to the impact of unexpected events – in the immediate or longer term, arising from external or internal factors – is an ongoing consideration for businesses. From the Compliance functions perspective, consideration of this in the context of regulation is the primary focus and a key part of the Compliance role is to ensure the board are aware of any such arising. Contributing to development of crisis management or disaster recovery planning within the firm at an appropriate level from a regulatory compliance perspective is necessary if the function is to be able to support the firm as needed should such risk manifest, including the reporting of where, why and how exceptions might occur and what the relevance of these are in the context of achievement of objectives.[29]

Human Nature
Finally, when conducting activities, Compliance will be faced with challenges that relate, quite simply, to human nature. There will always be those who rail against any form of constraint on their actions. It is impossible to fully regulate human behaviour – at best, regulation can tame this somewhat. There will always be those who are non-compliant, some who choose not to listen. The best systems and controls in the world will be useless if they are not followed, all of which have definite implications for the efficacy of Compliance activities. To as great a degree as possible, potentially problematic human behaviour should be curtailed by robust and effective systems and controls so as to encourage appropriate actions and minimise opportunities to act contrary to requirements. There should be clear consequences for non-adherence to these, supported by the board,

senior management and key stakeholders within the business. Repeat offences should be addressed and action taken against such offenders. If certain standards are set and adherence to these is regarded as mandatory, conscious decisions not to comply should be dealt with in order to reinforce the message that these are to be taken seriously.

Nevertheless, a wise Compliance professional will always recognise that human nature is a force to be reckoned with, and consider the relevance of 'people risk'.[30] They will build in measures to mitigate this while keeping an eye out for circumstances that might challenge these. Essentially:

- make it as straightforward as possible to comply
- as difficult as possible not to
- put in place adequate checks to ensure compliance
- challenge non-adherence
- take enforcement action where necessary.

In this, it is all about the approach to the role, which is the topic of our final set of Compliance challenges.

Approach

How compliance and the Compliance function itself is perceived and the challenges arising therefrom will be influenced by how the function operates day to day. In addressing this, emphasis should be on specific actions and approaches alongside the actual activities being undertaken. For example:

- *Approach*: Compliance professionals should exemplify through their own actions and attitude to their role the inherent aims of the function.
- *Conflicts of interest*: Maintaining awareness of potential or actual conflicts in the conduct of their role, taking steps to mitigate wherever possible and ensuring clarity in approach overall.
- *Relationship building*: As discussed in Part II and as must be apparent from earlier discussions on dealing with Compliance challenges in this chapter, focusing on enhancing relationships with those who have the greatest influence (either directly or indirectly) on others can be a very effective means of addressing negative perceptions. Think about whom and what to target: for example, what are the attitudes of key stakeholders towards Compliance? How does this manifest? What about issues such as the 'Mood from the Middle' in respect of others who influence attitudes?

Bringing all this to bear will be worth it, for challenges arising from or influencing how the Compliance function performs its role will never be too far away.

Culture

Take the culture of the firm, for example, which was discussed in detail in the previous chapter. Remember, 'Culture, more than rule books, determines how an organization behaves'.[31] As the beating heart of a firm, the very thing that makes it tick, its culture will shape the activities that are conducted within it and the attitude of all towards them. The attitude and approach of senior staff, from the board downwards, can have a defining impact on the culture of a firm and their views are ultimately reflected in the actions of the business. Should issues exist in relation to this, the Compliance function must work to challenge them. Where it is believed that the culture within a firm may not be helpful for the achievement of Compliance goals, an important part of the function's role will be in working to address this through their own activities and approach.

Awareness and sensitivity to this culture are key adapting to reflect requirements arising from it. For example, if the culture is extremely sales-focused, Compliance should consider what risks this might pose to the business and what measures are in place to mitigate these. They should factor this into their own risk assessment and subsequent approach, perhaps increasing checks in certain areas. Highlighting these issues during focused training would be useful, as would liaising with key personnel within business units, the board or senior management to address particular concerns, and so on and so forth. Awareness of the influence of culture on practices within the firm, and considering this within the approach taken by the function, will help meet this particular challenge.

Compliance activities, if not approached with sensitivity to the culture of the firm, can produce spectacularly negative results. In order to minimise the level of challenge:

- avoid taking a completely 'standardised' approach to Compliance activities
- Make efforts to understand the business perspectives and why they see things as they do.
- Consider what is appropriate for the firm, business unit, department, individual and so on and adjust accordingly, though remaining mindful of Compliance objectives.
- Reflect on the impact of the different Compliance scenarios discussed in Part II and the examples of wrongdoing or scandals we have looked at throughout this text, particularly those cases in Chapter 1.

Learn the lessons from these and take pains to avoid situations where Compliance operations will be perceived negatively.

Perception
Beyond issues of standing and credibility as previously touched on there is another important point to consider in examining how Compliance is perceived. This reflects the perceived view of where Compliance allegiances lie. Put simply, is the function viewed as a 'spy' for the regulator, there to feedback information on wrongdoing or incorrect behaviour on the part of the regulated firm? Of course not. But this view can provide something of a quandary for Compliance professionals. If this is an embedded perception, it can be particularly challenging. Once such a view has become entrenched amongst some or all key individuals within a regulated firm (particularly those with influence on others in one way or another), it will have a significant impact on interactions with the Compliance team. It might, for example, restrict the willingness of the business to share concerns or flag errors, for fear of this being passed straight on to the regulator with all the perceived connotations around that. With such obvious implications for the firm and for the efficacy of the Compliance function itself, this is a challenge that must be robustly

addressed (through judicious application of education and training throughout, for example) so that there is a more accurate understanding of the Compliance role and thus a greater willingness to cooperate between all parties concerned.

THE ULTIMATE COMPLIANCE PROFESSIONAL CHALLENGE?

Finally, a challenge that combines practicalities, activities and approach all in one – perhaps the ultimate set of challenges for the Compliance professional. Throughout their activities and their approach to their role, the Compliance function will flag issues to the board and senior management. They will raise concerns about potential compliance violations, ensure awareness of the possible consequences arising from these and recommend actions to address and challenge the business and the board where necessary. Throughout this, they will have documented their actions and their recommendations. If, having done all of this, over a protracted period they arrive at a position where they have serious concerns about an issue but are strongly of the view that it is not being addressed appropriately by those responsible for it, what then to do? Choices to respond are limited; essentially, this comes down to:

- *Wait it out*: to see if eventually the issue will resolve itself (but how long should one wait and what of the consequences of the issue continuing during this time)? The examples included in Appendix 5 might give some indication of the consequences of doing so ...
- *Walk away*: if the Compliance officer believes they and their concerns are not being taken seriously and despite their efforts they are not achieving results, they may choose this option.[32]
- *Whistle blow*: firms, sectors and jurisdictions have such schemes,[33] but what of consequences not only for the firm but also personally?

Given the consequences for both the function and the individual compliance professionals of any of these choices, the challenges in addressing them are many. With that in mind, consideration ought to be given to matters such as ensuring clarity around accountability and specifics in relation to responsibility, any personal liability implications (which will vary dependent upon jurisdiction and sector[34]) and mitigations (clarity of responsibility, insurance, and so on) necessary.

ENABLING COMPLIANCE

Attitudes towards compliance and Compliance will reflect those inherent in the Compliance function's performance and in that of the personnel who work within it. Though this chapter has identified a number of different challenges, elements of each challenge area are invariably reflected in others, as too are the mechanisms by which these might be addressed. More often than not, many of the day-to-day challenges faced by Compliance can be addressed or certainly mitigated to a notable degree through working with stakeholders. Taking action through adjusting work practices, training and education activities (particularly with management and key personnel) and working on relationship building are all valuable methods. However, we have seen a pattern emerging here regarding the impact that training and education activities together with advisory and guidance activities have on the efficacy of the Compliance role. This is where the efforts made in clarifying the role and benefits of the function, together with developing robust relationships with colleagues and others, will pay genuine dividends in helping to meet these challenges. It can also be seen that it is at times of challenge or difficulty that the skill of the personnel within the function really comes to the fore.

The benefits of an effective Compliance function – not only to the firm in which it is located but beyond it and to a wide range of stakeholders – should be evident by now. Actions to increase awareness of this should lie not only with the function itself, however, but with those very same stakeholders and the two of these in particular whose activities we have highlighted from the outset of this text as impacting significantly on the Compliance environment: the board of the regulated firm, and the regulator. How their actions, together with those of Compliance personnel themselves, can further enable the efficacy of the Compliance role, while also using their activities and approach for wider benefit, is the subject of our next and final chapter.

NOTES

1   Note that the 2013 survey was carried out between November 2012 and January 2013, comprising 800 Compliance practitioners, including Chief Executives and Heads of Compliance, from across 62 countries (spanning Africa, the Americas, Australasia, Europe and the Middle East) and spanning all financial services sectors (including bankers, brokers, insurers and asset managers). As previously highlighted, part of an ongoing series of annual surveys across similar respondents which since 2009 have provided useful insight into practical experience of the Compliance role.

2   Ibid., 'Financial Costs and Budget'.

3   The 2013 *Journal of Business Compliance* survey 'Measuring the value of compliance: Winning arguments for securing compliance budget …' was carried out in February and April 2013.

4   *Measuring the Value of Compliance: Winning Arguments for Securing Compliance Budget*, Smith-Meyer 2013.

5   For example, note the approach by SFO in the UK: www.sfo.gov.uk/publications/guidance-policy-and-protocols/guidance-for-corporates/evaluating-a-compliance-programme/. It is also interesting to note the approach in respect of particular types of compliance programmes, such as in respect of competition compliance programmes, as useful summary of which is provided here: www.reedsmith.com/en/perspectives/2020/09/should-compliance-programmes-enable-discounts-from-fines.

6   Recruitment firms often provide a useful source of information pertinent to recruitment of Compliance professionals. See the Barclay Simpson website for example: www.barclaysimpson.com/posts/tags-compliance.

7   Barclay Simpson, 2022, www.barclaysimpson.com/compliance.

8   The aforementioned Hammond and Walshe (2013) survey notes that 'competition for the most skilled staff will remain strong', while the 2022 survey identifies 'a significant need to recruit skilled and knowledgeable staff … with increased skill and experience comes a cost with these staff demanding more pay'.

9   Barclay Simpson's (2013) *Compensation and Market Trends Report 2013* highlights the fact that 'the average increase for Compliance professionals changing jobs is currently 17% while the average increase for those staying with their existing employer is 5%'. Note also this current salary survey insight: www.roberthalf.co.uk/salary-guide/details/compliance-analyst/london.

10   A survey by the US-based Society of Corporate Compliance & Ethics in June 2012 found that 60% of Compliance officers had considered leaving in the previous 12 months 'due to job related stress and frustration'. Anecdotally, this has continued and is often the reason cited for looking to change roles, either moving out of a compliance role or into a narrower one to reduce remit/risk.

11   An interesting insight into this is provided here: www.weforum.org/agenda/2022/02/what-do-employees-want-most-from-their-work-life-in-2022/, though there are many other publications on related topics.

12   Note the role of financial services HR departments in respect of the SM&CR and work in relation to this, for example.

13 Hammond and Walshe (2013), 'The Challenges Compliance Officers Anticipated in 2013', for example, and note Cost of Compliance surveys 2012, 2014, 2021 and 2022.

14 Ensuring relevant stakeholders are aware of the current hot topics and areas of focus – for example, including updates on key initiatives such as those discussed in Chapter 2.

15 For example, the US Foreign Corrupt Practices Act (FCPA) or the UK's Bribery Act 2010. See also www.sanctionsaml.com/extra-territoriality/ for additional commentary.

16 S.C. Blecker-van Eyk, 'The extraterritorial web', *Journal of Business Compliance*, 5, 2013.

17 Take, for example, the OFAC sanctions programme – home.treasury.gov/policy-issues/office-of-foreign-assets-control-sanctions-programs-and-information. Past sanctions imposed: RBS $100 million in December 2013, in 2012 HSBC $375 million and ING $619 million; more recently: 2022 Bitrex Inc. $24,280,829.20. Note the penalties and enforcement section on this website for further details.

18 For example, the FSAs Dear CEO letter *Review of Outsourcing Arrangements in the Asset Management Sector* of 11 December 2012. Available at: webarchive.nationalarchives.gov.uk/ukgwa/20130202001250mp_/http://www.fsa.gov.uk/static/pubs/ceo/review_outsourcing_asset_management.pdf.

19 Such as IMA's White Paper *Key Issues Arising for Asset Managers from the Regulatory Regime on Outsourcing* in May 2013 and FCA (2013f) report on its recent thematic review *Outsourcing in the Asset Management Industry: Thematic Project Findings Report* in November 2013. More recently note the FCA's Outsourcing and operational resilience guidance www.fca.org.uk/firms/outsourcing-and-operational-resilience which sets out implications and expectations in this area. Note also the FCA's DP22/3 Operational resilience: critical third parties to the UK financial sector www.fca.org.uk/publications/discussion-papers/dp22-3-operational-resilience-critical-third-parties-uk-financial-sector and the PRA's SS2/21 Outsourcing and third-party risk management: www.bankofengland.co.uk/prudential-regulation/publication/2021/march/outsourcing-and-third-party-risk-management-ss.

20 The changing nature of risk and risk management is pertinent here, as discussed in Chapter 3, with the impact of social media in the context of influences and influencers addressed Chapter 2 also relevant.

21 www.opriskglobal.com provides a helpful overview of the leading players in this area in the financial software sector. The Thomson Reuters *Fintech, Regtech and The Role of Compliance 2021* survey www.thomsonreuters.com/en-us/posts/investigation-fraud-and-risk/fintech-regtech-report-2021/ gives a useful insight into current practical challenges in this area, spanning topics such as growth, developing culture and challenges.

22 Such as those in Appendix 2, as previously discussed.

23 In Germany, the Federal Financial Supervisory Authority (BaFin) responsible for supervision of banks and financial services providers, insurance undertakings and securities trading stipulated in their Annual report for 2011 that 'In future, investment services enterprises wishing to engage certain employees in their sales operations will have to verify beforehand whether those individuals possess the necessary expertise and reliability. Besides investment advisers, who make up the most numerous group, sales representatives and compliance officers must also have minimum qualifications' (BaFin 2011). The UK example referred to in Part II provides a contrasting approach, together with an indication of more recent action in terms of the focus on head of Compliance and MLRO applicant competency and capability www.fca.org.uk/firms/approved-persons/heads-compliance-mlro-applicant-competency-capability.

24 Information on this case can be found by searching https://uk.practicallaw.thomsonreuters.com/ search under L & G v the FSA and see Legal & General: challenging the FSA.

25 FSA (2005).

26 www.gov.uk/government/news/independent-investigation-into-the-fcas-regulation-and-supervision-of-london-capital-finance-published.

27 www.thetimes.co.uk/article/bailey-apologises-as-report-slams-handling-of-scandal-fthg7jn5s.

28 questions-statements.parliament.uk/written-statements/detail/2020-12-17/hcws678.

29 As in the case of the coronavirus pandemic, for example, when regulation had to be agile to respond appropriately, with consequent impact on those regulated as they dealt with the day-to-day operational challenges within this. The UK's FCA provides an interesting podcast on this www.fca.org.uk/news/news-stories/chris-woolard-discusses-emergency-regulation-and-learning-coronavirus-crisis in which how they rapidly reprioritised work in light of this and implications for future business planning is discussed.

30 A good deal has been written on this specific area of risk and risk management, for example PWC provide some useful insight into this here: www.pwc.co.uk/services/human-resource-services/managing-people-risk.html.

31 The words of Warren Buffet, American businessman, philanthropist and considered the most successful investor of the twentieth century.

32 Being mindful, of course, of the relevant period of ongoing responsibility for holders of key positions are they have left their roles, which will differ by sector and jurisdiction.

33 This is becoming an increasingly political topic, and there are vast differences in attitudes to this across jurisdictions. An article in the *Journal of Business Compliance* 03-04/2014 provided an interesting round table debate discussing this different. Note the FCA www.fca.org.uk/firms/whistleblowing for the UK regulators stance on this, together with some useful practical case studies.

34 A useful summary of current positioning in respect of this is set out here: www.globalrelay.com/future-of-compliance-officer-liability/.

9

Enabling the Compliance Function

THE COLLECTIVE STAKEHOLDER ROLE

In this text, we have discussed the 'event reaction, event reaction, event reaction' regulatory approach to developments which has seemingly been endemic to our collective response to problems in this, or indeed any other, industry. As reports of new problematic events have emerged, requiring new actions to address them despite ongoing efforts to deal with the weaknesses identified in the previous problematic event, the calls for action inevitably become ever more urgent, encouraging a visible reaction ... and so we continue on. Reflect for a moment on the practical impact of the negative events of recent years on the financial services industry that we have discussed and how regularly the issue of problematic culture has featured; inevitably, therefore, addressing challenges relating to culture has increasingly been prioritised. In our renewed focus on positively changing the industry and in improving its culture overall, however, should we not focus on the role of *all* the different stakeholders in this, in maximising the contribution that can be made from them and use this to build a culture that is more reflective of what we, mutually, want? Might such joined-up thinking more effectively connect the many stakeholders who, as their collective name suggests, have a stake in the outcome of these endeavours and a real interest in ensuring these aims are met? Further enabling one of these, the Compliance function, which in performing its established role effectively means Compliance professionals operate at the core of business, is certainly a step towards this.

The Compliance function has, whether by design or simply from pragmatic need, carved out a role for itself that practically supports, on a day-to-day basis, the many aims that we, the wider stakeholders in the industry, have indicated we are collectively determined to achieve. What can be done to help them do so more effectively? To – in the words of the most recent *Cost of Compliance* survey of Compliance Practitioners – 'do more with less'. In considering this, we will focus specifically on the contribution that the three main influencers on the Compliance role can make:

- the regulators and, indeed, the wider regulatory environment, given their significant role in shaping the Compliance environment in which the regulated firm – and thus the Compliance function – operates;
- the regulated firm, given their significant role in shaping the operational environment in which the Compliance function carries out its role;

DOI: 10.4324/9781003431305-13

- and, of course, the Compliance function itself, which provides its own – not insignificant – influence on its activities and approach, driven by the Compliance professionals who work within it, who's influence extends far beyond that of the firm in which they are based.

ENABLING THE COMPLIANCE FUNCTION:
FROM THE OUTSIDE IN AND THE INSIDE OUT

Given its mandate, as we have seen throughout this text the activities and approach of the Compliance function can contribute significantly to the development of an appropriate culture within a regulated firm. In doing so, it can help embed an approach that not only achieves the function's main goal of assisting the firm in managing compliance and hence regulatory risk but as a consequence provide benefit to the regulatory environment as a whole. Consider the significance of the following activities and their positive impact not only on internal operations within a regulated firm but far more widely still:

- international bodies supporting initiatives that have a positive impact on the regulatory environment;
- regulators establishing appropriate regulatory approaches and creating effective regulatory structures;
- boards directing the management of their businesses to operate in a compliant manner;
- oversight and assurance functions supporting the board's approach;
- operational departments working in adherence to these requirements.

The creation and maintenance of an effective compliance culture within an individual firm have a positive 'spill-over' effect beyond that individual firm itself. For example, if one firm demonstrates such a culture and there are seen to be business advantages arising from this, others are more likely to adopt the same or a similar approach. They will do this with a view to achieving these same benefits, which in turn will be noted by other firms. And so this constructive cycle will continue, impacting positively on the wider regulatory environment, supporting regulatory aims. The more obvious demonstration of a compliant, integrity-focused approach and the publicising of it is increasingly likely in our new business paradigm that promotes this. This makes it more attractive for firms to work to realise and harness benefits. Conversely, it also makes it less attractive to keep such sources of success under wraps (so as to protect any perceived competitive advantage to do so, for example). It is in the demonstration of a real commitment to these issues that a firm will gain positive recognition in the current business climate and indeed from the regulator, whose relationship with the firm is key.

Effectively, there needs to be general encouragement towards a 'tipping point' within the industry where those who tend towards non-compliant-/non-integrity-focused approaches are the 'outliers'. Early adopters will have led the way and what was once less usual will increasingly become the norm. There are, however, practical issues to consider here in that the benefits of this will only be harnessed with a collective approach: there is little benefit to a firm to take a stance and be the 'first to the post' if others have no intention (or incentive?) to follow suit. The costs associated with this approach often cause firms to avoid being the front-runner unless there is a significant advantage to doing so. It's often a useful tactic to watch how others implement a new rule, see how the regulator responds to this and then make judgements on how implementation should be undertaken. There have been many examples in the past of firms investing resources in a particular approach only to find that requirements change, are withdrawn or are not widely adopted. This inevitably has cost implications for the firms involved who are then more wary of a similar approach next time round, learning to be more cautious in their approach for instance. An example of this was the Cookie Law[1] changes in the UK. Anecdotally, some firms actively elected not to be proactive in implementing these; instead, they watched what other firms did. In doing so, they observed that a surprising number of larger firms only went halfway to meeting the requirements, with no apparent consequences. They will inevitably take this into consideration in their own future decision-making. Such examples illustrate the importance of a joined-up approach to encouraging, establishing and embedding a compliant and integrity-focused culture within the industry; it has to be the majority that commit, or it is likely to fail.

There is much that can be done to further enable the Compliance function to play its part in this and in doing so more effectively help manage compliance and regulatory risk. This spans areas as wide-ranging as education, provision of support, the embedding of standards and so on. Each of the three main influencers highlighted has a contribution to make to developments in this regard. However, for all the reasons discussed it is important to remember that these contributions must remain connected, recognising that actions in relation to each have a crossover impact on others. Let us begin by considering the approach and activities of regulators and of the wider regulatory environment.

APPROACH AND ACTIVITIES OF THE REGULATOR AND WIDER REGULATORY ENVIRONMENT

These can be divided into two areas, broadly distinguishing between the impact *activities* will have on enabling the Compliance function versus that of their *approach* (although of course this latter point will strongly influence the former). How might the approach of these influencers and the impact of such influences be better channelled to create an environment where regulatory risk is more effectively managed?

Much has been done at an international level to make recommendations on and provide guidance about a host of topics intended to support the desired shift in attitudes and approach throughout the industry. Wide-ranging activities and output that include policy reviews, enhanced areas of focus, new legislation, additional prudential and conduct requirements and so on, have been targeted towards a host of linked topics, including regulation, governance, culture, ethics, standards, policy frameworks, supervision methodologies, the role of the board, the role of supervisors, internal controls, risk management, models of regulation, assurance methodologies and so forth. All of these influence and, in so doing, support the activities and approach of Compliance at a grass roots level. The development of the International Standard ISO 19600 *Compliance Management Systems – Guidelines* (replaced by ISO 37301:2021) is a good practical example of this. Given that it requires the involvement of representation from organisations in so many different jurisdictions, it well illustrates collective efforts to address perceived weaknesses and provide active solutions to do so. An interesting article[2] charted the development of this ISO and highlighted key areas of focus – it provided a fascinating insight into the continuing reach of compliance and the interest in, and need for, guidance on its management.[3]

At a national level, regulators state their commitment and active involvement in the initiatives at the international level, making much of their membership of, and contributions to, the many regulatory, quasi-regulatory or otherwise influential organisations discussed in Parts I and II. In doing so, they further emphasise their commitment to actions that support the generally agreed approach, while also undertaking action at the national level in support of this same goal. The previously cited complete overhaul of the regulatory system in the UK,[4] is a good example of this. So too is the widespread reform and active pursuit of wrongdoers involved in corporate scandals notable in the US over recent years. A further illustration is provided by the Dutch prudential supervisor DNB, who in 2011 'incorporated the "software of governance" into its supervisory methodology' within which

> greater emphasis … is placed on assessing and examining the (i) individual and collective behaviour patterns of CEO's and other board members, manager and staff and (ii) the effects of such observed behaviour on business performance and the company's risk profile.[5]

These examples and similar ones referred to elsewhere in this text do of course barely scratch the surface of the myriad of individual actions being taken by regulators and related bodies, by governments and global influencers around the world in pursuit of collective aims. They do, however, illustrate the fact that efforts are afoot from all sides and indicate the ramifications of these for the regulatory environment as a whole.

Let us narrow this discussion further now to focus on ideas around what can be done, specifically, to support the role of Compliance and, in so doing, support our collective wider goals. Note that in some jurisdictions efforts in these areas are more advanced than in others. While progress is steady, more can be done.

Approach

As a function that has (or should have!) ethics, standards and integrity hardwired into its DNA, Compliance is extremely well placed to support the ongoing efforts of regulators in these areas. Accordingly, regulators should support and champion the role of Compliance and of those who work within it, specifically the Compliance Officer. As the head of the function, the Compliance Officer has a great deal of influence over its efficacy, the translation of what the regulator is looking for and the level to which this is embedded in regulated firms. As we said right at the outset of this text, rules and enforcement are all well and good, but they are only effective if they are underpinned by ethics and integrity and genuinely effective mechanisms intent on developing and supporting these. This is where the efforts of the Compliance function have a greater contribution to make.

Recommended Activities in Support of This Approach[6]

Note that these will necessarily need to involve the actions of a number of stakeholders, dependent upon the particular activity referred to. However, in the first instance, these recommendations are directed primarily towards regulators, policymakers and influencers in the wider regulatory environment.

Higher Priority

1 Think about what we want from our Compliance function now and in the future in support of our collective aims. What do we expect of the function and the personnel within it? Set clear expectations of what is required in terms of practical issues such as independence, standing/seniority, reporting lines and resources, but also personnel issues, such as knowledge, training, experience, skills and attributes.[7]

2 Endorse formal and informal Standards[8] that support the role. Many jurisdictions have developed these or are in the process of doing so. These provide a benchmark that those working in compliance-related roles are required to meet in order to be considered to be appropriately qualified to perform the role. Such Standards are often accompanied by a set of Approved or Appropriate qualifications that can be undertaken in order to meet them, approved/endorsed by the regulator.

3 Support education and training activities. In many jurisdictions around the world, Compliance-related qualifications are becoming more common.[9] However, these would benefit from being more openly supported, perhaps through sponsorship programmes for individuals or for certain key organisations (SIFIs, for example), where establishing a core group of individuals specifically trained in this way would be recognised as beneficial not only to that firm but to the wider regulatory environment. Budget for this could be provided from a central fund, either at the national or international level, given the collective benefits to be gleaned from having better qualified and more able staff in such key positions in key firms.

4 At the international level, we have a single body that has specific responsibility for regulatory compliance-related activities, a 'Compliance Standards Professional Body' for example. A single body such as this at the international level (perhaps based in or linked to one of the existing international bodies currently championing developments in related areas, such as discussed in Chapter 2), supported by individual bodies at the national level, could act as a repository for all matters Compliance-related (standards, policies, recommendations, guidance, training, education, qualification and so on). Non-sector-focused, it could effectively be the conduit for regulators and regulated firms at these levels, coordinating efforts in this area or simply publicising work that is taking place in various sectors, jurisdictions and industries. A single source of information to go to and to learn from so that we can all benefit from developments taking place elsewhere and can save time in accessing this information. Note that it would be practical to consider this on a subject base (that is, Compliance) rather than solely on an industry or jurisdiction basis, along the lines of the Standards development approach, for example, which can draw from the expertise and experience of different industry sectors and jurisdictions. The agreement regarding the formation of a body such as the Banking Standards Board in the UK[10] went some way towards encompassing aspects of the purpose of such a body, but its focus in terms of aims and sector/national coverage is different. The points noted in its development, however, are of relevance.

5 Alternatively, set up a body with a narrower remit, some form of 'Advisory Council of Compliance Practitioners' perhaps, to act as an advisory panel to stakeholders on all matters Compliance-related when developments are taking place. Again, having such a body at the international level, supported by individual bodies at the national level, could act as a single point of contact and source of information/guidance.

6 Develop a blueprint at the international level for the content of a robust Compliance training programme that reflects internationally and nationally agreed standards and expectations of those in these roles. This would help standardise approach and set clear expectations. As well as knowledge requirements focused on Compliance role specifics, this could also include wider elements that support the role more broadly. This could include topics such as business law, economics and government policy, perhaps, together with practical elements such as auditing and investigation techniques. Experienced Compliance Officers could be invited to contribute. This said, it is important to note here that there are already many existing Compliance-related training and education programmes, both public and in-house within regulated organisations, with the latter becoming ever more the desired option so as to allow for tailoring specific to that organisation. More generally, programmes and qualifications are offered at all levels from entry through to master's stage, at global and national levels. They are linked to business schools and universities, are stand-alone, certificated or uncertificated. Some focus specifically on Compliance and regulatory compliance-related matters, while others include these within existing programmes (those focused on business, accounting, insurance and so on, for example). Many of these draw on existing guidance relating to the Compliance role to provide structure to their content, as well as include a practitioner element that translates the theoretical requirements into practical application. Some of these have a well-deserved and widespread reputation and a growing alumni as a result, while others are less well known. Using some of these as a base for the international blueprint and drawing on the experience of those who have developed them would be advantageous in terms of time and resource.

Essentially, what is being proposed here, in points 4–6 specifically, are all-stakeholder collective projects at the international level. Such projects should reflect the clear need for focus on all of the Compliance-related matters highlighted, recognising the wider benefit for the regulatory system that can be wrought from these. They should prioritise the desired areas of focus and make clear the requirements needed to achieve these. Ideally, such activity would be overseen independently by the body recommended but if such a body were not in place an alternative would be the formalisation of a qualification blueprint via an existing professional body or association that already has international reach and presence in numerous jurisdictions. Again, it may be practical to consider this on a subject basis (that is, Compliance) across industry sectors, which would assist from a funding perspective, rather than solely on a dedicated industry basis though the approach would of course necessarily be influenced by what was required (see point 1).

Returning now to other high-priority matters:

1. Require formal Continuous Professional Development (CPD), and make it mandatory for holders of all Compliance posts. The requirements should be specified and

tailored to the level of responsibility and be most rigorous for those at higher levels. This is necessary for the continued effectiveness of the function given the constantly changing environment in which it operates. There is a strong argument to be made that any Compliance professional who does not make ongoing efforts to maintain their knowledge and skills is not acting as a professional should. Compliance with CPD requirements could be assessed and monitored by the previously recommended Compliance Standards Professional Body.

2. Ensure an individual with practical (rather than only theoretical) regulatory compliance experience is present when high-level recommendations are made for policy development in these or related areas. This will allow for practical considerations to be more readily factored into planned developments. This would be an ideal role for a body such as the Advisory Council suggested above.

Medium to Longer-Term Priorities

1. Introduce a form of 'Oath' for compliance and risk professionals. Similar to the 'Bankers Oath' introduced in the Netherlands after the banking crisis,[11] with its focus on acting ethically, balance, complying with laws/regulations/codes, confidentiality, avoidance of abusing knowledge, acting openly and accountably and making efforts to improve/retain trust in society, might such an Oath provide a single distinct set of aims for the profession to coalesce behind?

2. Regulators and policymakers should fully engage Compliance professionals in developments within the regulatory environment that will or may impact upon their activities, encouraging their informal input and views based on their practical experience of life 'at the sharp end'. For example, the establishment of a panel along the lines of the practitioner or consumer ones that already exist in the UK could be established for those with Compliance oversight responsibility. This would help regulators and policymakers to more readily understand the challenges the regulations pose in implementation. Given the many competing pressures on the time of individuals in these key roles, this might be more practical via a scheme involving some form of a rolling invitation to participate. In this, different firms and individuals could be involved on a regular but periodic basis rather than continuously. This would also have the added benefit of keeping the views and input provided 'fresh' and so be more likely to be genuinely reflective of a broad range of views. More formally, one of the requirements of appointment to a senior Compliance role might be involvement in such a process and/or to periodically (say once every two to three years – again, mindful of the competing time pressures on individuals in these roles) produce a discussion paper on a specialist area of compliance knowledge or experience for the benefit of the regulator and/or other stakeholders within the regulatory environment. Again, this would contribute practitioner experience to the theoretical considerations which more often inform debate in this area.

3. Encouraging Compliance practitioner contributions to the development of regulatory standards in other jurisdictions or sectors, including collaboration between international regulatory bodies and Compliance professionals. This might include, for example, mentoring schemes between those in more experienced sectors/jurisdictions

with those who are less so, not only to firms within them but onto panels where policy is being developed. As an incentive, involvement in such projects could be factored into regulators' risk assessment frameworks for firms, with recognition as 'specialists' in this area and encouragement to share this specialism, being considered positively within the ongoing supervisory evaluation.

4. Give credit where effective compliance regimes are in place. Some jurisdictions[12] explicitly offer credit for their presence as part of the enforcement approach after a problem has been identified. However, it would be problematic to focus only on initiatives that gave credit *after* the fact. Regulators tend to factor the existence of compliance programmes into their overall supervisory risk assessment of the firm and so to a degree credit is already given for these. However, regulators (and governments) could do more to promote this type of action. At the least, publicly acknowledging those organisations with a robust compliance presence[13] further endorses the regulators' view that efforts in this area are important and worthy of resources. This would require some form of independent verification of what constituted 'robust' of course.[14] However, given this is part of what regulators themselves are looking to assess as part of their authorisation and ongoing supervisory process, that shouldn't prove too onerous if applied with the necessary caveats. Linked to this, we are all familiar with businesses being fined for regulatory failures, but could we also consider incentives to positively encourage the opposite? For example, at the governmental level, tax incentives could be awarded for having solid and effective compliance regimes – so supporting positive action in this area before a problem occurs, rather than taking this issue into account afterwards. Of course, such an approach would not be established without difficulty, but harking back to the collective approach theme that underpins this chapter, its practicality could reasonably be explored if there is a genuine will to do so.

5. Requiring regulatory staff secondments to compliance or risk roles in SIFIs for a period each year to help them gain a better (and continually refreshed) understanding of what practitioner life is like in an operational environment.

6. Take clear action against the board and senior management in firms found not to be supporting compliance requirements and the Compliance function. The potential for action ranging from education and training in the first instance right through to public sanction would help concentrate minds. Likewise (ever keen to promote positive initiatives) where firms are identified as being particularly strong in that area, this too should be promoted, perhaps encouraging some form of mentoring collaboration between firms or particular staff in firms whereby the stronger party is encouraged (to their benefit from a risk assessment point of view as noted above!) to assist the weaker.

Perhaps most importantly, regulators should support formal professionalisation[15] of the Compliance role. The level of industry and business knowledge, understanding and experience, together with the range of skills and attributes required to be effective in compliance roles is considerable. Operationally, as has been made clear in this text, it is at a level not dissimilar to in-house lawyers or accountants, with internal staff placing a similar level of reliance on the efficacy of these roles and regulators too being reliant on these. In many jurisdictions, however, these requirements are not fully recognised. Unlike more established professions, it is not necessary in all jurisdictions for Compliance officers or those working within the function generally to have specific compliance qualifications in order to be appointed to such a position. Often, the only requirement is that they are deemed to be appropriate for it and are generally 'fit and proper' to perform the role. Often the assessment of what constitutes 'appropriate' is left to the individual firm to decide. Increasingly, however, such assessments are coming under greater scrutiny by regulators to ensure individuals appointed to these key roles genuinely meet the required standards. Professionalisation of the role would be supported through the setting of *specific* qualifications and level of experience requirements as is the case in other recognised professions.

In addressing this topic, an article[16] published in the International Compliance Associations in-house journal concluded by setting out the reasons why it is important to professionalise the compliance role, summing up this need effectively and are worth repeating verbatim:

> Because it is needed. Because there is a lack of consistent interpretation and application of what is required of the discipline. Because stakeholders demand it. Because it can make a real different to businesses and the people who work within them. Because the risks associated with being a compliance officer can be seen to be as great as that which a lawyer undertakes. Because it is no longer the department it once was, a deterrent of business. Because it has evolved over time to mean something substantial and continues to grow with the number of individuals entering the role greater than any other financial services related discipline. Because it's about time.

Coming from an organisation which had at that time put thousands of individuals from around the world (currently with members in 157 countries) through professional certified compliance education programmes, it is well worth listening to, and it continues to be interesting to reflect on all these years later in light of developments since it was written. The only point to be added in supporting this is to emphasise the significant benefits to be gained for the industry, as well as for firms and individuals, of investing in these roles. To fail to do so would be an opportunity lost.

Of course, there are significant challenges to many of these ideas and one would not be so naive as to believe their implantation could be achieved *en masse* or without difficulty. Many are aspirational, goals to aim for, yet we need to recognise the benefits to be gained as well as acknowledge the difficulties in attaining them. We will return to this point in our conclusion; however, now we will look at further ideas for the development of the role by considering the approach and activities of regulated businesses.

APPROACH AND ACTIVITIES OF THE REGULATED BUSINESS

With management oversight as the hub of the risk control matrix and regulatory oversight as the exterior, positioned between the two in regulated firms lie matters spanning control, risk, security, resilience and quality assurance. Compliance activities play a pivotal role in supporting these. But it is only able to do so if the various components that contribute to the environment in which it operates (the Compliance environment) are supportive of it.

An interesting paper published back in 2009[17] described the 'Kumbaya' approach to Ethics and Compliance, which used an amusing scenario to illustrate a telling point. It described a scene whereby basic formal codes of conduct are established, an ethics officer is placed in charge, a training programme is introduced and some monitoring follows, with everyone then waiting expectantly for ... and suddenly, 'halleluiah!' with all those involved joining hands in a 'Kumbaya' moment that the desired good outcomes will result. It usefully made the point that 'there is a critical distinction between compliance and ethics programmes that have all the designated features on paper, and those that have real teeth and the potential for success'. There are many components to an effective compliance strategy and framework, with people and culture elements as important, if not more so, than the more concrete elements of the framework. The Boehme paper is a proponent of the view that 'an effective approach to integrity and corporate ethics starts with a senior level chief ethics and compliance officer who understand the compliance and ethics field, is empowered and experienced' because

> a well-implemented compliance and ethics programme doesn't spring from the void ex nihilo – it requires a strong leader to engage others in the organisation including powerful senior management, to surface and resolve issues and challenges, and to make a culture of transparency, accountability and responsibility a reality.

Those examples in Appendices 4 and 5 underline the consequences if that is not the case. Easier said than done of course and 'when compliance programmes have been mandated by government rules and regulations, programs have tended to develop in hyper-technical efforts devoid of senior level participation and commitment'. The author highlighted the output of a 'startlingly candid' white paper published in 2007[18] which flagged that 'a CECO[19] that serves as window dressing likely does more harm than good, especially in times of difficulty' and that their reporting line is the 'single biggest influence on his or her credibility within the organisation'. As we have seen over the ensuing decade, problems continue to arise against a backdrop of continued efforts in this field.

If compliance programmes are to move beyond merely hoping for the best in terms of effectiveness or indeed avoid the dangers of just being 'window dressing' in order to genuinely provide benefit, we need to consider carefully the path forward in embedding these within regulated organisations. Encouraging a focus on developing the culture within the firm is a logical step towards this. A still pertinent Deloitte paper *Cultivating a Risk Intelligent Culture: A Fresh Perspective*[20] provides a useful set of characteristics explaining that 'Risk culture encompasses the general awareness, attitudes, and behaviours of employees towards risk and how risk is managed. Risk culture is a key indicator of how widely risk management policies and practices have been adopted'. These span key areas including 'commonality of purpose, values and ethics; universal adoption and application; a learning organisation; timely, transparent and honest communications; understanding the value of effective risk management; responsibility – individual and collective; expectation of challenge', which bring together the points made on this topic throughout this text and demonstrates their positive impact on the firm's approach to it.

Approach

Clearly, in their day-to-day actions and discussions, the board and senior management should exemplify the objectives of the Compliance function by behaving in a manner that reflects these and supports its aims. This reinforces their commitment to the achievement of these and endorses the approach of the Compliance function and its personnel. In their interactions with stakeholders both within the firm and outside of it, their support of the function should be apparent through this endorsement. Essentially, the regulated firm in the person of the board (both executive and non-executive) should, like the regulator, continuously champion the role of the Compliance function and its personnel.

Recommended Activities in Support of This Approach[21]

Again, note that these activities will necessarily need to involve the actions of a number of stakeholders, dependent upon the issue at hand. However, in the first instance, these recommendations are directed primarily towards the board and decision-makers within regulated organisations.

Higher Priority

1 Define the Compliance role as a discrete, that is, independent, role, but one which is clearly part of the overall oversight and assurance framework within the organisation.
2 Ensure the individuals appointed to Compliance roles reflect requirements in terms of knowledge, experience, skills and attributes that are appropriate for effective performance within the Compliance environment in that firm.
3 Constructively set and support the development of a positive attitude towards compliance and Compliance through all forms of communication within the business and with relevant external stakeholders.
4 Endorse and contribute to the development of an appropriate culture that supports Compliance activities (including consideration of performance management, compensation structures and so on).
5 Ensure there is adequate financial commitment to compliance and Compliance – resource costs must be sustainable and appropriate.
6 Reporting lines involving the Compliance function should be appropriate and practical.

Medium-Term Priorities

1. Consider integration and visibility issues – where is the function located? Is it sufficiently in touch with the business to be able to perform its role effectively?
2. Invest in technology to assist the function to work efficiently and effectually.
3. Raise the profile of Compliance – encourage attendance at key meetings and visibility at events.

4. Have the head of the Compliance function not just reporting to the board, but being a senior level executive in their own right, particularly in larger businesses or those in key sectors.
5. Consider the seniority of key Compliance personnel, not only the head of the function, against those the function will be involved in monitoring – is there parity or might the business consider Compliance staff as inferior/less able because of their lowly rank (the likelihood of this will of course be influenced by the culture within the organisation) and therefore not really knowing what they're talking about, so be less likely to take note of them?
6. Link individual rewards for key business units to key compliance objectives.

Longer-Term Priorities

1. Provide practical support for the development of skills to improve performance in Compliance roles. For example, increasing opportunity for formal and informal skills development, both technical and softer, essentially with consideration to the various different day-to-day compliance activities. This might comprise encouraging, as part of the organisational policy and linked to the understanding of regulatory expectations in terms of what needs to be demonstrated by an effective compliance function/individual,[22] measures such as shadowing of more experienced colleagues, allowing less experienced staff to 'step up' in terms of their roles more frequently so as to gain exposure to the practical realities, and so on.
2. Encourage increased interaction and communication between Compliance personnel and those in the business units. For example, expanding beyond the recommended 'open door' policy between Compliance and the business to provide other mechanisms for general discussion around compliance and Compliance-related activity (such as ethical or cultural issues facing the firm, for example). Illustrations and case studies could be provided, building on lessons learned from breaches or other errors within the firm, or indeed cases publicised that involve other firms and how such issues might be avoided. Exploration of these and learning from them could focus on practical operational issues arising from them and how these might be addressed to ensure a better outcome.
3. Require periodic staff secondments (however brief or short-term) from key business units to Compliance or risk functions. Just as suggested regarding regulators having practical experience of life at the sharp end of Compliance within regulated firms, business staff will benefit from appreciating the Compliance role from this perspective.
4. Remember, boards can have Compliance focus on whatever they want, so use the skills and abilities of those in the function to the best advantage for the firm overall within the context of the function's remit.
5. Enhance learning and education opportunities around Compliance-related activities. For example, encouraging the scheduling of periodic question and answer opportunities (live or online) between the Compliance team and different areas of the business, perhaps focusing on a different topic each time, when staff are free (but not mandated) to attend.

Perhaps most importantly on a day-to-day basis once the Compliance function is up and running, the board should take note of and action the issues Compliance raise. As an extreme example of the potential consequences of not doing this, think of the impact of whistle-blowing for both firms and for any individuals involved. Why would any stakeholder in the business want problems to escalate to that degree given there are numerous stages prior to that where action could be taken and issues addressed?

APPROACH AND ACTIVITIES OF THE COMPLIANCE FUNCTION AND COMPLIANCE PERSONNEL

Notwithstanding that this is a role that can be so very challenging, the ranks of Compliance professionals, and the range of roles in which they are involved, are swelling. In financial services (and other) sectors and jurisdictions all around the world, individuals toil away in many different Compliance practitioner roles, from Heads of function with global remits in multinational companies through to junior Compliance assistants and indeed all the levels in between. Add to these those focused on education, training and research activities in the field and the reach of regulatory compliance professionals is significant, impacting on a whole host of linked areas. Numbers are increasing year on year and showing no signs of abatement, and a good thing too, if surveys on market and recruitment trends are to be believed, for Compliance professionals are more in demand than ever.[23] But (and there's always a but, isn't there?) *what*, exactly, are these staff needed for? There remains a lack of consistency in expectations of and attitudes towards compliance roles and that needs to be addressed.

How Compliance personnel can work to further enable the visibility and efficacy of their role, and in doing so support the betterment of the regulatory environment overall, can be divided into two broad areas for discussion: (1) approaches and actions carried out *collectively* by Compliance officers (plural) focused on developing and supporting the role while encouraging understanding of it, and (2) approaches and actions taken by *individual* Compliance officers (singular) for their own personal development. Let us begin with the first of these.

COLLECTIVE CONSIDERATIONS

Approach

Essentially, this comes down to collective action to achieve collective results. Many Compliance professionals are active in responding to consultations on intended regulatory initiatives that will impact on their sectors and the activities of the organisations within which they are based. More of them should do so. But what do they contribute to actually driving the agenda itself? Flagging issues that are of particular relevance in the performance of Compliance roles? Pushing forward on issues that are proving challenging or are creating difficulties? Generally, approaches to this tend to be on a much more limited and individual case-by-case basis. While there are certainly some groups that include practitioners whose activities do contribute in this way,[24] more could be done collectively. For example, with judgement being an ongoing component in the risk-based approach to regulatory supervision amidst an increasingly outcome-focused prioritisation in regulation, this will inevitably lead to greater challenges by firms and senior management: other than discussing this amongst themselves or within discussion-style groups,[25] is there more that could be done by Compliance personnel?

Professionalisation is another key consideration. Compliance is no longer an add-on to other roles (such as legal, accounting, audit, company secretarial and so forth); it is a professional role in its own right. It is therefore increasingly seen as an established career choice, with individuals actively choosing to enter it, rather than finding themselves allocated to this role as in days gone by. However, as previously highlighted, there is no single, clearly established development pathway for those wishing to work in Compliance-related roles as would be found in other professions. Compliance staff are recruited from multiple backgrounds, from the business, from internal audit, legal or accountancy roles for example.[26] This brings with it many positives given the wide-ranging skill set such staff are capable of contributing to the Compliance role. With that in mind, it could be argued that a development pathway has actually already been formed organically, as appointments from these disciplines are effectively indicative of the skills required to be effective in a Compliance role. Further efforts could be made to formalise this, however. As with all matters Compliance-related, the size, sector and complexity and so on of the firm in which the professional is to operate will strongly influence the extent and emphasis of requirements, but in short, it could be argued that a grounding in one or more of these disciplines is helpful prior to joining the ranks of the Compliance professional. As such, Compliance may not necessarily be a primary career path for all, but rather a secondary path for those already experienced or distinguished in one of the aforementioned fields. Is this an approach that could or indeed should become formally embedded, underpinning the development of the Compliance profession?

That said, what constitutes a profession? While much has been written on this subject, the aforementioned article focusing on the professionalisation of Compliance in *inCompliance*[27] neatly encapsulated this topic from the perspective of the Compliance professional themselves. It raised a number of salient points for the benefit of its intended audience: those who work within the compliance profession or aspire to. Put simply, professionalism = high standards, levels of knowledge and expertise beyond that of the non-professional.

But from an objective technical perspective, what is required to be viewed as a professional? Thus far, focus in the Compliance arena has been on several of these issues separately, but less so collectively. Will such an approach add to the collective regulatory burden of all stakeholders, already deemed by many to be significant and not rewarded by a genuine strengthening of the industry? Think also about what constitutes the hallmarks of a profession. Holding a certificate or qualification does not directly equate to the holder actually *being* a professional. Though important and indicative of study and/ or training in the relevant discipline, the presence of these alone does not mean someone is competent (or indeed remains so) but could certainly be seen as a passport to entry. For example, certification/qualification could be viewed as strong evidence of a demonstrable level of knowledge and understanding of an agreed set of topics at a particular time. On the flip side, nor does experience necessarily directly equate to competence, as experience gauged solely in terms of years served, for example, does not directly equate to relevant experience that is appropriate for a particular Compliance role, as these can vary hugely. Essentially, professional roles and our view of them are supported by a number of threads and we need to consider what we mean by this for the Compliance profession.

Of course, it is not only improving understanding and awareness of the Compliance role generally within the regulatory environment that we need to be cognisant of, as we discussed in detail in the previous chapter when we considered compliance challenges. Thinking about a collective approach within firms and considering how practitioners approach their activities, the aim should be to support Compliance objectives and in doing so reinforce the objectives of both the firm and the regulator.

Recommended Activities in Support of This Approach[28]

As before, note that these activities will necessarily need to involve the actions of a number of stakeholders, dependent upon the issue. However, in the first instance, these recommendations are directed primarily towards Compliance practitioners themselves and the discussion groups and associations that currently support them. Note that these inevitably pick up on recommendations under the earlier regulator and regulated firm sections in this text, but considering these from the viewpoint of the Compliance professionals adds valuable perspective.

Higher Priority

1. To professionalise or not – is more required? Should practitioners and those in supporting roles be agitating for formal recognition as a profession? Would that strengthen their position within regulated firms as they pursue their activities?
2. Embed the need for qualifications as a means of supporting experience within the Compliance role. Individuals joining this profession over recent years have flocked to qualifications in this field,[29] not least because of a desire for a better understanding of what this complex role consists of and where responsibilities lie. Would supporting such qualifications to become mandatory requirements be to the betterment of the profession overall? Is this something all would be supportive of or are there some who would resist (we have seen examples of this in the past with other sectors or professional roles where requirements for qualification were imposed)?
3. Consider Codes of Conduct or Codes of Ethics for the Compliance profession (or note the suggestion regarding a Compliance Profession Oath as highlighted under the section on regulators) – yes, these exist within individual bodies and associations (such as those set out in Appendix 2), but what about agreeing to these collectively as a means of uniting professionals in this area? Or should such approaches remain jurisdiction/ sector/firm specific? Would they or should they be voluntary or mandatory?
4. Network – networking is a vital collective action on the part of compliance professionals. As a means of supporting a whole host of related requirements including knowledge maintenance and development, sharing of experience and sharing of concerns, it is necessary and useful. Some embrace this wholeheartedly, some squirm at the very thought, and many find that time is against them in being able to

do this. But it *is* necessary and not just external networking, but networking within the firm in which the Compliance function is situated. For those who struggle with the idea of networking as a 'must do', they need to put aside preconceived notions of what it is and their possible past experience of 'good networkers' who appear to think this involves exchanges of multiple business cards or, more recently, building a vast number of connections on online networks. Instead, networking should be viewed as active relationship building: developing a support group, a mix of individuals who are willing and able to support each other to mutual benefit, utilising their own experience and areas of expertise to the benefit of others. If you assist others where you are able and both broaden and deepen your business relationships as you do so, without focusing specifically on what you will get back in return, you may be surprised at just how beneficial this will actually be. Fewer strong business relationships with those you can call on, and who can call on you, at times of need are far better in the longer term than scores of 'connections' with whom you don't actually have a relationship. This extends to networking within the organisation too, to great all-round benefit in enabling the performance of the Compliance role. As has often been said before in many different circumstances, people do business with people and if they have a relationship with someone they are more likely to want to do so in a mutually supportive way.

Networking should be viewed as active relationship building.

5. Attend events/round tables/seminars/conferences – provides opportunities to network and to contribute more widely to debates that impact on the regulatory environment. Hosting, as well as simply attending, can bring a different set of experiences that although potentially time-consuming may well be beneficial as a means of developing knowledge, skills and indeed contacts.
6. Join a professional association or network – provides opportunities for debate and support, as well as networking opportunities.

Medium to Longer-Term Priorities

1. *Learn from others*: all those working in Compliance-related roles need to learn from the past experiences (good and bad) of their predecessors, just as we encourage our firms to do.
2. *Share concerns*: conferences, panel discussions and networking events not only provide opportunities to mix with peers and debate current issues, they also provide fora to share concerns, put issues on the table and highlight challenges. Given the many pressures on their time, practitioners should ensure they make the most of these opportunities and encourage representatives of regulators, policymakers, research groups and educators in the field to attend. This will provide opportunities for them to fully understand the real experiences of those who are at the forefront of implementing requirements in the business world. This will help mitigate against developmental activity taking place in a 'practicality-free' vacuum which little considers the real-world consequences of what is being recommended or required.

Individual Considerations

Narrowing the focus now from collective Compliance approaches and activities, what can and should individual Compliance professionals be doing to enhance their own abilities and so further enable their effectiveness in this role? To be effective, not all individual actions need be focused directly on the role itself, rather these can be separated into those approaches and activities that predominantly enhance *performance* in the role (performance development) and those which develop the *person* (personal development), although of course this latter will ultimately enhance performance. Accordingly, suggested actions in support of individual considerations of role development are separated into two of these broad areas.

Performance Development

Higher Priority

1. *Maintaining industry and sector knowledge*: this should be high on any Compliance professional's 'To Do' list, not least for all the reasons discussed in Chapters 7 and 8. However, this is achieved not just via formal channels, but by less formal means. Membership of external bodies, professional associations and so on are invaluable in this respect, not only highlighting and thus encouraging awareness of the topics of the day and what others in a similar field are doing about them, but also recognising that the opportunity to share and hear the views of others helps consolidate one's own.

2. *Engaging with the business*: as a means of enabling the Compliance function, engaging with the business and being inquisitive about its activities and current areas of focus is probably the most beneficial on a day-to-day basis; it is this activity, after all, and the approach taken to it that helps embed a positive view of the function within the business (and indeed the view of the function of the business). This supports the Compliance function's all-round aims. Involvement in activities and projects, not only those that are directly related to work, helps encourage the view of the Compliance professional as being part of the business, as approachable, a team player. Learning/understanding how the business turns a profit and then contributing to that process within the remit of the role can help move individuals from roles in which they simply do the mechanics of the job to one in which they actively contribute to its effectiveness through a greater level of practical understanding.

3. *CPD*: in all its guises this should be an intrinsic part of any professional's working life. It is central to their being able to function effectively in their role, not just in terms of role-specific skills, but also in less tangible 'softer skills' for example. As with professional roles of any nature, those in positions such as Compliance must keep their knowledge up to date. They must have an awareness of new and emerging developments that might impact upon actions (such as technological advancements for example, that might lead to new types of or developments within products or services). Any professional interested in remaining effective within their professional sphere should prioritise this aspect of learning. Continuing development, building on experience, helps ensure that individuals working within whichever professions are able to do so effectively.

While many professionals accept CPD as something that will be of benefit to them and therefore as something they ought to build into their professional plans, some do not. There can be many reasons for this; sometimes, however, it can result from individuals feeling they have reached the pinnacle of experience in their particular field and that they no longer need to be tested or assessed in any way.

It is important, however, to remember that CPD takes many forms. It is not only achieved through formal activities but is often gained during work activities undertaken, with professionals developing as they work, and in doing so developing in the most directly practical way possible. In such cases, it may not be necessary to undertake a formal course to continue learning. Reading, analysing, understanding and implementing the latest regulations is therefore a form of CPD. However, what professionals need to regularly assess is what is necessary for their own professional development. They need to reflect on whether this is being met through their regular activities and if not, take action to address this via other means including, perhaps, specific training as referred to below.

> **Professionals need to regularly assess what is necessary for their own professional development.**

Medium to Longer-Term Priorities

1. *Training*: revised regulatory requirements, new business areas, management activities and so on, the Compliance professional's remit is often wide. Few commence their professional careers with the full range of knowledge and abilities that will allow them to perform effectively within their roles. Identifying knowledge and experience gaps, then focusing on plugging or developing these through appropriate activities, including targeted training where required, is to be encouraged. Working with those within the firm who can assist in this also provides another opportunity for relationship development.

2. *Mentoring*: from an individual perspective, this is an excellent way of developing our own skills and as such this has benefits for the mentor as well as for those mentored. Many organisations encourage this as part of their CPD approach. Whether to have or act as a mentor drawn from internally within the firm or alternatively locate an external mentor, however, is a decision for the individual. Given that such relationships can continue over many years, the relationship with the chosen mentor/mentoree may change over time. The key to productive mentoring relationships is mutual respect and appreciation of the benefits the relationship provides to both parties. Those who have experienced a positive mentor arrangement are fully in support of the advantages it can bring and encouraging of such relationships. They often note how these evolve over time, maturing from a student/tutor relationship in its early stages towards one of mutual professional colleague support as the student becomes more experienced over time. This of course shifts the premise of the relationship, yet it remains extremely worthwhile.

3. *Obtaining qualifications*: provides recognition amongst peers and in the eyes of employers and colleagues, while also providing opportunities for career advancement and the possibility of better remuneration. Though not a prime consideration for all (and as was discussed earlier, not necessarily a guarantee of competence) additional qualifications that address perceived knowledge and understanding gaps can be beneficial.

4. *Involvement in projects*: projects that focus on matters of relevance to the Compliance role, both within the firm and externally, provide a platform to share knowledge, influence development and can be a useful means of keeping up-to-date and developing further skills, as well as relationship building.

5. *Board meeting/board committee attendance*: for senior Compliance professionals, access to the board is critical. For those who are not quite at that level the opportunity to attend board or other key executive or non-exec committee meetings if at all possible (potentially as a form of 'shadowing' more senior colleagues perhaps) can be an extremely useful means of development. Such attendance builds on existing skills and attributes in a reasonably 'safe' environment: preparing for such meetings alone will provide a great deal of insight into more senior Compliance roles. Actual attendance at and potentially participation in (however terrifying this might be at first!) will stand individuals in good stead in terms of adding to their practical experience. One way of doing so might be to invite more junior members of the function to be minute-takers at such meetings or committees. In doing so, they have an active role in the meeting, requiring them to participate and engage, while having the opportunity to witness how the committee operates. This could be cited as a specific development opportunity and recorded on their Personal Development plans.

Personal Development Activities

In considering personal development activities, these have not been separated into different priorities as both the points noted are considered equally valuable in developing abilities within the Compliance role.

1. *Ongoing self-assessment*: Compliance professionals should be realistic. They need to regularly assess how the role, activities and approach of the function are perceived within the organisation and take action accordingly. This necessity should extend not only to the function overall but also to the self. Regular realistic consideration of one's own skill set, identifying areas that require attention and taking steps to address these, is a clear indicator of professionalism. Recognise that we are all learning all the time and that we have much to gain from doing so. In working towards our own professional improvement, we need to acknowledge that a single achievement is not the end of the learning journey but a step forward. Compliance is still a relatively young profession; there is a need for ongoing skills development within its ranks.

   Recognise that we are all learning all the time and that we have much to gain from doing so. In working towards our own professional improvement, we need to acknowledge that a single achievement is not then end of the learning journey but a step forward.

2. *Enhancing personal skills, attributes and behaviours*: focus should not only be on more fixed and tangible activities and the specific skills that relate to these, but also on the development of skills and enhancement

of attributes that support them. For example, developing social skills and confidence in different situations, or practical skills such as those involved in presentations, communication, handling conflict, investigations, negotiations and so on. This goes back to the role of Compliance being about people working with people. Much of this relies on influencing skills at the end of the day and a successful Compliance Officer *must* have these to be truly effective and accepted within the business. Knowledge can be gained fairly easily but developing the most useful approach, attitude and the people's skills that support them is much harder to achieve. In this the services of a Coach might be helpful.

There are so many personal benefits to be had from skill development, irrespective of whether these directly correlate to activity within the immediate role (it is useful to remember that there is always the next role to consider!). The above focuses on the positives, but there is also the point that Compliance professionals should fear a bad reputation, avoiding reprimands from the regulator that may result in personal fines, or actions within a firm that will negatively impact on the credibility of the function and thus the individuals within it. As to how developments in all these areas will further enable the Compliance function in its aims, these should be apparent: one staffed by a better informed, qualified, supported and up-to-date function is likely to be far more engaged in its role and effective in its task.

WHAT'S IN A NAME?

Consideration of the further enabling of the Compliance role would be incomplete without comment on the functions name. If ever there was an example of the name of a function overshadowing the benefits of that function, Compliance is it. Having outgrown its original formative purpose, to many, the name 'Compliance' still conjures up the image of the 'business police'. Shackled as it is to this name, many in Compliance functions struggle to slough off these negative perceptions, perceptions that are at odds with the currently accepted remit of this role and which do much to detract from its widespread benefits. For this reason, many Compliance functions are choosing to combine the dreaded 'C' word with other, more acceptably descriptive words such as ethics, for example. There are also clear interrelationships between objectives and activities of other areas within organisations such as governance and risk. The acronym 'GRC' – standing for governance, risk and compliance – is now widely recognised as an umbrella term in this area. Essentially, any wording that might alleviate the negative or inaccurate historical connotations of the word compliance and allow the benefits of such activities to shine through is increasingly being embraced.

AND FINALLY … A WORD OF CAUTION

As we have seen throughout this text, regulators and firms have increasingly recognised the need to consider what more can be done to protect or improve the culture we cultivate within our regulated organisations. This is where, increasingly, the benefits of the shift and/or expansion in the Compliance role to encompass an increasing range of support and advisory activities as well as those involving monitoring and reporting have, many believe, begun to pay dividends in embedding a more compliant and ethical approach within firms. This role as a promoter of improving compliance and ethical culture within the firm has direct consequences for the standards of conduct within that firm as a result. This has been an ongoing priority for regulated firms for a number of years now, spurred on and encouraged by the regulator's stated aims in this regard.

However, priorities within firms shift over time. In an article in the *Journal of Business Compliance*,[30] discussions with a number of senior Compliance professionals who had recently departed their roles were described. These suggested that at that time the Compliance role was *not* expanding in scope as would appear necessary, but instead increasingly returning to its monitoring and reporting roots. These findings supported anecdotal evidence from other practitioners who commented upon the increased interest of regulators at that time in demanding demonstrable evidence of compliance, with the resulting consequence for the prioritisation of Compliance activities within firms. More recently still, as highlighted in the *Cost of Compliance* surveys, the wide range of activities in which the Compliance function is involved, considered alongside a lack of resource and available skilled personnel, is providing increasing challenges to the achievement of objectives, with the necessary need for prioritisation of certain activities. Given the increasing need for demonstrable adherence to requirements, it may be that work in some areas is prioritised over other

> **Given the increasing need for demonstrable adherence to requirements, it may be that work in some areas is prioritised over other activity which may be less readily immediately measurable but nevertheless important, particularly in the longer term.**

activities which may be less readily immediately measurable but nevertheless important, particularly in the longer term. If this is indeed the case, such a shift towards a return to more of a 'ticking the box' prioritisation within firms in order to provide such evidence would inevitably impact on the broader role of Compliance. In some instances, it may tip the balance of activities away from the more supportive and advisory role into which it has moved.

What could be the consequences of this? The ability of Compliance personnel to focus on activities that supported the development and embedding of a more robust culture, that supported overall Compliance and business aims, is one that many Compliance practitioners and those in related roles believe has become increasingly effective in a practical sense. Many years of evolution of the role, including support for a Compliance function of increasing influence within regulated firms that benefits regulatory aims overall, far from progressing further to support the development of the ethical culture we are all agreed is currently a prime area of focus, could potentially be at risk.

In order for the benefits of Compliance to be fully realised, it is important that the Compliance role is carried out appropriately. Its remit, structure, approach, activities, personnel and the way in which all of these combine contribute to the level of the Compliance function's effectiveness in safeguarding the firm and the integrity of the markets in which it operates. As we have discussed throughout this text, the level of regulatory demand on businesses has expanded and continues to do so. As firms work to meet these, it would be unfortunate if positive steps forward were halted, or in some instances even reversed, as a result of a shift in regulatory focus and approach and consequent requirements within regulatory firms: an unintended consequence of a movement that was for all the right reasons. Any retrograde shift that lessens the focus of the Compliance role on support activities that help develop an appropriate culture within a firm will impact not only upon that firm but also beyond. With that in mind, the collective impact of regulatory trends on the aims of the jurisdiction and consequently on the aims of regulators should be recognised by us all. Regulators and legislators need to tread the path of reform with care, and boards and executives would do well to ensure that the organisation of their governance frameworks features high on their agenda of corporate priorities.

A FINAL THOUGHT TO END ON: JOINED-UP APPROACH = COLLECTIVE BENEFIT?

Competent Compliance professionals recognise that sometimes regulatory requirements can be problematic or challenging, even where the underlying will and belief in them is there. They are pragmatic in their approach, seeking to act as a practical and effective bridge between the stated aims and needs of both the regulator and the regulated firm in which they are based. They work with regulators by supporting the embedding of regulatory requirements, not only within the firm but more generally by endorsing them throughout their interactions in the regulatory environment; they work with the board to promote values of integrity throughout the business and support them in their efforts to meet the regulator's expectations.

Compliance professionals are pragmatic in their approach, seeking to act as a practical and effective bridge between the stated aims and needs of both the regulator and the regulated firm in which they are based.

Ensuring awareness of why regulation and compliance matters, improving perception of the Compliance role and focusing on what is needed at the regulator, firm and Compliance function/ personnel level to support this is crucial.

Ensuring awareness of why regulation and compliance matters, improving the perception of the Compliance role and focusing on what is needed at regulator, firm and Compliance function/personnel level to support this is crucial. All stakeholders should want to see effective Compliance regimes in place because the negligence of a firm in this regard is representative of an attitude overall. This brings us back to the issue of joined-up thinking and key themes for enabling the Compliance role and the way forward in pursuing collective goals flagged at the outset of this chapter:

• *The regulators and, indeed, the wider regulatory environment*: defining expectations; supporting standards development; creating a dedicated repository and resource for all matters compliance-related; promoting professionalisation of the regulatory role.

- *The regulated firm*: defining and supporting the standing of the regulatory compliance role within and without the business; providing appropriate resource; promoting activities; and developing an appropriate operational culture.
- *The compliance function and compliance professionals themselves*: promoting standards in the regulatory compliance role; encouraging professionalisation through experience, training, education and networking; promoting CPD as an ongoing requirement; encouraging ongoing self-assessment to assess developmental needs.

Yet we need to remain aware of the many challenges to achieving our collective goals in this respect, key amongst which are:

- Compliance officers are employed by firms, not regulators. Their salary – and indeed any bonus element that forms part of their overall remuneration package – is dependent upon their performance on behalf of that company, not on behalf of the industry or regulator.
- All these ideas have to be paid for. As an example, professionalising the role in itself will make it worth more, which could in turn make compliance more expensive.
- And of course, the more that regulators engage with regulated firms and Compliance practitioners, the greater the risk of potential for regulatory capture/loss of regulator independence, with all the resulting risks that might bring.

Nevertheless, the many positives to be gained must be balanced against such challenges and any potential downsides and any risks arising from these, as ever, must be managed as effectively as possible.

As has already been stated, many of the aims outlined are aspirational, yet these often simply reflect good business practice and we need to recognise the benefits to be gained from implementing them. As an industry, individuals should be looking to the actions of their fellows as the failings of one tend to be reflected as the failings of all. Collectively, each of these stakeholders in financial services must work to mutually support the activities of each other in pursuit of the common goal of restoring standards in the industry and, in doing so, restoring confidence in it. This can in part be achieved by further enabling an operational function that lies at its core which is focused on the management of a key risk within business that has wider implications than might initially be apparent. In bringing this text to its conclusion, this is our primary area of focus.

NOTES

1 Information Commissioners Office (IFO) (2012).
2 Sylvie Bleker and Dick Hortensius (Chairman and Secretary respectively of the Dutch Commission NEN on the development of the ISO standard on Compliance management), *Journal of Business Compliance*, 1, 2014.
3 *ISO 19600: 2014 Compliance Management Systems*. Available at: www.iso.org/obp/ui/#iso:std:62342:en/ and its replacement ISO 37301: 2021 www.iso.org/standard/75080.html.
4 As discussed in Part I.
5 Nuijts(2013)andalsonotecurrentwebsiteinformationinrespectofthis:www.dnb.nl/en/reliable-financial-sector/supervision-of-financial-institutions/supervision-of-governance-behaviour-and-culture/.
6 These are broadly grouped in priority order, separated into higher, medium and lower ranked priorities. Individual activities are not then specifically ranked within these broad groups, as the exact ranking would be reflective of the state of each individual jurisdiction.

7 Such as those discussed in Chapters 5 and 6. Note also the example from the UK regulator focused on Heads of compliance and MLRO applicants: www.fca.org.uk/firms/approved-persons/heads-compliance-mlro-applicant-competency-capability.

8 Such as the *National Occupational Standards in Compliance* and others referred to in Chapter 4.

9 For example, qualifications such as the ICA's International Diploma in Compliance is widely recognised as a benchmark qualification for those working in the industry, while others such as those offered by some of the other bodies noted in Appendix 2 are considered mandatory for employment in certain roles in certain sectors. In some jurisdictions wider measures to address education and training activities might also support developments in related areas, such as the UK expansion in Apprenticeships which include those in compliance and risk related areas. And there are of course some focused undertakings in this area, see for example the Irish Banking Culture Boards support of a new Professional Diploma in Leading Cultural Change and Ethical Behaviour in Financial services: www.irishbankingcultureboard. ie/professional-diploma-in-leading-cultural-change-and-ethical-behaviour-in-financial-services-2022–23/.

10 Formed in 2015, relaunched in early 2021 as the Financial Services Culture Board (FSCB) 'core remit has always been to help raise standards of behaviour and competence across the sector, for the benefits of customers, clients and society as a whole': www.financialservicescultureboard.org.uk.

11 Note the Dutch Banking Association and Code of Conduct introduced in 2009, followed by the Oath from 2015. This article provides useful background and commentary on views in relation to this: www.researchgate. net/publication/295179761_Swearing_to_be_a_good_banker_Perceptions_of_the_obligatory_banker's_ oath_in_the_Netherlands, while www.ing.com/About-us/Corporate-Governance/Dutch-Banking-Code. htm, including some interesting insight into application within a regulated firm.

12 For example, the Federal Sentencing Guidelines for Organizations www.ussc.gov/guidelines/organizational-guidelines were amended in November 2010, to allow that a convicted organisation might be eligible for a reduced sentence if it has established an effective compliance and ethics programme. Note another example here: www.deloitte.com/dl/en/pages/legal/articles/compliance-management-system.html. For a practical insight and a useful attachment detailing examples of discounts across different jurisdictions, note www. reedsmith.com/en/perspectives/2020/09/should-compliance-programmes-enable-discounts-from-fines.

13 Once noted during the regulators' authorisation and supervisory activities – obviously with the caveat that there are no guarantees and it is only that the organisation bears all the hallmarks of having such a regime!

14 Perhaps something similar to that offered by the International Compliance Association (see Appendix 2) which provides company certification services 'the process by which a firm's systems are assessed for conformity against ISO standards' www.int-comp.org/corporate/ica-risk/ica-audit-faqs/.

15 That is, formally establishing the role as a recognised profession along the lines of law, accountancy and so forth.

16 H. Langton, 'Taking the high road', in *inCompliance*, ICA's in-house journal, autumn 2013.

17 Boehme (2009).

18 Ethics Resource Center (2007).

19 Chief Compliance and Ethics Officer.

20 Deloitte (2012a), www2.deloitte.com/cbc/en/pages/financial-services/articles/cultivating-a-risk-intelligent-culture-in-fsi.html, note also the 2015 follow up www2.deloitte.com/content/dam/Deloitte/uk/Documents/ audit/deloitte-uk-erm-a-risk-intelligent-approach.pdf and current insights www2.deloitte.com/us/en/pages/ risk/topics/strategic-and-reputation-risk.html.

21 As with recommendations to regulators, policymakers and influencers in the wider regulatory environment these are broadly grouped in priority order, separated into higher, medium and lower ranked priorities. Individual activities are not then ranked further within these broad groups, as again the exact ranking would then be reflective of issues and requirements within each individual organisation.

22 Such as the previously noted FCA views on head of compliance and MLRO applicant competency and capability www.fca.org.uk/firms/approved-persons/heads-compliance-mlro-applicant-competency-capability with its flagging of experience to demonstrate competency and capability.

23 The previously discussed Cost of Compliance surveys highlight this, note also this article www.fnlondon.com/articles/compliance-staff-are-in-demand-firms-lure-with-salary-hikes-remote-working-and-company-equity-20220120 and the salary guide referred to therein for additional current insight.

24 Such as some of those noted in Appendix 2, for example.

25 Incidentally, some of these appear to have become more fractured in membership over time, separating into different sector groups as numbers have grown. This, while providing some benefit in terms of ensuring small

enough groups to encourage sharing of views and provide opportunity for contributions, has had the unfortunate consequence of diluting one of their initial aims, which was to learn from the related experiences of those in other sectors.

26 Note again the Michael Page and Barclay Simpson websites for information on the compliance role, qualifications, salaries and recruitment.

27 Langton (2013).

28 As with previous recommendations, above, these are broadly grouped in priority order, separated into higher, medium and lower ranked priorities. Individual activities are not then ranked further within these broad groups, as the exact ranking would reflect the requirements of different groups and individuals.

29 The ICA, for example, report steady increases year on year, with expansion into new jurisdictions, together with a significant increase in professional programmes being conducted in-house in addition to public courses.

30 A. Smith-Meyer, 'Blow the winds of change: The changing role of compliance', *Journal of Business Compliance*, 1, 2014.

Conclusion

This text was produced during a time of continuing upheaval in the global financial services industry, was subsequently refreshed, then revisited with a global pandemic in recent collective memory during a tumultuous year on the global and national stage. This allowed for consideration of specific developments over more than a decade, contrasting intent with achievement and findings then with now.

Progress in the achievement of aims has been definite, but mixed, clearer in some areas than others. As with so many crises and events previously, the pandemic inevitably tested regulation and its ability to be sufficiently flexible to effectively respond to the challenges arising, with views on efficacy dependent on a host of factors, including the views of individual stakeholders. In responding to these, matters both global and national have impacted recovery and shifted priorities, necessitating continual adaptation by firms and individuals. Seemingly never-ending challenges have presented themselves within this industry as in so many others, with action on the part of individual stakeholders often formulated whilst grappling with the very challenges that have prompted regular calls for change. Negative reports of regulatory omissions and/or weaknesses, crises in different sectors and jurisdictions, the emergence of a host of scandals and tales of wrong-doing across the corporate world; all of these have provided the backdrop to development of this text and the ever-evolving nature of the industry, with new and emerging factors contributing to its single most consistent feature: change. On the plus side, however, this text was also written and updated during a time that contained regular pockets of concerted, collective effort on the parts of international and governmental bodies, of regulators, policymakers, practitioners, researchers and educators across many different jurisdictions and sectors, of firms large and small, and, of course, of individuals working within them, to actively stem this tide of negativity. Each in different ways has put their energy into activities in support of this objective: the production of policy reviews and frameworks, new or enhanced legislation, additional prudential and conduct requirements, codes of best practice, guidance and recommendations on a whole host of linked topics, including governance, culture, ethics, standards, regulation, supervision methodologies, roles of boards and of supervisors, internal controls, risk management, revised models of regulation, assurance methodologies and so on. With this continuous positive swell of focus and prioritisation in the balance against the negative back-swell of difficulties and wrong-doing, it is hoped that through these combined efforts the mutual goals of

DOI: 10.4324/9781003431305-14

improving standards within the corporate world and of encouraging a more robust ethical culture within it will be achieved – or at the very least, much improved – to the benefit of us all.

At the outset of this text, we asked whether the efforts currently in play to address the many difficulties facing the industry would genuinely tackle some of the most significant areas of weakness apparent: namely, those of ethics and the integrity and actions of people, both collectively and individually. We reflected on the challenges of the more recent business climate, with its renewed focus on oversight and conduct, identifying regulatory risk as a significant risk for regulated firms and regulators alike. We explained how the management of this risk through the activities of the Compliance role, with its links to governance, operational risk management and its underlying support of ethical cultural development, is one of the most effective means of not only addressing this, but also the wider challenges facing the regulatory environment. As we move further into an era of business that is increasingly concerned with matters of integrity and ethics, that is supported by judgement-based proactive supervision and outcomes-focused regulation, and as we reflect on the impact of ongoing change within the regulatory environment that surrounds it, we ask what we should now expect of those who work in this challenging arena and what their role should be in supporting it.

The need to make more effective use of the Compliance function, particularly in this time of resourcing challenges across industry, is highlighted and, across this collective text, we have made our case in support of this view:

- we explored regulatory and compliance risk within the regulatory and Compliance environments and the various mechanisms in place to manage these;
- we provided background on the development of the Compliance function and the environment in which this took place and showed how it has adjusted to better serve the shifting needs of its operational Compliance environment, explaining how this in turn alters what is required of individuals to be effective in these roles;
- we looked at the roles of key stakeholders in this process – regulators, the board and senior management of regulated firms, and of Compliance personnel themselves – and considered their activities in support of this aim and how their approach can strongly impact on the Compliance function's efficacy;
- we reflected on why Compliance matters and who to, what the challenges to its successful performance can be and how the role can, in a practical way, be further enabled to achieve its objectives.

The role of Compliance in supporting collective efforts towards improvements in the financial services environment is substantial. Having emerged from its predominantly back office role of monitoring, it has taken its place as an established and worthy member of the oversight and assurance operations within regulated businesses. However, notwithstanding its unique role as the bridge between the regulator and the regulated business, the true benefits of its position as a conduit for the effective management of regulatory risk have yet to be fully harnessed. Developing as a recognised profession in its own right, with a growing number of experienced professionals working to create an environment in which the collective regulatory aims and objectives of both the regulator and the regulated firm can be channelled to the benefit of both, Compliance has a significant role to play in turning words into deeds. Empowering individuals and teams working within these roles will robustly support the stated collective aims of the industry and will play a pivotal role in demonstrating – internally, externally and to all stakeholders – a genuine commitment to addressing the behaviours and resulting problems of the past as the profession strives towards supporting the desired regulatory and business environments that exemplify the underlying regulatory aims of transparency, fairness and protection.

Appendix 1

Influential Bodies

The activities and output of a number of international bodies have a significant impact on the regulatory environment and, in turn, on the Compliance environment. Examples of those with the most influential remit and output are provided below in summaries extracted from their respective websites.[1]

European Central Bank (ECB) – Since 1 January 1999, the European Central Bank (ECB) has been responsible for conducting monetary policy for the euro area – the world's largest economy after the United States. The euro area came into being when responsibility for monetary policy was transferred from the national central banks of 11 EU Member States to the ECB in January 1999. Greece joined in 2001, Slovenia in 2007, Cyprus and Malta in 2008, Slovakia in 2009 and Estonia in 2011. The creation of the euro area and of a new supranational institution, the ECB, was a milestone in the long, complex and ongoing process of European integration.

The legal basis for the single monetary policy is the *Treaty establishing the European Community* and the *Statute of the European System of Central Banks and of the European Central Bank*. The Statute established both the ECB and the European System of Central Banks (ESCB) from 1st June 1998. The ECB was established as the core of the Euro system and the ESCB. The ECB and the national central banks together perform the tasks they have been entrusted with. The ECB has legal personality under public international law.[2]

Basel Committee on Banking Supervision (BCBS) – initially named the Committee on Banking Regulations and Supervisory Practices – was established by the central bank Governors of the Group of Ten countries at the end of 1974 in the aftermath of serious disturbances in international currency and banking markets (notably the failure of Bankhaus Herstatt in West Germany).

The Committee, headquartered at the Bank for International Settlements in Basel, was established to enhance financial stability by improving the quality of banking supervision worldwide and to serve as a forum for regular cooperation between its member countries on banking supervisory matters. The Committee's first meeting took place in February 1975, and meetings have been held regularly three or four times a year since.

Since its inception, the Basel Committee has expanded its membership from the G10 to 45 institutions from 28 jurisdictions. Starting with the Basel Concordat, first issued in 1975 and revised several times since, the Committee has established a series of international standards for bank regulation, most notably its landmark publications of the accords on capital adequacy which are commonly known as Basel I, Basel II and, most recently, Basel III.[3]

Bank for International Settlements (BIS) – the mission of the Bank for International Settlements (BIS) is to support central banks' pursuit of monetary and financial stability through international cooperation, and to act as a bank for central banks. To pursue their mission, they provide central banks with a forum for dialogue and broad international cooperation, a platform for responsible innovation and knowledge-sharing, in-depth analysis and insights on core policy issues and sound and competitive financial service. Established in 1930 the BIS is owned by 63 central banks, representing countries from around the world that together account for about 95% of world GDP. Its head office is in Basel, Switzerland and it has two representative offices: in Hong Kong SAR and in Mexico City, as well as Innovation Hub Centres around the world.[4]

Financial Action Task Force (FATF) – the global money laundering and terrorist financing watchdog. The inter-governmental body sets international standards that aim to prevent these illegal activities and the harm they cause to society. As a policy-making body, the FATF works to generate the necessary political will to bring about national legislative and regulatory reforms in these areas.

With more than 200 countries and jurisdictions committed to implementing them. The FATF has developed the FATF Recommendations, or FATF Standards, which ensure a coordinated global response to prevent organised crime, corruption and terrorism. They help authorities go after the money of criminals dealing in illegal drugs, human trafficking and other crimes. The FATF also works to stop funding for weapons of mass destruction.

The FATF reviews money laundering and terrorist financing techniques and continuously strengthens its standards to address new risks, such as the regulation of virtual assets, which have spread as cryptocurrencies gain popularity. The FATF monitors countries to ensure they implement the FATF Standards fully and effectively and holds countries to account that do not comply.[5]

The Task Force was given the responsibility of examining money laundering techniques and trends, reviewing the action which had already been taken at a national or international level, and setting out the measures that still needed to be taken to combat money laundering. In April 1990, less than one year after its creation, the FATF issued a report containing a set of *Forty Recommendations*, which were intended to provide a comprehensive plan of action needed to fight against money laundering.

In 2001, the development of standards in the fight against terrorist financing was added to the mission of the FATF. In October 2001 the FATF issued the *Eight Special Re*commendations to deal with the issue of terrorist financing. The continued evolution of money laundering techniques led the FATF to revise the FATF standards comprehensively in June 2003. In October 2004 the FATF published a Ninth Special Recommendations, further strengthening the agreed international standards for combating money laundering and terrorist financing – the *40+9 Recommendations*.

In February 2012, the FATF completed a thorough review of its standards and published the revised FATF Recommendations. This revision is intended to strengthen global safeguards and further protect the integrity of the financial system by providing governments with stronger tools to take action against financial crime. They have been expanded to deal with new threats such as the financing of proliferation of weapons of mass destruction, and to be clearer on transparency and tougher on corruption. The 9 Special Recommendations on terrorist financing have been fully integrated with the measures against money laundering. This has resulted in a stronger and clearer set of standards.[6]

Group of International Finance Centre Supervisors (GIFCS) – a long-established group of financial services supervisors with a core interest of promoting the adoption of international regulatory standards especially in the banking, fiduciary and AML/CFT arena.

The GIFCS was established in 1980. Its membership accounts for a market share of nearly 10% of global international banking assets. The Group has become a very positive contributor to promoting compliance among its membership with the Basel Core Principles for Effective Banking Supervision, the IOSCO Principles of Securities Regulation, and the Recommendations of the FATF. Through the publication of an international standard the GIFCS has also become recognised as a leading authority on the regulation of trust and company service providers, and the interface of these intermediaries with AML/CFT standards.

The Group's purposes are to: (1) Contribute to global financial stability through the support and adoption of international regulatory standards and the promotion of best practice where appropriate. (2) Apply its collective expertise to participate in change and effectively influence debate and consultation on evolving regulatory standards. (3) Provide mutual technical support to each other and a forum for promoting common interests.[7]

European System of Financial Supervision[8] – a network centred around three European Supervisory Authorities (ESAs), the European Systemic Risk Board and national supervisors. Its main task is to ensure consistent and appropriate financial supervision throughout the EU. As the European banking supervisor, the ECB closely cooperates with the ESAs, especially the European Banking Authority (EBA). The ESFS covers both macro-prudential and micro-prudential supervision.

Macro-prudential supervision – involves oversight of the financial system as a whole. Its main aim is to prevent or mitigate risks to the financial system.

- **European Systemic Risk Board** – responsible for macro-prudential supervision of the financial system in the EU. Although not part of the ECB, the ESRB is based at the ECB's offices in Frankfurt am Main, Germany, and the ECB ensures its Secretariat.
- **Tasks** – The main tasks of the ESRB are:
  - collecting and analysing relevant information to identify systemic risks
  - issuing warnings where systemic risks are deemed to be significant
  - issuing recommendations for action in response to the risks identified
  - monitoring the follow-up of warnings and recommendations
  - cooperating and coordinating with ESAs and international fora

Micro-prudential supervision – Micro-prudential supervision refers to the supervision of individual institutions, such as banks, insurance companies or pension funds.

- **European Supervisory Authorities** – The ESAs are the:
- European Banking Authority (EBA)
- European Insurance and Occupational Pensions Authority (EIOPA)
- European Securities and Markets Authority (ESMA)
- **Tasks** – The ESAs work primarily on harmonising financial supervision in the EU by developing the single rulebook, a set of prudential standards for individual financial institutions. The ESAs help to ensure the consistent application of the rulebook to create a level playing field. They are also mandated to assess risks and vulnerabilities in the financial sector.

The International Monetary Fund (IMF)[9] – works to achieve sustainable growth and prosperity for all of its 190 member countries. It does so by supporting economic policies that promote financial stability and monetary cooperation, which are essential to increase productivity, job creation, and economic well-being. The IMF is governed by and accountable to its member countries.

The IMF has three critical missions: furthering international monetary cooperation, encouraging the expansion of trade and economic growth, and discouraging policies that would harm prosperity. To fulfill these missions, IMF member countries work collaboratively with each other and with other international bodies.

The IMF fosters international financial stability by:

- **Policy Advice**
- **Financial Assistance**
- **Capacity Development**

International Organisation of Securities Commissions (IOSCO) – the international body that brings together the world's securities regulators and is recognised as the global standard setter for the securities sector. IOSCO develops, implements and promotes adherence to internationally recognised standards for securities regulation. It works intensively with the G20 and the Financial Stability Board (FSB) on the global regulatory reform agenda. OSCO was established in 1983. Its membership regulates more than 95% of the world's securities markets in more than 130 jurisdictions: securities regulators in emerging markets account for 75% of its ordinary membership.

The *IOSCO Objectives and Principles of Securities Regulation* have been endorsed by both the G20 and the FSB as the relevant standards in this area. They are the overarching core principles that guide IOSCO in the development and implementation of internationally recognised and consistent standards of regulation, oversight and enforcement. They form the basis for the evaluation of the securities sector for the Financial Sector Assessment Programs (FSAPs) of the International Monetary Fund (IMF) and the World Bank.

By providing high quality technical assistance, education and training, and research to its members and other regulators, IOSCO seeks to build sound global capital markets and a robust global regulatory framework.[10]

FURTHER

Other influential bodies which may be of interest, dependent upon industry sector, are the International Association of Deposit Insurers (IADI)[11] and International Association of Insurance Supervisors (IAIS).[12]

NOTES

1   Associations of regulatory authorities, either within groups of jurisdictions or at world level.
2   Based on extract from www.ecb.int/ecb/orga/escb/html/index.en.html.
3   See: www.bis.org/bcbs/history.htm.
4   Extracted from http://www.bis.org/about.
5   Extracted from http://www.fatf-gafi.org/pages/aboutus/.
6   www.fatf-gafi.org/about/historyofthefatf.
7   Extracted from www.groupgifcs.org/about/purpose-and-objectives.
8   Taken from www.bankingsupervision.europa.eu/about/esfs/html/index.en.html.
9   Adapted from www.imf.org/en/About/Factsheets/IMF-at-a-Glance.
10 Adapted from www.iosco.org/about/.
11 www.iadi.org/en/.
12 www.iaisweb.org.

Appendix 2

Associations, Organisations and Professional Bodies

This appendix provides links to and extracts from a number of associations, organisations and professional bodies whose offerings and activities will be of interest to Compliance professionals in respect of membership, training, education, networking and related matters. Some of these have a worldwide membership, others are jurisdiction, sector or subject specific.[1]

The Association of Professional Compliance Consultants (APCC)

The Association of Professional Compliance Consultants (APCC) is the body for compliance consultants who advise firms regulated in the UK. The APCC is active in enhancing the professional standards of compliance consultants and is recognised as a trade body by the FCA and other regulators. This provides our members with significant benefits in terms of direct access to the Regulators as well as business leads. The APCC often works in conjunction with the FCA to pilot or test new initiatives, and we also provide with valuable feedback on specific subjects as requested by them.

Members also benefits from our regular forums, technical briefings and interaction with other members. Members' are listed on the APCC website Directory which can produce potential new business for them and publically confirms their commitment to our professional standards. We also receive direct referrals from the FCA which often leads to new clients for our members.[2]

The Australian Financial Markets Association (AFMA)

The Australian Financial Markets Association (AFMA) was formed in 1986. Today we are the leading industry association promoting efficiency, integrity and professionalism in Australia's financial markets – including the capital, credit, derivatives, foreign exchange and other specialist markets.

We have more than 130 members, from Australian and international banks, leading brokers, securities companies and state government treasury corporations to fund managers, energy traders and industry service providers. Our role is to provide a forum for industry leadership and to advance the interests of all these market participants.

Promoting Best Practice

AFMA promotes best practice in financial markets so they can continue to contribute to Australia's economic health. We do this by:

- Effectively managing Australia's over-the-counter (OTC) markets;
- Developing widely accepted industry standards for transactional processing;
- Dealing with policy makers on effective regulation of Australia's financial markets to inspire investors' confidence; and
- Encouraging high standards of professional conduct through our professional development and accreditation programs.

Our Mission – Advancing Australia's Financial Markets

- Promote Australia as a global centre for financial services;
- Help members grow their businesses and contribute to Australia's economic wellbeing;
- Develop new markets for financial products;
- Encourage existing markets to reach their full potential;
- Lead and sustain effective management of OTC financial markets;
- Represent market participants in exchange-traded markets to ensure effective and efficient market processes and regulation;
- Encourage high standards of professional conduct;
- Develop individual expertise through professional development and accreditation programs; and
- Promote government policies and business conditions that support a strong financial sector. [3]

UK Finance

UK Finance is the collective voice for the banking and finance industry. Representing around 300 firms across the industry, we act to enhance competitiveness, support customers and facilitate innovation. We work for and on behalf of our members to promote a safe, transparent and innovative banking and finance industry. We offer research, policy expertise, thought leadership and advocacy in support of our work. We provide a single voice for a diverse and competitive industry. Our operational activity enhances members' own services in situations where collective industry action adds value.[4]

The British Virgin Islands Association of Compliance Officers (BVI ACO)

The British Virgin Islands Association of Compliance Officers ("BVI ACO") aims to foster a culture of compliance in the jurisdiction. It is the BVI ACO's ultimate goal to contribute to the reputation of the British Virgin Islands as a highly attractive and regulated international financial centre.

In doing so, the BVI ACO through its membership will promote the importance of compliance through various forums, encourage the sharing of information and exchange of ideas amongst the industry as well as with the policy makers and provide opportunities to the entire industry for professional development.

Every two years the members elect a council of seven members to represent them. These members meet once per month, or more frequently where required, to discuss the objectives of the BVI ACO.[5]

The Cayman Islands Compliance Association (CICA)

The Cayman Islands Compliance Association ("CICA") has been in existence since October 2000 as a not-for-profit organisation.
The formal objectives of CICA are to:

- Provide members with the information to assist with the implementation and maintenance of effective compliance and anti-money laundering programmes in their respective financial services organisation.
- Provide an open forum for sharing information and training.
- Identify common practices in the financial services industry and seek to raise the level of compliance in the financial services industry.
- Provide a forum for discussion of new legislation or required best practice relevant to the Cayman Islands financial services industry.
- Offer information on compliance and anti-money laundering issues.
- Provide an interface between senior management of member financial services organisations and regulators and law enforcement agencies.[6]

The Chartered Institute for Securities & Investment (CISI)

The Chartered Institute for Securities & Investment (CISI) is the leading professional body for securities, investment, wealth and financial planning professionals. Dedicated to professionalism since it emerged from the London Stock exchange in 1992, its purpose is to champion lifelong learning and integrity, raising individual standards of knowledge, skills and behaviour globally to enhance public trust and confidence in financial services.[7]

The Chartered Insurance Institute (CII)

The Chartered Insurance Institute (CII) are a professional body dedicated to building public trust in the insurance and financial planning profession. Our strapline Standards. Professionalism. Trust. embodies our commitment to driving confidence in the power of professional standards: competence, integrity and care for the customer.

We deliver that commitment through relevant learning, insightful leadership and an engaged membership. Our 125,000 members commit to high professional standards by maintaining continuing professional development and adhering to a published ethical code.

Our Royal Charter requires us to secure and justify the confidence of the public.[8]

CSI World Headquarters

CSI World Headquarters is a professional membership-based, organisation dedicated to advancing the techniques of big data, financial analysis and forensic investigation.[9]

The Guernsey Association of Compliance Officers (GACO)

The Guernsey Association of Compliance Officers (GACO) was formed in April 1999 with the following objectives:

- To provide a forum for discussion of governance, risk & compliance issues
- To provide information and other services to its members
- To assist other formal Guernsey bodies on governance, risk and compliance issues

GACO currently has a broad membership representing all businesses Regulated and Registered by the GFSC. This diversity of membership is reflected in the composition of the Committee, which has people with a range of backgrounds and experience covering all the elements of the financial services businesses in Guernsey. Committee members are elected for a two-year term of office by the members at the Annual General Meeting and can be assisted by co-opted members.[10]

The Ethics & Compliance Officer Association (ECOA)

The Ethics & Compliance Officer Association (ECOA) is a professional membership association and research institution with a focus on enhancing an organisation's compliance to the highest standards of ethics in the governance of their dealings. ECOA aims to encourage through advisement and consultation, to build and sustain a system that is proven to increase integrity in respective organisations' mandate. The association is also for individuals who are responsible for their company's ethics, compliance, and business conduct programs. Dedicated to building trust and corporate integrity in Africa, we help leaders create strong ethical workplace cultures and successful businesses that do the right thing.[11]

Hawkamah, the Institute for Corporate Governance

Hawkamah is a world-class corporate governance institute working to help in building sound organisations, corporate sector reform, strong banking and financial sector, good governance. Our vision is to see the MENA region enjoying healthy corporate governance environment and frameworks. Our mission is to assist companies to develop sound and globally recognised corporate governance frameworks. Hawkamah helps also in building qualified directors and top executives who are able to apply corporate governance in their organisations.[12]

Institute of Banking and Finance Singapore (IBF)

The Institute of Banking and Finance Singapore (IBF) was established in 1974 as a not-for-profit industry association to foster and develop the professional competencies of the financial industry. IBF represents the interests of close to 200 member financial institutions including banks, insurance companies, securities brokerages and asset management firms. In partnership with the financial industry, government agencies, training providers and the trade unions, IBF is committed to equip practitioners with capabilities to support the growth of Singapore's financial industry.

IBF is the national accreditation and certification agency for financial industry competency in Singapore under the Skills Framework for Financial Services, which were developed in partnership with the industry. Individuals who complete the IBF-accredited skills training programmes and meet the relevant criteria may apply for IBF Certification.[13]

Isle of Man Association of Corporate Services Providers (ACSP)

The Association of Corporate Service Providers (ACSP) was founded to further the development of the Isle of Man as an international centre for the provision of corporate and trust services. The ACSP was formed on 25 June 1999 with the primary objective of serving as the representative body for fiduciary, corporate management and administration services providers in the Isle of Man. The response from the industry was quite remarkable with a significant majority of those eligible for membership becoming members. With such an overwhelming level of membership the ACSP is effectively the trade body of the industry in the Isle of Man.[14]

Chartered Governance Institute UK & Ireland

The Chartered Governance Institute UK & Ireland assure world-class standards of governance by setting the international qualifying standard as the only chartered professional body dedicated to supporting governance professionals. As a lifelong learning partner, we help governance professionals to achieve their professional goals, providing recognition, community and the voice of our membership.

Membership of the Institute enables governance professionals to: Achieve recognition, Advance their careers, Commit to their continuing professional development, Uphold a code of conduct and ethics, Be at the forefront of the governance industry.[15]

The International Compliance Association (ICA)

The International Compliance Association (ICA) is the leading professional body for the global regulatory and financial crime compliance community. Since 2001, we have enhanced the knowledge, skills and behaviour of over 160,000 professionals, either through our internationally recognised portfolio of professional qualifications (awarded in association with Alliance Manchester Business School, the University of Manchester) or through accredited in-company training.[16]

Jersey Compliance Officers Association (JCOA)

The Jersey Compliance Officers Association (JCOA) was formed in 1997 with members comprising compliance officers, regulators and other professionals from the financial services industry. Our membership has grown steadily and the Association now has over 500 members from over 120 financial and associated institutions in Jersey.

The Association provides:

- Free members' meetings with high-quality speakers covering topical and relevant issues.
- A forum for discussing compliance issues and promoting good compliance practice;
- A cost-effective source of continuing professional development (CPD)
- Discounts on external events and professional courses
- A professional support network.[17]

The Jersey Bankers Association (JBA)

The Jersey Bankers Association (JBA) is the professional association of licensed banks in Jersey.

JBA membership encompasses all banks in Jersey, including UK clearing banks, private banks and a range of international banking groups.[18]

Asian Institute of Chartered Bankers (AICB)

The Asian Institute of Chartered Bankers (AICB) is the sole professional body for Malaysia's banking industry. Founded in 1977 as the Institute of Bankers Malaysia (or Institut Bank-bank Malaysia (IBBM)), it transformed into AICB in 2015 and today, has over 34,000 members. The Institute is governed by a council of representatives from Bank Negara Malaysia (BNM), The Association of Banks in Malaysia (ABM), and the Malaysian Investment Banking Association (MIBA).

Our aim is to elevate professional and ethical standards in banking by creating a workforce with the highest standards of professional conduct, knowledge and competence. AICB is the only institute in Southeast Asia that is authorised by the Chartered Banker Institute, UK, to award the Chartered Banker status.

We continue to engage with industry experts to ensure that our suite of qualifications remains relevant and future-proof, equipping bankers with the requisite skills and values to keep pace with the fast-evolving banking environment.[19]

The Institute of Risk Management (IRM)

The Institute of Risk Management (IRM) is the leading professional body for Enterprise Risk Management. We help build excellence in risk management to improve the way organisations work.

We provide globally recognised qualifications and training, publish research and thought leadership and set professional standards, which define the knowledge, skills and behaviours today's risk professionals need to meet the demands of an increasingly complex and challenging business environment.

IRM members work in many roles, in all industries and across the public, private and not-for-profit sectors around the world. We are independent and not-for-profit.[20]

The Investment Association (IA)

The Investment Association (IA) is the trade body and industry voice for UK investment managers. The UK investment management industry plays a major role in the economy, helping millions of individuals and families achieve their life goals by helping grow their investments (mainly through workplace pensions). In fact, 75% of UK households use an investment manager's services (knowingly or unknowingly). The industry also invests, billions of pounds in companies and the financing of transport networks, hospitals, schools and housing projects. The industry supports 122,000 jobs in the UK, including 13,900 in Scotland. It's the largest industry of its kind in Europe, and the second largest in the world, after America. Our members range from small, independent UK investment firms to Europe-wide and global players. Collectively, they manage over £10 trillion of assets on behalf of their clients in the UK and around the world. That is 12% of the £83 trillion global assets under management. We act as their voice and represent their interests to policymakers and regulators, and help explain to the wider world what the industry does.[21]

Society of Corporate Compliance and Ethics (SCCE)

The Society of Corporate Compliance and Ethics (SCCE) is a member-based association with 6,000+ compliance and ethics members worldwide. SCCE was founded in 2004 by Health Care Compliance Association (HCCA) to support compliance and ethics professionals across all industries. The vision of SCCE is to be the pre-eminent compliance and ethics association promoting lasting success and integrity of organisations worldwide. In 2011, SCCE incorporated with our founding organisation to form Society of Corporate Compliance and Ethics & Health Care Compliance Association (SCCE & HCCA).[22]

OTHER USEFUL WEBSITES

Risk.net

The world's leading source of in-depth news and analysis on complex markets

Risk.net explores topics in detail, assesses implications, speaks with practitioners, regulators and other stakeholders, and produces detailed analytical content.

Our users are able to make better, more informed decisions thanks to the information we provide.[23]

Thomson Reuters

Thomson Reuters is one of the world's most trusted providers of answers, helping professionals make confident decisions and run better businesses. Our customers operate in complex arenas that move society forward – law, tax, compliance, government, and media – and face increasing complexity as regulation and technology disrupt every industry.

We help them reinvent the way they work. Our team of experts brings together information, innovation and authoritative insight to unravel complex situations, and our worldwide network of journalists and editors keep customers up to speed on global developments that are relevant to them.

We're on a mission to help professionals advance their businesses and gain competitive advantage with the trusted answers only we can provide.[24]

NOTES

1 Note that those included are a sample provided for illustrative purposes only and the content of this list should not be relied upon as definitive: interested parties should research further the associations, organisations and professional bodies in respect of compliance, governance and risk that exist in their own jurisdiction and sector.

2 Extracted from and additional information available at: www.apcc.org.uk/the-apcc/what-is-the-apcc.

3 Extracted from and additional information available at: www.afma.com.au/aboutus.html.

4 Extracted from and additional information available at: www.ukfinance.org.uk/about-us.

5 Extracted from and additional information available at: www.bviaco.org/About-Us.

6 Extracted from and additional information available at: www.cica.ky/the-cayman-islands-compliance-association.

7 Extracted from and additional information available at: www.cisi.org/cisiweb2/cisi-website/about-us.

8 Extracted from and additional information available at: www.cii.co.uk/about/about-the-cii/the-chartered-insurance-institute/.

9 Extracted from and additional information available from: www.csiworldhq.com/about_us/.

10 Extracted from and additional information available at: www.gaco.org.gg/about/default.aspx.

11 Extracted from and further information available at: www.ecoass.org/about-us/.

12 Extracted from and additional information available at: www.hawkamah.org.

13 Extracted from and additional information available at: www.ibf.org.sg/about-ibf/about-ibf.asp.

14 Extracted from and additional information available at: www.acsp.co.im/.

15 Extracted from and additional information available at: www.cgi.org.uk.

16 Extracted from and additional information available at: www.int-comp.org.
17 Extracted from and additional information available at: www.jcoa.co.uk/.
18 Extracted from and additional information available at: www.jerseybankersassociation.com.
19 Extracted from and additional information available at: www.aicb.org.my.
20 Extracted from and additional information available at: www.theirm.org.
21 Extracted from and additional information available at: www.theia.org.
22 Extracted from and additional information available at: www.corporatecompliance.org.
23 Extracted from and additional information available at: www.risk.net.
24 Extracted from and additional information available at: www.thomsonreuters.com.

Appendix 3

Compliance Function – Best Practice Guidance

INTERNATIONAL BEST PRACTICE GUIDANCE

Based on the output of a variety of studies and consultations, several papers focusing on the Compliance function and compliance activities have been issued by some of the influential international bodies noted in Chapter 2. Widely recognised examples include:

Body	Paper
International Organisation of Securities Commissions (IOSCO)	*The Function of Compliance Officer* – July 2003[1]
Basel Committee on Banking Supervision (BCBS)	*Compliance and the Compliance Function in Banks* – 2005[2] *Implementation of the compliance principles: A survey* – August 2008[3]
IOSCO	*Compliance Function at Market Intermediaries* – March 2006[4]
European Securities and Markets Authority (ESMA)	*Guidelines on Certain Aspects of the MiFID Compliance Function Requirements* – July 2012 and most recent 2020[5]
International Organisation for Standardisation (ISO)	*ISO 19600:2014 Compliance management systems and most recent ISO 37301:2021 Compliance management systems*[6]

Although produced by bodies spanning multiple financial services sectors and jurisdictions internationally and with specific relevance to individual sectors and groups of regulated businesses, these papers have relevance to all regulated financial services firms, wherever located. Recommendations contained within them is indicative of good practice and will be reflected in the requirements of regulators in individual jurisdictions/ sectors because implementation of such guidelines into national requirements is usually overseen by regulators as part of their ongoing assessment of compliance in respect of the regulations that apply in their jurisdiction/sector. Accordingly, it is anticipated that all firms – both those directly required to adhere to the guidance and those who are not directly affected by it – would reference this guidance as a means of checking their own approach, allowing them to adjust it if necessary, depending on what is appropriate for their own organisation.

EXAMPLES OF NATIONAL BEST PRACTICE GUIDANCE

In addition to these international initiatives, at national level there is best practice guidance that is of relevance regarding the Compliance role in addition to statutory requirements set by national regulators. The following are examples of such guidance:

Body	Paper
National Occupational Standards (NOS)	*National Occupational Standards in Compliance* – 2006, updated 2011 and 2018[7]
British Standards Institute (BSI)	*Compliance Framework for Regulated Financial Services Firms – Specification*, British Standards BS8453:2011[8]

As with the international best practice guidance, the recommendations in these papers are not binding regulatory requirements. They are intended to provide interested parties with guidance on the most effective approaches to be taken in relation to the Compliance Function and the Compliance Officer's role.

NOTES

1 Accessible at: www.amvcolombia.org.co/attachments/data/20100630220810.pdf.
2 Accessible at: www.bis.org/publ/bcbs113.pdf.
3 Accessible at: www.bis.org/publ/bcbs142.pdf.
4 Accessible at: www.fsa.go.jp/inter/ios/20060510/02.pdf.
5 Accessible at: www.esma.europa.eu/sites/default/files/library/guidelines_on_certain_aspects_of_mifid_ii_compliance_function_requirements.pdf.
6 An overview can be accessed and the full standards purchased at: www.iso.org/standard/75080.html.
7 Accessible at: www.ukstandards.org.uk.
8 An overview can be accessed and the full standards purchased at: https://knowledge.bsigroup.com/products/compliance-framework-for-regulated-financial-services-firms-specification/standard.

Appendix 4

A Sector- and Jurisdiction-Focused Example of Scandals, Investigations, Compliance Related Findings, Fines, Reports, Recommendations, Action

HBOS[1]

In March 2012 the FSA confirmed in its Final Notice publication[2] that it had been conducting an enforcement investigation into HBOS, noting amongst other key issues that Bank of Scotland's control framework provided an insufficient challenge to the Corporate Division's strategy. The FSA had begun work on a report into the causes of the failure of HBOS in 2008 during the financial crisis (the start of this process was delayed by enforcement proceedings for fear of prejudicing the outcome, but commenced following completion of them).[3] The purpose of this review was to: (1) explain why HBOS failed and cover the FSA's supervision of HBOS and explain the focus of the enforcement actions; and (2) inform a wider internal and public understanding of the causes of failure during the crisis (to the extent not already covered by the RBS report).[4]

However, although due to be published in summer 2013, completion of the report was delayed.[5] Once published, it was intended to be subject to an independent review by the Treasury Select Committee which set out its scope in its *Independent Review of Financial Services Authority's Report on the Failure of HBOS – Terms of Reference*.[6]

One investigation that was completed in the interim, however, was the Parliamentary Commission on Banking Standards (PCBS)[7] *An Accident Waiting to Happen: The Failure of HBOS*, published in March 2013.[8] The commission 'decided to examine HBOS ourselves as a case study of banking failure, in order to identify lessons for our wider work on banking standards and culture'. Some of the points highlighted within this, particularly relevant to our focus in this text, relate to:

failures of internal control, failure of regulation, consequences of reduction in regulatory pressure, change in regulatory focus, scale and level of regulator engagement, the attitude of the firm towards the regulator, issues in respect of the role of the Board, levels of experience and skills of key personnel

A number of the findings in relation to this are, from a learning perspective, worth quoting in some detail. For example, it was noted in the PCBS report that 'The picture that emerges is that the FSA's regulation of HBOS was thoroughly inadequate'[9] and also that

> The experience of the regulation of HBOS demonstrates the fundamental weakness in the regulatory approach prior to the financial crisis and as that crisis unfolded. Too much supervision was undertaken at too low a level – without sufficient engagement of the senior leadership within the FSA. The regulatory approach encouraged a focus on box-ticking which detracted from consideration of the fundamental issues with the potential to bring the bank down. The FSA's approach also encouraged the Board of HBOS to believe that they could treat the regulator as a source of interference to be pushed back, rather than an independent source of guidance and, latterly, a necessary constraint upon the company's mistaken courses of action.[10]

From an objective standpoint it is interesting to note the attitudes of the various parties, both from a specific regulatory risk management perspective and in a wider cultural context.

Further it was observed that, as a result of this, the 'Regulatory failings meant that a number of opportunities were missed to prevent HBOS from pursuing the path that led to its own downfall',[11] although 'Ultimate responsibility for the bank's chosen path lies, however, not with the regulator but with the Board of HBOS itself'.[12] In respect of the Board of HBOS, in its conclusions the report made a particularly stark set of comments with relevance for our discussions in this text. Note the following in particular and reflect again on our discussions in Part II in respect of these topics:

> The corporate governance of HBOS at board level serves as a model for the future, but not in the way in which Lord Stevenson and other former Board members appear to see it. It represents a model of self-delusion, of the triumph of process over purpose.[13]

'There was insufficient banking expertise among HBOS's top management. In consequence, they were incapable of even understanding the risks that some elements of the business were running, let alone managing them'[14] and 'The non-executives on the Board lacked the experience or expertise to identify many of the core risks that the bank was running'.[15] The points regarding appropriate experience at a number of levels are particularly pertinent here, with the consequences running through the findings and linking, in my view, to a number of the key weaknesses flagged.

In November 2015, the PRA and FCA review into the failure of HBOS was finally ready.[16] In publishing, it was stated that

> The review concludes that ultimate responsibility for the failure of HBOS rests with the Board and senior management. They failed to set an appropriate strategy for the firm's business and failed to challenge a flawed business model which placed inappropriate reliance on continuous growth without due regard to risks involved. In addition, flaws in the FSA's supervisory approach meant it did not appreciate the full extent of the risks HBOS was running and was not in a position to intervene before it was too late.

This conclusion, in a nutshell, reinforces views expressed on what consequences can be when risks are not appropriately managed.

Collectively, the findings and subsequent views of those completing these investigations and reviews fed into the consequent demands for a fundamental overhaul of practice within the industry, with an increased focus on personal accountability, culture, and so on.

LONDON INTERBANK LENDING RATE (LIBOR)[17]

The manipulation of LIBOR (the global benchmark interest rate, seen as a measure of trust in the financial system) and the implications for Compliance activity more widely are well worth reflecting upon. A scandal – or rather, a series of scandals – details of which emerged and regulatory responses to which unfolded over a number of years from the late noughties into the mid-2010s, had significant consequences for the regulatory environment internationally, leading to widespread action at a number of levels involving multiple stakeholders.

Rumour and allegations of manipulation of this rate by traders at several banks (influencing the average rate offered) led to investigations into activity in this area. Ultimately a number of regulated firms (and some individuals) were fined by regulators as a consequence of this activity, seen as market manipulation, undermining one of the fundamental objectives of regulation of the markets, as discussed in Part I.

For our purposes in this text, it is useful to consider some of the fines levied in this case and reflect on comments made by regulators about the activities of the individual firms at that time[18]:

---

28 July 2014 – **The Financial Conduct Authority (FCA) has fined Lloyds Bank plc (Lloyds) and Bank of Scotland plc (BoS)**, both part of Lloyds Banking Group (LBG), £105 million for serious misconduct relating to the Special Liquidity Scheme (SLS), the Repo Rate benchmark and the London Interbank Offered Rate (LIBOR). £70 million of the fine relates to attempts to manipulate the fees payable to the Bank of England for the firms' participation in the SLS, a taxpayer-backed government scheme designed to support the UK's banks during the financial crisis. The £105 million total fine is the joint third highest ever imposed by the FCA or its predecessor, the Financial Services Authority, and the seventh penalty for LIBOR-related failures. Whilst the firms' LIBOR-related misconduct is similar in many ways to that of other financial institutions, the manipulation of the Repo Rate benchmark in order to reduce the firms' SLS fees is misconduct of a type that has not been seen in previous LIBOR cases. Tracey McDermott, the FCA's director of enforcement and financial crime, said:

> The firms were a significant beneficiary of financial assistance from the Bank of England through the SLS. Colluding to benefit the firms at the expense, ultimately, of the UK taxpayer was unacceptable. This falls well short of the standards the FCA and the market is entitled to expect from regulated firms. … The abuse of the SLS is a novel feature of this case but *the underlying conduct and the underlying*

failings – to identify, mitigate and monitor for obvious risks – are not new. If trust in financial services is to be restored then market participants need to ensure they are learning the lessons from, and avoiding the mistakes of, their peers. Our enforcement actions are an important source of information to help them do this.[19]

15 May 2014 – The Financial Conduct Authority (FCA) has fined Martin Brokers (UK) Ltd (Martins) £630,000 for misconduct relating to the London Interbank Offered Rate (LIBOR). Martins would have been fined £3,600,000 but for the fact that the firm was able to show that it could not pay a penalty of this amount in addition to the other regulatory fines that Martins faces in relation to LIBOR. Tracey McDermott, director of enforcement and financial crime, said:

> Interdealer brokers are expected to act as trusted intermediaries and are key conduits of market information. Martins abused this position of trust by providing false information to Panel Banks, with no regard for the integrity of the market. This is unacceptable behaviour from any market participant.... .
>
> The culture at Martins was that profit came first. Compliance was seen as a hindrance and the firm lacked the means to detect the "wash trades". In this environment, broker misconduct was almost inevitable. Similar cultural failings at other firms have caused havoc in the financial services industry. As we have said before, firms need to take their responsibilities to uphold market integrity seriously. If firms fail to heed these warnings then we will take action against them.[20]

29 October 2013 – Coöperatieve Centrale Raiffeisen-Boerenleenbank B.A. (Rabobank) fined 'for serious, prolonged and widespread misconduct relating to the London Interbank Offered Rate (LIBOR). The £105 million fine is the third highest ever imposed by the FCA or its predecessor, the Financial Services Authority, and the fifth penalty for LIBOR-related failures'. In the announcement which accompanied the publication of its final notice,[21] the FCA stated that

> Rabobank failed to act with due skill care and diligence; identify, manage or control the relevant risks; or meet proper standards of market conduct. This breached three of the FCA's fundamental principles for businesses, which underpin its objectives to ensure that markets function effectively, and to promote market integrity.

25 September 2013 – ICAP Europe Limited (IEL) £14 million for misconduct relating to the London Interbank Offered Rate (LIBOR), the first broking firm to be fined for failings relating to the benchmark and the fourth penalty for LIBOR related failures.

6 February 2013 – The FSA fined **The Royal Bank of Scotland plc** £87.5 million for misconduct relating to LIBOR.

19 December 2012 – **UBS AG** fined £160 million for significant failings in relation to LIBOR and EURIBOR by FSA. In total, UBS fined a total of $1.5bn (£940m) by US, UK and Swiss regulators for attempting to manipulate LIBOR,[22] agreeing to pay $1.2bn in combined fines to the US Department of Justice and the Commodities

Futures Trading Commission and 59m Swiss Francs to the Swiss Financial Market Supervisory Authority, in addition to the FSA fine.

27 June 2012 – The FSA fined **Barclays Bank plc** £59.5 million for misconduct relating to LIBOR and EURIBOR.

Further details about all these cases can be accessed via the FCA website (www. fca.org.uk).

Two of those fined for LIBOR failings (ICAP and Barclays) are now explored further, focusing particularly on compliance findings/failing and points of interest in relation to these. The detail provided here allows us to reflect on the effectiveness (or otherwise) of elements of the Three Lines model if applied to such operations within a firm.

ICAP Europe Limited (IEL)

The findings of the FCA investigation into ICAP Europe Limited (IEL) provide some useful practical insights into topics pertinent to our discussions in this text, particularly those in Chapter 5 on the Compliance Framework. In its announcement accompanying the issue of its Final Notice[23] the FCA flagged the point that 'IEL's risk management systems and controls were inadequate to monitor and oversee the relevant broking activity. There was *no effective oversight* of the brokers involved, which meant that they were able to conceal their misconduct. From October 2006 to November 2010, IEL did not audit the desk at the centre of the misconduct (the JPY Derivatives Desk)', and 'IEL's *inadequate systems, controls, supervision and monitoring meant that the brokers' misconduct went undetected and continued for several years*'. Amongst the points noted in the Final Notice[24] are issues with the Compliance structure – 'At certain times during the Relevant Period, one Broker, who had only one client, worked in an overseas IEL office which had no Compliance staff and was in a different country from the two different desks to which he reported'[25] – here we can see structural matters, systems and controls and monitoring weaknesses, control and risk management weaknesses, plus those relating to the visibility of the Compliance function, all as discussed in Part II, with it being observed that,

> for most of the Relevant Period, IEL had no Compliance staff based on the broking floors and IEL did not conduct a review of the JPY Derivatives Desk and further, had no Compliance staff at all in one of the overseas offices from which Broker 1, for a time, colluded with Trader A.[26]

There were issues also in respect of culture, of which one particularly pertinent finding was,

> For example, Brokers 1 and 2 have explained that it was unlikely that an IEL Broker would ever escalate to their Compliance department (or to the FCA) concerns about a client. Broker 1 said that it was not "realistic" to expect him to report Trader A's actions. He said, "I don't see any benefit, other than the fact we'd lose a line", "It's not up to me. I'm not a regulator ... I think if brokers brought everything to [regulators] then the brokers would end up having no clients ..."[27]

and 'One manager who was complicit in the collusion said,

> I go to Compliance, [and if a Trader] gets sacked, how many more lines have I got the next day? You have no lines … If you're known as a grass to traders, you're not going to do very well in terms of how many people want to talk to you …'.[28]

Consider each of these views in the context of our considerations around the interconnection of each element of the Compliance framework.

Barclays Bank plc

Consider the compliance findings/failings raised when Barclays were fined[29] by the then UK regulator, the FSA, in relation to their LIBOR submissions in June 2012. Some of the key points highlighted in this included:

> Compliance failures, compliance interaction and involvement, issues relating to the firm's internal controls, awareness of the Compliance role, awareness of compliance and Compliance requirements, Compliance action (or inaction), Problems relating to the flow of information to the Compliance function and from it, both internally and externally

Reflect on this with consideration to the Part II commentary in respect of working within an appropriate Compliance Framework.

In the wake of the regulatory fine and the unfolding of the LIBOR scandal more widely, *An Independent Review of Barclays' Business Practices*[30] was set up reporting to a non-executive committee of Barclays.[31] This independent review – the Salz Review – was published in April 2013. The review was broadly intended: To undertake a root-and-branch review of all of the past practices that have been revealed as flawed since the credit crisis started and identify implications for our business practices and culture going forward; To publish a public report of its findings; To produce a new, mandatory code of conduct that will be applied across Barclays.[32]

In its output, the review highlighted issues with: (1) the risk culture and control framework, and (2) the control function's independence and influence. It noted a range of weaknesses spanning:

> Reporting lines, culture and the risk culture, relationship management, challenges to the regulator, lack of representation of Compliance on key committees, status of Compliance, prioritisation of operational risk, independence of the function, risk management issues, problems with MI, attitude towards Compliance, effectiveness of Compliance training, dealing with breaches, escalation of these, escalation of issues generally, opportunities to challenge, skills and abilities of those in control functions (including Compliance)

Note the similarities here with those noted in the, unrelated, HBOS case flagged earlier. Consider how these span each element of the Compliance Framework set out in Part II, including the role of the many stakeholders within it.

Particularly notable in the findings from this review, for our purposes in this text, are the limitations on Compliance involvement and Compliance reporting lines. For example, Compliance did not contribute to Barclays' response to the BBA's review of LIBOR in 2008[33] and, as *The Salz Review* pointed out:

> For a key period in the run-up to and during the financial crisis (2006 to 2009), the membership of ExCo[34] was kept relatively small (four to six people) ... at times including only ... the Group Chief Executive, the Chief Finance Officer and the two 'cluster' Chief Executives. At that time, ExCo had no direct representation from smaller business units, or from functions such as Group Risk, Compliance, Legal or HR. The cluster arrangement was based on a decentralised system of accountability with a powerful leader for each of the "clusters".[35]

Even setting aside the practicalities around this, what does this suggest regarding the attitude of senior staff within the organisation towards each of these key functions?

London Interbank Lending Rate (LIBOR)[36] and the Regulatory Environment

As can be seen, there were a good number of investigations, findings and reports as a consequence of the LIBOR manipulation scandal. In the context of the compliance environment overall, some of the particularly pertinent points to note within these cases relate to:

> cultural indications and implications, actions of the Compliance function, escalation of issues, attitude towards compliance and Compliance (both within the firm and externally), weaknesses in internal controls, attitude of senior staff, standards, culture, plans for change, tightening of requirements, change of regulatory responsibility

A review which led directly to subsequent change and thus of particular interest to us was that commissioned by the Chancellor of the Exchequer and *The Wheatley Review of LIBOR: Final Report*, [37] was published in September 2012. The review worked to the following terms of reference[38]: (1) Reforming the current framework for setting and governing LIBOR, (2) Determining the adequacy and scope of sanctions to appropriately tackle LIBOR abuse, and (3) Whether similar considerations apply with respect to other price-setting mechanisms in financial markets, and provide provisional policy recommendations in this area.[39] The report provided a 10-point plan for comprehensive reform of LIBOR, with wider implications. Particularly relevant for this text, the report referenced the FSA Final Notice on Barclays in relation to which pointed out that:

> A firm must conduct its business with due skill, care and diligence (Principle 2) Compliance failures meant that inappropriate submissions and inadequate controls persisted. Barclays failed to conduct its business with due skill, care and diligence when considering issues raised internally in relation to its LIBOR submissions, thereby breaching Principle 2. LIBOR issues

were escalated to its internal Compliance function on three occasions, and in each case Compliance failed to assess and address them effectively.[40]

And, in its comments on the 'Limitations of the current governance framework', stated that 'oversight is insufficiently robust – specifically: internal compliance and systems and controls within contributing banks, or within BBA LIBOR Ltd, are not systematically overseen in order to provide assurance before any potential misconduct arises ...'.[41]

The Government accepted the recommendations of the Wheatley Review in October 2012. Following this, the Government published consultation on secondary legislation to implement these, seeking the views of the public and industry specifically in relation to: (1) bringing LIBOR within the scope of regulation; and (2) making the manipulation of LIBOR a criminal offence.

In March 2013, in one of the last actions before their transfer to the FCA, the FSA confirmed that both the administrator and the rate-setting process would be regulated. In the publication of *PS13/6: The Regulation and Supervision of Benchmarks*, [42] the FSA set out the requirements which included that administrators should 'appoint an individual, who is FCA-approved, to oversee the firm's compliance with the FCA's requirements for benchmark administration'[43] and 'appoint an individual, who is FCA-approved, to oversee the firm's compliance with the FCA's requirements for benchmark submission'. In publishing this, Martin Wheatley, who was about to take over as FCA chief executive, stated

> Confidence and trust are critical to financial markets ... That trust has been eroded by the Libor scandal and the recent enforcement action against several banks. These new rules today should help restore that faith and bring integrity back ....

The new regulation in place around LIBOR was not without some controversy, however, with concerns that the costs of this regulation would be significant. Some estimates suggested that 'Setting up a new administrator for Libor will cost £1.6m and running a properly regulated rate-setting process for the scandal-plagued benchmark is likely to cost an additional £1m a year'.[44]

JPMORGAN CHASE BANK N.A.

In our third example, we see again conduct and culture challenges both individual and collective, with manifestations of this more widely across the regulatory and business environments, in the UK and elsewhere.

In September 2013 JP Morgan Chase Bank N.A was fined £137,610,000 by the FCA regulator for serious failings relating to its Chief Investment Office's 'London Whale'[45] trades. In the announcement[46] which accompanied publication of the Final Notice, it was noted that the breaches occurred in connection with the $6.2 billion trading losses sustained by the CIO in 2012. These losses arose as a result of what became known as the 'London Whale' trades and in this announcement Tracey McDermott, the FCA's director of enforcement and financial crime, said:

> When the scale of the problems at JPMorgan became apparent, it *sent a shock-wave through the markets*. Maintaining the integrity of markets is a key part of our wholesale conduct agenda.

We consider JPMorgan's failings to be extremely serious such as to *undermine the trust and confidence in UK financial markets*. This is yet *another example of a firm failing to get a proper grip on the risks* its business poses to the market. There were *basic failings in the operation of fundamental controls* over a high risk part of the business. *Senior management failed to respond properly* to warning signals that there were problems in the CIO. As things began to go wrong, the firm didn't wake up quickly enough to the size and the scale of the problems. What is worse, they *compounded this by failing to be open and co-operative* with us as their regulator. Firms must learn the lessons from this incident and ensure that they have business practices, values and culture to control the risks in their businesses.

The FCA's announcement of the fine provided a summary of the key facts of the case and the level of international liaison with overseas regulators in conducting this case, noting that:

> This was a significant cross-border investigation ... JPMorgan also agreed to settle actions brought by the U.S. Securities and Exchange Commission, who imposed a financial penalty of $200 million and required the Firm to admit wrongdoing; the Office of the Comptroller of the Currency, who imposed a financial penalty of $300 million, and the Federal Reserve, who imposed a financial penalty of $200 million.

What was also notable in this case, as flagged by the Director of Enforcement and Financial Crime of the FCA Tracey McDermott in a speech[47] the month after the FCA Final Notice was issued, was that it 'revealed that, as late as 2012, the culture of greed and perceived invincibility that contributed to the crisis was alive and kicking within financial services firms ...'.

Particularly pertinent points to note in this case relate to:

> Information flow, escalation of issues, involvement of key individuals, involvement of Compliance, provision of key information and the action taken by the compliance function

NOTES

1 'HBOS timeline: An accident waiting to happen' published in *FT Advisor* (Shoffman 2013) in April 2013 provides a simple overview of the events prior to the HBOS debacle being made public, the events that unfolded around it as it became known and the subsequent fallout.
2 FSA (2012a).
3 Final Notice, Peter Cummings, 12 September 2012. Available at: http://www.fsa.gov.uk/static/pubs/final/peter-cummings.pdf.
4 FSA (2012c).
5 Treanor (2013).
6 Available at: http://www.parliament.uk/documents/commons-committees/treasury/Terms%20of%20Reference%20 HBOS%20review.pdf/.
7 The Commission and objectives discussed more fully in Part I of this text in our focus on calls to overhaul the industry post Global Financial Crisis.
8 UK Government (2013b).
9 Ibid., Point 83.
10 Ibid., Point 85.
11 Ibid., Point 86.
12 Ibid., Point 86.

13 Ibid., Point 91.

14 Ibid., Point 93.

15 Ibid., Point 94.

16 www.fca.org.uk/news/press-releases/publication-pra-and-fca-review-failure-hbos.

17 A BBC article 'Timeline: Libor fixing scandal' provides a most straightforward overview of the lead up to the LIBOR rigging scandal, the events that unfolded around it as it became known about and subsequent fallout. Available at: http://www.bbc.co.uk/news/business-18671255, 6 February 2013. A further article from the same source 'LIBOR: What is it and why does it matter?' provides a more thorough explanation around LIBOR specifically, how it was rigged and the consequences behind that (BBC News 2012).

18 Note that particular points have, for educational purposes, been emphasised in *italics* within this quoted and referenced material.

19 Lloyds Banking Group fined £105m for serious LIBOR and other benchmark failings|FCA.

20 Martin Brokers (UK) Limited fined £630,000 for significant failings in relation to LIBOR|FCA.

21 FCA (2013e).

22 Ibid.

23 FCA (2013a).

24 FCA (2013b).

25 Final Notice, Point 20.

26 Ibid, Point 84.

27 Ibid., Point 86.

28 Ibid., Point 87.

29 FSA 2012b.

30 *The Salz Review* (n.d.).

31 In order to put this in context, as highlighted previously, a BBC article 'Timeline: Libor fixing scandal' provides a most straightforward overview of the lead up to the LIBOR rigging scandal, the events that unfolded around it as it became known about and subsequent fallout. Available at: http://www.bbc.co.uk/news/business-18671255, 6 February 2013. A further article from the same source 'LIBOR: What is it and why does it matter?' provides a more thorough explanation around LIBOR specifically, how it was rigged and the consequences behind that (BBC News 2012).

32 Barclays' press release announcing the Review – 2 July 2012.

33 Available at: https://www.bba.org.uk/?s=LIBOR/.

34 The Executive Committee.

35 *The Salz Review*, Point 9.48.

36 A BBC article 'Timeline: Libor fixing scandal' provides a most straightforward overview of the lead up to the LIBOR rigging scandal, the events that unfolded around it as it became known about and subsequent fallout. Available at: http://www.bbc.co.uk/news/business-18671255, 6 February 2013. A further article from the same source 'LIBOR: What is it and why does it matter?' provides a more thorough explanation around LIBOR specifically, how it was rigged and the consequences behind that (BBC News 2012).

37 UK Government (2012b).

38 Ibid.

39 Available at: https://www.gov.uk/government/publications/the-wheatley-review/.

40 Ibid., Box C.2.

41 Ibid., Point C28.

42 FSA (2013b).

43 Ibid., p. 6.

44 'Libor regulation "to cost £1m a year"'. FT.com, 25 March 2013. Available at: http://www.ft.com/cms/s/0/a8f8e838–955a-11e2-a4fa-00144feabdc0.html?siteedition=uk#axzz2uDvcSuy8. In 2021 the FCA confirmed that 'all LIBOR settings will either cease to be provided by any administrator or no longer be representative', with allowance for transition. The Bank of England Governor Andrew Bailey stated "Today's announcements mark the final chapter in the process that began in 2017, to remove reliance on unsustainable LIBOR rates and build a more robust foundation for the financial system. With limited time remaining, my message to firms is clear – act now and complete your transition by the end of 2021.'

45 FCA (2013b).

46 FCA (2013c).

47 McDermott (2013b).

Appendix 5

Spotlight on the Compliance Officer

This appendix details a selection of regulatory fines of Compliance Officers from the past decade, highlighting findings and failings relating to these.[1]

FCA Fines Sigma Broking Limited £530,000 and Bans and Fines Its Former Directors Following Market Abuse Reporting Failures2

Press Releases First published: 06/10/2022 Last updated: 06/10/2022

Sigma Broking Limited (Sigma) has been fined £531,000 for failing to make reports crucial in fighting potential market abuse and three directors have been fined amounts totalling over £200,000, two of whom have also been prohibited. Between December 2014 and August 2016, Sigma did not report, or failed to report accurately, 56,000 contracts for difference (CFD) transactions to the FCA. It also failed to identify 97 suspicious transactions or orders that it should have reported to the FCA. Many of Sigma's failings had their origins in the inadequate governance and oversight provided by Sigma's board of directors. As a result, the FCA has issued prohibitions against two of Sigma's directors, Simon Tyson (former Chief Executive and director) and Stephen Tomlin (former director),[3] preventing them from holding significant management functions in firms regulated by the FCA. They have also been fined £67,900 and £69,600, respectively. Matthew Kent, a current director, has also been fined £83,600.

Mark Steward, Executive Director of Enforcement and Market Oversight, said:

> Firms must accurately report their transactions and bring any suspicious activity to our attention. Sigma failed to do this, which left potential market abuse undetected. Those failures came from the top and two directors have been banned from holding senior positions in financial services, as a result. Accurate transaction reporting and effective surveillance are crucial tools in identifying dodgy dealing that undermines clean markets. These bans and the scale of the fines we have imposed demonstrate our determination to ensure firms – and those who lead them – meet the reporting standards we expect.

Five Individuals Banned and Fined for Causing Losses to Pension Customers4

Press Releases First published: 09/05/2022 Last updated: 09/05/2022

The FCA has prohibited five directors of financial advice firms from working in financial services and fined them over £1 million, after they caused significant losses to pension customers. The decisions follow an extensive 300-page judgement issued by the Upper Tribunal in which the five directors unsuccessfully challenged the FCA's decisions.

The Tribunal found Andrew Page, Thomas Ward, Aiden Henderson, Robert Ward and Tristan Freer had failed to act with integrity having either acted dishonestly or recklessly. Each had been directors at failed financial advice firms (Financial Page Ltd, Henderson Carter Associates Limited, and Bank House Investment Management Limited) who provided unsuitable advice to over 2,000 customers causing them to place their pensions in high-risk financial products in self-invested personal pensions in which Hennessy Jones, an unauthorised firm, had a significant financial interest. These customers had been referred to them by Hennessy Jones which was also involved in designing the pension advice process used by these firms. This scheme caused significant losses of over £50 million to over 2,000 consumers who have been compensated now by the Financial Services Compensation Scheme. As well as the negative impact on consumers, this also affected other financial services firms which have to contribute to the costs of the FSCS. The Tribunal found that all the five individuals allowed their 'instincts and values to be overridden' and their judgement to be compromised for personal financial gain. They failed to scrutinise where their customers' pension funds were being invested. The scale of these shortcomings has led to very large penalties being imposed for directors of small IFA firms.

Mark Steward, Executive Director of Enforcement and Market Oversight at the FCA said:

> No reputable financial adviser should recommend that people put their entire pension savings in high-risk investments. Customers were misled into believing that they would get independent and impartial advice, but their interests were reprehensively betrayed in this case. This case also places firms' relationships with unauthorised introducers in the spotlight. All firms should pay heed and scrutinise these relationships to ensure standards of integrity, due diligence and fair treatment of customers are uppermost.

FCA Fines Compliance Oversight Officer for Pension Transfer Failings5

Press Releases First published: 14/07/2017 Last updated: 14/07/2017

The Financial Conduct Authority (FCA) has today fined David Watters £75,000 for failing to exercise due skill, care and diligence in his role as compliance oversight officer, firstly at FGS McClure Watters (FGS) and then Lanyon Astor Buller Ltd (LAB). Following an investigation, the FCA found that Mr Watters failed to take reasonable steps to ensure that the process in place at FGS and LAB, for giving advice on Enhanced Transfer Value (ETV) pension transfer exercises, was adequate and met regulatory standards. This led to a serious risk of unsuitable advice being given to customers of FGS and LAB about the merits of transferring their pension, from a defined benefit (DB) to a defined contribution (DC) scheme, as part of an ETV pension transfer exercise.

Approximately 500 customers that received advice from FGS or LAB transferred their pensions from a DB scheme to a DC scheme, with a combined value of approximately £12.7 million. In many cases, it may have been unnecessary for customers to leave their DB schemes, thereby losing their guaranteed benefits. Mr Watters failed to give sufficient consideration to whether the advice process was compliant; he did not take reasonable steps to gain a sufficient understanding of the relevant regulatory requirements; and did not obtain an appropriate third party review of the processes to ensure compliance. Mr Watters also failed to take reasonable steps to ensure that advisers were properly monitored to reduce the risk of unsuitable ETV pension transfer advice being given to customers. ETV exercises incentivise customers to transfer their pensions. During these exercises, it is vital that customers considering giving up their guaranteed benefits are given suitable advice on the real benefits and consequences so that they can properly conclude whether a transfer is in their best interests. Mark Steward, Executive Director of Enforcement and Market Oversight said: 'It was Mr Watters' responsibility to take reasonable steps to put in place a compliant advice process. His failure to do this placed customers at risk of needlessly losing valuable benefits for their retirement'. LAB has agreed to contact affected customers and where loss has been caused, it will pay appropriate redress.

FCA Fines Compliance Officer and Broker Whose Actions Enabled Market Abuse to be Committed in October 2010[6]

Press Releases First published: 08/08/2013 Last updated: 17/09/2013

The Financial Conduct Authority (FCA) has fined David Davis, senior partner and compliance officer of Paul E Schweder Miller & Co, £70,258, and Vandana Parikh, a broker at the same firm, £45,673, for failing to act with due skill, care and diligence in the period leading up to the illegal manipulation of the closing price of securities traded on the London Stock Exchange (LSE) by Rameshkumar Goenka, a Dubai based private investor, in October 2010. Goekna was fined $9,621,240 (approximately £6 million) by the Financial Services Authority (FSA) on 11 November 2011 for market abuse. It was the largest fine imposed by the FSA on an individual.

In April 2010 Goenka was introduced to Parikh to execute trades in Gazprom and Reliance securities in LSE closing auctions. A series of conference calls took place during which Goenka asked whether the closing price of Gazprom Global Depository Receipts (GDRs) could be raised by placing strategic orders. Parikh explained the impact that the size and timing of various orders might have on the closing price. However, although the matter progressed, an unforeseen announcement about Gazprom caused the price to drop unexpectedly on the intended trading day and the proposed trading was abandoned. The FCA has concluded that Parikh failed to act with due skill, care and diligence by explaining the process of manipulation to Goenka without recognising the risk that this posed and without proper challenge or enquiry as to his intentions. Further, although Parikh speculated that Goenka had a related structured product she did not discuss this possibility with her compliance officer. The FCA has imposed a penalty of £45,673 on Parikh. In October 2010 Goenka took the knowledge gained during the Gazprom preparations and used this as the basis for a successful strategy to illegally manipulate the closing price of Reliance and enabled him to avoid a loss of $3.1m on a related structured product. Parikh suspected but did not know that Goenka had an underlying structured product. Parikh informed Davis that she had concerns about the proposed Reliance trading with the result that Davis became involved and monitored the trading. Although Davis was not aware of Goenka's desire to manipulate the price nor that he in fact held a linked structured product, he was aware of sufficient information to constitute clear warning signals and failed to take preventative steps before authorising the trades. Furthermore, Davis did not report the trading as suspicious after the event. The FCA has concluded that Davis failed to act with due skill, care and diligence by failing to challenge the instructions for Reliance and by failing to refuse to accept the orders to trade. Davis held senior management positions at Schweder Miller and was responsible for compliance oversight. The FCA has withdrawn his Significant Influence Functions (SIF) and prohibited him from holding those functions in future. The FCA has imposed a penalty of £70,258.

Tracey McDermott, Director of Enforcement and Financial Crime, said: 'The FCA's actions against the two persons whose actions, or lack of, assisted Goenka make it clear that every individual involved in a chain that leads to trading must proactively challenge suspicious behaviour and ensure it is reported. The collective failure of Parikh and Davis to recognise the warning signs and react accordingly meant they unwittingly enabled his manipulation to take place.

> All approved persons have a duty to help the FCA in its fight against market abuse, and must be vigilant in spotting, challenging and reporting market abuse. That did not happen here. Instead, Goenka's manipulative strategy was allowed to proceed unchallenged. This falls far short of our expectations of approved persons.

The Final Notices published today should be read in conjunction with the Final Notice issued to Goenka in 2011. The FCA has also today published a Decision Notice in relation to the same matter.

John Douglas Leslie[7]

Date: 26 July 2013

1. Action

1.1. For the reasons given in this Notice, the Authority hereby:
(a) imposes on Mr Leslie a financial penalty of £28,000; (b) withdraws the approval granted to Mr Leslie to perform CF4 (Partner), CF10 (Compliance Oversight) and CF11 (Money Laundering Reporting) at Leslie & Nuding; and (c) makes an order prohibiting Mr Leslie from performing any significant influence function in relation to any regulated activity carried on by any authorised person, exempt person or exempt professional firm.

1.2. Mr Leslie agreed to settle at an early stage of the Authority's investigation. He therefore qualified for a 30% stage 1 discount under the Authority's executive settlement procedures. Were it not for this discount, the Authority would have imposed a financial penalty of £40,000 on Mr Leslie.

2. Summary of Reasons

2.1. The Authority sanctions Mr Leslie for breaches of Statement of Principle 6 in performing the significant influence controlled functions CF4 (Partner) and CF10 (Compliance Oversight) during the relevant period. Mr Leslie also held CF11 (Money Laundering Reporting) during the relevant period. 2.2. Mr Leslie breached Statement of Principle 6 by failing to discharge adequately his responsibility to control the distribution of prospectuses for three UCISs to retail investors and thereby failing to exercise due skill, care and diligence in managing the business of Leslie & Nuding. 2.3. As a direct result of his incompetent approach to his responsibilities, prospectuses were issued to approximately 2,900 retail investors without an adequate assessment of their eligibility for UCIS promotions having been made. In total, approximately 880 investors invested €38 million in the three UCISs on a non-advised basis. The UCISs fell into financial difficulties from 2006 and the investors' original investments may now be virtually worthless. 2.4. Mr Leslie has failed to meet minimum regulatory standards in terms of performing significant influence functions with due skill, care and diligence. He is not fit and proper to perform significant influence functions at any authorised person, exempt person or exempt professional firm. Accordingly, the Authority has decided to impose the Prohibition Order on him. 2.5. This action supports the Authority's regulatory objectives of protecting consumers and enhancing the integrity of the financial system.

The FCA Censures Catalyst Investment Group Limited for Misleading Investors and Fines Former Compliance Officer[8]

4 October 2013

Catalyst

Catalyst offered bonds issued by Luxembourg-based ARM to investment intermediaries and independent financial advisers (IFAs) in the UK, who in turn promoted and sold them to retail investors. ARM applied for a licence to issue the bonds from the Luxembourg financial regulator, the CSSF. Catalyst knew that ARM had applied for a licence in July 2009, and had been asked to stop issuing bonds by the CSSF in November 2009 pending a decision. However, Catalyst continued to accept funds from investors without disclosing ARM's position, or the risk that ARM could be liquidated if its licence application failed. This should have been included in Catalyst's marketing material for ARM bonds. Catalyst also wrote to IFAs and investors on separate occasions suggesting that ARM's licence application was voluntary, but did not spell out the implications if the licence wasn't granted. To ensure consumers are properly protected, the FCA expects firms and individuals to act with integrity, and communicate clearly and fairly with their customers. Catalyst didn't follow these principles, exposing investors to significant risks without their knowledge.

Tracey McDermott, the FCA's director of enforcement and financial crime, said: 'Catalyst showed a reckless disregard for investors' interests, exposing them to significant risks. We expect firms, and their senior managers, to put customers' needs first – and will take tough action against those who fall short of our standards'.

Alison Moran

Alison Moran, Catalyst's former compliance officer, has been fined £20,000 for failing to act with due skill, care and diligence. Although she was aware of the issues with ARM's licence in December 2009, she failed to ensure this was properly communicated to investors. UK investors have invested £54 million in ARM bonds, including £17.1 million in un-issued ARM bonds, and may lose a significant part of their investment. Those affected should refer to the Financial Services Compensation Scheme for details of how and when to make a claim for compensation.

The Financial Services Authority (FSA) Has Publicly Censured Gracechurch Investments Limited (Gracechurch) for Misconduct, Including Using Pressure-Selling Tactics with Customers to Invest in the Shares of Small Companies, Resulting in Client Losses of at least £2 million. The FSA Would Have Fined Gracechurch £1.5 million Had the Firm Not Been in Liquidation[9]

20 December 2012

The FSA has decided to fine Sam Thomas Kenny, the former chief executive of Grace-church, £450,000 and prohibit him from holding a position in the financial services industry. Kenny has referred the matter to the Upper Tribunal where the FSA and Kenny will be able to present their case. The Tribunal will then determine the appropriate action for the FSA to take in relation to Kenny, which may be to uphold, vary or cancel the FSA's decision. Subject to the Tribunal's decision, the FSA has found that Kenny personally pressurised, or misrepresented material facts to clients and in his role as chief executive Kenny trained and encouraged his staff to pressure clients. Gracechurch's brokers used pressure sales tactics to coerce its clients to invest in risky small company stocks which were listed on AIM and PLUS or not listed at all. The firm misrepresented, for instance, the financial performance of stocks both orally and in writing. Brokers ignored requests for further information and protests that clients had no funds to invest. In at least one case a broker claimed that the recommendation was based on inside information. Between 1 April 2008 and 4 November 2009, Gracechurch advised approximately 340 clients to buy about £4 million of small company stocks. Gracechurch's clients would have lost 72% of the amount they had invested in eight of the top ten stocks (based on financial volume) sold by the firm if they had held those small-cap stocks until 12 October 2011. The firm also provided the FSA with false dates for internal committee meetings and deliberately withheld a recording of a non-compliant advised sales call requested by the FSA. Finally, the firm knowingly employed someone in a senior position who was not approved by the FSA and who was linked to pressure-selling tactics.

The FSA has also prohibited former Gracechurch compliance officer Carl Peter Davey from working in the financial services industry. The FSA would have fined Davey £175,000 if it were not for the serious financial hardship that such a fine would cause him. As compliance officer, Davey was also involved in the deliberate withholding of the non-compliant advised sales call requested by the FSA. Despite Davey's efforts to improve the firm's systems and controls, the monitoring of advised calls by the firm's brokers was inadequate and brokers were regularly making misrepresentations about stocks to clients.

Tracey McDermott, director of enforcement and financial crime at the FSA, said:

> High pressure sales tactics and systematic misrepresentation to clients are wholly unacceptable practices. The FSA will not tolerate firms coercing clients into buying financial products or services that aren't suitable for them. Senior management of stockbroking firms should be clear that the buck will stop with them.

The Financial Services Authority (FSA) Has Fined Alexander Ten-Holter, Trader and Former Compliance Officer at Greenlight Capital (UK) LLP (Greenlight)

27 January 2012

£130,000 for failing to question and make reasonable enquiries before selling Greenlight's shareholding in Punch Taverns plc (Punch) ahead of an anticipated significant equity fundraising by Punch in June 2009, and prohibited him from performing Compliance Oversight and Money Laundering reporting functions.[10] The FSA has also fined Caspar Agnew, a trading desk director at JP Morgan Cazenove, £65,000 for failing to identify and act on a suspicious order from Greenlight to sell Punch shares that allowed the firm to be used to facilitate insider dealing or market abuse. As a result of his failings JP Morgan Cazenove failed to identify the trade as suspicious and report it to the FSA.

Ten-Holter

On 9 June 2009, Ten-Holter received an order to sell Greenlight's entire shareholding in Punch despite being made aware that Greenlight had spoken to Punch management a matter of minutes before its decision to sell. The Greenlight analyst who gave the sell-order told Ten-Holter that Punch management would have told them 'secret bad things' had they signed a confidentiality agreement and the analyst thought that Greenlight had potentially a window of a week before the stock 'plummets'. This should have alerted Ten-Holter to the risk that Greenlight may have been in receipt of inside information. Ten-Holter took no steps to satisfy himself that the order was not based on inside information, despite the clear risk that it was. In fact, Greenlight had received inside information in the course of the call with Punch management and had based its decision to sell on that inside information. Ten-Holter simply executed the order, instructing Agnew to sell on behalf of Greenlight. On 15 June 2009, Punch announced a fundraising of £375 million. Following the announcement, the price of Punch shares fell by 29.9%. Greenlight's trading had avoided losses of approximately £5.8 million for the funds under Greenlight's management. This should have again prompted Ten-Holter to question and make enquires regarding the order to sell. Instead, he took no action to satisfy himself that Greenlight's trading had not been based on inside information in relation to the fundraising. Ten-Holter failed to act with due skill, care and diligence despite his knowledge of the suspicious circumstances surrounding Greenlight's sale of its shares. In addition to imposing a fine of £130,000, the FSA has concluded that he is not fit and proper to act as a compliance officer. The FSA expects compliance officers to be vigilant for signs that transactions may be improper, to investigate and, if not satisfied as to the propriety of the transaction, to prevent the trade.

Agnew

Agnew's misconduct related to his dealings with Greenlight between 9 and 12 June 2009 when he was instructed by Ten-Holter to sell 11.4 million Punch shares, which constituted over 4% of its issued share capital. This represented approximately 68% of all trading in Punch shares over that period. Agnew failed to act with due skill, care and diligence especially because he became aware of the possibility that there had been a pre-marketing of Punch shareholders prior to the unscheduled announcement, and that major shareholders were likely to have obtained inside information through pre-marketing. Shareholders contacted during such a pre-marketing exercise are not allowed to trade on receipt of that inside information. Agnew failed to identify and alert JP Morgan Cazenove, his employer, to the possibility that the trade was being conducted on the basis of inside information and as a result no Suspicious Transaction Report (STR) was submitted to the FSA. Agnew thought that Greenlight was simply fortunate in the timing of its transactions.

Tracey McDermott, acting director of enforcement and financial crime, said:

> Ten-Holter's approach to compliance oversight was wholly inadequate. Serious compliance failures of this nature can have a dramatic effect on the orderliness and integrity of the markets. Agnew was an experienced trader, so should have been suspicious of this transaction and aware of his responsibilities to report it. Tackling market abuse and insider dealing is not just an issue for the regulator. Compliance professionals and staff on sales and trading desks play a key role in assisting the FSA in detecting and preventing market abuse. Approved persons should be in no doubt as to their responsibilities in this area and the FSA will not hesitate to take tough action where they fall down on these.

The Financial Services Authority (FSA) Has Fined Dr Sandradee Joseph £14,000 and Banned Her from Performing Any Significant Influence Function in Regulated Financial Services for Breaching Principle 6 of the FSA's Statements of Principle for Approved Persons[1]

22 November 2011

Joseph was Compliance Officer at Dynamic Decisions Capital Management (DDCM), a hedge fund management company based in London (and Milan). In the wake of the collapse of Lehman Brothers, the investment strategy adopted by DDCM for the fund it managed resulted in losses totalling approximately 85% of the fund's total assets under management. To conceal the losses, in late 2008, a senior employee at DDCM entered into a number of contracts, on behalf of investment funds managed by DDCM, for the purchase and resale of a bond (the Bond). Various investors raised concerns that the Bond was of doubtful provenance and legitimacy, and DDCM's Prime Broker resigned as a result of its concerns. Joseph failed to consider the reasons for the Prime Broker resigning and despite being aware of the investors' concerns about the Bond she failed to properly investigate those concerns or act upon the information. In doing so, Joseph did not engage with her responsibilities as Compliance Officer and therefore failed to act with due skill and care. She relied wrongly on another employee of DDCM, and on her belief that external lawyers were instructed and would have acted on concerns as appropriate.

Tracey McDermott, acting director of enforcement and financial crime, said:

> Joseph's failure, as Compliance Officer, to challenge a colleague, investigate and act on the information she received, resulted in DDCM and the FSA being unable to take appropriate action Joseph took far too narrow a view of her role as a Compliance Officer. She failed to understand the importance of her role and the wider regulatory obligations it brings. The FSA is committed to driving up standards across the industry and will take robust action against those who do not meet our standards.

Joseph agreed to settle during the course of the FSA investigation. She therefore qualifies for a 30% reduction on her financial penalty. Were it not for this discount, the FSA would have imposed a financial penalty of £20,000 on Joseph.

NOTES

1. These are drawn from the UK's Financial Conduct Authority (FCA) and their predecessor the Financial Services Authority (FSA) websites. Fully referenced, they are presented as a sample for illustrative and learning purposes only. More information on each case accessible via the FCA website link provided. Interested parties should also research instances of such findings and failings reported elsewhere, both more widely and in their own jurisdiction/sector in order to draw out any further learning points arising from these.
2. www.fca.org.uk/news/press-releases/fca-fines-sigma-broking-limited-530000-and-bans-and-fines-its-former-director.
3. Note he was also the holder of CF10 at Sigma during the period referred to.
4. www.fca.org.uk/news/press-releases/five-individuals-banned-and-fined-causing-losses-pension-customers. Note amongst these individuals held the CF10 position in respect of different firms.
5. www.fca.org.uk/news/press-releases/fca-fines-compliance-oversight-officer-pension-transfer-failings.
6. www.fca.org.uk/news/press-releases/fca-fines-compliance-officer-and-broker-whose-actions-enabled-market-abuse-be.
7. www.fca.org.uk/your-fca/documents/final-notices/2013/john-douglas-leslie.
8. www.fca.org.uk/news/catalyst-investment-group-limited.
9. Can be found via the national archives webarchive.nationalarchives.gov.uk/, search under Carl Peter Davey.
10. Can now be found via the national archives webarchive.nationalarchives.gov.uk/, search under Ten-Holter.
11. Can now be found via the national archives webarchive.nationalarchives.gov.uk/, search under Sandradee Joseph.

Bibliography

A significant volume of background reading contributed to the development of this text: academic and practical, populist and specialist, from focused reports to wide-ranging reviews, together with speeches, opinion pieces, commentaries, online blogs and discussions, produced by a vast array of stakeholders from right across the regulatory environment – an intentionally eclectic mix of influencers whose contributions influenced the development of the regulatory and compliance environments and thus the development of the compliance role. For information and reference purposes, this bibliography contains a robust representative example of this reading; however, it is by no means exhaustive.

Adamson, C. 2012. 'Regulating in a new era of professionalism: What does the FSA want to see from the industry?'. Speech at the IEA's 15th Annual Conference, 14 June 2012. Available at: http://www.fsa.gov.uk/library/communication/speeches/2012/0614-ca.shtml/

Adamson, C. 2013. 'The importance of culture in driving behaviours of firms and how the FCA will assess this'. Speech by Clive Adamson, Director of Supervision, the FCA, April 2013. Available at: http://www.fca.org.uk/news/regulation-professionalism.

BaFin. 2011. *BaFin Annual Report 2011*. Bonn and Frankfurt am Main: BaFin. Available at: http://www.bafin.de/SharedDocs/Downloads/EN/Jahresbericht/dl_annualreport_2011.pdf?_blob=publicationFile/

Bagehot, W. [1873] 1999. *Lombard Street: A Description of the Money Market*. New York: Wiley & Sons.

Bailey, A. 2012. 'Basel III: The big issues'. Speech at the Seventh City of London Swiss Financial Roundtable, 27 April, Mansion House, London.

Bailey, A. 2013a. 'The new approach to financial regulation'. Speech at the Chartered Banker Dinner 2013, Edinburgh, 1 May.

Bailey, A. 2013b. 'Challenges of prudential regulation'. Speech at the Society of Business Economists Annual Dinner, London, 13 June.

Bailey, A. 2013c. 'Regulating international banks'. Speech at British Bankers Association Annual International Banking Conference, London, 17 October.

Baldwin, R., Cave, M. and Lodge, M. 2010. *The Oxford Handbook of Regulation*. Oxford: Oxford University Press.

Bank for International Settlements (BIS). 2005. *Compliance and the Compliance Function in Banks – 2005*. Available at: http://www.bis.org/publ/bcbs113.pdf/

Bank for International Settlements (BIS). 2006. *International Convergence of Capital Measurement and Capital Standards: A Revised Framework – Comprehensive Version (Commonly Referred to as 'Basel II').* Available at: http://www.bis.org/

Bank for International Settlements (BIS). 2008. *Implementation of the Compliance Principles: A Survey.* Basel Committee on Banking Supervision (BCBS). August. Available at: http://www.bis.org/

Bank for International Settlements (BIS). 2011. *Principles for the Sound Management of Operational Risk.* BCBS, June. Revised version March 2021. Available at: http://www.bis.org/publ/bcbs195.htm

Bank for International Settlements (BIS). 2012b. *Core Principles for Effective Banking Supervision.* BCBS, September. Available at: http://www.bis.org/publ/bcbs230.htm/

Bank for International Settlements (BIS). 2012c. *Framework for Dealing with Domestic Systemically Important Banks (D-SIBS).* 11 October. Available at: http://www.bis.org/publ/bcbs233.htm/

Bank for International Settlements (BIS). 2013a. *Methodology for Assessing and Identifying Global Systemically Important Banks (G-SIBs) Regulatory Consistency.* 3 July. Available at: http://www.bis.org/publ/bcbs255.htm/

Bank for International Settlements (BIS). 2013b. *Liquidity Stress Testing: A Survey of Theory, Empirics and Current Industry and Supervisory Practices.* Available at: http://www.bis.org/publ/bcbs_wp24.htm/

Bank for International Settlements (BIS). 2014a. *External Audits of Banks: Final Document.* BCBS, March. Available at: http://www.bis.org/publ/bcbs280.htm/

Bank for International Settlements (BIS). 2014b. *Supervisory Framework for Measuring and Controlling Large Exposures: Final Standard.* April. Available at: http://www. bis.org/publ/bcbs283.htm/

Barclay Simpson. *Compensation and Market Trends Report.* Available at: http://www.barclaysimpson.com/compensation-market-reports-2013/

Basel Committee on Banking Supervision. 2011. *Principles for the Sound Management of Operational Risk.* Basel Committee on Banking Supervision, June. Available at: http://www.bis.org/publ/bcbs195.htm/

Bazeley, S. and Haynes, A. 2007. *Financial Services Authority Regulation and Risk-Based Compliance,* 2nd edn. London: Tottle Publishing.

BBC News. 2009. 'Timeline: Credit crunch to downturn article'. August. Available at: http://news.bbc.co.uk/1/hi/7521250.stm/

BBC News. 2012. 'LIBOR: What is it and why does it matter?'. December. Available at: http://www.bbc.co.uk/news/business-19199683/

Biegelman, M.T. 2008. *Building a World-Class Compliance Program: Best Practices and Strategies for Success.* Chichester: John Wiley & Sons.

Black, J. 2004. *The Development of Risk Based Regulation in Financial Services: Canada, the UK and Australia.* Available at: http://www.lse.ac.uk/collections/law/staff%20publications%20full%20text/black/risk%20based%20regulation%20in%20financial%20services.pdf/

Black, J. 2008. London School of Economics and Political Science, Presentation to OECD, 1 December. Available at: http://www.oecd.org/gov/regulatory-policy/44800375.pdf/

Blundell, J. and Robinson, C. 1999. *Regulation without the State.* IEA Occasional Paper 109. London: Institute of Economic Affairs.

Blustein, P. 2005. *And the Money Kept Rolling in.* New York: Public Affairs Books.

Boehme, D. 2009. 'From Enron to Madoff: Why many corporate compliance and ethics programs are positioned for failure'. Compliance Strategists LLC, RAND Conference, March. Available at: http://www.compliancestrategists.org/wp-content/uploads/2012/09/March-5-2009-Boehme-PDF-Download.pdf/

Bootle, R. 2009. *The Trouble with Markets: Saving Capitalism from Itself.* London: Nicholas Brealey Publishing.

Boyes, R. 2009. *Meltdown Iceland: How the Global Financial Crisis Bankrupted an Entire Country.* London: Bloomsbury.

British Standards Institute (BSI). 2011. *Compliance Framework for Regulated Financial Services Firms – Specification, British Standards BS8453:2011.* Available at: http://shop.bsigroup.com/en/ProductDetail/?pid=000000000030210205/

Brummer, A. 2008. *The Crunch: The Scandal of Northern Rock and the Escalating Credit Crisis.* London: Random House.

Callioni, P. 2008. *Compliance and Regulation in the International Financial Services Industry: Turning Compliance into a Competitive Advantage.* Global Professional Publishing Ltd.

Caprasse, D., Laurent, J. and Reed, W. 2008. 'Three lines of defence: How to take the burden out of compliance'. *PWC Insurance Digest*, April.

Carney, M., Tucker, P., Hildebrand, P., de Larosière, J., Dudley, W., Turner, A. and Ferguson Jr., R.W. 2011. *Regulatory Reforms and Remaining Challenges.* G30 Occasional Paper 31. Washington, DC: Group of Thirty. Available at: http://www.group30.org/images/PDF/ReportPDFs/OP81.pdf/

Central Bank of Ireland. n.d. *Introduction to PRISM.* Central Bank of Ireland. Available at: http://www.centralbank.i.e./regulation/processes/prism/Pages/default.aspx/

Chartered Banker Professional Standards Board. 2014a. *CB: PSB Consults on Leadership Standard for Professional Bankers.* January. Available at: http://www.cbpsb.org/news/news_detail.cb-psb-consults-on-leadership-standard-for-professional-bankers.html/

Chartered Banker Professional Standards Board. 2014b. *Exposure Draft of the Leadership Standard for Professional Bankers.* (CB: PSB). January. Available at: http://www.charteredbanker.com/news/news_detail.cbpsbconsultation.html/

Compliance Institute South Africa. n.d. 'What is compliance?'. Compliance Institute South Africa. Available at: www.compliancesa.com/profession.asp/

Cooper, G. 2008. *The Origin of Financial Crises: Central Banks, Credit Bubbles and the Efficient Market Fallacy.* Petersfield: Harriman House.

Cooper, J. 2006. 'The integration of financial regulatory authorities: The Australian experience'. J. Cooper, Deputy Chairman of the Australian Securities and Investments Commission, September. Available at: http://www.asic.gov.au/asic/pdflib.nsf/LookupByFileName/integration-financial-regulatory-authorities.pdf/$file/integration-financial-regulatory-authorities.pdf/

Cowan, M., Camfield, H., English, S. and Hammond, S. 2014. *State of Internal Audit Survey 2014: Adapting to Complex Challenges?* London: Thomson Reuters Accelus.

Darcy, K.T. 2013. 'Ethics and compliance: Birth of a profession'. *Journal of Business Compliance*, 36 (3/4): 36–45.

Davies, H. and Green, D. 2008. *Global Financial Regulation: The Essential Guide.* Cambridge: Polity.

Dehesa, G. de la. 2010. *Twelve Market and Government Failures Leading to the 2008–09 Financial Crisis.* Occasional Paper No. 80. Washington, DC: Group of Thirty. Available at: http://www.group30.org/images/PDF/ReportPDFs/OP80.pdf/

Deloitte. 2012a. *Cultivating a Risk Intelligent Culture: A Fresh Perspective.* October. Available at: http://www.deloitte.com/assets/Dcom-Australia/Local%20Assets/Documents/Industries/Financial%20services/Cultivating%20a%20Risk%20Intelligent%20Culture_September_2012.pdf/

Deloitte. 2012b. *A Path to Integration: An Integrated Compliance Solution.* October. Available at: http://www.deloitte.com/assets/Dcom-UnitedKingdom/Local%20Assets/Documents/Services/Audit/uk-audit-integration.pdf/

Doherty, C. 2012. 'Rating the agencies'. *Businesslife.com*, April–May.

English, S. and Hammond, S. 2012. *Cost of Compliance 2012.* London: Thomson Reuters Accelus.

English, S. and Hammond, S. 2014. *Cost of Compliance 2014.* London: Thomson Reuters Accelus.

Ernst & Young. 2012. *Turn Risks and Opportunities into Results: Exploring the Top 10 Risk and Opportunities for Global Organizations.* Global Report 2012. Available at: http://www.ey.com/

Publication/vwLUAssets/The_top_10_risks_and_opportunities_for_global_organizations/ $FILE/Business%20Challenge%20main%20 report-%20SCORED.pdf/

Ernst & Young. 2013a. *Financial Crime Compliance: Key Findings from Ernst & Young 2012 Financial Crime Compliance Survey.* Ernst & Young/ICA.

Ernst & Young. 2013b. *Insights on Governance, Risk and Compliance Series.* December. Available at: http://www.iia.nl/SiteFiles/EY-Maximizing-value-from-your-lines-of-defense.pdf/

Ernst & Young. 2013c. *Maximising Value from Your Lines of Defense: A Pragmatic Approach to Establishing and Optimising Your LOD Model.* December. https://www.ey.com

Ernst & Young. 2013d. *Turn Risk and Opportunities into Results: Global Report.* https://www. ey.com

Ernst & Young. n.d. 'Why implement a LOD model? Maximizing value from your lines of defense'. Available at: http://www.ey.com/GL/en/Services/Advisory/Maximizing-value-from-your-lines-of-defense/

Ethics Resource Center. 2007. *Leading Corporate Integrity: Defining the Role of the Chief Ethics and Compliance Officer.* August. Available at: http://www.ethics.org/files/u5/CECO_Paper_UPDATED.pdf/

European Banking Authority (EBA). 2011. *Guidelines on Internal Governance (GL44).* September. Available at: http://www.eba.europa.eu/documents/10180/103861/EBA-BS-2011–116-final-EBA-Guidelines-on-Internal-Governance-(2)_1.pdf/

European Securities and Markets Authority (ESMA). 2012. *Guidelines on Certain Aspects of the MiFID Compliance Function Requirements* – July. Available at: http://www.esma.europa.eu/system/files/2012–388.pdf/

FBI. 2012. 'Peter Madoff, former Chief Compliance Officer and Senior Management Director sentenced in Manhattan Federal Court to 10 years in prison'. December. Available at: www.fbi.gov.

Financial Conduct Authority (FCA). 2013a. *FCA Final Notice 2013: ICAP Europe Ltd.* September. Available at: http://www.fca.org.uk/your-fca/documents/final-notices/2013/icap-europe-ltd/

Financial Conduct Authority (FCA). 2013b. *ICAP Europe Ltd Final Notice.* September. Available at: http://www.fca.org.uk/static/documents/final-notices/icap-europe-limited.pdf/

Financial Conduct Authority (FCA). 2013c. 'JPMorgan Chase Bank N.A. fined £137,610,000 for serious failings relating to its Chief Investment Office's "London Whale" trades'. FCA news article, September. Available at: http://www.fca.org.uk/news/consumers/jpmorgan-chase-bank-na-fined/

Financial Conduct Authority (FCA). 2013d. *The FCA's Response to the Parliamentary Commission on Banking Standards.* October. Available at: http://www.fca.org.uk/static/documents/pcbs-response.pdf/

Financial Conduct Authority (FCA). 2013e. *FCA Final Notice 2013: Coöperatieve Centrale Raiffeisen–Boerenleenbank B.A. (Rabobank).* October. Available at: http://www.fca.org.uk/your-fca/documents/final-notices/2013/fca-final-notice-2013-rabobank/

Financial Conduct Authority (FCA). 2013f. *Outsourcing in the Asset Management Industry: Thematic Project Findings Report.* November. Available at: http://www.fca.org.uk/static/documents/thematic-reviews/tr13-10.pdf/

Financial Conduct Authority (FCA). 2014a. *FCA Risk Outlook 2014.* March.

Financial Conduct Authority (FCA). 2014b. *Business Plan 2014/15.* March.

Financial Reporting Council. 2012. *UK Corporate Governance Code.* London: Financial Reporting Council. Available at: http://www.frc.org.uk/Our-Work/Publications/Corporate-Governance/UK-Corporate-Governance-Code-September-2012.aspx/

Financial Service Authority (FSA). 2002. *An Ethical Framework for Financial Services.* FSA Discussion Paper 18, October. London: Financial Services Authority. Available at: http://www.fsa.gov.uk/pubs/discussion/dp18.pdf/

Financial Service Authority (FSA). 2005. 'FSA statement regarding the Legal & General judgment'. Press release, January. Available at: http://www.fsa.gov.uk/library/communication/pr/2005/004.shtml/

Financial Service Authority (FSA). 2011. *Dear CEO Letters Providing Guidance on Issues Relating to Remuneration*. FSA Finalised Guidance, October.

Financial Service Authority (FSA). 2012a. 'FSA publishes censure against Bank of Scotland plc in respect of failings within its Corporate Division between January 2006 and December 2008'. Press release, March. Available at: http://www.fsa.gov.uk/library/communication/pr/2012/024.shtml/

Financial Service Authority (FSA). 2012b. *Final Notice: Barclays Bank Plc*. Available at: http://www.fsa.gov.uk/static/pubs/final/barclays-jun12.pdf/

Financial Service Authority (FSA). 2012c. 'Update on FSA report into the failure of HBOS'. Statement, 12 September. Available at: http://www.fsa.gov.uk/library/communication/statements/2012/hbos.shtml/

Financial Service Authority (FSA). 2012d. *Journey to the FCA*. October. Available at: http://www.fca.org.uk/static/documents/fsa-journey-to-the-fca.pdf/

Financial Service Authority (FSA). 2012e. 'UBS fined £160 million for significant failings in relation to LIBOR and EURIBOR'. Press release, December. Available at: http://www.fsa.gov.uk/library/communication/pr/2012/116.shtml/

Financial Service Authority (FSA). 2013a. *FSA Business Plan 2012/13*. March.

Financial Service Authority (FSA). 2013b. *Policy Statement 13/6: The Regulation and Supervision of Benchmarks*. March. Available at: http://www.fsa.gov.uk/static/pubs/policy/ps13-06.pdf/

Financial Service Authority (FSA). n.d. *Building the New Regulator*. Available at: http://www.fsa.gov.uk/static/pubs/policy/bnr_progress1.pdf/

Financial Skills Partnership. 2011. *Job Profile: Compliance*. Available at: http://www.directions.org.uk/profiles/compliance/

Financial Stability Board (FSB). 2010. *Promoting Global Adherence to International Cooperation and Information Exchange Standards*. March. Available at: http://www.financialstabilityboard.org/publications/r_100310.pdf/

Financial Stability Board (FSB). 2012a. *Increasing the Intensity and Effectiveness of SIFI Supervision*. November. Available at: http://www.financialstabilityboard.org/publications/r_121031ab.htm/

Financial Stability Board (FSB). 2012b. *Update of Group of Global Systemically Important Banks (G-SIBs)*. November. Available at: http://www.financialstabilityboard.org/wp-content/uploads/r_121031ac.pdf?page_moved=1/

Financial Stability Board (FSB). 2012c. *Global Adherence to Regulatory and Supervisory Standards on International Cooperation and Information Exchange: Status Update*. November. Available at: http://www.financialstabilityboard.org/2014/12/global-adherence-to-regulatory-and-supervisory-standards-on-international-cooperation-and-information-exchange-status-update-3/

Francke, A. 2014. *Management: How to Make a Difference and Get Results*. Upper Saddle River, NJ: FT Publishing.

Friedman, A.L. 2007. *Ethical Competence and Professional Associations*. Bristol: PARN.

Friedman, A.L. 2012. *Continuing Professional Development: Lifelong Learning of Millions*. London: Routledge.

Gapper, J. and Denton, N. 1996. *All that Glitters: The Fall of Barings*. London: Penguin.

Gittleman, S. 2012a. 'US compliance officers need clarity on status as "supervisors", industry professionals say'. Article on *Reuters.com* blog, May.

Gittleman, S. 2012b. 'Whistleblowing is a duty if internal calls unheeded, US bailout overseer tells compliance officers'. Interview at the Financial Regulatory Forum, 31 July. Available at: http://blogs.reuters.com/financial-regulatory-forum/2012/07/31/interview-whistleblowing-is-a-duty-if-internal-calls-unheeded-u-s-bailout-overseer-tells-compliance-officers/.

Goodhart, C.A.E. 2009. *The Regulatory Response to the Financial Crisis*. Cheltenham: Edward Elgar Publishing.

Group of Thirty (G30). 2008. *The Structure of Financial Supervision: Approaches and Challenges in a Global Marketplace*. Washington, DC: Group of Thirty. Available at: http://www.group30.org/images/PDF/The%20Structure%20of%20Financial%20Supervision.pdf/

Group of Thirty (G30). 2012. *Toward Effective Governance of Financial Institutions.* Available at: http://www.group30.org/images/PDF/TowardEffGov.pdf/

Group of Thirty (G30). 2013. *A New Paradigm: Financial Institution Boards and Supervisors.* Washington, DC: Group of Thirty. Available at: http://www.group30.org/images/PDF/Banking_Supervision_CG.pdf/

Hammond, S. and Walshe, J. 2012. *Cost of Compliance Survey 2012.* London: Thomson Reuters Accelus.

Hammond, S. and Walshe, J. 2013. *Cost of Compliance Survey 2013.* London: Thomson Reuters Accelus.

Information Commissioners Office (IFO). 2012. *The EU Cookie Law (e-Privacy Directive).* May. Available at: http://ico.org.uk/for_organisations/privacy_and_electronic_communications/the_guide/cookies/

Information Security Management. n.d. 'What is information security and why is it important?'. Information Security Management. Available at: http://www.informationsecuritymanagement.co.uk/info-security.php/

Ingves, S. 2012. 'SIFIs: Is there a need for a specific regulation on systematically important financial institutions?'. Speech by S. Ingves, Chairman of the Basel Committee on Banking Supervision, January. Available at: http://www.bis.org/speeches/sp120120.htm/

Ingves, S., Lind, G., Shirakawa, M., Caruana, J. and Ortiz Martínez, G. 2009. *Lessons Learned from Previous Banking Crises: Sweden, Japan, Spain and Mexico.* G30 Occasional Paper 79. Washington, DC: Group of Thirty. Available at: http://www.group30.org/images/PDF/OP79.pdf/

Institute of Internal Auditors. 2013. *The Three Lines of Defense in Effective Risk Management and Control.* Available at: http://www.iia.org.au/sf_docs/default-source/member-services/thethreelinesofdefenseineffectiveriskmanagementandcontrol_Position_Paper_Jan_2013.pdf?sfvrsn=0/

Institute of Risk Management (IRM). 2002. *Risk Management Standard.* Institute of Risk Management. https://www.irm.org

International Association of Insurance Supervisors. 2012. *Insurance Core, Principles, Standards, Guidance and Assessment Methodology, International Association of Insurance Supervisors (2011, updated 2012).* Available at: http://hb.betterregulation.com/external/Insurance%20Core%20Principles,%20Standards,%20Guidance%20and%20Assessment%20Methodology%20(as%20amended%2012%20October%202012).pdf/

International Compliance Training. n.d. *International & UK Diplomas in Compliance and Governance, Risk & Compliance (GRC).* Available at: http://www.int-comp.com/

International Monetary Fund (IMF). 2014. *World Economic Outlook (WEO) Update.* Available at: http://www.imf.org/external/pubs/ft/weo/2014/update/01/index.htm/

International Organisation for Standardisation (ISO). 2014. *ISO 19600:2014 Compliance management systems.* Available at: https://www.iso.org/obp/ui/#iso:std:62342:en/

IOSCO. 2003. *Function of the Compliance Officer* – July. Available at: http://www.iosco.org/library/pubdocs/pdf/IOSCOPD160.pdf/

IOSCO. 2006. *Compliance Function at Market Intermediaries.* March. Available at: http://www.fsa.go.jp/inter/ios/20060510/02.pdf/

IOSCO. 2010. *Objectives and Principles of Securities Regulation.* June. Available at: http://www.iosco.org/library/pubdocs/pdf/IOSCOPD323.pdf/

Irwin, A.S.M. and Choo, K.K.R. 2014. *The Future of Technology in Customer Identification & Relationship Risk.* London: Thomson Reuters Accelus.

Jones, B. and Kavanagh, D. [1979] 1998. *British Politics Today.* Manchester: Manchester University Press.

Kahneman, D. 2011. *Thinking, Fast and Slow.* London: Penguin Books.

Kearney, A.T. 2013. *Back to Business: Optimism and Uncertainty.* The 2013 A.T. Kearney Foreign Direct Investment Confidence Index. London: A.T. Kearney. Available at: http://www.at-kearney.com/documents/10192/1464437/Back+to+Business+-+Optimism+Amid+Uncertainty+-+FDICI+2013.pdf/96039e18–5d34–49ca-9cec-5c1f27dc099d/

KPMG. 2012. *The Future of Compliance: Compliance Functions as Strategic Partners in the New Regulatory World*. July. Available at: http://www.kpmg.com/UK/en/IssuesAndInsights/ArticlesPublications/Documents/PDF/Advisory/future-of-compliance.pdf/

Krell, E. 2011. 'Too much information, not enough analysis'. *Business Finance*, 27 September. Available at: http://businessfinancemag.com/technology/too-much-information-not-enough-analysis/

Krogerus, M. and Tschappeler, R. 2011. *The Decision Book: Fifty Models for Strategic Thinking*. London: Profile Books.

Lambert, R. 2014. *Banking Standards Review*. May. London: Banking Standards Board.

Langton, H. 2013. 'Taking the high road', *inCompliance*, Autumn.

Lawton, D. 2012. 'MiFID II: A regulators viewpoint'. Speech by D. Lawton, FSA. January. Available at: http://www.fsa.gov.uk/library/communication/speeches/2012/0130-dl.shtml/

LRN. 2012. *Can We Talk? What Chief Compliance Officers and Boards Should Be Discussing*. LRN White Paper, 2012.

LSE. 2012. *Financial Regulation in General Equilibrium*. LSE discussion paper. Available at: http://www.lse.ac.uk/fmg/workingPapers/discussionPapers/fmgdps/dp702AXA9.pdf/

Luijerink, D. 2008. *Corporate and Financial Fraud*. KMPG and The Institute of Chartered Accountants in England and Wales, CCH.

Maharaj, A. 2012. 'Rise to the challenge: Become a compliance officer'. March. Available at: corporatesecretary.com.

McCleskey, S. 2010. *When Free Markets Fail: Saving the Market When It Can't Save Itself*. Hoboken, NJ: John Wiley & Sons.

McDermott, T. 2013a. 'Enforcement and credible deterrence in the FCA'. Speech at the Thomson Reuters Compliance & Risk Summit, London, 18 June. Available at: http://www.fca.org.uk/news/speeches/enforcement-and-credible-deterrence-in-the-fca/

McDermott, T. 2013b. 'Financial services regulation and enforcement: Recent developments and emerging issues'. Speech at the NERA Economic Consulting seminar, London, 9 October. Available at: http://www.fca.org.uk/news/speeches/financial-services-regulation-enforcement/

Michael Page Financial Services. 2013. *Salary Survey 2013*. Available at: http://www.page.com/disciplines/banking-and-financial-services.aspx/

Miles, R. 2014. *Risk Culture and Conduct: Biases & Good Behaviour*. London: Thomson Reuters Accelus.

Mills, A. 2008. *Essential Strategies for Financial Services Compliance*. Chichester: John Wiley & Sons.

Moody's Analytics. 2011. *Basel III New Capital and Liquidity Standards – FAQs*. 1 March. Available at: http://www.moodysanalytics.com/Insight/Regulations/Basel-III/Basel-III-Publications/

Morris, C.R. 2008. *The Trillion Dollar Meltdown*. New York: Perseus Books.

Morris, S. 1995. *Financial Services: Regulating Investment Business*, 2nd edn. London: Sweet & Maxwell.

Murphy, J.E. and Leet, J.H. 2007. *Building a Career in Compliance and Ethics*. Minneapolis, MN: Society of Corporate Compliance & Ethics.

National Occupational Standards. [2006] 2011. *National Occupational Standards in Compliance*. Available at: http://www.int-comp.org/attachments/nos-comp-june-11.pdf/

Newton, A. 1998. *The Handbook of Compliance: Making Ethics Work in Financial Services*. London: Mind to Matter Publishing.

Nuijts, W.H.J.M. 2013. 'Supervision of behaviour and culture: An effective response to governance and risk management problems within financial institutions'. *Journal of Business Compliance*, 6: 5–21.

Office of the Superintendent of Financial Institutions (OSFI). n.d. *Supervisory Framework: The Office of the Superintendent of Financial Institutions (OSFI)*. Available at: http://www.osfi-bsif.gc.ca/Eng/Docs/sframew.pdf/

Oprisk Software. 2013. *Oprisk Software Profiles 2012/2013*. Available at: http://viewer.zmags.com/publication/4762ab68#/4762ab68/2/

Organisation for Economic Co-operation and Development (OECD). 1999. *Principles of Corporate Governance*. OECD.

Organisation for Economic Co-operation and Development (OECD). 2010a. *Good Practice Guidance on Internal Controls, Ethics, and Compliance*. Adopted 18 February 2010. Available at: http://www.oecd.org/investment/anti-bribery/anti-briberyconvention/44884389.pdf/

Organisation for Economic Co-operation and Development (OECD). 2010b. *Policy Framework for Effective and Efficient Financial Regulation*. OECD. Available at: http://www.oecd.org/finance/financialmarkets/44362818.pdf/

Pagliari, S. (ed.). 2012. *Making Good Financial Regulation*. Guildford: Grosvenor House Publishing Limited.

Palmer, A. 2012. 'Compliance has emerged as a growth industry in the UK'. Article in *Cityam. com*, 20 November.

Phillips, M., Cruikshank, I. and Friedman, A. 2002. *Continuing Professional Development: Evaluation of Good Practice*. Bristol: PARN.

Pricewaterhouse Coopers (PWC). 2010. 'Romanian banking banana skins 2010'. *The CSFI Survey of Bank Risk*. Centre for the Study of Financial Innovation, Pricewaterhouse Coopers.

Pricewaterhouse Coopers (PWC). 2013. *Right First Time: Staying ahead of the Conduct Agenda*. Available at: http://pwc.blogs.com/files/conduct-right-first-time.pdf/

Prudential Regulation Authority (PRA). 2012. *The PRA's Approach to Banking Supervision*. October. Bank of England, Prudential Regulation Authority.

Prudential Regulation Authority (PRA). 2013. *The Prudential Regulation Authority's Approach to Insurance Supervision*. April. Available at: http://www.bankofengland.co.uk/publications/Documents/praapproach/insuranceappr1304.pdf/

Punch, M. 1996. *Dirty Business: Exploring Corporate Misconduct*. London: SAGE Publications.

Regulatory Excellence Forum. 2012. *Common Approach to Competency for Regulators*. November. Available at: http://www.regulatorsdevelopment.info/grip/sites/default/files/project-overview.pdf/

Reinhart, C.M. and Rogoff, K. 2009. *This Time is Different: Eight Centuries of Financial Folly*. Princeton, NJ: Princeton University Press.

Reuters. 2012. 'Enforcement against Citibank serves as reminder that compliance counts in product development'. April. Available at: reuters.com.

Resources Global Professionals. 2010. *FTSE 100 Resources Governance Index 2010*. Available at: http://www.resourcesglobal.co.uk/content/uk/docs/rgi/RGI_FTSE_Report2010.pdf/

Resources Global Professionals. 2011. *FTSE 100 Resources Governance Index 2011*. Available at: http://www.resourcesglobal.co.uk/content/uk/docs/rgi/RGI_FTSE_Report2011.pdf/

Rumelt, R. 2011. *Good Strategy/Bad Strategy: The Difference and Why It Matters*. London: Profile Books Ltd.

Russo, T.A. and Katzel, A.J. 2011. *The 2008 Financial Crisis and Its Aftermath: Addressing the Next Debt Challenge*. G30 Occasional Paper 82. Washington, DC: Group of Thirty. Available at: http://www.group30.org/images/PDF/OP82.pdf/

Sants, H. 2009. 'Delivering intensive supervision and credible deterrence'. Speech at the Reuters Newsmakers event, London, 12 March. Available at: http://www.fsa.gov.uk/library/communication/speeches/2009/0312_hs.shtml/

Sants, H. 2010. 'Reforming supervisory practices: Progress to date'. Speech at the Reuters Newsmakers Event, London, 13 December. Available at: http://www.fsa.gov.uk/library/communication/speeches/2010/1213_hs.shtml/

Sants, H. 2011. 'The future of banking regulation in the UK'. Speech, June. Available at: http://www.fsa.gov.uk/library/communication/speeches/2011/0629_hs.shtml/

Sants, H. 2012a. 'Delivering a twin peaks regulatory model within the FSA'. Speech at the British Bankers' Association briefing, London, 6 February. Available at: http://www.fsa.gov.uk/library/communication/speeches/2012/0206-hs.shtml/

Sants, H. 2012b. 'Update on the regulatory reform programme and European issues'. Speech, February. Available at: http://www.fsa.gov.uk/library/communication/speeches/2012/0207-hs.shtml/

Sants, H. 2012c. 'Delivering effective corporate governance: The financial regulators role'. Speech at Merchant Taylors' Hall, London, April. Available at: http://www.fsa.gov.uk/library/communication/speeches/2012/0424-hs.shtml/

Securities and Exchange Commission (SEC). 2010. 'Kathleen Griffin named SEC's first Chief Compliance Officer'. SEC News Release, April. Available at: http://www.sec.gov/news/press/2010/2010–50.htm/

Seidman, D. 2011. *How: Why How We Do Anything Means Everything.* Hoboken, NJ: John Wiley & Sons.

Shoffman, M. 2013. 'HBoS timeline: An accident waiting to happen'. *FT Advisor,* 11 April. Available at: http://www.ftadviser.com/2013/04/11/regulation/regulators/hbos-timeline-an-accident-waiting-to-happen-2vKyj16VSJ3SYRo5TZdrUL/article.html/

Smith, G. 2012. 'Why I am leaving Goldman Sachs'. *New York Times,* 14 March. Available at: http://www.nytimes.com/2012/03/14/opinion/why-i-am-leaving-goldman-sachs.html/

Smith, M.J. 1999. *The Core Executive in Britain.* London: Macmillan.

Smith-Meyer, A. 2013. 'Measuring the value of compliance: Winning arguments for securing compliance budget'. *Journal of Business Compliance,* 3/4: 72–81.

Solicitors Regulation Authority. 2011. *Outcomes-Focused Regulation at a Glance.* October. Available at: http://www.sra.org.uk/solicitors/freedom-in-practice/OFR/ofr-quick-guide.page/

Taleb, N.N. 2007. *The Black Swan: The Impact of the Highly Improbable.* London: Random House.

Tarantino, A. 2006. *Manager's Guide to Compliance.* Hoboken, NJ: Wiley.

Tarantino, A. 2008. *Governance, Risk, and Compliance Handbook.* Hoboken, NJ: Wiley.

Taylor, C. 2005. 'The evolution of compliance'. *Journal of Investment Compliance,* 6 (4): 54–58.

Telegraph. 2012. 'The US fiscal cliff explained'. *The Telegraph,* 16 November 2012. Available at: http://www.telegraph.co.uk/finance/financialcrisis/9682597/The-US-fiscal-cliff-explained.html/

The Salz Review. n.d. See (PDF) Salz Review An Independent Review of Barclays' Business Practices | patricia banda - Academia.edu

Treanor, J. 2013. 'HBOS report delayed to end of year'. *The Guardian,* 18 July. Available at: http://www.theguardian.com/business/2013/jul/18/hbos-report-delayed-chairman-fca?cmp=wp-plugin/

Turner, A. 2012a. 'Financial risk and regulation: Do we need more Europe or less?'. Speech at the Central Bank of Ireland Conference on 'Financial Regulation: The Response to the Crisis', Dublin, 27 April. Available at: http://www.fsa.gov.uk/library/communication/speeches/2012/0427-at.shtml/

Turner, A. 2012b. 'The regulation of shadow banking'. Speech, September. Available at: http://www.fsa.gov.uk/library/communication/speeches/2012/0902-at.shtml/

UK Government. 1985. *Financial Services in the UK: A New Framework for Investor Protection.* Government White Paper, January.

UK Government. 2011. *A New Approach to Financial Regulation: Building a Stronger System.* HM Treasury, February. Available at: https://www.gov.uk/government/uploads/system/uploads/attachment_data/file/81411/consult_newfinancial_regulation170211.pdf/

UK Government. 2012a. *Common Approach to Competency for Regulators.* Better Regulation Delivery Office, 13 September. Available at: https://www.gov.uk/government/publications/common-approach-to-riskassessment/

UK Government. 2012b. *The Wheatley Review of LIBOR: Final Report.* Gov.uk, September. Available at: https://www.gov.uk/government/uploads/system/uploads/attachment_data/file/191762/wheatley_review_libor_finalreport_280912.pdf/

UK Government. 2013a. *Creating Stronger and Safer Banks Policy.* Gov.uk, April. Available at: https://www.gov.uk/government/policies/creating-stronger-and-safer-banks/

UK Government. 2013b. *An Accident Waiting to Happen: The Failure of HBOS*. Parliamentary Commission on Banking Standards, Fourth Report of Session 2012–13, Volume I: Report, together with formal minutes. London: The Stationery Office. Available at: http://www.publications.parliament.uk/pa/jt201213/jtselect/jtpcbs/144/144.pdf/

UK Government. 2014a. Serious Fraud Office. 'Further charges in LIBOR investigation'. Press release, February. Available at: http://www.sfo.gov.uk/press-room/latest-press-releases/press-releases-2013/further-charges-in-libor-investigation.aspx/

UK Government. 2014b. *Banking Standards Review*. Committee on Standards in Public Life. March. https://www.gov.uk/government/publications/committees-response-to-sir-richard-lamberts-banking-standards-review-consultation/

UK Government. n.d. National Crime Agency (NCA). *The SARs Regime*. Available at: http://www.nationalcrimeagency.gov.uk/about-us/what-we-do/specialist-capabilities/ukfiu/the-sars-regime/

UK Government. n.d. *The Wheatley Review*. Information, Gov.uk, various dates. Available at: https://www.gov.uk/government/publications/the-wheatley-review/

UK Parliament. 2010. *Credit Rating Agencies*. Available at: http://www.parliament.uk/business/committees/committees-a-z/commons-select/treasury-committee/inquiries1/parliament-2010/credit-rating-agencies/

UK Parliament. 2013. *Changing Banking for Good: Report of the Parliamentary Commission on Banking Standards – Volume 1: Summary, and Conclusions, and Recommendations*. 12 June. Available at: http://www.parliament.uk/documents/banking-commission/Banking-final-report-volume-i.pdf/

US Office of the Comptroller of the Currency (OCC). 2012. Available at: www.occ.treas.gov/about/who-we-are/index-who-we-are.html

Walker, D. 2009. *A Review of Corporate Governance in UK Banks and Other Financial Industry Entities: Final Recommendations*. HM Treasury, November. Available at: http://webarchive.nationalarchives.gov.uk/+/http:/www.hm-treasury.gov.uk/d/walker_review_261109.pdf/

Ward, S. 2013 [updated 2015]. *Financial Services Compliance Elective Module*. Available at: http://charteredbankermba.bangor.ac.uk/CBMBA.php.en/

Wheatley, M. 2013a. 'Human face of regulation'. Speech at the London School of Economics, London, 10 April. Available at: FCA website http://www.fca.org.uk/news/speeches/human-face-of-regulation/

Wheatley, M. 2013b. 'Modelling integrity through culture'. Speech at the FCA Markets Conference 2013, 19 November. Available at: http://www.fca.org.uk/news/firms/modelling-integrity-through-culture/

Wright, A. (ed.). 2000. *The British Political Process*. Abingdon: Routledge.

Zoromé, A. 2007. *Concept of Offshore Financial Centers: In Search of an Operational Definition*. IMF Working Paper. Washington, DC: International Monetary Fund. Available at: http://www.imf.org/external/pubs/ft/wp/2007/wp0787.pdf/

Websites

Australian Prudential Regulation Authority, www.apra.gov.au
Bank for International Settlements, www.bis.org
Barclay Simpson, www.barclaysimpson.com/compliance/
Better Regulation, http://hb.betterregulation.com/
Centre for the Study of Financial Innovation (CSFI), http://csfi.org/
Drucker Institute, www.drucker.institute
European Central Bank (ECB), www.ecb.europa.eu/ecb/orga/escb/html/index.en.html
The European Corporate Governance Institute (ECGI), www.ecgi.global
Financial Conduct Authority (FCA), www.fca.org.uk
Institute of Risk Management, www.theirm.org

Journal of Business Compliance, www.journalofbusinesscompliance.com

Journal of Financial Regulation and Compliance Management, www.emeraldinsight.com

Michael Page Financial Services, www.page.com/disciplines/banking-and-financial-services. aspx

Moodys Risk Management, http://moodysriskmanagement.com/

Organisation for Economic Co-operation and Development (OECD), www.oecd.org

Resources Global Professionals, www.resourcesglobal.co.uk/index.php/client-services/rgi/rgi-results

Index

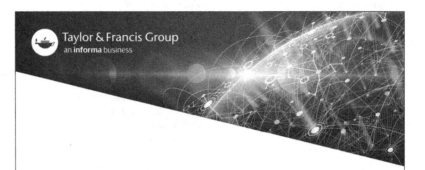

Printed in the United States
by Baker & Taylor Publisher Services